Spirit of Revolution

Spirit of Revolution

Ireland from below, 1917–23

John Cunningham & Terry Dunne

EDITORS

FOUR COURTS PRESS

Typeset in 11pt on 13.5pt AGaramondPro by
Carrigboy Typesetting Services for
FOUR COURTS PRESS LTD
7 Malpas Street, Dublin 8, Ireland
e-mail: info@fourcourtspress.ie
and in North America for
FOUR COURTS PRESS
c/o IPG, 814 N Franklin St, Chicago, IL 60610

A catalogue record for this title is available
from the British Library.

ISBN 978–1–80151–038–7 hbk
978–1–80151–118–6 pbk

SPECIAL ACKNOWLEDGMENT

The editors and publisher would like to acknowledge the support for
this publication by the Moore Institute, University of Galway.

Printed in England
by CPI Antony Rowe, Chippenham, Wilts.

Contents

A spirit of revolution? Introductory reflections   7
Terry Dunne and John Cunningham

'The change was not to be in symbol only but also in substance':
    contested freedoms in the Castlecomer coalfield   21
Anne Boran

A 'bolshie spirit'? Agrarian mobilizations in Co. Galway in 1920   44
Johnny Burke

A 'soviet at Galway'? William J. Larkin, Stephen Cremen and the town
    tenant mobilization of May 1922   59
John Cunningham

'Strike out for yourselves': land and labour from the Boyne to the
    Barrow   79
Terry Dunne

'Eager to produce food': the United Irish Plotholders' Union   97
Mary Forrest

'The only people who would take a risk': maritime workers and the
    Irish Revolution   114
Brian Hanley

The 'dreaded menace of the Red Flag': the Munster soviets of 1922   132
Dominic Haugh

'Famous only as far as the wanders of a lame dog': the Volunteers of
    Moygownagh C Company   156
Liam Alex Heffron

'They were the coming men – Ireland's hope': the mobilization of
    agricultural labourers in Maugherow, Co. Sligo, 1917–20   179
Moira Leydon

'No such sight has been seen in Belfast since Dissenter and Catholic
 united in 1791': the Workers' Union and the Belfast Labour Party 197
Fearghal Mac Bhloscaidh

'More militant than the men': women's activism, class and
 revolution in Kerry 217
Kieran McNulty

'They felt it was their duty to stimulate that discontent': women at
 the Irish Trade Union Congress, 1916–23 231
Theresa Moriarty

'Welcome back Jim': the mobilization of Dublin workers on the
 return of James Larkin in 1923 245
Gerry Watts

List of contributors 261

Index 263

A spirit of revolution? Introductory reflections

TERRY DUNNE AND JOHN CUNNINGHAM

In March 1919, David Lloyd George, last prime minister of the United Kingdom of Great Britain and Ireland, wrote in confidence to the Paris Peace Conference:

> The whole of Europe is filled with the spirit of revolution. There is a deep sense not only of discontent, but of anger and revolt, amongst the workmen against prewar conditions. The whole existing order in its political, social and economic aspects is questioned by the masses of the population from one end of Europe to the other.[1]

For Lloyd George, the 'spirit' manifested itself in different ways: 'In some countries ... the unrest takes the form of open rebellion; in others ... it takes the shape of strikes and of a general disinclination to settle down to work – symptoms ... just as much concerned with the desire for political and social change as with wage demands.'[2] Lloyd George's comment was prompted by anxiety about the post-war world, that out of hubris the victorious powers might cause social unrest to mutate into outright revolution.

More generally, given the circumstances in early 1919, it was hardly surprising that there was a 'disinclination to settle down to work' as if nothing of consequence had happened. The experience of the war had produced a sense of alienation among many of those who fought in it, whether as 'volunteer' or conscript, while the terrible slaughter in the trenches and elsewhere had subdued or diverted the popular patriotism that greeted the outbreak of the conflict in almost every country. Even before the war ended, economic adversity on the 'home front' prompted popular resistance, alongside the revival and intensification of the labour militancy – and indeed of the labour consciousness – that had characterized the immediate pre-war period. Moreover, with the collapse of four major empires between 1917 and 1922, with the formation of new nation states, and with the proclamation of a novel form of political organization by the triumphalist Bolsheviks, it was inevitable that the previous order of things would be questioned, even in those

---

1 David Lloyd George, *Fontainebleau memorandum (some considerations for the peace conference before they finally draft their terms)*, 25 Mar. 1919. 2 Ibid.

places where the constitutional architecture of the pre-war world survived more or less intact. Social discontent was reflected in a variety of ways, including in the extent of support for the soviet republics declared in Germany and Hungary in late 1918 and 1919, in the protracted syndicalist-led factory occupations in Italy, as well as in the Seattle general strike and the Boston police strike of 1919. For its part, the British empire was shaken by manifestations of an insurgent spirit from Egypt, to Iraq, to India. In the Ireland of those years, where the political foundations were conspicuously insecure, there was an almost universal questioning of the condition of things, expressed in a variety of ways, including in demonstrations, strikes, cattle drives, and the seizure by crowds of people of agricultural and industrial property. Moreover, just as Lloyd George was composing his memorandum to the Paris Peace Conference, his government was being challenged by the separatist administration established by the revolutionary Dáil Éireann on 21 January 1919.

The term 'revolution' has increasingly been applied to the Irish events of 1917–23. Nonetheless, any real sense of a spirit of revolution seems to have evaporated from the social memory of the period, and even from the academic scholarship. In the social sciences, definitions of revolution understand it as necessarily involving mass participation. For Eric Hobsbawn, there had to be 'the element of mass mobilization, without which few historians would identify a revolution as such.'[3] Yet the dominant narrative of the Irish Revolution largely ignored the popular seizures and protests – where a 'spirit of revolution' was most evident – in favour of a narrow focus on the demand for formal national independence. Mass mobilization was elided in favour of the élan of a military elite. With a few notable exceptions, the historiography has emphasized either small-scale military engagements or high politics, while the social movements that accompanied and often underpinned them have been overlooked or downplayed. A perceived conservative outcome is projected backwards in time to preclude any radical political content. Moreover, working-class people are largely written out of the history, in a manner similar to the longstanding exclusion of women – an exclusion that thankfully has been challenged, especially in the recent past.

And it was not just the scattered struggles of workers, rural as well as urban, and 'congested' small farmers that were ignored, but also the several coordinated trade union interventions which manifestly assisted the separatist cause. Notable examples were the Irish Trade Union Congress's anti-conscription strike of 23 April 1918, widely observed throughout most of the

---

3 E.J. Hobsbawm, 'Revolution' in Roy Porter and Mikuláš Teich (eds), *Revolution in history* (Cambridge, 1986), pp 5–46 at 9.

country, which contributed greatly to preventing the implementation of conscription in Ireland, and the two-day general strike of April 1920 which obliged the British government to release hunger-striking republican prisoners, to the great detriment of British security efforts during the following months.[4]

A particularly significant trade union intervention was the munitions embargo of May to December 1920, placed by unionized transport workers on the movement of British military equipment, which greatly impeded the operations of Crown forces. The idea of the embargo was suggested by the action of London dockers who refused to handle weaponry destined to be used against the soviet administration in Russia. First, Dublin dockers, and then railway workers in various parts of the country applied the anti-militarist policy to Irish circumstance: up to 1000 railway workers and 500 dockers were dismissed or suspended from their jobs for taking part. Defying the military, those involved risked their lives as well as their livelihoods in defence of the republic.[5] The importance of the embargo was recognized at the time – for Nevil McCready, commander of the British army in Ireland, it was a 'serious setback to military actions' – but it had a minimal impact on the historiography of the Irish Revolution. More than fifty years ago, Martin O'Sullivan, a retired train driver and a veteran of the embargo, found it 'almost impossible to believe that those important events were not recorded in any recent history of Ireland in the years 1920 onwards to the present day'. In an effort to correct what he was sure was an oversight, he contacted the national broadcaster RTÉ and all the universities in the state. He received no reply. Indignation led him to write his own account of 'How railwaymen defied an empire', which was eventually published in the *Irish Independent* during August 1967.[6]

An enormous amount has been published on the subject of the Irish Revolution since Martin O'Sullivan put pen to paper in 1967 but the imbalance that he complained of has not been corrected.[7] This is not unconnected with the fact that, in large measure, the movements and the people discussed in this volume were defeated and demoralized. From the

---

4 See Emmet O'Connor, *A labour history of Ireland, 1824–2000* (Dublin, 2011), pp 109–15, and John Dorney, 'An unnecessary number of graves? The road to the Truce of July 1921', in *The Irish story*, https://www.theirishstory.com/2021/05/19/an-unnecessary-number-of-graves-the-road-to-the-truce-of-july-1921/#.Yx8X2b_MJy1 [accessed 20 Apr. 2023]. **5** Peter Rigney, *How railwaymen and dockers defied an empire: the Irish munitions embargo of 1920* (Dublin, 2021). **6** Martin O'Sullivan, 'How railwaymen defied an empire', *Irish Independent*, 13 Aug. 1967. The articles were published together in a scholarly journal after the author's death: Martin O'Sullivan, 'The Irish munitions strike of 1920', *Cathair na Mart: Journal of the Westport Historical Society*, 11 (1990), 132–6. **7** The neglect of the episode by historians was remarked upon as long ago as 1979 by Charles Townshend. See his 'The Irish railway strike of 1920: industrial action and civil resistance in the struggle for independence', *Irish Historical Studies*, 22:83 (1979), 265–82.

mid-1920s, according to Bill O'Brien, a Co. Tipperary rural worker writing decades later in the ITGWU periodical *Liberty*: 'members of the Union "got the bird" properly, employers took it out on our men wholesale. When men applied for a job, they were bluntly told, "We want no Union men here," or, more often, "We want no Transport Union men here".'[8] Alongside the coercion of the rural labourers, the consent of the congested farmers was secured through ameliorative land redistribution. And, just as it was with access to services and social supports more widely, the redistribution was accomplished through patronage and clientelism, involving the political parties descended from the pro- and anti-Treaty factions.[9] The emerging narrative of the Irish Revolution served to legitimize the scraggy reality of a profoundly unequal society with the closing off of the radical possibilities of 1917–23. For a dissident minority, dissatisfaction with the outcome of the revolution came to be focused almost exclusively on the six counties of Northern Ireland, seen through the prism of the unresolved national question. This too determined how the past was remembered. The Border Campaign-era memorialization of Padraig Mac Gamhna (otherwise Paddy Gaffney, anti-Treaty Labour TD elected for Carlow–Kilkenny in 1922), at Killeshin, Co. Laois, for instance, is a sculpture of a uniformed Volunteer, alluding to his role in the Carlow Brigade Active Service Unit, while eliding his interests in trade unionism and agrarian reform.

The question of resources is important to the shaping of social memory. Martin O'Sullivan was not, in a phrase of his time, an ordinary five-eighth, but a prominent figure in his locality with national status in his trade union. Yet he had to battle to have some attention drawn to the part that he and his fellow railway workers played in the events of 1920. Powerful institutions in Irish society (including academia) were not interested in engaging with a broader understanding of what made up the Irish Revolution. Particular types of stories were preferred. Tales of derring-do had an intrinsic appeal, but they also served to depoliticize the struggles. The fact was that the lived reality of colonial underdevelopment – poverty, unemployment, emigration – continued to characterize the situation post-1922. Gunsmoke and bravado in the popular literature of revolution offered escapism, but the movements of the revolutionary era had tried to grapple with the social conditions. Such movements represented a radicalism that conservative mid-twentieth-century Ireland had little time for.

8 Bill O'Brien, 'A trade unionist looks back', *Liberty* (ITGWU periodical) (Oct. 1952). 9 See Terence Dooley, *'The land for the people': the land question in independent Ireland* (Dublin, 2004), pp 57–131; and Tony Varley, 'The politics of "holding the balance": Irish farmers' parties and land redistribution in the twentieth century' in Fergus Campbell and Tony Varley (eds), *Land questions*

The first draft of the history of the period was the memoirs of participants, the most highly regarded of which is Ernie O'Malley's *On another man's wound*. Admired for its literary value, there is also an ethnographic aspect to O'Malley's writing, his IRA role as a travelling organizer bringing him in touch with unfamiliar rural worlds. Every so often he interrupted his autobiographical account with comparatively terse segments on the wider political situation. These reveal a revolution quite different from that in the rest of the text. O'Malley appeared to recognize a lacuna that was there when he wrote, somewhat ruefully:

> The movement as a whole was hostile to labour claims even though labour had helped to prevent conscription, had not contested the last election, and was refusing to carry armed troops … [W]e knew where our sympathies were: with the labourer and small farmer in the country, the worker in the city … I could feel my annoyance at the conviction of purely revolutionary workers who stood outside the nationalist movement, and a certain amusement at their arguments.[10]

O'Malley's insight here was exceptional however. More broadly, there were a number of key institutions that were critical to the shaping of the social memory of the revolutionary period. One of these was *The Kerryman* newspaper, which serialized accounts of guerrilla struggle in its pages and subsequently republished them in the collections, *Rebel Cork's fighting story, Kerry's fighting story, Limerick's fighting story* and *Dublin's fighting story*. In the introduction to the recent republication of the Limerick volume Ruán O'Donnell points to the 'problematic themes' that had to be grappled with in its production – not least 'the anomalous experience of a city "soviet" in 1919'.[11] For its part, Tom Barry's *Guerrilla days in Ireland* (1949) was first serialized in the *Irish Press,* the party newspaper of Fianna Fáil.

Popularly, the traditional nationalist version of history has been assailed by revisionism in recent decades. This actually has not greatly influenced the conceptual space of what constituted the revolution; in fact, the very same territory has been occupied. In his keystone article, 'The geography of revolution in Ireland', Peter Hart specifically defined the revolution in relation to the extent of IRA violence in proportion to population: 'The Cork brigades alone were responsible for 28 per cent of all of the IRA's victims, thereby

in modern Ireland (Manchester, 2013), pp 238–65.   **10** Ernie O'Malley, *On another man's wounds,* new Anvil Books edition (Dublin, 1979), p. 144. For further discussion of O'Malley, see Aidan Beatty, 'An Irish Revolution without a revolution', *Journal of World-Systems Research,* 22:1 (2016), 54–76.   **11** *Limerick's fighting story: told by the men who made it* (Cork, 2009), p. 19.

earning pre-eminent notoriety, They and neighbouring units made Munster the heartland of the revolution …'.[12] In this respect, for all the controversy, there is no difference between the gun-centric perspective of Hart and the old gun-toting glamour of the popular histories. Hart's approach, most influentially in his monograph *The IRA and its enemies* (1998), represented a step back from David Fitzpatrick's study of Clare (1977), a social history of the period which was far more attentive to agrarianism, to the labour movement, and to the *ancien regime* in the county.[13] The problem with a local case study however, especially one of as particular a county as Clare, was that its conclusions are not readily applicable to other counties. The configuration of social forces, for example, was very different in counties with high levels of paid employment in agriculture. It might be noted that Fitzpatrick's and Hart's studies both reflect the period in which they were written. As well as coinciding with the 'turn' to social history, Fitzpatrick's work was written at a time of upsurge in labour militancy and other forms of unrest in the 1970s, while Hart was writing when the ascendancy of neoliberalism had appeared to eclipse the organized working class as a dynamic factor in western societies.

It is a matter of regret that specialist works by such as Emmet O'Connor and Conor Kostick, and studies of metropolitan Dublin and Cork by Padraig Yeates and John Borgonovo, respectively, have not informed the wider discourse on the period to the extent that they might have.[14]

The military memoir genre was effectively institutionalized in the form of the Bureau of Military History (BMH) – a state-directed oral history project of the 1940s and 1950s.[15] The project gathered 1773 witness statements, eventually released in 2003 and made available online in 2012. Not surprisingly, they have greatly influenced writing on the revolutionary period over the past twenty years. As the name suggests the BMH had a particularly militaristic focus. It was conducted under the auspices of the Department of Defence, based at least partly on Military Service Pension records. It is notable that only a select few witness statements are concerned with civilian roles –

12 Peter Hart, 'The geography of revolution in Ireland, 1917–1923', *Past & Present*, 155:1 (May 1997), 142–76 at 146.   **13** Peter Hart, *The IRA and its enemies: violence and community in Cork, 1916–1923* (Oxford, 1997); David Fitzpatrick, *Politics and Irish life, 1913–1921: provincial experiences of war and revolution* (Dublin, 1977).   **14** Emmet O'Connor, *Syndicalism in Ireland, 1917–1923* (Cork, 1988); Conor Kostick, *Revolution in Ireland: popular militancy, 1917 to 1923* (London, 1996); Padraig Yeates, *A city in turmoil, Dublin 1919–1921* (Dublin, 2012); John Borgonovo, *The dynamics of war and revolution: Cork city, 1916–1918* (Cork, 2013).   **15** See Daniel Ayiotis, *The Military Archives: a history* (Dublin, 1922), especially pp 125–9; Eve Morrison, 'Bureau of Military History witness statements as sources for the Irish Revolution', Military Archives, https://www.military archives.ie/collections/online-collections/bureau-of-military-history-1913-1921/wp-content/uploads/ 2019/06/Bureau_of_Military_witness_statements-as_sources_for_the_Irish-Revolution.pdf [accessed 1 June 2023]; Diarmuid Ferriter, '… in such deadly earnest', *Dublin Review*, 12 (2003), 36–64; Fearghal

and in some instances evidence givers who were involved in both labour and paramilitary mobilization spoke on the latter, but not the former.

The example of David Hall, Officer Commanding 1st Brigade, Meath IRA, is instructive. In his witness statement he mentioned in passing his role in Sinn Féin electioneering and Sinn Féin courts and the Dáil loan. He made no reference at all to his involvement, first, in the Back to the Land movement and the Meath Labour Union, or, then, to being secretary of the largest Irish Transport and General Workers' Union (ITGWU) branch in Co. Meath during the 1919 farm strike, or, for that matter, his election as a Labour member of Dunshaughlin Rural District Council in 1920, of which body he was elected chair. Hall's activist career would culminate in his election as a Labour Party TD between August 1923 and September 1927 (see Terry Dunne's article in this volume), but little of that strand of it was captured by the Bureau of Military History.[16] It is not even a matter of military versus civilian roles. Some civilian roles were considered worthy of recording. The silence in Hall's witness statement is in quite the contrast to the voluminous recounting by Kevin O'Shiel of his role in the Dáil courts dampening of the Western agrarian protests of 1920 (see Johnny Burke's article in this volume). The impact of this tendency in the primary sources on recent historiography is indicated by the following pronouncement in a recently published survey article: 'It is difficult to identify a qualitative leap forward in popular mobilization for the period 1913–23'.[17] Thus, the anti-conscription strike, the munitions embargo and the outbreak of agrarian militancy of 1920, the unprecedented waves of strikes, the Munster soviets, are consigned to seeming irrelevance.

The Irish Republican Army of course was itself a mass movement, as borne out in this volume by the articles dealing with communities in north Sligo, north Mayo and north Kilkenny. But of the tens of thousands of its volunteers, only a minority were armed. And the range of actions shown in brigade reports indicates that for the most part, volunteers were involved in low level sabotage, intimidation, raids for arms – activities similar to those carried out by nineteenth-century agrarian militants, with the key qualitative difference being that their endeavours were directed against the state. In this regard, one might give the example of the activity reported by Co. Laois brigade officers for the nineteen-member Rathdowney company during 1919/20:

McGarry, '"Too many histories": the Bureau of Military History and Easter 1916', *History Ireland*, 19:6 (2011) 26–9. **16** Bureau of Military History, Witness Statement 1539, David Hall; 'David Hall (1891–1960)' in Charles Callan and Barry Desmond, *Irish labour lives: a biographical dictionary of Irish Labour Party deputies, senators, MPs and MEPs* (Dublin, 2010), p. 112. **17** Marc Mulholland, 'How revolutionary was the "Irish Revolution"', *Éire-Ireland*, 56:1–2 (2021), 139–75 at 148.

> Co-operation with other Companies in the destruction of Errill, Borris-in-Ossory and Garron RIC Barracks. Collected 14 shot guns and ammunition. Film Machine showing war pictures in Rathdowney destroyed. Warned JPs from attending Courts. Held Sinn Féin Courts. Collected money to purchase rifles. Raided Mail Car on several occasions. Raided trains and destroyed Government property. Blocked and trenched roads several times. Held up RIC Attendant a few yards from Barracks and took her away, and several other minor operations.[18]

With regard to the dominant narrative of the revolutionary period one must acknowledge the part played by the Catholic Church from the late 1920s to the 1960s, in determining what was acceptable to remember. During protracted 'red scares', phenomena like soviets could not be publicly commemorated – or even named.[19]

We must also consider the role of the political context of the 1950s in shaping the social memory of the 1920s. There is not a major archive independent of the state and there is a marked contrast today between the digitization of some archives and the inaccessibility of others. Most notably, while the BMH witness statements are easily available, the records of the Land Commission – which have the potential to greatly add to an understanding of the social history of the revolution – remain closed to researchers. It would be naïve not to see political decision-making in this, even if this was not necessarily always particularly calculated. It is hardly coincidental that flows of funding have been made available for the heroic pre-history of the two main political parties who have interchangeably governed over the history of the state. Indeed, in the 1940s and 1950s politicians were essentially funding their own personal biographies (and, given the prevalence of political dynasties, there is an element in the contemporary period of them funding their personal genealogies). Although there are certainly animated controversies, these reflect imagined affinities with conservative or centrist forces in the Ireland of the revolutionary period, while the radical upsurge goes unstated. Essentially, more often than not, arguments in the public sphere about the proposed commemoration of the Royal Irish Constabulary, apparent attacks on Protestants or Irish involvement in the 1914–18 war are arguments by proxy

---

18 Military Archives, Brigade Activity Reports, Report for 1919/1920 on Rathdowney company, 3rd Battalion, Leix Brigade, submitted by Thomas F. Brady, O/C Leix Brigade, and Laurence P. Cummins, vice commandant, 3rd Battalion. **19** See Mike McNamara, 'Remembering the Limerick soviet of 1919' in John Cunningham, Francis Devine and Sonja Tiernan (eds), *Labour history in Irish history: Irish Labour History Society 50th anniversary essays* (Dublin, 2023), pp 234–8.

about the more recent conflict in the North. They frequently reflect little engagement with what went on in the 1910s and 1920s.

Reference above to Kevin O'Shiel's role draws attention to the scale of the agrarian movement that swept the western counties in the spring and early summer of 1920. Indeed, the number of reported 'agrarian outrages' was greater in 1920 than in any year since the height of the land war of 1879–82. The focus of the movement however was not the same as in the nineteenth century. Increasingly, from the period of the 'ranch war' of *c.*1904–10, mobilizations were concerned with the redistribution of agricultural land rather than with landlord-tenant relations.[20] In parts of the west, according to the future minister for justice, Kevin O'Higgins, grazing land 'became a common and everyone's stock was on everyone else's land'.[21] Undoubtedly the movement was tumultuous, but it was not quite the free-for-all implied by O'Higgins: the land seizures and cattle-drives of 1920 were redistributive in purpose, and the instigators were farmers whose holdings were uneconomic, and landless neighbours who wished to secure a future for themselves in rural Ireland. Frustrated by the failure of the land legislation of the preceding decades to address their particular concerns, their targets were mainly grazing farms – on which the extensive type of agriculture practiced had long been considered anti-social. However, in his article here on the community of Moygownagh in north Mayo Liam Alex Heffron shows that acquisitiveness might trump idealism in such conflicts.

Members of Sinn Féin and the Irish Volunteers participated in the agrarian militancy, but, wishing to conciliate the better-off in society, the leadership of the national movement quickly intervened to bring it to a halt, inaugurating land courts, and deploying IRA units to stop seizures and to return occupied land. Though a rather different view was taken of labour militancy in 1920 – especially of actions such as the munitions embargo that greatly benefited the independence struggle – in time strikes would also come to be regarded as inimical to the interests of the emerging state. This is among the developments traced by Dominic Haugh in his article on the Munster soviets of 1921/2.

The efforts of labour and social historians notwithstanding, the dominant version of the Irish Revolution remains two-dimensional at best. With this volume, the editors hope that their selection of local and regional case studies with a focus on mass participation will reveal that a 'spirit of revolution' was widespread in Ireland in the period 1917 to 1923, a spirit that in hindsight

---

20 See Fergus Campbell, *Land and revolution: nationalist politics in the west of Ireland, 1891–1921* (Oxford, 2005), pp 85–123.   **21** Cited by David Jones, 'The issue of land redistribution: revisiting *Graziers, land reform and political conflict in Ireland*' in Campbell and Varley (eds), *Land questions*, pp 117–48 at 128.

appears remarkable in its heterogeneity of origin and principle. If movements arose which were guided by adherents of the Revolutionary Socialist Party and of the Irish Workers' League, others were led by activists in the GAA and Sinn Féin, such as Bernard Meehan of Maugherow, Co. Sligo, who is introduced in Moira Leydon's article in this volume. Other manifestations still, equally vibrant and vital, such as the Town Tenants League and the United Irish Plotholders' Union, the latter discussed in Mary Forrest's article, had their roots and connections in Redmondism. It is the broad-based and multi-faceted processes of mobilization and radicalization, leading to an expansion of imagined possibilities, that make up what we mean here by revolution.

* * *

If, as Lloyd George put it, there was a 'deep sense not only of discontent, but of anger and revolt, amongst the workmen', the conduit through which much of it was expressed was the trade union movement, the most dynamic element of which was the ITGWU. Reduced to a low ebb by its defeat in the Dublin lockout of 1913–14, and hindered in regrouping by the calling up of many of its remaining members to the army later in 1914, and by the loss of key figures including the absent James Larkin and the executed James Connolly, the ITGWU nonetheless underwent a revival from 1917. A generalized upturn in union recruitment arose at that time from wartime economic conditions, with the membership of unions affiliated to the Irish Trade Union Congress, rising from about 100,000 in 1916 to 225,000 in 1920. Extremely high levels of inflation – by one calculation, prices rose by 124 per cent between August 1914 and December 1916[22] – had the effect of reducing the purchasing power of wage earners, obliging them to seek increases. Beneficiaries of economic demand and of price increases during 'the most hectic period of agricultural prosperity in Ireland's history', in Louis Cullen's judgment, were farmers, especially large farmers.[23]

At the same time, near-full employment and government regulation of the economy to ensure food production combined to improve the bargaining power of labour. Particularly significant regulatory measures were the Corn Production Act of 1917, legislating for compulsory tillage, and the establishment of the Agricultural Wages Board in the same year. To secure their new entitlements, agricultural labourers revived some of the inert rural labour associations of the pre-war period, but these were pushed aside by, or

22 Central Statistics Office, *Life in 1916 Ireland: stories from statistics*, 'Wholesale price index in Ireland, 1914 to 1918 (note)': https://www.cso.ie/en/releasesandpublications/ep/p-1916/1916irl/economy/ie/ [accessed 22 June 2022].   23 L.M. Cullen, *An economic history of Ireland since 1600*

absorbed into, the ITGWU. That union grew from about 5000 members in 1916 to 100,000 in 1920. Of the 100,000, up to 60,000 were agricultural labourers, so that the ITGWU reached into small towns and villages over most of the island.[24] In May 1920, the *Manchester Guardian* reported on how Ireland had been transformed to an extent that made it almost unrecognizable to anyone who had spent a decade away from it:

> Another new factor in the West of Ireland is the rapid march of organized labour. The returned Irishman would notice in his old market town a rich crop of buttons or badges on the coats of the younger men. These are not the badges of the [United Irish] League or of Sinn Fein but of trade unionism, usually of the ITGWU. He would also notice if he peered into the old shop windows that it would be far easier to buy a photograph of James Connolly than of De Valera. The ITGWU, Connolly's body, is particularly active all over the country, and penetrates to such remote spots as Clifden, the far end of the desert of Connemara ... This is a small-holders country, and employed agricultural labourers are few but in the land where hired labourers are to be found, this union is busy organizing them.[25]

The influx of agricultural workers transformed the social character of Irish trade unionism, which had during most of its history been dominated by skilled male workers. The character and the trajectory of the transformation is illuminated in several articles in this volume. Anne Boran's study of a mining community in rural Kilkenny untangles the different and sometimes conflicting ambitions of several social classes during this period of upheaval.

Significantly also, women workers became organized to a far greater extent than formerly. Theresa Moriarty's article shows how women fought to have their voices heard in the councils of the Irish Trade Union Congress (Congress) while Kieran McNulty discusses the ways gender issues presented themselves during the period in Co. Kerry. At the same time, the success of manual workers in securing increases that were equal to or greater than the rate of inflation attracted the attention and the affiliation of white collar workers, who had previously remained aloof from labour. Notable in this regard was attendance for the first time of delegates from the Irish National Teachers' Organisation at the 1918 Congress.

(London, 1971), p. 171. **24** O'Connor, *A labour history of Ireland*, pp 102–11. **25** Special Correspondent, East Clare, 'Sinn Fein's fight for temperance; rise of trade unions; coming conflict with the Church', *Manchester Guardian*, 13 May 1920.

As trade unionism was extending its reach into new social categories, it was also undergoing a radicalization. Contributing to this was the success of strike action, as well as the rise in insurgent nationalism and anti-war sentiment. Influential among the more activist element was a perception that the working class had taken charge in revolutionary Russia and that this might be also be achieved elsewhere. As the modernist Irish language writer Pádraic Ó Conaire wrote at the time: '*As an lucht oibre, as lucht na Boilséibhiceachta atá muinín ag an pobal i ngach tír leis an tsíocháin chaoin a thabhairt den Eoraip … agus le saol nua uasal a thógáil do na daoine a thiocfas inár ndiaidh.* [It is the labour movement, the Bolsheviks, that the people trust to establish a benign peace in Europe … and to build a satisfying new life for those that come after us]'. In Ó Conaire's native Galway, such thinking found expression through a branch of the Town Tenants' League, which is examined in John Cunningham's article

James Connolly's concept of the Workers' Republic informed Irish understandings of developments in Russia, and Connolly was also a martyr of the Irish Republic declared at Easter 1916. ITGWU leaders such as William O'Brien and Cathal O'Shannon embraced the several elements of Connolly's legacy, while drawing on his writings to inform and validate their approach to political and material circumstances. In its expansionist phase, the ITGWU was relatively decentralized with local initiative in the ascendant, initiative supported and guided by platform speeches and union periodicals including the *Watchword of Labour.* At the same time, the union headquarters in Dublin, Liberty Hall, came to epitomize the ITGWU ideal.

The cover image of Liberty Hall, by the Dublin Jewish artist Harry Kernoff, shows Liberty Hall as it was in the 1930s, door open and a hub of daily life in the north inner city. Previously the Northumberland Hotel, it was acquired by Jim Larkin and opened in late February 1912, serving as a centre of culture, education and entertainment as well as of union administration. No explanation of the name was given at the time. It occurs in Oliver Goldsmith's *She stoops to conquer* but ITGWU historian Desmond Greaves hypothesized that Larkin took it from a popular adventure novel of his boyhood, *Mr Midshipman Easy* by Frederick Marryat.[26]

Through associations with the 1913 lockout and the 1916 Rising, through the Citizen Army and in other ways, the building came to represent the Workers' Republic. For those with power and property to lose, and those they influenced, Liberty Hall was a source of dangerous and destabilizing doctrines – in an exchange of letters during August 1919 in the *Irish Independent* the

---

26 C. Desmond Greaves, *The Irish Transport and General Workers' Union: the formative years, 1909–1923*

prevalence of 'Liberty Hall methods' in counties Tipperary and Meath was denounced.[27] To Lieutenant-Colonel Loftus Bryan of Wexford, a national leader of the Irish Farmers' Union, it seemed in May 1920, that 'there were at least three governments proposing to run the country – one of them in Dublin Castle, another he thought in Harcourt Street [Michael Collins's Finance ministry] and the other in Liberty Hall …'.[28] Fearing that their interests would suffer in 'the conflict between these different governments', Bryan urged that farmers 'take a hand in the game themselves' and later, towards the end of May 1920, he was prominent among those announcing the establishment of a Farmers' Freedom Force with the declared objective of breaking 'the recent embargo by Liberty Hall on the exports of pigs, bacon and butter'.[29]

For the hundred thousand or so who flocked into the ITGWU between 1917 and 1920, Liberty Hall represented an aspiration for a levelling up to a more equal and equitable society. In Drogheda, in Galway, in Sligo, and elsewhere members showed its resonance by applying the name to union buildings in their own towns.[30] Further afield in 1919, Marcus Garvey named the New York headquarters of his Universal Negro Improvement Association (UNIA) Liberty Hall, in acknowledgment in part at least of its iconic predecessor in Dublin. The name would be used subsequently for UNIA buildings throughout the United States.[31] For its part, Garvey's movement would intercede in disputes between Irish and black longshoremen in an episode examined by Brian Hanley in his article on the roles of maritime workers in the Irish Revolution.

The idea represented by Liberty Hall changed as conditions changed. A post-war economic downturn from 1920/1 led to unemployment and a decline in union membership. A consequent retrenchment and restructuring brought about a great reduction in the union staff throughout the country, a centralization of operations, and a more cautious approach generally.[32] For a more combative element of the movement, Liberty Hall came to represent bureaucracy and inertia, prompting rancorous splits in the movement, most dramatically 'the battle for Liberty Hall' that followed James Larkin's return to Ireland in 1923, and is treated here by Gerry Watts.[33]

(Dublin, 1982), p. 343, n. 10.   **27** 'Liberty Hall methods', *Irish Independent*, 4, 6 Aug. 1919. **28** Quoted in the *Irish Farmer*, 8 May 1920.   **29** Ibid.; *Nationalist and Leinster Times*, 29 May 1920. **30** 'Letters to the Editor', *Drogheda Independent*, 8 May 1920; 'New ITGWU secretary elected', *Connacht Tribune*, 24 June 1922; Greaves, *Irish Transport and General Workers' Union*, p. 79. **31** Robert A. Hill et al. (eds), *The Marcus Garvey and Universal Negro Improvement Association Papers*, vol. I: *1826–August 1919* (Berkeley, 1983), p. lxxii.   **32** See Francis Devine, *Organizing history: a centenary of SIPTU, 1909–2009* (Dublin, 2009), pp 93–9.   **33** For accusations of bureaucracy and inertia, see 'Unemployed tactics', *The Workers' Republic*, 7 Jan. 1922; 'Bureaucrats of Liberty Hall', *The Workers' Republic*, 22 Apr. 1922; 'Bounce Beaver O'Brien, *Workers' Republic*, 5 May 1923.

Even at its height, Liberty Hall's authority had geographical limits, for the ITGWU's presence was patchy north of a line connecting Sligo and Dundalk. In most of Ulster, the British-based Workers' Union (WU) organized the categories of workers catered for elsewhere on the island by the ITGWU. Faced with similar economic conditions, the WU expanded rapidly from 1918, parallel with the ITGWU, reaching across the sectarian divide and channelling rank-and-file militancy, but with its position challenged by burgeoning loyalism and partition. Its trajectory is among the matters considered by Fearghal Mac Bhloscaidh in his chapter on Belfast labour.

* * *

In completing this book, our greatest debt is to the contributors, who stayed with the project through various drafts and editorial pauses.

The volume originated in discussions prompted by a conference, 'Labour, Gender and Class in the Struggle for Irish Independence', held at the University of Galway in November 2019. This was a Decade of Centenaries event, jointly organized by the Irish Congress of Trade Unions and the Irish Centre for the Histories of Labour and Class (based at the university's Moore Institute), and supported by the Department of Culture, Heritage and the Gaeltacht. Our thanks to the Congress, to the Department, to the University, to the Institute and to the Centre, as well as to the Irish Labour History Society, which generously assisted with conference preparation, and to the Department of Sociology, Maynooth Univeristy, which hosted a seminar exploring the major themes of this book.

Most of the contributors featured here presented thought-provoking local case studies at the conference, which the editors considered had the makings of an interesting and original volume.

In addition to the contributors, we wish to thank the following who assisted us in various ways in seeing this project to fruition: John Borgonovo, Sarah-Anne Buckley, Fergus Campbell, Dan Carey, David Convery, Olivier Coquelin, Mary Corcoran, Francis Devine, Mary Harris, Kate Kernoff, Fintan Lane, Mary McAuliffe, Mary Muldowney, Richard McElligott, Gerard Madden, Conor McCabe, Emmet O'Connor, Pól Ó Dochartaigh, Martha Shaughnessy, Tony Varley, Whyte's Auction Rooms, Padraig Yeates.

'The change was not to be in symbol only but also in substance': contested freedoms in the Castlecomer coalfield

ANNE BORAN

This chapter examines social relations in the Castlecomer coalfield in the period 1917–23. It will focus on four dominant groupings – miners, carters, farmers and businesses – considered to be of key relevance to mobilization and action in the context of the struggle for independence. It argues that the social structures were reflected in the leadership, roles, ideologies and organizational goals of local organizations set up to respond to aspirations for freedom. This being so, notions of freedom were contested and in practice involved a conflict of interest between the collective organizations to further independence goals and individual group interests, particularly those of labour. This was also reflected in the Civil War factions and in the aftermath of the conflict at local level. Those with least bargaining power in the social hierarchy tended to have their interests marginalized and unresolved by the 'freedoms' offered in post-independence Ireland.

The class context of the Castlecomer area

Although the focus of the study is on social relations between miners, carters, farmers and businesses, the colonial/imperialist context of location and time is of significance. In 1917 the Castlecomer coalfield was still dominated by the Wandesforde estate that had survived from the seventeenth to the twentieth century despite resistance from the native O'Brenan clan, an ancient tribe or sept of Ossory, who had held the north Kilkenny lands of Idough, from medieval times.[1] Through the patronage of Thomas Wentworth, appointed lord deputy of Ireland in 1632 under Charles I, the lands were ceded to the Yorkshire Wandesforde family. The family survived many uprisings.[2] Although, by 1917, the 22,000 acres of farmland had been sold to

---

1 The O'Brenans contested the loss of their lands through the courts during the seventeenth century and generally made a nuisance of themselves, by helping themselves to stock on what they regarded as their land, until finally denied possession under William of Orange. 2 The Wandesfordes were forced to flee during the 1641 and 1798 rebellions. In the latter the big house and part of the town of Castlecomer were destroyed. Miners from Doonane (on the border with Laois) joined Father

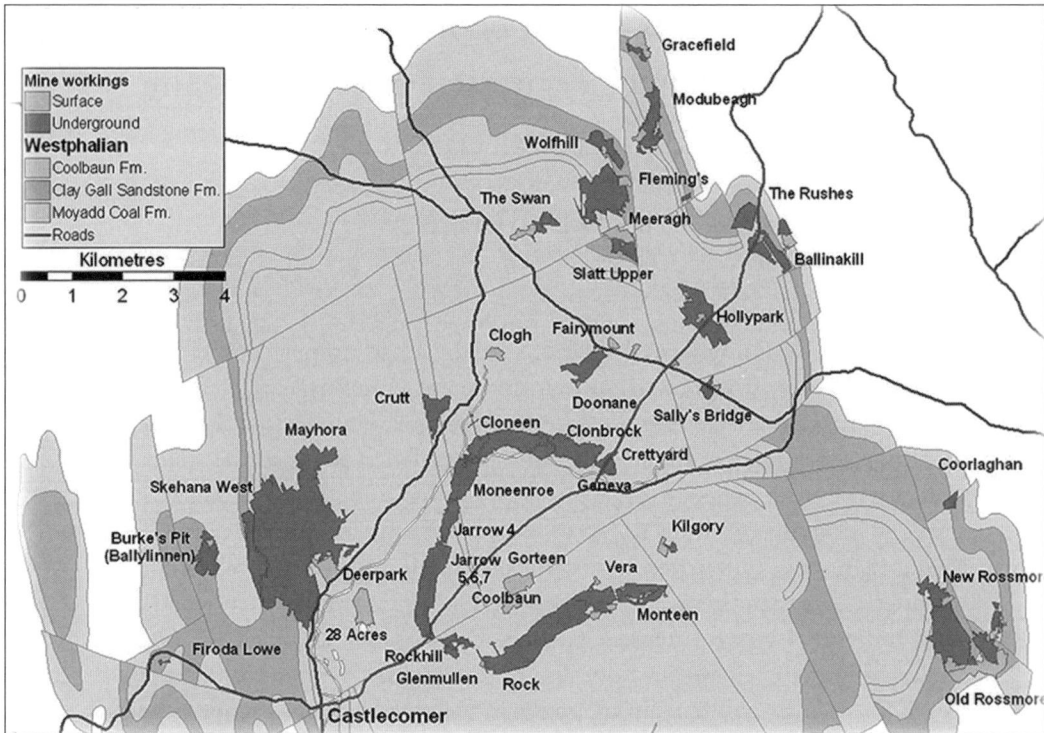

1.1 Leinster coalfield.

the Land Commission and distributed to small farmers in the area, the mines mainly remained under Wandesforde control. Richard Henry Prior-Wandesforde who inherited the estate in 1892 was an intransigent employer, hostile to organization and militancy amongst his employees and resistant to demands for higher wages or better working conditions. He was keen, however, to modernize mining operations and agriculture and was enthusiastic about the co-operative movement of the day, establishing co-operative creameries in the town of Castlecomer and at Crettyard and co-operative stores at Massford. He also established the Agricultural Bank in the town of Castlecomer.

The chapter will proceed to look in turn at the position in the community of (i) miners, (ii) carters, (iii) farmers and (iv) business and professionals.

Murphy's Wexford men when they marched into Kilkenny to fight Asquith and his troops in 1798. Lady Anne Ormonde (Wandesforde) rebuilt the town and big house on her return to Castlecomer adding an army barracks and the Market House (William Corrigan, *The history and antiquities of the diocese of Ossory* (4 vols, Dublin, 1905), vol. i, p. 159).

(i) The miners

Although numbers of miners rose and fell over time, depending on the challenges faced in individual mines, the political context of the day and the dissatisfactions experienced by the workforce, approximately 500–600 miners and 300 coal carters worked the last section of the Jarrow Seam in four pits in 1917.[3] They were Jarrow Number 7, Vera, Monteen and Rock pits. By this time, production was fully wage-labour based, which had not always been the case historically. The Skehana seam, discovered and worked briefly before the First World War, dominated production in the 1920s, especially at Deerpark which was sunk in 1924. This mine would become the centre of mining in the district until its closure in 1969. It produced good quality almost sulphur-free anthracite.

A strong tradition of mining families stretched back for generations and created a mining culture, with sons joining fathers in the mines at age 14, bonded by solidarity and trust, and with a clear identity relating to an occupation that involved dangerous work underground. They possessed a working-class consciousness related to the industry of mining, but as a rural-based industrial workforce they lacked, perhaps, the mutual collective support that is possible for urban industrial workers. The Castlecomer miners had a history of rebelliousness and involvement in Whitefeet (Whiteboy) activities in the nineteenth century.[4] They reacted against the deep mining reforms imposed by Charles Wandesforde that involved bringing in pitmen from Newcastle. They opposed the resulting mine closures, unemployment and insecurity by striking, sabotage and attacks on the incomers. This found a forceful expression in clashes at Cloneen in the coalfield on 25 November 1831, when an attempt was made to free eight Whitefeet prisoners who were being taken under army and police escort to Kilkenny. Coal carters, with the support of miners, put a roadblock in place at Cloneen turnpike, using two lines of loaded carts fastened together and about 300 local people pelted the 40-strong escort with stones and missiles. The escort opened fire on the crowd with live ammunition, killing five and wounding more than forty.[5] Shortly afterwards a mine manager was brutally murdered at Doonane pit in front of many witnesses.[6]

3 National Library of Ireland (NLI), Prior-Wandesforde Papers, Collection List 173, MS 48,346/10.
4 For more detailed discussion of Whitefeet activity and links to miners see T.M. Dunne, '"Humour the people": subaltern collective agency and uneven proletarianization in Castlecomer colliery, 1826–34', *Éire-Ireland*, 53:3 (2018), 64–92, and T.M. Dunne, 'Gentlemen regulators: landlord/tenant conflict and the making of moral economy in early nineteenth-century Ireland', *Rural History*, 31:1 (2020), 17–34. **5** *Chutes Western Herald*, 1 Dec. 1831. **6** *Kilkenny Moderator* (henceforth *KM*), 22 Mar. 1832.

While in such cases there is evidence of collective action, in the power structures of the early nineteenth century, power inequalities existed within the mining community. Master colliers had some leverage over workers and labour relations because they contracted labour for the mine owner. They also supplied provisions, the cost of which were deducted from workers' wages, all of which gave them power to manipulate the miners who depended on them for employment and provisions.[7] The master colliers and the carters (who carried coal) had a level of independence and resources not possessed by miners in general and were accused of pilfering coal. They risked losing out under the reforms being imposed by Charles Wandesforde. Dunn, the mine engineer, in 1844, laid the blame for much of the stealing at the door of the master colliers, who could sell the extra coal without the landlord taking a cut. Carters would have been complicit in this process. Prevention meant extra expenditure on watchmen.[8] Ordinary miners often suffered the consequences of their resistance against those in power.[9] Direct confrontation was unlikely to achieve success against an armed enemy whereas intimidation often proved more effective. When, after the Cloneen incident, the toll collector was arrested, presumably because of collusion in the blockade, attempts to replace him were unsuccessful because of local intimidation.[10]

The Famine reduced the local population by almost half in the mid-nineteenth century and helped Wandesforde to clear his lands of sub-tenants, cabins and excess labour. Later the miners learned the value of boycott from the fiery Clogh curate, Fr O'Halloran, who defended them in their strike action in 1881. They rebelled against having to mine 24 cwts of coal in order to be paid for 1 ton (20 cwts) to take account of waste and small coal. O'Halloran presided over a meeting of 200 miners and management and negotiated an agreement of 22 cwt to the ton.[11] He encouraged co-operation between farmers and miners.[12] In 1907 the miners attempted to unionize into a Miners' Federation.[13] They were, however, led in the main by non-miners

---

7 Children's Employment Commission (1841): *Reports by Frederick Roper, Esq., on the employment and conditions of children in mines and manufacturing.* Republished by Picks Publishing (1998), p. 23.
8 Matthias Dunn, *An historical, geological and descriptive view of the coal trade of the north of England to which is appended a concise notice of the peculiarities of certain coal fields in Great Britain and Ireland; and also a general description of the coal mines of Belgium, drawn up from an actual impression* (Newcastle upon Tyne, 1844), p. 147. 9 Tom Lyng, *Castlecomer connections: exploring history, geography and social evolution in north Kilkenny environs* (Kilkenny, 1984), p. 253. 10 National Archives Ireland (NAI), Martin Kenny to Henry William Paget, lord lieutenant, 22 Apr. 1832, CSO/RP/1832/1795. He claimed compensation for loss of income on his contract to collect tolls at Cloneen turnpike. 11 *Kildare Observer*, 24 Sept. 1881. 12 Fr O'Halloran was chairman of the Clogh Land League Association and co-opted miners to save the harvest of an imprisoned farmer Mr Barron. He facilitated support of £30 from the Land League for the miners who went on strike to get proper recompense for the weight of the coal extracted. *Kildare Observer*, 23 July 1881, 24 Sept. 1881. 13 *Kilkenny*

with their own political ambitions within the Home Rule or United Irish League (UIL) milieu. These men failed to serve the miners' interests, and despite many strikes and disputes, they were met by intransigence from Wandesforde. Finally, in 1918, they unionized under the Irish Transport and General Workers' Union (ITGWU). The founding members were Ned Mahon (a local miner) and Cathal O'Shannon, an early member with William O'Brien of the Socialist Party of Ireland.[14] That was significant, because the union and its members identified with both the socialist ideals of its founder James Larkin and the socialist republican ideas of James Connolly who worked for the ITGWU from 1911 onwards. He brought his aspiration to create an industrial union across all industries (including rural wage workers) and his belief that independence should mean more than simply a change of political masters but should challenge 'the power dangerous to freedom that goes with ownership'.[15] As William O'Brien pointed out in Kilkenny in 1918: 'Some people who were making a good thing out of their labour talked about the freedom of Ireland, but there could be no such freedom as long as the majority of the people – the workers – were ground down in slavery'.[16]

Although likely to have encompassed a range of left-wing views, evidence suggests that the miners mobilizing at that point in time aspired not only to better wages and conditions but also to a new independent nation that would include social and work-based freedoms as well.[17] They were ready for collective action in the workplace and in the fight for an independent Ireland. Branch membership in Castlecomer in 1918 was 89 and in Gazebo (later called Moneenroe), where the majority of miners lived, it was 223. A year later the Gazebo membership was 529 (presumably with Castlecomer membership incorporated).[18]

(ii) The carters

By the 1900s there were about 300 carters carrying coal from the mines to the local population and to Carlow, Kilkenny and Athy, where it could be transported further afield by river or rail. Although an inherent part of the mining economy, the interests of the carters and the miners were by no means the same. They sometimes engaged in collective action with the miners (as in

People, 2 Nov. 1907; Francis Devine, 'The Irish Transport and General Workers' Union in Carlow and Kilkenny, 1918–1930', *Old Kilkenny Review* (2017), 147–71. **14** Lyng, *Castlecomer connections*, pp 256–7. **15** James Connolly, *Labour in Ireland, the re-conquest of Ireland* (Dublin, 1917), pp 326–53. **16** 'Organizing labour in Kilkenny', *The Kilkenny Moderator and Leinster Advertiser*, 10 July 1918. **17** Martin Maguire, 'Labour in County Louth, 1912–1923' in Donal Hall and Martin Maguire (eds), *County Louth and the Irish Revolution, 1912–1923* (Dublin, 2017), pp 59–85. **18** Devine, 'ITGWU in Carlow and Kilkenny', p. 12.

the Doonane example above), sometime in separate collective action. They were mobile, well remunerated for carting coal long distances, 8*s.* (shillings) to 10*s.* per ton from the pit head to Kilkenny (15 miles), and 8*s.* per ton to Carlow (12 miles) in 1917. Wandesforde claimed that Welsh coal could be delivered to Kilkenny for 8*s.* a ton giving it an unfair advantage over Castlecomer coal.[19] Carters also provided a useful function in carrying information and ideas as well as coal in their travels. They had a distinct identity, linked to mining and miners but distinguished from the miners by ownership of substantial equipment (carts) and animals. The former had to be sturdy to tolerate poor roads, long distances and heavy weights, and the latter healthy and well cared for, requiring sufficient land, housing and food for their needs. Evidence suggests they were ambitious to expand their stock when opportunities presented themselves. For example, when the railway line was extended to Castlecomer in 1920 but had not yet been extended to Deerpark (it took another 12 months), some 20–25 carters carried coal from the terminal of the aerial ropeway at Deerpark to Castlecomer to be loaded onto the train. According to the mine manager Mr Whittaker, most of these had 3 carts each and some had 6 carts each. They were paid 9*s.* 3*d.* per ton.[20] Their location in class terms could perhaps be seen as a distinct fraction of the working class or even as at a transitional phase, at least in their aspirations, to non-working-class status. Accurate categorizations are very tricky to make in such circumstances.

Carters were forceful in reacting to threats to their way of life as shown by the Cloneen incident in the previous century. They organized separately under the Castlecomer Coal Carriers Association in 1905, again with direction from politically ambitious outsiders who were not themselves carters. Signed up at the first meeting were 102 persons from Castlecomer parish, 207 persons from Clogh parish and 76 persons from Kilkenny.[21] Wandesforde fought hard and successfully for a railway that would make distribution easier and make the coal more competitive with imported coal from Britain. He saw the carters as problematic, 'owing to very heavy thefts of coal on the road and extortionate charges for loading'. He also claimed there was excessive breakage from double handling and tried to substitute tractors and lorries for carters before the railway extension was built. Substitution was not successful due to the state of the roads. Wandesforde hoped to save 6*s.* per ton on the cost of delivery with railway transportation.[22] The carters saw this as a direct threat, particularly when the branch line was extended to Deerpark in 1921. There the coal from the aerial ropeways could be graded and loaded directly on to

19 *Kilkenny Journal*, 7 Mar. 1917. 20 *Kilkenny People*, 1 July 1922. 21 *Kilkenny People*, 9 Dec. 1905. 22 Prior-Wandesforde Papers, Pit papers, annual report 1918.

the train. They saw themselves as a distinct category from the miners because of their flexibility and bargaining power, given the limited transport facilities in operation at the time.

(iii) The farmers

Richard Prior-Wandesforde arranged a land purchase agreement under the 1903 Land Act whereby the land was sold to Castlecomer estate tenants for £175,555 at 3½ per cent.[23] By 1914 local farmers had achieved their key goal of landownership and although they faced annuities to repay government loans for the land purchases, landownership gave them status, a means of self-provisioning and a measure of security beyond wage labour.[24] Many were still economically marginal, however, as landholding figures for Kilkenny demonstrate. Out of the total number of landholdings (12,522) in Kilkenny county, 9,400 were over 1 acre in size and the average size of farms was 19 acres or approximately 7.7 hectares.[25] However, a quarter of all landholdings were of less than one acre which made it difficult, if not impossible, to make an adequate living by farming alone.

Most small farmers in north Kilkenny and on the borders of Laois and Carlow depended on the mines for enough income to survive. Generally, the small farmers took surface rather than underground work and opted out of the collieries at key times in the farming cycle. Some also worked in coal carting, which gave additional flexibility and mobility.[26] They had a pride in the ownership of the land despite many being very poor and saw themselves as of higher status than the miners. They had educational aspirations for their children, determined that their sons would not become miners. This was made difficult because of the lack of secondary educational facilities for boys in Castlecomer, the nearest schools being the Christian Brothers or St Kieran's in Kilkenny city or the Christian Brothers in Carlow (the former 15 miles from Castlecomer town and the latter 12 miles). This involved a commitment to bicycle or bus travel over the distance and a deferral of potential earnings at a young age.

Small farmers also differed from the landless miners in that they had succeeded in achieving the major objective of landownership. During the tithe war (1830–6) farmers, big and small, and miners with potato plots were united in resistance to the payment of tithes to support the Protestant clergy. Charles Wandesforde, who had only one-sixth of his estate requiring tithe

23 Lyng, *Castlecomer connections*, p. 141. **24** The author's great grandfather Nicholas Boran was registered as owner of 31 acres, 2 roods and 39 perches in 1912. **25** Central Statistics Office (CSO), *Life in 1916 Ireland, stories from statistics* (Government of Ireland, Dublin, 2016), p. 13. **26** The author's grandfather, George Boran, was a small farmer and carter.

payments, was one of the first landlords to adopt the Tithe Composition Act of 1823 and 1824 (made compulsory in 1832), the effect of which was to lower the payments of small farmers (20 acres and under) and to extend tithe payments to larger landholding in pasture.[27] It was reported that in Castlecomer parish, collectors could not safely enter certain townlands and no one could be found to execute warrants.[28] This marked a success for collective action for small farmers and those miners affected by tithes. The Whitefeet organization served the interests of both miners and farmers in that it used severe sanctions to further their interests if necessary. In 1838, tithes were reduced by 25 per cent and made payable by the landlord.

Many farmers joined the Land League and the Gaelic League, gaining valuable experience and honing skills that they subsequently drew on when mobilizing and organizing in the revolutionary period. Their aspirations now focused on national independence, on acquiring more land if possible and ensuring a future outside mining for all their sons. In the longer term, the children of small farmers did not usually enter mining but pursued education beyond the age of 14, some to third level. Many entered professions or emigrated. Only a small minority of farmers were able, however, to live either by farming alone or by combining farming with additional enterprises like pub ownership, mechanical services or haulage. Those outside that group could not be regarded as capitalist farmers in the full sense of the word in that they had insufficient land for independent sustenance and depended on hiring their labour to the mine owner to support their survival. Ian Roxborough, in an analysis of the role of small rural producers ('peasants') in revolutionary situations, notes their conservatism in general and their dependence on outside (often urban-based) leadership. He claims that 'the peasantry is not a class: it is a conceptual category'. Depending on the agrarian system there will be a distinct set of social classes.[29] Smallholdings worked by the owner with family labour and dependent on mining income characterized most farms in the Castlecomer coalfield. Land reform in such a system would tend to widen social divisions, concentrating some holdings into larger and viable capitalist farms but expelling the poorer smallholders to become landless wage labourers.[30] The fact that there was a source of industrial wage labour in the

---

27 Michael O'Hanrahan, 'The tithe war in County Kilkenny, 1830–1834' in Nolan and Whelan (eds), *Kilkenny: history and society* (Dublin, 1990), p. 485. Kick-started by Fr Martin Doyle of Graiguenamanagh, Co. Kilkenny, who encouraged his parishioners not to pay tithes and to prevent the sale of sequestered animals taken in lieu of payment, the anti-tithe movement spread throughout Kilkenny and beyond, the Whitefeet providing a mechanism for enforcement. **28** NAI, Edward Power to Sir William Cosset (under secretary) CSO/RP/1832/940. **29** Ian Roxborough, *Theories of underdevelopment* (London, 1979), p. 95. **30** Ibid., p. 99.

area nevertheless allowed many farmers to have a foot in both landownership and wage labour.[31]

(iv) Business and professionals

The social structure included another key sector, the business community who fit more easily into a middle or lower middle-class categorization – local shops, pubs, construction, maintenance and service businesses, mainly located in the town of Castlecomer but including a network of rural pubs and small shops scattered around the townlands. Included in this group I would add professionals – priests, doctors and teachers – who had status and access within the community and so could exercise influence on action. Shopkeepers and businesses frequently had a background in farming, and rural pubs generally also had a farm attached. Even some businesses in the town (e.g. butchers) also owned farms. Business interests often had family involvement in the Land League movement, the Gaelic League and cultural revival activities – a background they shared with farmers.

They often assumed a mediation role especially in relation to the mines and miners, because they depended on miners' wages for survival. They had status, were organizationally active and played a significant role in the independence movement. Their children were often sent to boarding schools and became professionals of varying kinds. One shopkeeper in Castlecomer had a family of 10 children, all of whom were educated to secondary or tertiary level and later entered various professions – dentistry, chemistry, teaching, veterinary, public service and the priesthood, as well as shopkeeping. Some priests and doctors were active supporters of IRA activities, such as Fr Michael MacNamara of Moneenroe, Dr Farrell, Castlecomer, who trained Cumann na mBan activists in first aid, and Dr Dunne, Castlecomer, who had worked with Welsh miners and was aware of the dangers to health of their way of life. Teachers inspired and informed activists and fostered cultural revival activities such as Irish language and history classes that were instrumental in strengthening national and Irish identity. Many witness statements attest to their influential role in shaping their nationalist thinking.

Not all priests were supportive of national independence movements, however. Canon O'Halloran, PP Castlecomer, was a friend of Wandesforde and very anti-IRA. In the 1914 Kilkenny County Council elections, he, together with Revd Grant, CC Castlecomer, and Revd M. Power, PP Clogh, supported R.H. Prior-Wandesforde (also deputy lieutenant, Kilkenny) in his

---

31 Lenin's typology of Junker (large scale) and Kulak (small farmer) paths to agrarian development do not fit the Irish context neatly but the latter can provide insights into what might be expected to happen in relation to an area with a majority of smallholdings. **32** *Freeman's Journal*, 27 May 1914.

nomination for a seat on the Council against John Fogarty, UIL candidate.[32] Fogarty was a Redmondite and Wandesforde was described as a Unionist, although when asked to define his position with reference to Home Rule, he said, 'I shall endeavour to make the measure a success if and when it becomes the law of the land'.[33] Their strong support was justified, the priests argued, to a large meeting held after Mass in Clogh on 30 May 1914, because of his contribution to the district. He provided employment in his coal mines for 500 men, thus helping to stem emigration, brought a Rural Bank to the area to support farmers and businesses and also a creamery. They were keen to point out that Home Rule would not suffer because of support for a unionist since it was already 'guaranteed'.[34] Local Volunteers also appear to have bought into that analysis, supporting Wandesforde over Fogarty, who had been critical of the clergy's assumed 'dictatorship rights' at parish level. Fogarty was supported by Redmonite loyalists.[35] Wandesforde won the seat and his wife Florence was returned for Moneenroe as a rural district councillor. The strength of clerical support and their open antagonism towards Fogarty probably ensured Wandesforde's success. This support would soon change, however. In the meantime, he was busy organizing recruitment to the British army on the eve of war.

Collective goals and means

Almost all the above groups shared the goal of national independence and of dislodging the British but what that independence would involve was open to different interpretations. For those 'politically conscious miners' inspired by Connolly it meant workers being at the heart of an independent Ireland with structures that regarded them as more than mere cogs in production. They wanted real recognition of their role in society, good working conditions and pay – in other words social as well as political, freedom. For the business community, it meant a say in the control of state resources and an assertion of cultural, including religious, distinctiveness and difference from Britain. For farmers, it was similar, but the core was secure ownership of land, loan repayments that they could afford and a future share of prosperity for their children.

The First World War provided the context for attacking a weakened enemy and, with the attempt to extend the military draft to 18-to-41-year-olds in Ireland in April 1918, Sinn Féin expanded to approximately 1,354 clubs with 112,000 members by the end of 1918.[36] A Sinn Féin club was set up in

33 *Kilkenny People,* 6 June 1914. **34** *Kilkenny People,* 30 May 1914. **35** Deputy Commissioner Garrett Brennan, Witness Statement 1601, 30 Mar. 1957, p. 3. **36** Pauric Travers, *Settlements and*

Castlecomer in 1917 to canvass against conscription and to get candidates elected to local government. In July 1918 it drew 5,000 to the Square, Castlecomer, to protest against the draft. A triumphant Sinn Féin won 73 of the 105 House of Commons seats in the 1918 general election and declared independence and established Dáil Eireann on 21 January 1919. The subsequent name change from Irish Volunteers to Irish Republican Army (IRA) was an important symbolic move. The rebels were thereby laying claim to being an army defending its country and this gave added impetus to local mobilizations for independence which had begun in the townlands in the hills around Castlecomer, particularly in Crutt and the Swan, from 1914 onwards.[37]

Organizations for struggle

The creation of IRA army structures led to the establishment of a brigade at Kilkenny county level with seven battalions. In north Kilkenny, the 3rd Battalion comprised 11 companies from the farming, business and mining communities. Command of the 3rd Battalion changed frequently. James Culleton was the first commandant, and he was succeeded by Patrick J. Fleming (1918), George Dwyer (1920), Michael Fleming (1921) and Garrett Brennan (1921). The leadership down to captain level came mostly from the larger farmers and the business communities. The only exception was Company H (Coolbawn), captained by a miner, John Love.

Cumann na mBan activists frequently came from the same families as male activists, such as the McGuire sisters (part of a group of 10 members in Crutt) and the Flemings of the Swan. Cumann na mBan activists provided support, raised funds through organizing dances and concerts, and carried communications between companies.[38] As with the men of the farming class, they had more freedom of movement than women tied to miners' shifts, although, when called upon for quick decisions, miners' wives also proved very competent. One oral account of the timely intervention of a miner's wife was that of Mrs Loughlin from Moneenroe, who, when the Royal Irish Constabulary (RIC) visited with little warning, plunged a gun into a pot of boiling potatoes to prevent them finding it.

Here we look at (i) direct action and (ii) the establishment of alternative institutions.

divisions: Ireland, 1870–1922 (Dublin, 1988), p. 109. **37** Bureau of Military History, Witness Statement (BMHWS) 1271, Patrick Dunphy, p. 2. **38** BMHWS 1271, P. Dunphy, Addendum, p. 1.

(i) Direct action

The Castlecomer area had assets that could be used in operations co-operatively by the different groups. Miners smuggled out explosives from the mines and used their skills to set the charges.[39] Shopkeepers used the tool of boycott against the RIC and Black and Tans in the town.[40] Farmers had the flexibility to move around, hide arms on isolated farms, hold meetings and train activists. They were not easily monitored. The hills surrounding the collieries provided an ideal setting, combining isolation, inaccessible terrain and a network of narrow roads and laneways that gave activists an advantage over the RIC. Significant actions included mail robberies, the trenching of roads to interrupt the RIC and Black and Tan movements, temporary kidnap of jury members serving on assizes in Kilkenny, reprisals against informers, the seizing of weapons from farmers holding them for agricultural purposes (about 40 were seized), or from RIC members, as well as the planning and execution of ambushes.[41] Orders to destroy RIC barracks led to the successful burning of Crettyard barracks (unoccupied) by B Company (Crutt) and Newtown barracks (already abandoned by the RIC) by L Company (Newtown) on Easter Sunday 1920. There were also attacks on Castlecomer barracks (still occupied) by D Company (Castlecomer) on 8 May 1921, on Ballyragget barracks (occupied) by C Company (Ballyouskill) on 23 May 1921 and on Clinstown barracks (occupied) by I Company (Conahy) on 17 May 1921. None successfully dislodged the occupants but they certainly unsettled them.

The actions in the Castlecomer area were of some significance in the independence struggle but were weakened by two factors. The leadership came in most cases from the farming and business section and was not representative of the whole community.[42] More importantly, most of the ambushes and attacks failed (there was a catalogue of planned ambushes where the RIC took alternative routes, changed their schedule or did not turn up). Operations seemed to be undermined by 'leaky' networks that, it was suspected, warned the military of planned IRA operations through 'loose talk' in pubs or through informers.[43] Garrett Brennan said that 'it looked as if the enemy were getting information about our plans and an old Fenian said that the family of one of the prominent men in the IRA had been traitorous in the Fenian days ... the IRA man could be no good.'[44] The man was edged out of the organization,

39 BMHWS 1271, P. Dunphy, p. 8. Dunphy claims that a miner, Carroll, smuggled out 2 cwts of gelignite over a period. Other miners smuggled out blasting powder and fuses. **40** BMHWS 1601, Garrett Brennan, pp 7–8. **41** Ibid. **42** The one exception in the chart (fig. 1.2) is that of H Company, Coolbawn, captained by John Love, a miner. **43** Brennan (WS 1601) gives an example of two town residents, a baker and a carpenter, overheard discussing the attack on the Castlecomer barracks in a public house frequented by military and police, in which they discussed positions taken by the attackers and named names. **44** Ibid., p. 21.

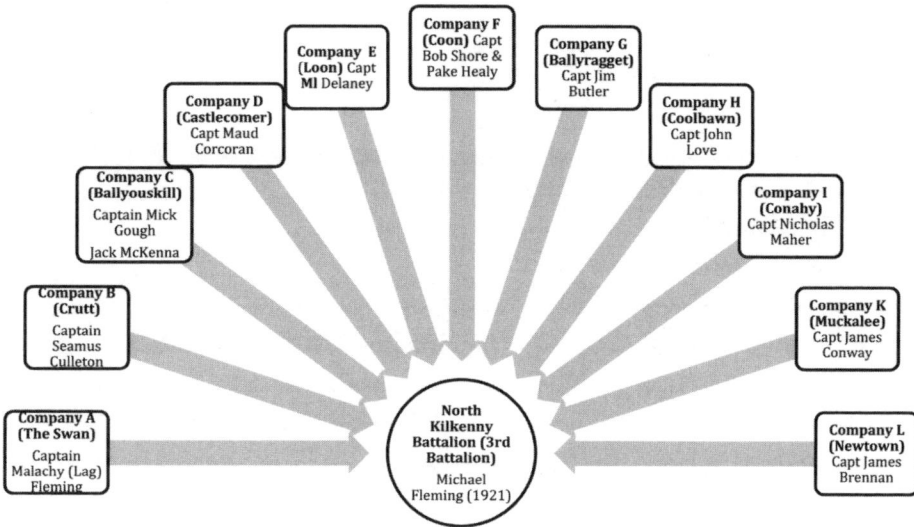

1.2 North Kilkenny Battalion IRA, 1921.
Adapted by the author from data provided in Lyng, *Castlecomer connections* (1984).[45]

which points to the 'long' memories and historical mistrust that could operate even when no proof was provided.

The chart above shows the structure of the North Kilkenny 3rd Battalion in 1921, though the leadership changed often because of arrests and imprisonments during the War of Independence. The diagram illustrates comprehensive area organization into companies across north Kilkenny combining cross class co-operation and diversity, in mining and non-mining areas of operation including in Castlecomer town.

(ii) Creation of alternative institutions and legal system

Alongside the IRA structures, the creation of Dáil courts in June 1920 was another factor in the freedom struggle. They replaced Sinn Féin arbitration courts set up in 1919 to fill the vacuum caused by the republican-imposed boycott of the British court system. Disputes were to be settled by respected local figures, including teachers, doctors, priests and community leaders, including trade unionists. By July 1921 there were over 900 parish, and seventy district courts in operation throughout Ireland. They operated in secret, in this area from the priest's house in Moneenroe, the hall at Chatsworth and Jack Lyng's forge at Crotenclogh.[46] Fr McNamara, the

45 Lyng, *Castlecomer connections,* Appendix 1.   **46** Lyng, *Castlecomer connections,* p. 151.

1.3 Oath of Allegiance of the Dáil court in Clogh parish.
Signed by Seamus Culleton, Thomas Campion, Micheál MacConMara
(Fr Michael McNamara) and Seán Pleamonn (John Fleming) (Clerk).[47]

Moneenroe curate, was president of the court; John Fleming, a farmer and IRA activist, was its clerk; James Culleton (farmer and IRA captain) and Thomas Campion (miner, ITGWU organizer and IRA activist) were members. It therefore drew on a cross-section of the community and was a concrete expression of an Irish alternative court system that could be experienced in practice. In reality, it dealt mainly with minor issues, imposing sanctions such as agricultural work or turf cutting on defendants. The Oath of Allegiance signatories demonstrate this combination of backgrounds – farmers, miner/union leader and priest. Note the Irish form of the signatures – an assertive statement of Irish identity as opposed to a colonial one. Internal IRA military courts, on which officers served, dealt with more serious issues

47 My thanks to Fonsie Meally (Castlecomer) for this copy.

such as animal cutting or collaboration with the RIC.[48] An example of this process was the case of a farmhand, Michael Cassidy, who was accused of being an informer and of having led the RIC to the farm of Jim Conway, O/C of K Company (Muckalee). Not finding him, the RIC set fire to his haybarn. Michael Cassidy was subsequently shot by two armed and masked men at his place of work, sending a clear message to actual or potential informers.[49] It is not difficult to see how there might have been some overlap and confusion between the two judgment systems in practice.

Divergent interests

Although the Castlecomer area had social groups sharing the same over-arching goal of independence, the underlying divergent interests of the different classes in the area could weaken action and lead to conflicts of interest. I shall illustrate this by reference to three events, (i) the Coolbawn ambush, (ii) the miners' strike of 1921, and (iii) the destruction of the aerial ropeway that carried coal from outlying mines to a central location at Deerpark.

(i) The Coolbawn ambush, 18 June 1921

Although the miners were very engaged in the War of Independence, they did not have the flexibility of farmers or of the business community who had the capital resources of shops, farms and other assets to fall back on. The Coolbawn ambush was an example of conflicting interests at play. It echoed Dan Breen's attack on an explosives convoy at Soloheadbeg in January 1919 at the start of the War of Independence. Up to this point the IRA had been prohibited by GHQ from attacking the mines or convoys carrying explosives to the mines because of Wandesforde's threat to stop production should this happen. Closure would put some '500 miners and 200 coal carriers out of work as well as cutting off the fuel supply for an area of about 15 miles square'.[50] The IRA leadership, Brigadier George Dwyer in particular, was determined to make a mark and change national perceptions that Kilkenny operations in the independence fight were lightweight. According to Lyng (1984), 'George was itching for Dublin [wanted to work at GHQ] at the time, but Dublin told him to show some action in Kilkenny first'.

---

48 See original statements on the Michael Cassidy killing at: http://www.bloodysunday.co.uk › shot-by-ira-as-spies [accessed 3 May 2023]. 49 BMHWS 1601, Garrett Brennan, p. 14. 50 BMHWS 1601, Garrett Brennan, p. 13.

Dwyer had been appointed Kilkenny Brigade Commandant after Ernie O'Malley was arrested in Inistioge in 1920 while carrying a list of brigade and battalion officers' names, the consequence of which was that the entire command was picked up by the RIC, leaving much disorganization in its wake.[51] Dwyer faced a difficult challenge in the circumstances. He proposed to attack an explosives convoy destined for Vera pit and got permission from GHQ to do so. The interests of miners were disregarded, and their futures put in jeopardy.[52] The ambush was a disaster due to a catalogue of errors: failures of communication, disagreements about the attack and location, no-shows by some companies, non-participation by the battalion commander and other organizational lapses. These led to a surprise counterattack by the RIC and Black and Tans and to the deaths of two IRA men. The allocation of I Company (Conahy) to monitor movements and to corral passing carts on market day was a mistake in that its members lacked local knowledge, did not know the residents and allowed the passage of the farm hand Sandy Bradley to his work at Finsboro farm (the home of the Unionist Dreaper sisters Florrie and Rebecca). This resulted in the military being alerted by Florrie and the tables being turned on the ambushers. Finsboro farm, near Coolbawn, was subsequently burned out by H Company (Coolbawn) and the sisters, whose lives and those of their animals were spared, soon left for England. They were awarded £5,000 in damages in October 1921.[53]

(ii) The 1921 strike in the mines

The miners had pressing work problems, but action on them was not supported by the IRA. In September 1921, 600 miners went on strike when Wandesforde attempted to reduce wages after the removal of wartime subsidies. The colliers marched to Kilkenny, carrying a red flag to a demonstration presided over by William O'Brien, Cathal O'Shannon and other labour leaders. The ITGWU organizer Seamus O'Brien made revolutionary threats about taking over the mines.

> I want to say something about the magnificent body of men that marched in from Castlecomer. They have thrown down the challenge to another autocrat who says that not only does he own the soil of Ireland, but what is under the soil of Ireland. It is up to you to say that you will not allow that tyranny to prevail in the district of Castlecomer. We have men able to run the mines in Castlecomer without any domestic or

51 Annie Ryan, *Comrades inside the War of Independence* (Dublin 2007), pp 211–13. 52 BMHWS 1601, Garrett Brennan, p. 23. 53 *Freeman's Journal,* 20 October 1921; *Kilkenny People,* 10 June 1922.

foreign interference, and we propose in the near future to open up these mines and run them (applause), and the quicker they get into business and negotiations with the Irish Transport and General Workers' Union, the better for all concerned.[54]

Cathal O'Shannon, drawing on James Connolly, pointed out to the gathering that if 'foreign rule and the foreign flag were to be changed and another put in its place, the change was not to be in symbol only but also in substance, and it should change everything'. William O'Brien added: 'When the national question was settled it would be for them to link up every section of workers under the banner of freedom, that freedom which would bring the greatest benefit to the toilers of this country'.[55]

Wandesforde however resisted. The miners then kidnapped two mine managers who 'disappeared' for a couple of months. Wandesforde appealed to the IRA for help in finding them and they responded by arresting and questioning four miners' leaders. In November the strike went to arbitration and the managers were released unharmed on 17 November 1921. There is no evidence that the strike or kidnappings achieved anything, but a surviving handwritten letter makes clear that support for the miners was not regarded as being in the interests of the IRA despite expectations.[56]

HQ 3rd Batt.
26/9/21

Brigade Orders
Copy.

The following is a copy received from Brigade HQ
I am in receipt of yours with enclosure from A Coy. You must please inform this man that it is not for him to decide on Headquarters' orders. You will see that protection is guaranteed and given as decided. The merits or demerits of the strike is outside our province and the IRA cannot side with any one party on such a question. There is too much at stake for this matter to be treated lightly.
P.S. You will please see that the following instructions are carried out if not stringent action will have to be taken.

Adj. 3rd Batt.
Kilkenny Brigade
I.R.A.

---

54 *Kilkenny People*, 8 Oct. 1921, p. 6.   **55** Ibid.   **56** With thanks to Fonsie Meally, Castlecomer, for a copy of the letter.

A newspaper notice indicated that it was settled through the intervention of Dáil Éireann. It stated simply that the strike had been settled, had lasted 8 weeks and that 600 men were involved.[57] It may have been naïve to expect solidarity from the IRA on the basis of miners' contributions to IRA action in the neighbourhood.

(iii) Destruction of the aerial ropeways

On 9 February 1922, the day that the Black and Tans left Castlecomer barracks for good, 80 masked and armed men attacked the aerial ropeway connecting Vera, Rock and Deerpark collieries with the depot serving the new railway branch at Deerpark. They burned the engine house and cut the steel rope in several places. There was a further attack in July of that year. The IRA's response was to declare martial law 'on the Parish of Clogh, the Parish of Doonane and that portion of Castlecomer Parish lying to the north of the town of Castlecomer' so that people had to remain indoors between 10 p.m. and 5 a.m. unless in possession of a permit signed by Battalion Commander Garrett Brennan or Vice Commandant Seamus Culleton.[58]

Carters were believed to be responsible. They feared the loss of their livelihoods because the combination of the new railway, which had just been extended to Deerpark, and the aerial ropeway greatly facilitated the carrying of coal further afield. The new transportation system would reduce their work to simply serving local community fuel needs. The carters' destruction of the ropeway caused up to three months unemployment and drove many young men, including my father, Nixie Boran, into the newly formed Free State army.[59] Many were also forced to compete for road work against farmers in March 1922 when James Campion led a delegation of 100 unemployed ITGWU miners to pressurize for an allocation of road repairs by direct labour instead of by contract, which usually went to farmers. Seamus Culleton and Sean Fleming, now representing the county council, debated the case and it was decided that 19 works would be contracted out and 17 would go to direct labour. The deputation also made a case for small farmers with only five or six acres of land who had 'barely enough to keep the hunger out of their stomachs'.[60] Local union members were furious with the carters and denied any involvement in the ropeway attack. In a letter to the *Kilkenny People* the branch secretary of the ITGWU made his members' feelings known in no uncertain terms:

---

57 *Nenagh Guardian*, 19 Nov. 1921.   **58** *Kilkenny People*, 11 Feb. 1922, p. 5.   **59** Nixie Boran, a miner, joined the Free State army in Kilkenny with his brother Martin in June 1922 just before the outbreak of the Civil War.   **60** *Kilkenny People*, 4 Mar. 1922.

That we the miners and workers generally of the Castlecomer collieries condemn the outrage on the aerial ropeway in the strongest manner possible, seeing that this outrage has thrown hundreds out of employment, and we wish to make it known to the public that none of the employees encouraged, aided or abetted this outrage.

(Signed) Thomas Campion, branch secretary.[61]

The picture is of a divided mining community with divergent interests and ambitions, unsupported in work-based action by the IRA and, in the perception of the mining community, defended poorly by a divided and perhaps over-extended national trade union movement. After their strike failure in 1921 union membership in the coalfield dropped from 529 in 1919, to 343 in 1921, to 200 in 1922, to 182 in 1923. This was followed by a continuing decline year on year until it sank to just 14 in 1928.[62]

The execution of Connolly after the Easter Rising and the involvement of the Irish Citizen Army in the 1916 Rising conferred a nationalist legitimacy on Labour but subsequently the independence movement lacked Connolly's guidance to maintain the centrality of his vision within it.[63] So, although trade unionism expanded strongly towards the end of the decade, militarism carried greater sway in the War of Independence and subsequent settlements. Larkin's absence in America and divisions within the ITGWU meant that the labour movement lacked the strong political leadership that might have avoided a narrowing of focus to that of a 'wages' movement' between 1916 and 1921.[64] Under those conditions the carters, confronting a threat to their way of life, could only employ the tools of the weak and try to resist change by violent but ultimately fruitless means. This was particularly true if not supported by formal organizations such as the IRA, prepared to back up their threats with serious action as in the case relating to action for independence. In this case the carters lacked both miners' and IRA support.

Truce and Civil War

Although some of the older IRA activists found it impossible to slot into the Free State army and Civic Guards, most of the leaders of the 3rd Battalion did so. An audit of loyalties printed in the *Irish Independent* in April 1922 asserted that, of the 3rd Battalion, 'Comdt., Vice Comd. and Q.M. and all

---

61 *Kilkenny People*, 18 Feb. 1922, p. 18.   **62** Francis Devine, 'The Irish Transport and General Workers' Union in Carlow and Kilkenny, 1918–1930', *Old Kilkenny Review* (2017), 12.   **63** Emmet O'Connor, *A labour history* (Dublin, 1992), p. 93.   **64** Ibid., p. 97.

Companies were loyal'.[65] A census of the North Kilkenny Brigade by Adjt Sean McEvoy listed a total of 679 members before the Civil War broke out, 139 of whom had joined during the Truce. This recruitment aimed, it was alleged, to bolster numbers in favour of a Free State position. From the ranks of the brigade, 109 entered the regular army or Garda Síochána, which might give some indication of their allegiances. However, in view of the long periods of unemployment in the mines, many were glad of secure employment. In reality, there was considerable soul-searching among members of the North Kilkenny Brigade.[66]

Michael Delaney, C/O of E Company (Loon), having been sentenced by court martial to 2 years' imprisonment in Winchester prison because of his activities in the 3rd Battalion, emerged from prison after the Treaty disturbed by the new political realities. In Delaney's words:

> Culleton, C/O B Company (Crutt), explained that they had gone into debt in town and if they did not toe the line on the Free State side, they could not get the necessary money to pay the traders who had supplied them with food etc. for the last few months. So, they were going to be Free Staters and that was that. I bid them good evening, turned on my heel and walked away. As I turned to close the door, I saw every man looking at me as if wondering what they themselves should do.[67]

An anti-Treaty faction made up of escapees from Castlecomer jail attempted to organize resistance in the area in September 1922. They blew up Dysart bridge on the Castlecomer–Kilkenny road. Some 45 men from this faction then wandered the area, sleeping rough in cow barns and commandeering food from locals, from whom they got a mixed reception. All the time they were pursued by former companions from the Free State side who knew the personalities and landscape well. In an attempt to prevent all-out war between the factions, Fr McNamara, CC of Moneenroe, organized a meeting between Free State fighters and republicans. He persuaded the latter to give up their arms and disband, threatening not to protect them if attacked by the Free State side.[68] A handful went on to fight with anti-Treaty forces. P.J. Fleming, A Company (Swan), fought in Wexford and Mike Brennan, B Company (Crutt), in Tipperary, while significant support was provided on the

---

65 *Irish Independent*, 8 May 1922, p. 6.   **66** Figures are extracted from data put together by Lyng, *Castlecomer connections*, p. 415. Based on his interviews with local combatants and an audit by Adjt Sean McEvoy (no reference included).   **67** Seamus Culleton cited in Lyng, *Castlecomer connections*, p. 174.   **68** Lyng, *Castlecomer connections*, p. 177.

home-front by sheltering republicans being pursued or 'on the run' and by hiding arms, helping with communications and providing financial support where possible.[69]

Kilkenny was not the locus of much Civil War action, although General Prout used the city as his control centre for South-Eastern Command which combined the 47th Free State Battalion (Kilkenny), the 14th Battalion (Waterford), the 25th Battalion (Tipperary) and the 41st Battalion (Wexford). He gradually made inroads into Wexford, Waterford and Tipperary as the superior resources of the Free State eroded republican strength and positions, thereby pushing the anti-Treaty combatants into the hilly areas and eventually towards the Glen of Aherlow in the closing stages of the Civil War.

Miners had less flexibility of movement and tended to offer more local support. Choice of which side to back was often conflicted or dependent on personal loyalty to the IRA leadership at battalion and company level. There was often movement from one side to the other during the Civil War. My father Nixie Boran, who joined the Free State army days before the Civil War began because of strife in the mines, switched sides when, as part of the 25th Battalion, he was posted to Clonmel to fight the anti-Treaty units led by Dan Breen, Dinny Lacey, Séamus Robinson and other well-known Republican leaders. He spent six months fighting alongside Breen and was one of the last to be picked up in the Glen of Aherlow, on 8 May 1923, after the Civil War ended. Unlike Breen, who had been arrested in the Glen three weeks earlier, Nixie was sentenced to death for desertion from the Free State army and for being found with a rifle and ammunition. He managed to escape before execution and spent the period before the amnesty on the run.[70]

Post-Civil War

In the meantime, production in the Castlecomer mines was shifting to the Skehana seam, where the anthracite was regarded as being among the best in the world, but the pits were beset with problems of faults and flooding. Wandesforde complained about a problematic workforce in the initial pit, prone to absences because of the distances of travel from home to work.[71] Miners' housing was located close to former mines on the old Jarrow seam. A court case exemplified some of the continuing tensions between management

69 Dan Breen and Sean Hogan were sheltered by the McGuires of Crutt before the Civil War when on the run from the RIC and it appears that most of B Company Crutt remained republican supporters throughout the Civil War. **70** Anne Boran, *Challenge to power: Nixie Boran, freedom and the Castlecomer miners* (Dublin, 2021). **71** NLI, Castlecomer Collieries, annual report, 1922, Prior Wandesforde Papers, annual reports, 1922–28, 173 MS48346/20, p. 2.

and the workforce. Check-weighman Power, of Skehana mine, tried to exercise
some authority as a worker representative by threatening the pit manager
Addison that if he did not pay a worker for a job that the manager asserted
he had not done, he would, in the manager's words: 'Smash my face in. He
said he would fetch me out of my house at night, put a rope around my neck
and take me to some secret place … that he would take my body and dance
on my corpse'.[72]

Power discovered, however, that such methods no longer worked. 'These
courts are your own and we are your servants', he was told. 'At the same time
our very first and primary duty should be the protection of the people … The
time for taking people away to unknown destinations is at an end and the
time for dancing on people's corpses is also at an end.' While recognizing that
the manager was a difficult and cantankerous man, the court found in his
favour and made it clear that the Saorstát would be 'impartial' in such
matters.[73] Clearly, Power, like those before him who had found the system
skewed in favour of the powerful, tried the old methods of threat of violence
to 'persuade' and failed. They would have to find more effective methods of
fighting their cause.[74]

Returning to Castlecomer when it was safe to do so, Nixie Boran found
that little had changed in the mines. Many of those on the losing side in the
Civil War found opportunities closed to them unless they had farms to fall
back on or sympathizers prepared to help. That is not to say that all with
leadership positions in the Free State did not help former companions or those
known to them. It would not go down well with family members if those with
power to do so did not help a family member in trouble because of their
political stance. There is evidence, for example, that Fr MacNamara of
Moneenroe tried to negotiate terms for the return of Nixie Boran to the area
while he had outstanding garda charges against him.[75] The gardaí rejected his
representations because Nixie had thwarted their attempts to arrest him, and
they considered him to be troublesome.[76] Strongly influenced by the left of
the IRA and by Connolly's thinking, and having networked with activists such
as Peadar O'Donnell, who argued for a socialist small farmer/workers'
republic, he and a committed group of miners were determined to force
change. Independence had made little difference to the lives of the miners (or
indeed of farm labourers). Their interests were still marginalized and unmet
by the 'freedoms' offered in post-independence Ireland. In 1923 they faced
recession and a Free State located firmly on the side of owners of farms and

---

72 *Kilkenny People*, 23 Dec. 1922. **73** Ibid. **74** Ibid. **75** *Kilkenny People*, 3 Nov. 1928.
76 Nixie was Garrett Brennan's first cousin. Garrett rose in the ranks of the army and then of the
gardaí and may well have been helpful in the background.

businesses and prepared to use force to defend their rights above those of labour. This ultimately motivated them to set up their own communist-inspired trade union in the 1930s.[77]

Conclusions

This essay has suggested that notions of freedom were contested. In practice this involved conflicts of interest between different groups about the meaning of freedom and about the priorities to be set for an independent Ireland. The unity of purpose, that united activists across occupations and across classes to achieve independence, hid tensions, which dissolved into open factionalism and enmity in the bitterness of the Civil War and its aftermath. The dominant power structures continued to reflect the interests of those with more resources and status and those who managed to control the resources of the new state. Although it could be argued that the rationale of 'political freedom first' made logical sense, in practice, the nature of the freedoms on offer continued to reflect the interests of those inspired by a narrow nationalism in which the interests of labour were not a priority either at national level or in the Castlecomer coalfield.

77 Boran, *Challenge to power*, passim.

A 'bolshie spirit'? Agrarian mobilizations in Co. Galway in 1920

JOHNNY BURKE

In his memoir of his time as a Dáil court judge, Kevin O'Shiel described land agitators he encountered in Co. Roscommon in 1920 as having a 'bolshie spirit'.[1] 'Bolshie', derived from Bolshevik, was used to describe a deliberately uncooperative or obstructive individual, as well as someone with radical or revolutionary tendencies. In the spring of 1920, a wave of agrarian unrest broke out across the west of Ireland and was described as 'spreading like a prairie fire'.[2] Some Catholic bishops and Sinn Féin leaders feared that this agrarianism could jeopardize not only the struggle for national independence, but the existing social order by threatening the right to private property.[3] The bishop of Clonfert, preaching on 'land hunger' in a sermon in May 1920, remarked that communism would take hold if those in authority failed to intervene.[4] In his analysis of land conflict in the west, Fergus Campbell identifies 'radical impulses' in agrarianism and notes that Co. Galway already had a 'tradition' of agrarian agitation.[5] David Fitzpatrick, in his study of Co. Clare, describes many IRA operations there as 'thinly disguised land seizures which Dublin headquarters had neither the ability nor perhaps the intentions to prevent'.[6] This essay will analyse agrarian agitations throughout Galway in the spring of 1920 to establish what motivated large groups of rural dwellers to take action. Some victims of agitations will be examined to uncover the part they played and the reactions of Catholic Church and IRA leaders will be considered. The essay will also examine measures taken by Dáil Éireann to contain agrarianism in the short term and consider how the 1920 outbreak acted as an expedient to effective land legislation in the Irish Free State.

As early as 1863 leading Fenians were uncomfortable with the land question, holding the view that peasant proprietorship, as with the resolution of other grievances in society, could only be achieved after national independence.[7] However, Fenians were among those involved in agrarian

---

1 Bureau of Military History, Witness Statement, Kevin O'Shiel, 1770. See also Fergus Campbell and Kevin O'Shiel, 'The last land war? Kevin O'Shiel's memoir of the Irish Revolution (1916–21)', *Archivium Hibernicum*, 57 (2003), 155–200. 2 O'Shiel, WS 1770. 3 Fergus Campbell, *Land and revolution: nationalist politics in the west of Ireland, 1891–1921* (Oxford, 2005), p. 284. 4 *Connacht Tribune* (henceforth *CT*), 1 May 1920. 5 Campbell, *Land and revolution*, p. 227. 6 David Fitzpatrick, 'The geography of Irish nationalism 1910–1921', *Past and Present*, 78 (1978), 119. 7 Samuel Clark, *Social origins of the Irish land war* (Princeton, 1980), p. 202.

mobilizations organized and politicized under the auspices of the Land League in 1879. Phillip Bull contends that in this period, 'a united and powerful political leadership [emerged] to exploit agrarian discontent ... [which] represented distinct and powerful elements of Irish political life.'[8] In the early twentieth century, there was considerable agitation in the west by impoverished tenants. As a result, influential farmers, politicians and some graziers took control of agrarian mobilizations under the auspices of the United Irish League (UIL) and encouraged agitation against landlords and graziers. Ultimately, agrarian action was undermined by the cleavage between different farmer classes and by influential leaders who decided that Home Rule was to take precedence over land reform.[9] A grazier (sometimes called a rancher) was usually a businessman or large farmer who had the capital to rent grazing land at auction on 'conacre', an 11-month lease, usually beginning on 1 May and ending on 1 April the following year.[10] Thus the smallholder was generally priced out.

If land reform was to succeed, land that was rented by large farmers and businessmen would have to be relinquished and given to farmers of small uneconomic holdings. While the Land Acts of 1903 and 1909 had enabled all farmer classes to purchase their holdings, there remained the problem of large tracts of grazing land nestled among poor uneconomic smallholdings, which were unavailable for redistribution or sale for those in need. Along with uneconomic holdings, Fergus Campbell outlines other reasons that formed the basis for large-scale agrarian mobilizations in 1920. Restrictions on emigration during the Great War meant there were more 'non-inheriting' young men seeking land; prices for agricultural produce, which had been abnormally high, had by 1920 decreased significantly. Moreover, IRA attacks on RIC barracks increased early in 1920 and numbers became depleted in rural Galway as policemen retreated to larger towns, allowing people to mobilize more freely.[11] Up to this, the RIC had largely contained agrarian agitations.[12]

There was a strong element of continuity in Galway agrarianism. Connections between the Galway secret society (an agrarian organization led by Tom Kenny of Craughwell), Sinn Féin and the Irish Republican Brotherhood had developed during the so-called ranch war of 1906–8 and on to the Galway rising in 1916. This undercurrent of agrarian influence characterized the Volunteer organization after the Rising with many of the

8 Phillip Bull, *Land, politics and nationalism: a study of the Irish land question* (New York, 1996), p. 86. **9** Tony Varley, 'A region of sturdy smallholders? Western nationalists and agrarian politics during the First World War', *Journal of the Galway Archaeological and Historical Society*, 55 (2003), 129. **10** David Seth Jones, *Graziers, land reform and political conflict in Ireland* (Washington DC, 1995), p. 123. **11** Campbell, *Land and revolution*, pp 47–8. **12** Terence Dooley, *'The land for the people': the land question in independent Ireland* (Dublin, 2004), pp 38–9.

participants becoming major IRA figures by 1920.[13] The role of the Congested Districts Board (CDB) is also important. The CDB was established in 1891 to tackle poverty on the western seaboard by creating viable holdings and improving infrastructure. In 1909 the CDB was given the extra burden of land redistribution.[14] However the British Treasury stopped the Board's funding for the duration of the Great War, fuelling discontent among those seeking land.[15] The Board was often accused of being partial to graziers by renting untenanted land to them at premium prices, particularly during the Great War as the Board sought to maximize profits.[16]

Galway had a significant number of smallholdings. The Land Commission (established in 1881 to facilitate the fixing of fair rents and subsequently the purchase of holdings by tenants) defined in 1921 an uneconomic holding as roughly 20 acres of 'reasonable' land.[17] Table 1 shows farm sizes over a number of decades.

Table 1. Galway Farm Sizes[18]

YEAR	1–5 acres	5–15 acres	15–30	30–50	50–100	Total
1905	4,400	12,200	9,000	3,700	2,300	31,600
1910	4,200	12,200	9,700	4,000	2,400	32,500
1915	3,000	9,800	9,400	4,700	2,500	29,400
1930	1,800	6,900	9,000	6,700	3,200	27,600

The years 1905–10 show little change, but from 1910 to 1930, the figures show a gradual but significant fall in holdings of 1–30 acres and an increase in holdings of 30–100 acres. Taking 1915 as the closest reference point to 1920, farms in the 1–15 acre bracket constitute 43.5 per cent of the total holdings of 1–100 acres – a significant number of smallholdings, where land quality was often poor. David Seth Jones advises caution in interpreting holding size. In some cases, census returns showed that graziers held a number of smaller holdings in different areas rather than one large one, 'thus disguising the true extent of ranch farming'.[19]

The RIC report for Galway West Riding (which includes a large portion of north Galway and some of south Galway) for January 1920 stated:

13 Campbell, *Land and revolution*, pp 171–89, 218–24 and 244–5.   **14** Ciara Breathnach, *The Congested Districts Board of Ireland, 1891–1923: poverty and development in the west of Ireland* (Dublin, 2005), p. 175.   **15** Dooley, 'The land for the people', p. 31.   **16** Campbell, *Land and revolution*, p. 239.   **17** Dooley, 'The land for the people', pp 8–9 and 29.   **18** Central Statistics Office, 'Farming since the Famine, 1847–1996', Table 9.   **19** Jones, *Graziers, land reform*, p. 55.

There is considerable agrarian unrest in the county on the part of persons who want lands that they cannot get and this unrest is accompanied by grave acts of intimidation instanced by firing shots at persons, firing into dwelling houses, malicious injuries to property, threatening letters and notices.[20]

A common method of agitation was cattle driving, which first became widespread during the ranch war of 1906–8.[21] The effects of cattle driving were two-fold. First, the act of removing the stock of an uncompromising landlord or grazier was empowering for the drivers; it emboldened them and created a community spirit. Second, it caused financial loss to the owner due to the resulting stress and weight-loss in the cattle.

The agitations

Identifying those who carried out agitations is challenging since participants were rarely named. Nevertheless, similarities between incidents are notable. In early April at Rahoon, walls, gates and pillars were knocked on lands belonging to several different landowners.[22] Castlegrove House near Tuam was surrounded by approximately 200 men demanding that the owner T.F. Lewin give up his lands for division. Extensive cattle-drives were reported across the north-eastern part of the county, where 'about 1,500 men raided all the grasslands [driving cattle from graziers' land] over a wide area from Creggs to Castleblakeney in one direction and as far as Dunmore in another.'[23] Even Catholic Church property was not immune, as about 80 acres of grazing land which had been bequeathed by its late owner to the archdiocese of Tuam was cleared of stock.[24] In Annaghdown parish there were grievances against James Gunning Alcorn, a large landowner, a justice of the peace, and the high sherriff of Co. Galway. On 30 March a large crowd, reportedly between 200 and 300, converged on Alcorn's premises and demanded that he surrender land to them. When he refused, he was taken a short distance to the shore of Lough Corrib where he was ordered to sign an agreement to surrender land or he would be drowned. He was reported to have resolutely refused to sign any document, although he did give a verbal undertaking to surrender some land.[25] These agitations reveal that smallholders, motivated by the belief that some extra land would allow them to climb out of economic despair, acted collectively

20 National Archives of Ireland, RIC confidential reports, 1 February 1920, CO 904/111. 21 Campbell, *Land and revolution*, pp 101–2. 22 *CT*, 17 Apr. 1920. 23 Ibid., 10 Apr. 1920. 24 Ibid. 25 Ibid., 3 Apr. 1920.

with neighbours in a similar situation, to accelerate the stagnant process of land reform.

At Ballinasloe Crimes Court on 24 April 1920, three men were charged with unlawful assembly on 9 April, having been arrested committing the illegal act of driving thirty cattle and 180 sheep from the lands of Mrs Anny Jones at Ashford on the northern outskirts of Ballinasloe. The arresting policeman testified that at least thirty men had participated in the drive. In the gallery of the courthouse, the men had a large following of supporters and the judge had to warn them to cease cheering for the accused. The men were convicted and sentenced to three months imprisonment, despite pleas from the defence that they would be needed on their farms. In the course of the proceedings, it was revealed that the accused had farms of eight, ten and fifteen acres, while Mrs Jones' parcel of land from which the stock were driven contained 400 acres. When the men were on their way to the station for the journey to Galway jail, 'they received another reception, hundreds of people cheering them again and again'. The tricolour flew at the front of the demonstration.[26] This case demonstrates the popularity and level of approval within the farming community for direct action. Indeed the waving of the tricolour may have signified that the fight for land redistribution went hand in hand with the fight for independence. Maura Cronin argues that it was difficult to understand 'in such a disturbed and politically-charged atmosphere [whether] Sinn Féin exploited agrarianism or agrarianism exploited Sinn Féin'.[27]

Uneconomic smallholders also mobilized on their own initiative, showing a spirit of solidarity where no 'land committee' was evident. A farm near Killimor was divided by locals who had been waiting several years for land redistribution and they used thirty ploughs to till it. It is likely that the land was held by the CDB, hence the delay. In another case, a man who held four acres from which a tenant had been evicted agreed to give it up. The next morning, locals reinstated the original evictee and began ploughing the land for him.[28] In his analysis of land conflict, Phillip Bull writes: 'the land agitations of the late nineteenth-century display the survival and re-expression of a still fundamental identification with a tradition of protest based on an alternative moral legitimacy.'[29] The examples here indicate what Campbell may have meant by 'radical impulses': smallholders uniting and taking collective action to correct what they perceived to be an injustice.

A common aspect of the agitation process involved a deputation or 'land committee' visiting a landholder/grazier and delivering a verbal or printed

---

26 Ibid., 1 May 1920.   27 Maura Cronin, *Agrarian protest in Ireland, 1750–1960* (Dundalk, 2012), p. 51.   28 *CT*, 17 Apr. 1920.   29 Bull, *Land, politics and nationalism*, p. 119.

notice to make land available to local smallholders. This usually included an explicit or implied threat of violence. Who were on these committees? Earlier in the century, land agitators were usually affiliated with the UIL. However, between 1917 and 1920, the UIL diminished at the same time as Sinn Féin clubs proliferated. Fergus Campbell contends that several Sinn Féin clubs in the county took over lands for redistribution among congests in 1918 and 1919. Some senior members of these clubs had previously been active in the Galway secret society. There is strong evidence to suggest secret society involvement in the 1920 agitations, given that some former members became active in the local Sinn Féin club, although it was confined to the Craughwell area.[30] Experienced activists usually became leaders of community actions such as land agitations. In one example, the chairman of Ballinasloe Urban District Council, Michael Manning, led 'a large crowd' who visited a number of farms in the Portumna area, where livestock was driven and replaced by smallholders' stock.[31]

Community approval was again evident when a deputation visited landowner Henry Howard of Meelick, to demand that he give up land. Howard agreed to consider their wishes and 'perhaps give it up on 1 May'. The deputation, travelling in nine sidecars, was loudly cheered when parading through Eyrecourt.[32] Clearly, this was a popular action. On 8 April, James Howard of Moorfield, Eyrecourt, an owner of some 200 acres, was asked by a deputation to give up a separate rented farm of 163 acres, which he was renting from the CDB. His response was, 'not a perch, until you shoot me'. He also received a threatening letter stating that he would face the same fate as Mr Shawe-Taylor (a large landholder who was killed in March, discussed below).[33] Howard's cattle were then driven from his land to his house by a large crowd, which he confronted with a shotgun. Howard was disarmed and assaulted by members of the crowd, some of whom were arrested and later appeared in court. Their solicitor James Kearns stated that nine tenants lived on the perimeter of this CDB-owned grass farm. They had been waiting a number of years to receive an increase to their smallholdings and graziers had been 'fighting tooth and nail' to retain these grass farms at the expense of local smallholders.[34]

At Knockferry, Oughterard, around 200 men mobilized on foot, on horseback and in sidecars, visiting a number of graziers who held land on the Ross estate. The graziers agreed to give up their tenancies and the deputation then headed for Ross House to meet the owner Mrs Taylor who was absent. Agreement was reached, through her manager, that Mrs Taylor would meet

30 Campbell, *Land and revolution*, pp 243–5. **31** *CT*, 17 Apr. 1920. **32** Ibid. **33** Ibid. **34** Ibid., 19 June 1920.

the deputation at a later date for the purpose of selling land to local people. The men then proceeded to a number of other graziers in Rosscahill and forced them to sign declarations stating that they would give up land by 1 May.[35] Nell Kinneavy, a publican in Rosscahill, had her house raided and had shots fired at it because, it was alleged, she refused to take her cattle off Ross estate and give the land to more deserving smallholders.[36] On the other side of the county Patrick Collins of Moylough, who held a number of farms, had first been given notice by about 20 men to remove his stock. When he failed to comply, his cattle were driven by a large number of people. Afterwards he received another notice stating: 'If you intend to come back to either of the farms you are driven from, you will get what [Shawe-] Taylor got'.[37] The irony of issuing notices to landlords/graziers was not lost on smallholders. After all, the legal notice was the first step a landlord took in evicting tenants in post-Famine Ireland. Nineteenth-century evictions were strong in the collective memory of the people and Michael Davitt describes this sentiment:

> Process-serving, being the preliminary legal step to eviction, was necessarily obnoxious to the tenants. It was the dreaded herald of ejectment, of the driving of a family from its home and means of labour and subsistence, and the 'process-server' had always been, next to the 'informer', a detested instrument of landlord oppression and of English law in Irish peasant feeling.[38]

The reversal of this process by smallholders and the landless produced a popular feeling of agency that inspired them to participate in agrarian mobilizations. These examples reveal that most agitations were motivated by the same concern – economic necessity. Many agitations were instigated and led by a local 'land committee'. It can also be seen that in many of these agitations, the intention of the agitators was to purchase extra land rather than confiscate it. The sizeable numbers of mobilizations throughout the county, and the substantial endorsement by rural communities, reveal a 'spirit of revolution' – a phenomenon in keeping with the general state of the country at that time.

The IRA

Although Sinn Féin actively supported land agitations through local branches and clubs during 1917 and 1918, the leadership soon realized that this could

35 Ibid., 3 Apr. 1920. 36 Ibid., 24 Apr. 1920. 37 Ibid., 8 May 1920. 38 Michael Davitt, *The*

alienate larger nationalist farmers.[39] Leading Sinn Féiners Arthur Griffith and Cathal Brugha voiced their opposition to land confiscations and the involvement of Volunteers in them. David Fitzpatrick's contention that many agrarian actions in Clare were 'thinly disguised IRA operations' is also borne out in Galway to an extent. For example, Frank Shawe-Taylor, a well-known figure in agricultural circles in Galway, was killed on 3 March 1920, most likely by the IRA, following his rebuttal of a deputation a short time earlier. In an oral testimony from 1990, former Volunteer Paddy Kelly of Athenry defined the attack as an IRA assassination and stated that after the attack, Volunteers Christy Daly and Larry Lardner, who had led the deputation, fled to Co. Tipperary and stayed there until the Truce of 11 July 1921. Furthermore, Kelly claims that Shawe-Taylor was 'alright' and that it was his chief employee who had convinced him to defy the deputation, most likely in the hope that he would obtain some of Shawe-Taylor's land.[40]

In an ambush at Killaclogher, near Skehana, in June, a party of RIC men who were protecting landowner James Hutcheson was ambushed by the IRA. Three of the attackers were part of a deputation who had visited Hutcheson the previous February requesting him to surrender his 160-acre farm to congests. Furthermore, some high-profile IRA members who were also members of estates committees (established around the county in February 1920 to petition landlords and graziers to sell their holdings) were known to be active in land agitations in south Galway.[41] In Belclare near Tuam, later in 1920, IRA Volunteers divided the lands among several tenants in the absence of the owner, Colonel Denis Bernard, who was on active duty with Crown forces in Co. Cork at the time.[42] This could also be an example of Campbell's 'radical impulses' – a land confiscation with the purpose of benefiting smallholders. At Barbersfort in the parish of Killererin the Volunteer executive purchased a holding using Volunteer funds. They divided the land among uneconomic smallholders and in the process prevented a 'grabber' from securing the land.[43] Therefore some local Volunteer units recognized the difficulties of uneconomic smallholdings and acted to alleviate the pressure on congests.

In a letter to Michael Collins, Fr T. O'Kelly described the deteriorating situation in south Connemara:

fall of feudalism in Ireland or the story of the Land League revolution (London, 1904, reprint, 2019), p. 213. **39** Campbell, *Land and revolution*, p. 246. **40** *The Castle Lambert tapes: the assassination of Shawe Taylor* https://athenry.org/record/the-castle-lambert-tapes-tape-6-the-assassination-of-shawe-taylor-473/ [retrieved 12 Aug. 2021] and *Tuam Herald*, 6 Mar. 1920. **41** Campbell, *Land and revolution*, pp 264–6. **42** Johnny Burke, 'Revolution and the land question in north Galway, 1920–1923' (MA thesis, NUI Galway, 2020), pp 18, 44. **43** Bureau of Military History, Witness

The Volunteers … claim to do all kinds of things in the name of the Irish Republic. Every Sunday there is a notice on the chapel gate or nearby, warning the public from doing so and so under gravest penalties. The chief victim a cousin of Padraic O'Mailles [sic] (Sinn Féin TD for Connemara and IRA leader) is rigidly boycotted. His servants had to leave him, his windows have been broken, nobody dares to go to his shop except at night … One item in dispute is a 15 acre island belonging to the man I mentioned. They did not even ask him for it, but put up a notice that nobody was to let him have a boat to get to it.[44]

Apart from the implication O'Kelly's letter and the other incidents mentioned above, there is little evidence of IRA Volunteers abusing their powers for personal gain. Neither were they leading a campaign of agrarianism, but rather facilitating smallholders in certain localities to obtain land.

Targets of agitations

A number of targets of land agitations have been identified here. Census records show that Mrs Anny Jones of Ballinasloe, the Horsmans and Howards of south-east Galway and Frank Shawe-Taylor were members of the Church of Ireland. Others, like high sheriff James Alcorn, Patrick Collins and Nell Kinnevey, were Catholics.[45] The issue of sectarianism has been analysed by Conor McNamara who concluded that although there were tensions and long-held grievances against landowning Protestants in Galway, 'there is no evidence of any systematic attempt at persecution of any social group … [and] one's religion counted for little where land was coveted'.[46] However, other factors can be considered, such as long-running campaigns of intimidation and the issuing of threats. In January 1918, Alcorn was shot as he travelled to Mass in Corrandulla. Despite receiving injuries to his neck and face he attended Mass and afterwards made a defiant speech outside the church. It was reported that a widow and her two sons were under notice of eviction from Alcorn and although one of the sons was arrested in connection with the shooting, he was released without charge.[47] On 31 March 1918, a steward employed by Alcorn was shot in the leg near Alcorn's residence. He was hospitalized, but died of an infection on 11 April. The motive offered by police was that Alcorn had

Statement, Sean O'Neill, 1219.   **44** National Archives of Ireland, letter from Fr T. O'Kelly to Michael Collins, DE/2/25 (012).   **45** 1911 Census, household schedules.   **46** Conor MacNamara, *War and revolution in the west of Ireland, 1913–1922* (Newbridge, 2018), pp 161–2, 175.   **47** *CT,* 12 Jan. 1918.

recently refused to give land on the conacre system.[48] Alcorn claimed damages through the courts a number of times for cattle driven and for damage to gates. He complained that he would have to get a man from Galway to repair the damage as he could not get anyone in his local area to do it.[49] This suggests that Alcorn was also the victim of a boycott. In the light of the prolonged campaign against him, Alcorn could be seen as obdurate in the face of strong local discontent.

Obduracy was also apparent in the Eyrecourt area. This region of the county had a history of land conflict and the Horsmans and the Howards showed a similar reluctance to Alcorn and Shawe-Taylor when asked to give up some land. In June, the Portumna court heard from the defence solicitor of five men accused of assaulting James Howard that they only wanted his rented farm and not his farm of residence. The solicitor, James Kearns, also stated that Howard would be fully compensated for any losses and that the accused, who lived adjacent to the land, were desperate smallholders.[50] Edward Horsman was known in the Eyrecourt area for taking the lands of evicted tenants. He was mentioned at a UIL meeting in 1917 along with another individual, T. Williams, as being in possession of lands from which a Mr P. Madden and a Mrs Killeen had been evicted.[51] Frank Shawe-Taylor also remained steadfast. With regard to land, he was described as 'an obstinate and unyielding character' and he once reportedly said 'if he had to surrender land, he would give it to ex-soldiers'.[52] As early as 1912, at a sporting event on the Tiaquin estate, a number of locals objected to Shawe-Taylor's presence, owing to the fact that he had refused to relinquish some land in the Castlelambert area.[53] In 1914, he was under police protection and had received compensation for damage to property and farm implements.[54] These examples highlight long-standing grievances. Overall, the main victims of land agitations were large landowners, many of whom had unyielding personalities and appeared oblivious to the plight of smallholders and the growing momentum of political and agrarian discontent.

Reactions to agitations

The repercussions of Shawe-Taylor's killing were strongly felt and the community of larger landowners became alarmed with many fearing for their lives. Kevin O'Shiel described this effect:

---

48 Ibid., 20 Apr. 1918.   **49** Ibid., 7 Feb. 1920.   **50** Ibid., 19 June 1920.   **51** Ibid., 28 Apr. 1917.
52 Ibid., 6 Mar. 1920.   **53** Ibid., 19 Oct. 1912.   **54** Ibid., 20 June 1914.

Eastbound trains brought to Dublin terrified landowners who came looking to the Dáil for protection, many of whom urged it to set up, immediately, independent land courts to check the outbreak. It was ... a strange anomaly that amongst the first persons to advocate the setting up of a Dáil judiciary were, not the Sinn Féiners ... but harassed landowners, mainly strong unionists and opposed to the Dáil, in principle.[55]

In another letter to Michael Collins, the aforementioned Fr O'Kelly wrote:

The mind of the people was being diverted from the struggle for freedom by a class war, and there was a likelihood that this class war might be carried into the ranks of the Republican Army itself, which was drawn in the main from the agricultural population and was largely officered by farmers' sons.[56]

O'Kelly's fear that land conflict could cause a split in Volunteer ranks was also raised by James Haverty in his unpublished memoir. A native of Springlawn, Mountbellew, Haverty was a veteran republican and O/C of the Mountbellew company of the IRA, as well as being an egg merchant and a farmer. He stated his belief that land agitations had the potential to split the IRA, simply because of the high proportion of farmers' sons involved therein. Haverty recounted an incident in his locality where he intervened at a meeting of agrarian agitators. As an IRA leader he ordered them to cease their actions in the name of the Republic.[57]

Catholic leaders made their feelings known in sermons during the spring. In April 1920, the bishop of Galway, Thomas O'Dea, spoke on land agitation at the Galway Pro-Cathedral:

The desire for land has become feverishly active ... Within limits, it is a legitimate desire ... It is good for all that the grazing ranches, now deteriorating from neglect, should be broken up, and tilled, and so made more productive. The young men, too, need a living and the division of the grazing ranches among them has the further advantage that it reverses the foolish and iniquitous policy of wholesale clearances after the famine, and brings the land back to the people.[58]

55 Campbell and O'Shiel, 'The last land war?', 169.   56 Quoted in Michael Laffan, *The resurrection of Ireland: the Sinn Féin party* (Cambridge, 1999), p. 315.   57 University of Galway Archives, James Haverty memoir.   58 *CT*, 10 Apr. 1920.

Although acknowledging the need for land reform, the bishop also invoked the absolute right of the individual to property ownership: 'it is immoral and unjust to seek land which a man not only lawfully owns, but which he has a right to keep, in spite even of the public need for land'.[59] In May, the bishop of Clonfert, Thomas O'Doherty, conceded that land reform was urgent and that the CDB had to shoulder much of the blame: 'a man cannot be justly forced to give up what he lawfully possesses without adequate compensation … even if he agrees to part with his property, the price must be a just one … If this principle is violated the door is open to communism'.[60] While some bishops preached alarmingly about the spread of communism, it was clear that the fear was exaggerated, especially when most smallholders were willing to pay for land – albeit on their own terms.

Arbitration courts

The practice of dealing with land disputes through arbitration was not new and had been practiced in the countryside for generations. Heather Laird, in her study of 'subversive law', reveals 'the existence of an alternative system of control capable of replacing without necessarily replicating the official legal system.'[61] These processes emerged from the ground up and those in authority were compelled to find solutions to popular unrest, lest their interests be endangered. In land disputes, arbitration courts emerged during the nineteenth century and were usually presided over by local community leaders such as the clergy and politicians. Agreements were reached beforehand that opposing sides in the dispute would abide by any rulings reached by the court. In that context, it is interesting that the *Connacht Tribune* reported as follows in April 1920:

> A large meeting of young men from districts in North Galway, was held in the Town Hall, Tuam, on Sunday, when it was decided to take action to prevent the wholesale driving of stock, particularly in cases of severe hardship. The majority of those present favoured the setting up of an arbitration court to hear applicants seeking a division of lands, and this was agreed upon.[62]

Throughout April, in many parishes, arbitration courts were established and the general feeling was that they were a success in that rulings were abided

---

59 Ibid.　60 *Tuam Herald*, 8 May 1920.　61 Heather Laird, *Subversive law in Ireland, 1879–1920: from 'unwritten law' to the Dáil courts* (Dublin, 2005), p. 16.　62 *CT*, 10 Apr. 1920.

by.[63] This success, in the midst of an agrarian crisis, was noted by Sinn Féin leadership in Dublin. Dáil Éireann minister for agriculture, Art O'Connor, travelled to Galway in May and together with Kevin O'Shiel met with James Haverty in Ballinasloe and informed him that the minister for home affairs Austin Stack would shortly issue a declaration bringing the courts officially under Dáil control.[64] The next big step in addressing agrarianism was the setting up of a series of land conferences. During the first of these held in Roscommon on 9 May, Sinn Féin officials determined that land redistribution should be brought under Sinn Féin control. Succeeding conferences during the month revealed formal Sinn Féin policy, that land would be redistributed, that landowners would be adequately recompensed and that no violence or intimidation should be used.[65] Kevin O'Shiel describes the origins of the land courts:

> Conditions in the West proved to be much more serious than we had anticipated, so serious indeed that the people themselves … took matters into their own hands and established arbitration courts to check the chaos. Those arbitration courts sprang up, as it were, from the hearts of the people, without the direct sanction of any government, in order to cope with an emergency which threatened to overwhelm the whole structure of society.[66]

Even O'Shiel conceded that the courts originated from the grassroots; it was the people who organized and administered an age-old system of justice. The Land Settlement Commission established in September 1920 under the guidance of Art O'Connor was the first serious step in addressing the land question.[67] The part played in the Irish Revolution by smallholders and the landless in 1920 was embedded in the minds of future Free State leaders and culminated in the Land Act of 1923. However, the Free State government could not contain further agrarian mobilizations without the army and in January 1923 established the Special Infantry Corps to deal specifically with both agrarian and labour radicals.[68] According to Terry Dunne, 'the Free State was to respond with a more biting repression and a more generous reform'.[69]

63 Ibid.   **64** Haverty memoir.   **65** Campbell, *Land and revolution*, pp 255–7.   **66** O'Shiel, WS 1770.   **67** Dáil Éireann Debates, 17 August 1921, vol. 5, no. 2.   **68** John Dorney, '"Rough and ready work" – the Special Infantry Corps' https://www.theirishstory.com/2015/10/15/rough-and-ready-work-the-special-infantry-corps/comment-page-1/ [retrieved 13 June 2021].   **69** Terry Dunne, 'The cattle drives of 1920: agrarian mobilization in the Irish Revolution' https://www.theirishstory.com/2020/11/24/the-cattle-drives-of-1920-agrarian-mobilisation-in-the-irish-revolution/ [retrieved 13 June 2021].

While the Land Act established a new Land Commission and introduced compulsory purchase of estates, it did not go far enough for many farmers, particularly due to certain restrictions on estate purchase. As a consequence, further reform was introduced under Fianna Fáil in 1933 effectively reducing bureaucracy and the process of land redistribution continued for most of the twentieth century.[70]

Conclusion

The extensive agrarian mobilizations throughout Co. Galway in the spring of 1920 showed that collective action by smallholders and the landless contributed significantly to increased land redistribution. High numbers of smallholdings in Galway, many of which were of poor quality, as well as the significant amount of ranches remaining, were a major cause of discontent. Delays in the process of land reform, which was mostly the responsibility of the CDB, was also a key factor. While these were long-standing causes of periodic outbreaks of agrarianism, more immediate factors combined to provoke the wide-ranging mobilizations of 1920. The presence of more young men due to stagnant emigration, the sharp decline in post-war agricultural prices and declining numbers of police in the countryside were notable factors. However, the intensity of agrarianism in 1920 was most likely caused by the climate of national rebellion or a 'spirit of revolution'.

While many leading Sinn Féiners and Catholic clergy declared that agitations were simply land confiscations, this study has shown that smallholders believed they had an entitlement to a share of large holdings in their locality and were willing to purchase the land they claimed. The most common agrarian tactic was to establish a land committee, visit a large landowner, and persuade him to sell his holding to locals in need of extra land. Almost always, some sort of coercion was present. Catholic clergy, who regarded agrarian mobilizations as the confiscation of property, generally understood the plight of those who took such actions and called for land reform measures to alleviate economic suffering. The victims of agitations varied somewhat, but most were large landowners and/or graziers who were determined to retain their holdings. This obstinacy in the face of the obvious economic needs of the general rural population led to land conflict.

Arbitration courts emerged and spread throughout parishes across the county and many land issues were already settled by the time Dáil Éireann took control and officially established Dáil courts in June 1920. Dealing

70 Dooley, *'The land for the people'*, p. 103.

initially with land disputes, the courts quickly developed into a propaganda weapon in the fight for national independence, especially after the IRA was deployed to enforce judgements. IRA involvement in agrarianism was complex, given that the majority of Volunteers were farmers' sons and some community leaders feared that this would split the Republican movement. However, assertive policing by the IRA in arbitration and Dáil court cases suggests that members' involvement in land agitations were at low levels. The impact of the 1920 agrarianism was such that it forced the Republican government to act. Containment measures including land conferences, the establishment of a Land Settlement Commission and the takeover of arbitration courts led to a decrease in agitations. During the Civil War, the Free State government used force to prevent further agrarianism but its commitment to effective land legislation resulted in the 1923 Land Act shortly after the Civil War ended. Although agrarian protests continued throughout the 1920s and forced various amendments, the 1923 Act formed the basis for land reform well into the twentieth century.

A 'soviet at Galway'? William J. Larkin, Stephen Cremen and the town tenant mobilization of May 1922

JOHN CUNNINGHAM

On the approach of noon on 25 May 1922, hundreds of followers of the Town Tenants' League (TTL) marched behind a fife and drum band to Galway's Town Hall. It was Ascension Thursday, a Catholic holiday, so more people were available than on an ordinary working day. They were demonstrating support for a TTL deputation, which had been invited to meet urban councillors to discuss a proposed new housing scheme.[1] The march was the culmination of a week of activity during which support for TTL demands had been canvassed at dozens of outdoor meetings where tenant grievances were aired by the local TTL leader, Stephen Cremen, and by a visiting national figure, William J. Larkin. The grievances included the dilatoriness of the urban council in providing housing, high rent levels, and the unsympathetic legal system. Significantly, the mobilizations took place in the latter part of the interval between the signing of the Anglo-Irish Treaty and the outbreak of the Civil War, so they reflected discontent with the orientation and attitude of the incoming Irish administration rather than with the receding British order.

With regard to the treatment of those who had joined the League's rent strike – called to reduce rents to 1914 levels – Cremen had earlier criticized the local courts at a meeting in Eyre Square: 'The courts in Galway are strongly behind the landlords and are a damned sight worse than the old courts... [T]he people should have the right to select their own justices and the right to recall them if they did not act properly'.[2] Larkin took up the theme at the same meeting:

> Who made the laws under which you live at the present time? The thieves of the country. Who robbed you of every right you ever possessed, and continues to do it today? What law are you under? ... Why are we not under the Brehon Code if we have an Irish government?

---

1 'The "soviet" at Galway', *Connacht Tribune* (henceforth *CT*), 27 May 1922. The episode was treated in John Cunningham, 'The soviet at Galway and the downfall of Dunkellin', *Cathair na Mart: Journal of the Westport Historical Society*, 10 (1990), 115–23. 2 'Town tenants', *CT*, 27 May 1922.

Is it because there are too many clauses in that code which are favourable to the tenantry? … Are there slum owners on the bench in Galway? … No parish or district justice should preside here or in any town in Ireland unless he is put there by the people, who make the laws for Ireland.[3]

Press reports of speeches delivered by Cremen and Larkin, and of actions initiated by them, are the main sources of information about the proceedings of the week. From the enthusiastic participation of large numbers, however, it can be inferred that these orators were articulating the indignation of working-class Galwegians at the housing shortage and at the repeated breaches of promises to address it. The events also reveal a distrust of the capacity of the political and legal authorities to transcend the class interests that bound them to property owners, and to act justly in relation to tenant householders.

In Eyre Square, three evenings prior to the events of Ascension Thursday, both Cremen and Larkin drew attention to the monument to Lord Dunkellin, 22 feet high, which towered over their proceedings. Dunkellin, Ulick Canning de Burgh (1827–67), an MP for Galway and the brother of the notorious last earl of Clanricarde, was a descendant of the Anglo-Norman family that had established Galway in the thirteenth century. Following his early death, the Galway aristocracy had raised a subscription, and commissioned eminent sculptor, John Henry Foley, to fashion a bronze figure, which, perched on a plinth of Aberdeen granite, was unveiled in 1873. In the belief that the Clanricarde tenantry had been levied to pay for it, and in the context of Clanricarde's unpopularity, there were occasional calls over the decades to remove it from the Square.[4] For Cremen and Larkin, as for populist orators before them, the monument was a symbol of landlordism. 'It is better for you to tear that statue out of the square', urged Larkin, 'and leave the place free for the children'. 'Why', he continued, 'was there not the statue of Padraic Pearse or James Connolly there?'[5]

Due to the absence of Dr Thomas Walsh, council chair, the Ascension Thursday meeting between councillors and TTL representatives was cancelled. Greatly irritated, Cremen and Larkin led their supporters, band, instruments and all, into the chamber, packing it 'to suffocation'. In an exchange with councillors, during which it was admitted that the new scheme had been drafted by a single individual – by implication the absent Walsh – Larkin accused the council of undemocratic 'star chamber methods', and declared: 'Your council is obsolete, and we are going to take the chair'.

---

3 Ibid.   **4** No title, *Dublin Weekly Nation*, 3 Oct. 1885; 'Galway town commissioners and Lord Dunkellin's statue', *Dublin Daily Express*, 8 Oct. 1886; No title, *Galway Observer* (henceforth *GO*), 3 June 1922.   **5** 'Town tenants', *CT,* 27 May 1922.

3.1 Statue of Lord Dunkellin, older brother of the notorious last Lord Clanricarde, erected in Eyre Square, Galway, in 1873, and removed in the course of town tenant agitation in May 1922. Courtesy of the National Library of Ireland.

In a development described by the *Connacht Tribune* as 'The "Soviet" at Galway', the TTL next 'took possession' of the council chamber, and, with the exception of Labour's Rea and Colohan, the councillors left the building.[6] To cheers, Larkin declared: 'The scheme for Galway is the abolition of slums, and the erection of thousands of cottages for everyone in need of them in Galway.'[7]

6 Ibid.   7 'Urban council invaded', *GO,* 27 May 1922.

The commandeering of the chamber marked the beginning of four days of militant gatherings, revolutionary speeches, the seizure of houses, and iconoclastic gestures which involved thousands of people and left a permanent mark on the townscape. This article looks at the mobilization in detail, revealing something of the moral economy of housing at that time, and examining the political connections and trajectories of the key personalities.

Galway itself was a market town and administrative centre, with little in the way of industry or opportunity. With a population that had declined at every census since the Famine, there were only 13,255 Galwegians in 1911. Reflecting its circumstances, labour had not sunk deep roots there, but there were traditions of popular protest and it had a reputation for disorder. For the essayist Robert Lynd, writing in 1912, it was a 'wild, fierce and most original town', quintessentially Irish and more distinctively so than any other city or town, a place 'where the people are not allowed to make law and order for themselves and therefore seem to look on law and order as a superfluous thing'.[8]

If William J. Larkin's declared aim – the provision of houses for 'everyone in need of them' – was ambitious, it was widely held during those years. There was an urban housing crisis, and the ill-housed in Galway, as in other towns and cities, were impatient. Rural housing had been addressed by the Labourers Acts – championed by Irish nationalist politicians – under which almost 50,000 houses with tillage gardens had been built in the three decades prior to the First World War (see pages 88–9 in this volume). The attendant rhetoric and political debate copper-fastened the belief that decent housing was a moral right. With no effective champions, however, the urban working class remained largely in squalor. Artisan dwellings legislation had provided only for better-off workers, and though a Housing of the Working Classes Act (1908) promised to assist labouring families, only limited progress had been made by local authorities by the outbreak of the war. In the aftermath of the war, there appeared to be an urgency about improving the condition of the working class. As one Irish Unionist MP put it: 'Not only is bad housing largely responsible for the drink evil … but it is largely at the back of that greater evil, Bolshevism, and the extreme socialism that is stalking through Europe today …'.[9]

Also anxious to neutralize the spirit of revolution was Lloyd George, whose promise to provide half-a-million 'homes fit for heroes' in Britain was advanced by the Addison Act (1919). A parallel scheme for 50,000 houses in

8 Robert Lynd, *Galway of the races: selected essays* (Dublin, 1990), p. 60. For nineteenth- and early twentieth-century social unrest, see John Cunningham, *'A town tormented by the sea': Galway: 1790–1914* (Dublin, 2004), passim.   **9** Major O'Neill, MP, cited in Murray Fraser, *John Bull's other homes:*

urban Ireland had the barely-concealed objective of 'killing Sinn Féin with kindness'. Sinn Féin dared not obstruct such a popular scheme in a context where it needed working-class support as well as the co-operation of a growing labour movement. Accordingly, the Dáil administration urged local authorities to take advantage of it. By February 1920, almost a hundred of the 127 Irish municipalities had submitted outline schemes to the Local Government Board, the Galway Urban Council among them.[10] Developments in 1920 – the rise of violent conflict; the outcome of the local elections of January and June – halted progress. British state agencies placed political conditions on financing, conditions unacceptable to the great majority of local authorities, which, following the local elections, transferred their allegiance to Dáil Éireann. Those in need of housing were again disappointed. The issue could not be ignored, however, and the Provisional Government, anxious to mollify Labour in the aftermath of the Treaty, announced a 'Million Pound Scheme', providing for a modest 2150 urban houses, in March 1922.[11] This was the scheme that was being considered at the time of the Galway town tenants' mobilization of April–May 1922.

With housebuilding having fallen between the stools of contending authorities, there was uncertainty also on other fronts. British forces had left in February, leaving pro- and anti-Treaty blocs competing for influence. The Galway events of May 1922 may be located in the context of a wave of labour and social unrest during these months – including the Munster soviets – prompted by a squeeze on wages and by a determination to make a stand in circumstances where the tide seemed to be going out for labour.[12] In March in Limerick city, in an episode discussed below, a Workers' Housing Association placed destitute families in houses vacated by British soldiers. In early May in Roscrea, Co. Tipperary, in a bravura display of 'Soviet power' according to the *Freeman's Journal*, there was an episode similar to the Galway usurpation of Ascension Thursday, when Irish Transport and General Workers' Union (ITGWU) organizers Martin Cunningham and Phil O'Neill, frustrated at the district council's refusal to concede a wage increase, led road workers into the council chamber, declared a provisional council 'in the name of the Workers' Republic', and awarded the assembled workers a wage increase.[13]

state housing and British policy in Ireland, 1883–1922 (Liverpool, 1996), p. 196. **10** Fraser, *John Bull's other homes*, p. 225; Conor McCabe, *Sins of the father: tracing the decisions that shaped the Irish economy* (Dublin, 2011), pp 13–24; 'Urban council', *CT,* 14 June 1919, 14 Feb. 1920. **11** Fraser, *John Bull's other homes*, pp 278–80. **12** See Emmet O'Connor, 'Syndicalism, industrial unionism, and nationalism in Ireland' in Steven Hirsch and Lucien van der Walt (eds), *Anarchism and syndicalism in the colonial and postcolonial world, 1870–1940* (Leiden, 2010), pp 193–224; and Olivier Coquelin, 'Class struggle in the 1916–23 Irish Revolution: a reappraisal', *Études irlandaises*, 42–3 (2017), 23–36. **13** *Freeman's Journal* (henceforth *FJ*), 11 May 1922. The Roscrea incident is mentioned in Conor

For those concerned about housing, the legal environment was very important. If there were 'slum owners on the bench', as alleged by William J. Larkin, tenants would be hampered in asserting their rights. In Galway's courthouse, surmounted by the lion and unicorn symbolic of British authority, rival systems of justice had overlapped, with the petty sessions of the old order and the republican district court each sitting there during February 1922.[14] In the Treaty itself there were indications that the new state would dispense with the democratic features of the revolutionary-era Dáil courts. These features were familiar from a number of widely circulated pamphlets, including *Judiciary* published by Dáil Éireann early in 1919, which decreed that justices should be elected by local conventions of delegates from Sinn Féin, the Volunteers, Cumann na mBan, trades councils and parish councils.[15] Evidently recognizing that the *Judiciary* horse had bolted, Stephen Cremen contended in April 1922: 'You may see the post offices painted green but you should recollect that is not freedom – that is only paint on boxes. You may also have the law books with green covers on them, but inside there are seven hundred and fifty years of oppressive laws'. Cremen was reiterating a point frequently made by labour orators during these years – that a simple Republic was not adequate to the needs of labouring families; that it was necessary to hold out for a Workers' Republic. Consciously, or unconsciously, he was echoing James Connolly, who had written in 1909: 'If you remove the English army to-morrow, and hoist the green flag over Dublin Castle, unless you set about the organization of the Socialist Republic your efforts would be in vain. England would still rule you …'.[16]

Cremen, Larkin, and the town tenants movement

Stephen Cremen and William J. Larkin were relatively obscure figures, pushed into leadership positions in the volatile conditions of 1922–3, and returning to obscurity thereafter. They were just two of the many hundreds during the revolutionary period who found themselves at the front of crowds and movements, but whose experiences left little evidence in the historical record. The travails of Cremen and Larkin provide glimpses of the aspirations of a segment of labour-oriented social radicals and of the disposition of an urban working class at a critical moment of state formation.

Kostick, *Revolution in Ireland: popular militancy, 1917–1923* (Cork, 2009), p. 202. **14** 'Galway District Court', *CT,* 11 Feb. 1922; 'Petty sessions', *CT,* 18 Feb. 1922. **15** Mary Kotsonouris, *The winding-up of the Dáil courts, 1922–1925: an obvious duty* (Dublin, 2004), pp 6–23. **16** 'Town tenants', *CT,* 8 Apr. 1922. Connolly quote from *The Harp,* 1 Mar. 1909.

With regard to the Town Tenants' League, established in 1904 (succeeding House Leagues active from the mid-1880s), its objective was to gain for town tenants entitlements similar to those sought by the Land League and its successors for tenant farmers, including security of tenure, reasonable rent and right to purchase. A celebrated struggle was that of Martin Ward, a Loughrea shopkeeper evicted in 1905/6 by the earl of Clanricarde. The League had connections with the Irish Parliamentary Party, its leaders being William Field, a Dublin MP who professed to be a 'labour nationalist', and J.M. Coghlan Briscoe, a member of Dublin Corporation.[17] A connection with Redmondism was maintained into the Free State era.[18] The TTL aspired to represent the interests of all urban tenants: 'from the shopkeeper to the well-paid tradesman who pays a high rent ... to the poorly-paid toiler who pays three or four shillings a week for a few square yards'.[19] In reality, interests often clashed, with the shopkeeper, for example, frequently being landlord to the 'poorly-paid toiler'. A case in point was the Galway branch founded in 1905, which reputedly 'had a committee formed of landlords'.[20] In 1911, it was the threatened eviction of an Eyre Square grocer-publican that prompted a TTL revival.[21] A further effort at a revival in 1920 fell flat, and it was left to Stephen Cremen to take up the reins in March/April 1922, when it unquestionably became a movement of the 'poorly paid toiler', its meetings held in Liberty Hall, the local ITGWU headquarters.[22]

Cremen was branch secretary of the ITGWU in Galway, and his championing of the housing question suggests pressure from the union grassroots. Born in 1881, his family had a long-standing address in Raleigh Row in the town. His father, already an army pensioner at Stephen's birth, retained that status twenty years later. Bridget Cremen, mother of eleven children of whom at least five were dead by 1911, was a brushmaker, as was Stephen and his two post-school age siblings in 1901.[23] A significant but rapidly declining occupation in late nineteenth-century Galway, brushmaking was mostly carried out on a piece-work basis in the workers' homes.[24]

---

17 Noel McDonnell, 'The Ward eviction, 1906' in Joseph Forde et al. (eds), *The district of Loughrea: vol. 1: History, 1791–1918* (Loughrea, Co. Galway, 2003), pp 551–7; B.J. Graham and Susan Hood, 'Town tenant protest in late nineteenth- and early twentieth-century Ireland', *Irish Economic and Social History,* 21 (1994), 39–57. 18 Martin O'Donoghue, *The legacy of the Irish Parliamentary Party in independent Ireland, 1922–1949* (Liverpool, 2019), pp 26, 43–4, 91. 19 Quoted in Conor McNamara, '"A tenants' league or a shopkeepers' league?": urban protest and the Town Tenants' Association in the west of Ireland, 1909–1918', *Studia Hibernica,* 36 (2009–10), 135–60. 20 'Town tenants: Galway branch', *CT,* 8 July 1911. 21 Ibid. 22 'Apathetic town tenants', *CT,* 12 June 1920; 'Town tenants', *CT,* 8 Apr. 1922. 23 Stephen Cremen, birth certificate, 15 Oct. 1881; household schedules for Cremen, Raleigh Row, 1901 and 1911. 24 'What Galway can do', *Galway Express,* 21 Jan. 1888. According to census returns there were still 61 brushmakers in Galway in 1901,

Stephen was short and stocky, and something of his temperament may be inferred from his imprisonment for a few weeks for assault in 1902.[25] In 1903, he emigrated to the United States. Ten years later, working as a pipe-fitter and living in Dedham near Boston (notable later for the Sacco and Vanzetti trial), he applied for naturalization. Though registering for the draft in Dedham early in 1918, he chose to join the British merchant navy towards the end of the war.[26]

Returning to Galway following demobilization, Cremen was elected secretary of the Galway branch of the ITGWU on its establishment in November 1919, indicating prior union experience in Boston. The ITGWU was the largest, most dynamic and most militant union in Ireland at that time, but it was very late in establishing itself in the town of Galway. The obstacle was the Liverpool-based National Union of Dock Labourers (NUDL) which, having gained a foothold in 1912, organized categories of workers that might otherwise have joined the ITGWU.[27] At the founding meeting in the Town Hall, organizer Séamus O'Brien denounced the NUDL as 'an English union' and appealed to Galway workers on a nationalist basis:

> You are looking for political freedom, and you are wearing the badges of the slave around Galway. How can you expect political freedom when you are not able to achieve industrial freedom without going to the foreigner and asking, 'Can I do this, Jimmy-so-and-so?' [referring to James Sexton, NUDL leader].[28]

The initial recruits to the ITGWU were in the Galway Woollen Mills, among non-academic staff in the university, and in catering, sectors in which the NUDL had not made inroads.[29] Consistent with the nationalist rhetoric quoted above, the new branch associated itself with Sinn Féin, Cremen announcing within weeks of its formations that its premises were in the Sinn Féin hall on Prospect Hill, where it remained until the premises was burned out by Crown forces in March 1921.[30] Because of the association with Sinn

but only two in 1911.   **25** General register of prisoners, Galway 1902. I am indebted to Dara Folan for drawing my attention to this and other details on Stephen Cremen.   **26** United States naturalization petitions, Massachusetts, 1913; World War One draft registration cards – Stephen Joseph Cremen transcript; Britain: Merchant Seamen, 1918–1941.   **27** For detail of labour mobilizations prior to the establishment of the ITGWU branch see Linda Thompson, 'Strikes in Galway' in David Fitzpatrick (ed.), *Revolution? Ireland, 1917–1923* (Dublin, 1990), pp 130–43. **28** 'Transport Union', *CT,* 22 Nov. 1919.   **29** C. Desmond Greaves, *The Irish Transport and General Workers' Union: the formative years, 1909–1923* (Dublin, 1982), pp 255–7.   **30** See John Cunningham, '"A great believer in the *Internationale*": a British trade union in Galway, 1911–1936' in John Cunningham and Niall Ó Ciosáin (eds), *Culture and society in Ireland since 1750: essays in*

Féin, ITGWU officials were harassed and obliged to operate out of hiding.[31] Fractiousness characterized the relationship between the new union and the established labour movement in the town. On the industrial front, the ITGWU was thwarted when it tried to replace the NUDL in Thomas McDonogh & Sons, Galway's leading employer. Politically, the ITGWU ran a joint slate with Sinn Féin in the urban elections of January 1920, while other Labour candidates aligned themselves with an old guard of Redmondite businessmen.[32] In June 1920, Cremen was a runaway poll-topper for Labour in the elections for the district council and poor law guardians.[33]

Aged 40 in 1922, the same as Cremen, William J. Larkin had a degree of prominence in the tenant movement in Dublin. Like his namesake, the ITGWU founder, Larkin was born in England to Irish-born parents, but there is no indication that the two men were related. The family moved to the father's native Dublin, and in the 1901 census, William was returned as a messenger. By 1911 he was a 'clerk – unemployed'.[34] In the years prior to the First World War, he hit the headlines for militant Catholic actionist activities.[35] In 1913, he was among those who obstructed the passage to Liverpool of children of locked-out Dublin workers under the so-called 'Kiddies' scheme'.[36] No evidence was found of prior interest in housing questions but towards the end of 1916, he was prominent in a newly established Dublin Tenants' Association (DTA), dedicated to securing 'Cottage Homes and Allotments for the People'.[37] There were precedents in rural Ireland for the demand for working-class housing with gardens, but DTA publicity indicates that the garden city movement was also an influence. Larkin later characterized the DTA as an 'advance guard' of tenant agitation, prepared to engage in more militant action than the TTL.[38] He maintained a profile in Dublin, contributing to newspapers, and was occasionally prosecuted for obstructing evictions. In June 1919, he was physically assaulted by a future head of Irish governments, William T. Cosgrave, while giving evidence at a Dublin housing enquiry.[39] He told an audience in Galway that 'he had stood twenty-seven

honour of Gearóid Ó Tuathaigh (Dublin, 2015), pp 197–218. **31** Gilbert Lynch and Aindrias Ó Cathasaigh, *The life and times of Gilbert Lynch* (Dublin, 2011), pp 36–8. **32** Cunningham, 'A great believer in the *Internationale*', p. 205. **33** 'Urban guardians', *CT*, 5 June 1920. **34** Household schedule for Larkin, Sherrard Avenue, 1901 and 1911. **35** 'Crusade in Dublin', *FJ*, 19 May 1913; 'Scene in city theatre', *Irish Independent*, 7 Mar. 1914. **36** Dónal Ó Drisceoil, 'Sex and socialism: the class politics of immorality in pre-First-World-War Ireland', *Saothar: Journal of Irish Labour History*, 40 (2015), 19–29. **37** 'The Dublin Town Tenants' Association', *Evening Herald* (henceforth *EH*), 6 Nov. 1916; 'Housing problem', *EH*, 9 Dec. 1916. **38** Dublin Town Tenants' Association, *Stop the tragedy of Dublin* (Dublin, 1918); 'Tullamore tenants', *Offaly Independent*, 1 Jan. 1927. **39** 'W.T. Cosgrave involved in violent affray during Dublin housing inquiry', *Century Ireland*, *https://www.rte.ie/centuryireland/index.php/articles/wt-cosgrave-involved-in-violent-affray-during-dublin-housing-inquiry* [accessed 26 May 2022].

times in the dock in Dublin'.[40] Though influenced by the pervading labour radicalism of 1918–21, his pronouncements indicate that he retained strongly Catholic ideas of social justice.[41] Prior to his visit to Galway in May 1922, he was involved in the Limerick City Workers' Housing Association (LCWHA) – evidently initiated by the local ITGWU early in 1922, and supported, if uneasily, by the Trades Council.[42]

Limerick was a very different place to Galway at that time, with three times the population, a solid industrial base, and a strong labour tradition. A notable upholder of that tradition, Councillor John Cronin, president of the Limerick soviet strike committee in 1919, was an early spokesperson for the LCWHA, but Larkin soon took over that role. That such prominence was given to a stranger to Limerick is curious, and it may indicate that local leaders did not wish to be held accountable for militant activity.[43] The significant intervention by the LCWHA was the seizure of 27 houses in Garryowen, following their evacuation by departing British non-commissioned officers. Already, approaches had been made by the Trades Council and by the LCWHA to Ebrill, the local solicitor who was an agent for the owners of the properties. Eventually, according to Larkin:

> Finding that matters were leading nowhere, and the houses were being deliberately left idle despite the shocking conditions prevailing … we again approached Mr Ebrill and told him … [that] as children were being exposed to dire hardship and in fact being left in surroundings opposed to moral obligations, we would only have to take possession and await a reasonable consideration of our case.[44]

On the night of 13 March 1922, the Garryowen houses were seized by the LCWHA and families in need of housing placed in them. The seizure occurred during a period of intense activity by the Association, with large crowds attending meetings at the O'Connell monument in support of demands for 'additional and much improved accommodation'.[45] It was Larkin who took

40 'Give work before it is too late', *EH*, 23 June 1917; 'Hard hitting essentials', *EH*, 4 Sept. 1917; 'Battle of Mercer Street', *FJ*, 11 Dec. 1917; 'Sent for trial', *FJ*, 22 Dec. 1917. See also 'Town tenants', *CT*, 27 May 1922.   **41** Thomas Keane, 'Class, religion and society in Limerick city, 1922–1939' (PhD, Mary Immaculate College, University of Limerick, 2015), pp 27–33, 38–9.   **42** Tom Crean, 'Crowds and the labour movement in the south-west' in Peter Jupp and Eoin Magennis (eds), *Crowds in Ireland, c.1720–1920* (London, 2000), pp 249–68 at 263–4.   **43** Keane, 'Class, religion and society in Limerick city', pp 32–3.   **44** 'The Garryowen houses: statement by the Housing Association', *Limerick Leader* (henceforth *LL*), 25 Oct. 1922.   **45** 'Limerick's housing needs', *LL*, 13 Mar. 1922, 'City housing' and 'Commandeering of city houses', *LL*, 17 Mar. 1922. The *LL* reported that the seizure took place on Tuesday night, 14 March; Larkin later dated it 13 March.

the lead in the seizures. Three houses on O'Connell Street were occupied some days later and more occupations were threatened. Larkin stated in May that the LCWHA had by then placed tenants in 70 vacant houses.[46] Circumstances in Limerick, with both pro- and anti-Treaty forces taking the measure of each other, gave the LCWHA relative freedom of action during the spring of 1922.[47] Interestingly in light of Galway developments, Larkin prepared an LCWHA invasion of the council chamber in June following a slight from councillors, but was dissuaded by armed police.[48] Larkin's arrival in Galway, it is likely, was on foot of an invitation from members of the Galway TTL who had become aware of his activities in Limerick.

'Pulled down and drowned, amidst plaudits of thousands'

As several thousand people gathered in the Square on Ascension Thursday evening for the scheduled TTL meeting, two men were sawing at the base of the Dunkellin statue. When that job was done, others tied a rope around the neck of the figure, and to great applause pulled it to the ground. Thereupon Cremen, Larkin, and Paul Kiely, TTL secretary, mounted the empty plinth. Cremen, exultant, urged that 'every symbol of its kind in Ireland' be removed and a monument to 'a good Irishman' put in its place. More speeches followed, and when they finished, the statue was dragged through the town behind a marching band playing reels and hornpipes. Thousands followed the procession to Nimmo's Pier by the Claddagh, a mile distance from the Square. There, Larkin took charge: 'Let it go boys, and may the devil and all rotten landlordism go with it.' As the statue was lowered into the sea, the band struck up 'I'm forever blowing bubbles' to the great amusement of the crowd. Reporting on this 'bold and drastic stroke of the town tenants', the *Galway Observer* summed up the proceedings in its sub-heads: 'The Dunkellin monument – Symbol of landlord tyranny – Pulled down and drowned – Amidst plaudits of thousands'.[49] The wry acquiescence apparent in the *Observer's* coverage reflected the predominant attitude of Galwegians towards the event. As was noted at the time, there were bodies of pro-Treaty police and soldiers stationed within a few hundred yards of the Square, as well as anti-Treatyites, yet there was no intervention to preserve the statue.[50]

At a further meeting on the following evening, it was declared that Eyre Square – named for a landlord – was henceforth to be known as Father Griffin

46 'Town tenants', *CT,* 27 May 1922. **47** John O'Callaghan, *Limerick: the Irish Revolution, 1912–1923* (Dublin, 2018), pp 103–6. **48** Crean, 'Crowds and the labour movement', p. 265. **49** 'The Dunkellin monument', *GO,* 27 May 1922. **50** 'Dunkellin events', *GO,* 3 June 1922; 'Thursday

Square, in honour of the popular local priest killed by Crown forces in November 1920.[51] As for Dunkellin, he was already in a furnace, a place 'to which he was best accustomed'. And it would not stop there, said Larkin, for the tenant movement would ensure that the lion and unicorn, symbolic of alien authority, would be removed from the courthouse. For its part, the obsolete urban council would be replaced by a tenant-friendly body at a further meeting on Sunday. After the speeches, and the burning of the effigy of a landlord, the crowd lined up behind the fife and drum band, and proceeded to Eyre Street, where an unoccupied house, owned by Joseph Young OBE, a prominent local figure and an active Unionist, was seized. A needy family was installed. The band next led the crowd to Magdalen Terrace, where another house was seized and occupied, this one the property of the Magdalen Asylum.[52] Doubtless, there was a deliberate political point in the choice of properties – one owned by a prominent Anglican and the other by a Catholic religious order.

Denunciations followed. For the *Tuam Herald*, 'it was nauseating and disgusting [that] a wild crowd … vented their blind rage on a bit of bronze and made their once historic city a byword for reproach'.[53] Closer to the centre of things, Dr Thomas Walsh, whose absence on Ascension Thursday had led to the angry invasion of the council chamber, spoke out at the following meeting of the urban council. Walsh was a university lecturer in pathology, a prominent figure in the Gaelic League, a founder of Sinn Féin in Galway, a long-time urban councillor, and an internee in Frongoch following the 1916 Rising.[54] Claiming, with justification, a record of active sympathy with Labour 'before Messrs Larkin and Cremen were heard of in Galway', he nonetheless drew on rhetoric of a type frequently deployed by critics of social protest – the people involved 'were not labourers but were always keeping up the corners and would not work if they got work', and they included some that had 'smashed up the Volunteer Hall' at the time of the split in the Volunteers in 1914, and that had thrown missiles at him and others following their arrest in 1916.[55] Referring to reports that 'the "Soviet" was established', Walsh pronounced that it was 'the duty of every decent citizen to get his back up against that thing,' continuing: 'I believe it was boasted that neither [pro- or anti-Treaty] force would interfere, and that the Bolsheviks could do what they liked, but I understand that if they try it again they will be mistaken.'[56]

evening's incident', *CT*, 3 June 1922.   **51** 'Demonstration in Galway', *Cork Examiner*, 27 May 1922. **52** 'Town tenants', *CT*, 3 June 1922.   **53** 'Galway notes', *Tuam Herald* (henceforth *TH*), 3 June 1922.   **54** John Cunningham, '"Something that is new and strange": the 1911 Irish Trade Union Congress in Galway', *Journal of the Galway Archaeological and Historical Society*, 64 (2012), 169–82 at 178.   **55** 'Thursday evening's incident', *CT*, 3 June 1922.   **56** Ibid.

The destruction of the monument was denounced in several Galway churches on Sunday. For Canon Nestor, preaching in the Pro-Cathedral:

> Such an act was a grave violation of the fourth and seventh commandments – of the fourth as a usurpation of lawful authority, and of the seventh in the wanton destruction of property by men who did not own it … Whosoever statue it was, it was the property of the citizens of Galway, and the only authority in town that could lawfully remove it is the urban council as representing the citizens. By what right then did those men take it on themselves to pull down and destroy this statue? The deed savours of Bolshevism. In other words it is the deed of men who recognize no authority but their own. It is well to take this opportunity of pointing out that there are doctrines being preached in Galway lately which are in direct opposition to the teachings of Catholic theology, and therefore rank heresy.[57]

With the reproaches of Canon Nestor still ringing in their ears, the tenants returned to Eyre Square on Sunday afternoon for the advertised elections. Responding to the priest, Larkin stated: 'Bolshevism is the purest ring from the bell of the people's call for justice … I am proud of being a Catholic but twice as proud of being an Irish Bolshevick'. The business of the meeting was then announced in the following resolution:

> In public meeting assembled at Fr Griffin Square, we the tenants of Galway, having deposed the existing useless body of councillors of the urban district of Galway on Ascension Thursday 1922, hereby approve and appoint the following councillors for Galway as the council best fitted to act for the people, the new council to operate from May 29, 1922.[58]

The new body would convene on the following Wednesday in 'the people's council room', and council employees were urged to produce the documents necessary for the proceedings. Twelve men were nominated, three for each of the urban wards, but it is not possible to establish whether all had agreed to be nominated. With regard to Cremen and to Paul Kiely, a motor driver and active trade unionist who had been prominent in the TTL, to NUDL branch secretary William Carrick, and to stonemason J.J. McNamara, who had all actively participated in the proceedings, one can be reasonably certain. With

---

57 'Bolshevism', *CT*, 3 June 1922.   **58** 'Town tenants', *CT*, 3 June 1922.

regard to Labour councillors Colohan and Rea, to printer and former Trades Council president, James Pringle, and to Flynn and McGowan of the Ex-Servicemen's Association, there can be no such certainty. It is noteworthy that none of those nominated was a woman, and indeed that all of those named in connection with the entire affair were men. Women participated in the public meetings, including an unnamed 'lady' who reportedly 'mauled' a heckler, but they were not given any prominence, surprisingly in the light of Cremen's acknowledgment that there had been 'more "gis" in the women at the time of conscription than in the men'.[59]

Following the elections to the council, a slate of seven justices was adopted – all from the list of councillors – who were to ensure 'that all foreign law be abolished and replaced by the people's will'. And that was that, more or less. William J. Larkin announced his departure in a conciliatory letter to the local papers, rather different in tone to his speeches:

> I do appeal to all sections in the name of humanity to do all that humanly lies in them to eradicate slums and to take children into homes fit for them to live in and to thrive in ... Plenty of local material is available, and idleness is rampant. My friends in the Press I too sincerely thank for their great help and kind cooperation in the noble cause for better homes, and I do appeal for an earnest generous campaign by the Press to take Galway's sons out of a slough of rottenness and idleness into a hive of activity and health-giving environment. If there were good clean homes and work, there would be less shuddering by gentlemen at the prolific, profane use of the Name of Names. In God's name, let us rise to better things.[60]

By the time the letter was published, the authorities had evicted the TTL occupiers from the two seized houses and restored them to their legal owners. And when Cremen and J.J. McNamara arrived at the town hall for the scheduled meeting of their people's council on the Wednesday, they found their way obstructed by an armed guard. Armed guards were also deployed for a period outside the meetings of the established urban council, lest there be repeat of the 'soviet'.[61]

59 Ibid.   60 'Mr Larkin's farewell', *CT*, 3 June 1922.   61 In a review of the *Tribune*'s coverage of the 'fight for freedom' its sister paper later published excerpts of reports from the period, including Cremen and McNamara's effort mentioned above. The original was not located. See 'Urban council "abolished" and Dunkellin statue dumped into river', *Connacht Sentinel*, 1 June 1954.

Aftermath

In the aftermath of the purported soviet, increased membership was claimed for the Galway TTL while Cremen assisted an ITGWU colleague in establishing a TTL branch in Clifden.[62] The League in Galway was greatly dependent on a single individual however, and Cremen had urgent priorities which distracted him from the tenants' cause. In June, having left or been forced out of his union position, he was arrested at the request of union headquarters in Dublin, and charged with refusing to surrender branch accounts. Denying an ITGWU accusation that he was preparing to establish a rival union, he protested that he was having the books audited to protect himself against charges of financial impropriety.[63] On surrendering the books, he was released. Denial notwithstanding, Cremen had announced the formation of an Irish Mechanics' and General Workers' Union (IMGWU) within a week, citing developments in the ITGWU – excessive centralization and a crack-down on independent-minded officials, specifically mentioning J.J. Hughes, who had been purged from the union by William O'Brien in 1921.[64]

ITGWU branches in Athenry and Tuam, and part of the Galway branch, defected with Cremen, giving the IMGWU a solid enough position in the county for a time.[65] For his former union's *Voice of Labour*, unsurprisingly, he was 'the ratting branch secretary who became an official of the shopkeepers' Town Tenants' League'.[66] Indeed when things settled down, the IMGWU office in Shop St served also as the office of the TTL.[67]

Cremen also remained at odds with the emerging state, and on or around 1 September 1922, he was detained for some weeks when he issued posters accusing the Free State military of 'Black and Tannism' and, characteristically, remarked to the officer chiding him: 'Michael Collins was a big man and he got potted, and Commandant Brennan [the local military commander] should not think that he was so high and mighty either'.[68] To secure his release he signed an undertaking that 'as secretary of the Galway Tenants' Association and general secretary of the Irish Mechanics' and General Workers' Union [he would] not pursue a policy to which the Commanding Officers of the Galway

62 'Clifden Town Tenants' Association', *CT,* 17 June 1922. **63** 'Refusal to submit books', *CT,* 24 June 1922. **64** 'Athenry Labour Union', *CT,* 1 July 1922. For Hughes and the 'purge' see Francis Devine, *Organizing history: a centenary of SIPTU, 1909–2009* (Dublin, 2009), pp 93–9. **65** 'Irish Mechanics' and General Workers' Union', *TH,* 9 Sept. 1922; 'Athenry IT and GW union' *CT,* 14 Apr. 1923; 'Committee on prices', *CT,* 31 Mar. 1923; 'Contract v direct labour' *CT,* 14 Apr. 1923; 'County officials', *CT,* 23 June 1923; 'Labour's opposition', *CT,* 26 Aug. 1923. **66** 'Galway', *Voice of Labour,* 28 Oct. 1922. **67** 'The Galway Town Tenants' Association', *CT,* 28 Oct. 1922. **68** 'The arrest of Mr Cremen', *CT,* 9 Sept. 1922.

area or General Headquarters object.'[69] The grandstanding did not impress a local branch of the Communist Party, which accused Cremen of conceding wage cuts and of selfishly weakening the movement by his split while 'preaching the tenets of Industrial Unionism' and 'posing as the personification of a Revolutionist'.[70] The communists may have been correct in discerning some circumspection in Cremen's disposition following his release from Free State custody. Certainly the statements he issued for the TTL were low key, describing negotiations and representations on behalf on individual tenants rather than addressing the broader housing question.[71]

By the spring of 1923, efforts were being made by the TTL national headquarters and local individuals to establish a new Galway unit which would exclude Cremen and his 'mushroom branch'.[72] This was part of a wider restructuring which would culminate in the nomination of town tenant candidates in the 1923 general election, including old Redmondite Thomas Sloyan in the Galway constituency. For Cremen, it was a time when there were difficulties also on the IMGWU front, and in that context there were efforts to make common cause with Jim Larkin in the months after his return from the United States.[73] Nothing seems to have come of that, and Cremen, with his IMGWU and his TTL, had disappeared from view by the end of 1923.

Cremen was next located in Coventry, England, in 1926, where he established a small business as a wardrobe dealer and evidently had a tempestuous personal life. He would hit the headlines for the last time in 1931 when he survived an assault during which he had his throat slashed by a razor, wielded by the ominously named Daisy Cleaver. (He subsequently married his attacker, and she would be his heir in 1956.)[74]

William J. Larkin's trajectory was somewhat less melodramatic. Following his departure from Galway, he returned to Limerick, where the saga of the 'commandeered houses' rumbled on, with the installed families remaining in occupation. Under pressure from the LCWHA, the Corporation increased the rates (a property tax) to support house construction, but the overwhelming majority of councillors refused to countenance acquiring the commandeered houses.[75] Matters were brought to a head in mid-December, when the agent Ebrill had one of the occupiers evicted, prompting LCWHA resistance,

---

69 'Mr S.J. Cremen and the national forces', *CT*, 23 Sept. 1922.   **70** 'Galway news: the bosses advance', *Workers' Republic*, 17 Nov. 1923.   **71** 'The Galway Town Tenants' Association', *CT*, 28 Oct. 1922; 'Get back your overpaid rent', *CT*, 11 Nov. 1922.   **72** 'Long suffering', *CT*, 10 Mar. 1923; 'Galway town tenants awakening', *CT*, 31 Mar. 1923; 'Position of town tenants', *CT*, 31 Mar. 1923. **73** 'Bossism at HQ', *Irish Worker*, 30 June 1923.   **74** 'Wounding charge: alleged attempt to murder', *Coventry Evening Telegraph*, 25 Feb. 1931; England and Wales marriages, 1935.   **75** Keane, 'Class, religion and society', pp 36–7.

including confrontations with members of the new Civic Guard. Larkin and others faced assault charges, but they were however acquitted.[76] Frustrated, Larkin appealed to the bishop of Limerick to arbitrate, citing the papal encyclical *Rerum novarum* in his letter. Considering this to be impertinent, Bishop Hallinan publicly scolded Larkin for his 'profane and irreverent appeal to the authority of the Encyclical of Leo XIII on the condition of the working classes', and accused him of leading 'some of my people into the evil course of seizing by violence and holding the property of their neighbour against his will'.[77] By-passing Larkin and the LCWHA, the bishop engaged directly with tenants through January 1923, brokering a compromise under which some families were permitted to remain in possession, but were required to sign a declaration stating that the initial seizure was 'subversive of all social order, and opposed to the principles, that we, as good Catholics are bound to stand by.'[78] The LCWHA chose to interpret this as a partial victory, and on 19 January 1923, it arrogated a function of the Corporation by presenting Larkin with a golden key and awarding him the freedom of the city at a well-attended meeting in the town hall.[79]

In August 1923, Larkin stood as an independent in the seven-seat Co. Limerick constituency, where he received 466 votes, 1 per cent of the total. His performances subsequently as an independent tenant advocate in Dublin North were somewhat better – 1012 in June 1927; 823 in September 1927 – but not close to taking a seat. He earned a month imprisonment in 1925 for leading resistance to an eviction, and continued to represent the Tenants' Association from an office in Lower Abbey St for the remainder of his life.[80] Prominent in a Davitt memorial event in 1931, he denied any connection between his association and the Communist Party two years later.[81] Interestingly, in light of the Dunkellin affair, he was an advocate for the removal of Nelson's Pillar.[82] At his death in 1954, an obituary acknowledged that he 'was a very active worker in the interests of the working classes, particularly in regard to housing conditions' and the 'removal of tenements'.[83] His first visit to Galway was for the 1922 events, and there is no indication that he ever returned.

76 Ibid., pp 44–5. **77** Ibid., p. 41. **78** Ibid., p. 47. **79** Ibid., p. 49. **80** 'Abusive language: William J. Larkin sentenced to one month', *EH*, 11 Dec. 1925; 'Dublin Port', *EH*, 13 July 1928; 'Dublin housing', *EH*, 3 Feb. 1938. **81** 'Davitt's anniversary', *CT*, 13 June 1931; 'Irish Communist Party', *Irish Independent*, 9 June 1933. **82** 'Nelson Pillar', *EH*, 19 June 1925; 'Everything seemingly understood', *EH*, 2 Dec. 1926. **83** 'Mr William J. Larkin', *Irish Independent*, 6 Jan. 1954.

Conclusion: 'a burst of patriotism'?

The episode then was a four-day-wonder in a place where there had been comparatively little labour militancy, and where the major agent of labour militancy, the ITGWU, was comparatively weak. So frustrated however were Galway's working-class people at the housing situation that they used the unpromising vehicle that was the TTL to get their voices heard. Commencing with the occupation of the council chamber on Thursday, the protest was practically over before its last act on Sunday afternoon – the selection of 'people's' councillors and justices in the renamed Fr Griffin Square. The authorities took care to ensure that the people's council did not meet, and the episode had little discernible impact, either with regard to expediting council housing or to leaving a mark on local memory.[84] While the Dunkellin statue was sometimes discussed in the local press in the following decades, the context of its removal was seemingly forgotten, and when it was mentioned, it was as a purely nationalist affair. In the dominant narrative of the revolutionary period, social struggle was delegitimized or occluded, so when the toppling of Dunkellin was remembered at all it was as 'a burst of patriotism of the type that led recently to the blowing up of the Nelson Pillar in Dublin', as one commentator put it in 1966.[85] Occasions when the Dunkellin statue was remembered included when a replacement monument was erected in the Square in 1935 to writer Padraic Ó Conaire – a 'good Irishman' as urged by Cremen in 1922 – and when Dunkellin's granite plinth was used for a memorial to local republican activists in the village of Castlegar in 1951.

The relative lack of impact had a number of causes: the transient character of the town tenants' movement in Galway; the other demands on the time of the leaders of the struggle; and, not least, the practical difficulties of conducting a social agitation in a context of civil war. As a visiting organizer, Larkin can hardly be faulted for returning to Limerick, where he directed a significant struggle of his own through the remainder of 1922. If Cremen had the greater responsibility insofar as it was he that had brought the TTL into being, circumstances in the aftermath of the soviet, including his acrimonious departure from the ITGWU, his incarceration by pro-Treaty authorities, and the threat that he would be detained indefinitely if he engaged in further militant action, meant that he was constrained in conducting the tenant movement, though he did keep it ticking over for a time.

---

84 James Kerrigan, 'Case study' in 'The provision of social housing in Ireland in the 1920s and 1930s: a case of pragmatism over ideology' (MA history thesis (minor), NUI Galway, 2019), pp 35–43.
85 'On the Square', *CT,* 7 May 1966.

So how do the events discussed here relate to the other mobilizations of 1918–22 that were characterized as soviets? The soviet (meaning 'council' in Russian) as instruments of workers' power were associated with the Russian Revolution and the term was applied post-1917 to radical initiatives by workers in a number of countries which generally included an effort by those involved to claim political or economic authority. While it was understood that workers had taken over government in Russia, detailed knowledge of what this meant in practice was scant, so there was considerable variety in the manifestations of 'Bolshevism'. In labour activist circles in Ireland, the Russian Revolution was interpreted as being consistent with James Connolly's concept of the Workers' Republic, and those aspiring to put it into effect assumed that this would be achieved by a 'bottom up' syndicalist-style movement (as opposed to a highly centralized party, Bolshevik-style party).[86] As it was put by Padraic Ó Conaire, the labour-connected Irish language writer whose statue would later replace Dunkellin's in the Square: 'In the future, there will be one big union, one big industrial army ... which will ensure that all that is produced in a country is under the control of its working class people'.[87] The soviets in Ireland during the period were in most cases workplace seizures – some of them involving multiple seizures over a wide area and for a period of months such as the Cleeve's Munster soviets discussed by Haugh in this volume. These were operated generally by councils of workers, which continued and in instances even expanded production. Occupied premises were used as bargaining chips in negotiations with employers, and were handed back when these were concluded, though a wider ambition for workers' control is evident in the Munster events of 1922.[88] The 'Soviet at Galway' was clearly part of a wider movement in the spring of 1922. Any claim to include it among the soviets of the period lies in the efforts of those involved to claim civic authority on behalf of Galway's working-class tenants – by taking over the council chamber, declaring the council 'defunct', and replacing the councillors (and justices) with trade union and tenant representatives. The 'soviet' designation was applied at the time by detractors

86 Emmet O'Connor, *A labour history of Ireland, 1824–2000* (Dublin, 2011), pp 106–8, 121–5; Danny Gluckstein, *The Western soviets: workers' councils versus parliament, 1915–1920* (London, 1985), passim. **87** Ó Conaire wrote: 'Aon chumann mór amháin, aon arm mór tionsclaíoch amháin, a bheas ann san am le theacht, go gcuirfear an cuspóir a luadh cheana i ngíomh, go mbeidh gach déantús dá bhfuil sa tír i seilbh lucht a oibrithe.' For Ó Conaire, see Aindrias Ó Cathasaigh, *Réabhlóid Phadraic Uí Chonaire* (Baile Átha Cliath, 2007). **88** See Olivier Coquelin, 'Cleeve's soviets: "socialism from below" in revolutionary Ireland, 1920–1922' in Francis Devine and Fearghal Mac Bhloscaidh (eds), *Bread not profits: provincial working class politics during the Irish Revolution* (Dublin, 2022), pp 144–60; Emmet O'Connor, 'Munster labour in "the red flag time": a regional exception' in Devine and Mac Bhloscaidh (eds), *Bread not profits,* pp 129–43.

of the endeavour – the *Connacht Tribune* and urban council chair Thomas Walsh – just as it had been in the case of the Limerick soviet of 1919. It was a designation which was however apparently embraced by the principal actors – in Larkin's public identification as 'an Irish Bolshevick', and in Cremen's socialist republican rhetoric.

The dramatic features of the soviet at Galway were symbolic – almost carnivalesque – in character, from the removal of the statue, to the renaming of the square (and arguably the naming of councillors and justices that were never likely to carry out the functions of these offices). That the intention may have been more far-reaching, however, is indicated by William J. Larkin's involvement in the concurrent large-scale appropriation of houses in Limerick. The appropriation of two houses by the TTL in Galway shows at least a disposition to follow the Limerick example.

'Strike out for yourselves': land and labour from the Boyne to the Barrow

TERRY DUNNE

This chapter surveys farm workers' mobilizations in the east of Ireland as a means of exploring how the labour movement in the revolutionary period approached what has been called the agrarian question of labour.[1] That question was a debate about what policies to adopt in situations where agriculture consisted, to some degree, of small-scale units of production, operated in part by family labour. This was a major international issue in the period, one of obvious relevance on an island where agriculture was the main industry and where wage workers were not the majority of the agrarian workforce.[2] In the early 1920s there was considerable discussion within the ranks of the Irish workers' movement around co-operative marketing, collective forms of landownership, the provision of garden plots to farm workers, and the re-distribution of farmland. The chapter will conclude with a look at the ramifications of these different policies on a local level and at the relationship between the workers' movement and the new state.

The aim is to have a survey of the agrarian question of labour as it manifested in this particular place at this particular time, not to deal with all aspects of the workers' movement, or to say everything that could be said about the agrarian policy discussions within the Irish labour movement. Nonetheless there will be an introduction to the study area and overviews of both the local movements and the wider policy discussion. Regarding the latter, specific attention will be given to exploring the particular rationality of farm labourers' demand for land – both because it has been misinterpreted in the scholarly literature and because it was what was popular among the rural branches of the Irish Transport and General Workers' Union (ITGWU). The specificity of the study area, the more markedly proletarian nature of its agrarian workforce relative to other parts of Ireland, offers a particular vantage point. From here, it is possible to understand the demand for land as emanating from the lived experience of the working class as opposed to an atavistic irruption of repressed peasant DNA; that is to say people were not

---

1 A. Haroon Akram-Lodhi and Cristóbal Kay, 'Surveying the agrarian question (part 1): unearthing foundations, exploring diversity', *Journal of Peasant Studies*, 37:1 (2010), 177–202.   2 For examples see: Paul Frölich, *Rosa Luxemburg* (London, 1994), p. 250; Massimo Salvadori, *Karl Kautsky and the*

confusing themselves for farmers, as is claimed in David Fitzpatrick's study of Clare in the revolutionary period.[3] In great part the farm workers' mobilization of the years between 1917 and 1923 was a wages movement, and was related closely to the exigencies of the 1914–18 war.[4] These dimensions have been the major focus of the scholarly literature to date. This chapter re-focuses attention on to how wage workers fitted into the politics of land and on the deeper roots of their mobilizations.

The agrarian economy in Dublin, Kildare and Meath

The specific area examined here is the east central lowland, an unfamiliar mouthful perhaps, but an essential effort to capture a physical and social geography that transcends county boundaries. Hence the focus on river valleys in the title. Nonetheless counties had a reality in state administration and oftentimes the organizational forms of civil society, and most frequently what will be referred to here are counties Dublin, Kildare and Meath.

What most characterized this broad area was a long-term concentration of the highest-value farms. It is this that accounts for the concentration in the area of a comparatively high proportion of wage earners as part of the agricultural workforce. To some extent the presence of particularly labour-intensive branches of production played a significant role in this also.

According to the Department of Agriculture's statistics for 1912 only in Dublin did the number of permanent adult male farm employees exceed the number of farm family members working in agriculture.[5] In Dublin this was also true for the adult female farm workforce. In most counties the disparity was even greater among women. Elsewhere, only in Meath and Kildare does the inclusion of the temporarily employed tip the proportionate balance in favour of the wage worker category. Agriculture in these counties was, in relative terms, unusually proletarian.

We might say there are two relevant variables, first the size of farms, and second the extent of area under crops. By the 1930s, about 43 per cent of land in Kildare was in farms of over 200 acres, with Meath coming in at 40 per cent of land in such farms.[6] As area does not necessarily co-relate with value, it is worth noting that this region has consistently a pronounced clustering of the highest-value farms reaching back at the very least into mid-nineteenth century.[7]

socialist revolution 1880–1938 (London, 1990), pp 48–59.   **3** David Fitzpatrick, *Politics and Irish life, 1913–21: provincial experience of war and revolution* (Cork, 1998), pp 196–7, 205.   **4** Emmet O'Connor, *Syndicalism in Ireland, 1917–1923* (Cork, 1988), pp 33–44.   **5** Department of Agriculture and Technical Instruction for Ireland, *Agricultural statistics, Ireland, 1912*, 'Report and tables relating to Irish agricultural labourers', p. 40.   **6** Terence Dooley, '*The land for the people': the land question in independent Ireland* (Dublin, 2004), p. 137.   **7** T. Jones Hughes, 'The large farm in

In 1914 Dublin had just over 40 per cent of its land under crops (including hay), Kildare over 25 per cent, and Meath almost 21 per cent. In the case of Dublin, in particular, this was significantly more than western counties, e.g., the equivalent figure for Galway was 15.4 per cent.[8] However, this quantitative evidence over large geographic areas can obscure – the classic big farm of the west was an expanse of grazing held on a short-term lease. Here cattle were fed over the summer, 'brought-on' to be 'finished' further east. It seems winter fodder was more a necessary factor for the 'finisher'. How much of the cropped area in the west was on small farms operated by family labour? Moreover, the compulsory tillage introduced by the government to address the exigencies of war particularly targeted the large-holder and so had more impact in counties like Meath and Kildare. It is the areas that had both large farms and some form of crops that, at the minimum, required harvesting, which would have a large proportion of wage workers in agriculture. There were further particularities of production that are worth noting. South Kildare, along with parts of Louth and Laois, were cereal-growing areas. Dublin, in common with all urban hinterlands at the time, had market-gardening areas. So again we can expect particular concentrations of wage workers in these areas around these particularly labour-intensive branches.

The main centres of market gardening in Dublin were Crumlin, Rush and Clonsilla, but, as well as in those places, in north Co. Dublin more generally farmers would have grown vegetables, especially in the more tillage-orientated north-east.[9] Rush, in particular, as a coastal area, had particular environmental advantages – less frost and access to that important natural fertilizer, seaweed. Vegetable production was labour intensive and these farms would have had more employees than usual. That said, units of production were actually of varying scale and Rush seems to have had a lot of smallholders. An extreme, but illuminating, contrast is given by the Delany 500-acre grazing farm in Dunshaughlin, Co. Meath, with its two employees, set next to the 72-acre Butterly market garden, near Blanchardstown, Co. Dublin, with at least fifteen employees.[10] The point has also been made that Dublin farm workers lived in small towns or villages and this residential clustering facilitated their organizing. While this was true of Dublin, it was also true, to some extent, elsewhere.[11]

nineteenth-century Ireland' in Dáithí Ó hÓgáin and Alan Gailey (eds), *Gold under the furze: studies in folk tradition presented to Caoimhín Ó Danachair* (Dublin, 1982), pp 93–100. **8** Department of Agriculture and Technical Instruction, *Agricultural statistics, Ireland, 1914*, 'General abstracts showing the acreage under crops and the numbers and descriptions of live stock in each county and province, 1913–14', pp 14–17. **9** G.O. Sherrard, 'Commercial horticulture in Éire', *Scientific Horticulture*, 7 (1939), 119–38. **10** W.E. Vaughan, 'Farmer, grazier and gentleman: Edward Delany of Woodtown, 1851–99', *Irish Economic and Social History*, 9 (1982), 67. **11** Gerard Hanley, '"Let

Farm strikes 1913 to 1924

Over the summer of 1913 there was a recruitment campaign conducted by the ITGWU in the farming areas of Co. Dublin. There were meetings and rallies in such places as Balbriggan, Baldoyle, Clondalkin, Crumlin, Swords, Blanchardstown and Lucan.[12] On 21 June 1913, the *Irish Worker* ran a front page commentary on the campaign, urging:

> workers of County Dublin, the remedy is in your own hands to improve your present unenviable lot. Strike out for yourselves, locking together the different districts in one solid organization, and I promise you if you do so that before the next harvest moon appears you will be in receipt of better wages, you will have received your half holiday on Saturday, and you will be on the right road to better housing accommodation and more land for yourselves, your wives, and families in the future.[13]

The goal of 'better housing accommodation' is significant, as this was the moment of transition from the infamous 'fourth-class' housing of the nineteenth century to modern council cottages. 'Fourth-class' houses were single-roomed dwellings with walls and roofs of perishable materials.[14] Although the number of 'fourth-class' houses per se had already undergone steep decline, in fact there was little to separate the more inferior variants of 'third-class' housing from the kinds of dwellings we associate today with the Great Famine. A discussion of the goal of 'more land' is what the main body of this chapter will be concerned with. The *Irish Worker* article is clearly addressed to a male audience – 'more land for yourselves, your wives, and families' – but it actually speaks to wider interests in a way a purely wage-centred focus would not have. The house, yard, and garden were at the centre of what was seen as women's work. The house, most obviously, was at the heart of the labour of the reproduction of labour power, i.e., the raising of new workers and the renewal of capacities of the current workers. The subsistence production and petty trade of the garden was similarly gendered as female. The realization of the goal of 'better housing accommodation and more land' offered women some financial independence and a reduction of their expenditure of labour.[15]

the harvest go to blazes": farm labourers in north County Dublin and the 1913 lockout', *Studia Hibernica*, 40 (2014), 135–64 at 146. **12** *Irish Worker*, 7, 14, 28 June, 12, 19 July, 9 Aug. 1913. **13** Ibid., 21 June 1913. **14** F.H.A. Aalen, 'The rehousing of rural labourers in Ireland under the Labourers (Ireland) Acts, 1883–1919', *Journal of Historical Geography*, 12:3 (1986), 287–306; Enda McKay, 'The housing of the rural labourer, 1883–1916', *Saothar: Journal of Irish Labour History*, 17 (1992), 27–38. **15** Jonathan Bell and Mervyn Watson, *Irish farming life: history and heritage*

This summer campaign saw strike action during the beginnings of the harvest in August and then – as farmers joined hands with the city employers – was met by the great Dublin lockout of 1913.[16] Some farm workers were among the last groups of workers to return, defeated, to their places of employment.[17]

The Meath Labour Union in the pre-war period, rather than representing employees to employers, was more concerned with lobbying for local government action on cottage construction and direct labour, i.e., employment in road maintenance of council workers as opposed to sub-contractors.[18] It did play a more conventional trade union role with regard to those council workers. It was a Meath version of the more Munster-orientated Irish Land and Labour Association. The post-1916 wages movement was a departure in this instance. Nonetheless, the issues of direct labour, and cottages – or more particularly their gardens – remained important.

So in the resumed farm worker mobilization from March 1917 onwards, the Meath Labour Union was listed in police records as having twenty-five branches and 1264 members.[19] This was in the new context of state intervention to meet the First World War food supply crisis with wage arbitration and compulsory tillage. Particularly across the east and south of the island there was a range of local wage demands in the spring of that year, and later the revival of old organizations and the establishment of new ones.[20] Some of these eventually formed a larger cross-country organization, the Irish Agricultural and General Workers' Union, but it, and almost all of these local bodies, eventually folded into the ITGWU.[21]

(Dublin, 2014), pp 39–45. **16** *Irish Worker*, 16 Aug. 1913; Hanley, 'Farm labourers in north County Dublin', p. 162. **17** The 1913 movement is comparatively well researched: Eugene A. Coyle, 'Larkinism and the 1913 County Dublin farm labourers' dispute', *Dublin Historical Record*, 58:2 (2005), 176–90; Cormac Murphy, 'Revolution and radicalism in County Dublin, 1913–1921' in Myrtle Hill and Sarah Barber (eds), *Aspects of Irish studies* (Belfast, 1990); Christopher Lee, '"The principal rallying-ground for the Larkinites" – the Swords riot of 1913', *The Irish story*, https://www.theirishstory.com/2013/07/15/the-principal-rallying-ground-for-the-larkinites-the-swords-riot-of-1913/#.YfHaDvzLdyo [accessed 20 Apr. 2023]; Christopher Lee, '"Shot down like a dog": the Finglas riot of 1913', *The Irish story*, https://www.theirishstory.com/2013/04/23/shot-down-like-a-dog-the-finglas-riot-of-1913/#.YfHaEvzLdyo [accessed 20 Apr. 2023]; Christopher Lee, 'Frank Moss – a forgotten labour leader of 1913', *The Irish story*, https://www.theirishstory.com/2013/09/11/frank-moss-a-forgotten-labour-leader-of-1913/#.YfHaJvzLdyo [accessed 20 Apr. 2023]. **18** Francis Devine, 'Under a green flag: the Meath Labour Union, 1906–1922, victim of the red flag's advance' in Francis Devine and Fearghal Mac Bhloscaidh (eds), *Bread not profits: provincial working-class politics during the Irish Revolution* (Dublin, 2022), pp 65–84. **19** National Library of Ireland, The British in Ireland, series one, Colonial Office 904/102, 'Inspector general's confidential report for the month of March, 1917, together with county inspectors' reports for the same period', 11 Apr. 1917 (microform, original in the National Archives of the United Kingdom). **20** Ibid. **21** Francis Devine, *Organizing history: a centenary of SIPTU, 1909–2009* (Dublin, 2009), p. 906.

The ITGWU made its first appearance in the borders of Laois and Kildare not on farms but in sawmills in Portarlington. A lockout against the union there began in December 1917 and rumbled on through the first half of 1918. Labour historian C.D. Greaves argued that the lockout had the 'unintended effect of arousing interest in trade unionism in three counties'.[22] In 1918 most of the Co. Dublin branches comprised of overwhelming majorities of agricultural workers – this was true of branches in Baldoyle, Blanchardstown, Donabate, Finglas, Lucan, Lusk, Skerries and Swords.[23] However, as with the more diverse pattern in Portarlington, the Balbriggan branch had 120 members in the woollen mills, while Clondalkin's large detachment of general labourers may have included workers in quarries, paper mills or tile works, as well as farming.[24]

In the membership census of mid-summer 1918 the only ITGWU branch in Meath was in Navan, and was a non-agricultural one, while the branches in Kildare were in the north of the county rather than the south.[25] In both cases this likely reflected the strength of local labour organizations. Undoubtedly the headline-grabbing event concerning agricultural labourers in these counties in these years was the victorious Meath and Kildare strike of the summer of 1919. This has received comprehensive narrative treatment elsewhere, but it is useful to compare it with later conflicts – and with the success then for the labour movement in comparison to later defeats.[26] Additionally, it is worth bearing in mind that while Kildare and Meath saw the most overt conflict in that year, events there forced the pace of negotiations in adjacent counties, and so in that respect the strike was only the most prominent part of a broader conflict.

Comparing industrial action in Meath and Kildare in 1919 with that in south Kildare in 1922 to 1923, or Dublin in 1924, may seem redundant. After all the latter took place in the very different economic circumstance of the slump and after the removal of the Great War emergency measures such as compulsory tillage. However, one can see the role of the collective agency of organized social groups if one delves deeper. First, in a self-sabotaging hubristic

22 C. Desmond Greaves, *The Irish Transport & General Workers' Union, the formative years, 1909–1923* (Dublin, 1982), p. 192. **23** Census of membership forms for branches of the ITGWU consisting of forms that were returned and completed starting with Arklow and ending with Youghal and are compiled in alphabetical order, 1918 (National Library of Ireland/William O'Brien (1881–1968) Papers, 1898–1969/MS 13,948/120). Online at: http://catalogue.nli.ie/Record/vtls000628987/ HierarchyTree. **24** Ibid. **25** Ibid. **26** Terence M. Dunne, 'Emergence from the embers: the Meath and Kildare farm labour strike of 1919', *Saothar: Journal of Irish Labour History,* 44 (2019), 59–68; Terry Dunne, '"Meath is rich, Meath's workers are poor": the Kildare and Meath farm labour strike of 1919', *History Ireland,* 27:4 (2019), 36–8; Aidan Gilsenan, '"Arrant Bolshevism"? 1919 farm labourers strike in Meath', *Ríocht na Midhe,* 32 (2021) 239–68.

move on the part of the farmers' association in Kildare in 1919, it escalated to open dispute in the weeks before harvest, that is, the time of maximum labour demand. More astutely in south Kildare in 1922 they engineered conflict in the slack winter period. The 1919 strike in both Meath and Kildare was characterized by direct action on a far more extensive scale than simply the withdrawal of labour suggested by the term 'strike', namely secondary picketing that shut down the trade conducted by recalcitrant farmers. In the early 1920s in particular farmers' groups started to mimic these tactics and aimed at stopping the trade of dissident farmers who had settled with their workers, and even at shutting down the petty trade conducted by labourers.[27] Hence, in 1924 the Dublin cattle market was patrolled by rival sets of pickets.[28] While in 1919 industrial conflict was policed by the Royal Irish Constabulary, with the establishment of the Free State in 1922 this role was taken on by the Free State military, and the latter were notably more partisan. Finally, in the 1919 victory the role of solidarity action by other workers was decisive – specifically by dockers and drovers who refused to handle tainted goods, while potential action by railwaymen was held in reserve. By 1923 by contrast the moment of confident exuberance had passed, which is not to say that it was impossible that a more unified approach could have been taken. It is worth noting here as well that annual wage agreements were buttressed with annual episodes of industrial action, there were for instance strikes in Meath and Dublin in the springtime of 1922 and again in 1923.[29]

The demand for land

In the wake of the 1919 strike one of the key branches involved, that in Athy in south Kildare, made a resolution on housing that concluded:

> We also demand that in future all labourers provided with houses be allotted four statute acres, and the tenants of such houses get the same in order that the poor man may be in a position to have a sup of milk as well as vegetables for his family.[30]

That is to say that new council cottages would have four acres and people already in council cottages would have their plots expanded. The 'sup of milk' is mentioned because four acres would allow for the keeping of a cow as well

27 Terry Dunne, 'Labour in Laois: lockout in Portarlington, farm strike in Clonaslee' in Devine and Mac Bhloscaidh (eds), *Bread not profits*, pp 32–44. **28** *Evening Herald*, 6 Mar. 1924. **29** *Voice of Labour*, 18 Mar. 1922, 17 Mar. 1923. **30** *Nationalist and Leinster Times*, 8 Nov. 1919.

as the more usual vegetable plot, pigs and poultry. This was broadly the same objective that we have already seen in the early days of the movement in Dublin.

In the scholarly literature the demand for land is sometimes cast as a backward-looking glance, harkening after an idealized peasant past.[31] At times there is a conflation between this demand among farm workers and the separate, but concurrent, movement of smallholders concentrated in the west of Ireland. The goal of acquiring larger plots was a goal of expanding what we would now call the 'social wage', the 'social wage' meaning the non-pay related supports of workers' living standards such as public health care provision or public housing. It is necessary to have an appreciation of what a difference that a small piece of land brought to people's everyday lives. A memoir from Narraghmore in south Kildare paints a vivid picture of what a garden meant to the family of a farm worker in the 1930s: 'We had our own plot of about half an acre in the large, fenced garden behind the house and we sowed vegetables and potatoes every year to sustain the family.' That vegetable plot also fed a pig which was 'a significant profit and a crucial means of added revenue for the household'; additionally, the mother of the household also reared turkeys 'to supplement our income at Christmas time … the money was used to purchase clothing and footwear for a rapidly increasing family'.[32]

Note also that the goal of the provision of public housing with attached gardens was a goal of independence. The Narraghmore description is about housing and land supplied by an employer – and a regular feature in accounts of strikes in the period is the prospect of eviction from such so-called 'tied' properties. Even further necessitating access to land was the temporary or seasonal nature of a lot of agricultural employment. Moreover, possession of land also made for a source of sustenance less subject to inflationary pressures.[33] To understand the alternative of privation, we can look at the case of a Co. Louth family who featured in a parish priest's letter to the national press. The priest claimed that the

> taste of butter, jam, marmalade, eggs or bacon is unknown to this family … [a] substantial meal is never placed on the table. It is the usual tea and dry bread, or bread moistened with some of the ¼ lb. of margarine or 1lb. of dripping that is served up to the family. The potato garden is small and the produce is quickly consumed.[34]

31 Fitzpatrick, *Politics and Irish life*, op. cit.   **32** Michael Delaney, with Daragh Ó Conchúir, *The time of our lives: a social history of Narraghmore parish, 1925–1955* (self-published, n.d.), pp 15–16. **33** *Voice of Labour*, 30 Aug. 1919.   **34** *Irish Independent*, 20 Aug. 1919.

He also noted that the family had mostly cast-offs as clothing, with the mother re-fashioning for the children some of the clothes she received as a domestic servant in her youth. The above diet is that of the wife and children. The adult male received dinner at work, and that plus 30 shillings a week meant his pay was within the average band and not exceptionally low. The successful strike in 1919 in Kildare, for instance, increased the basic rate in north Kildare to 34s. and in south Kildare to 32s., and left perquisites, such as the daily dinner received by the employee in this case, to agreement in individual workplaces.[35] Incidentally, in the wake of efforts principally in Meath and Kildare, the basic rate set in Louth rose to 32s. 6d.[36] The gendered dimension is pretty apparent, in terms of who was most disadvantaged by the situation in the Louth case, and whose work was most assisted by the garden in the Narraghmore case. How representative were these two cases? What makes them representative is the recurrent popularity of the demand for larger cottage gardens. Additionally, the ITGWU was also representing its members as leasers of conacre tillage plots from farmers.[37] While one could argue this problem of poverty could be solved by a struggle for higher wages, arguably that struggle was just keeping up with inflation, and access to publicly provided land provided a greater security and a necessary supplement to wage-based incomes. This could be seen as a public subsidy to support low wages, but the provision of land was at the expense also of the employing class, as it was, after all, farmers' lands being re-distributed.

The search for an agrarian policy

In 1922 the Irish Trade Union Congress and Labour Party (ILP&TUC) appointed two representatives to the new Irish Free State's Commission on Agriculture. To prepare, the ITGWU distributed a questionnaire to all its rural branches to ascertain members' views on prospective agrarian policy. The survey received one hundred replies, which 'indicated fairly general agreement on certain matters' including the desire for 'a substantial increase in the size of labourers' plots'. Indeed this and the extension of unemployment insurance are the only matters mentioned in the summary in the 1923 Congress report. The report was dismissive towards these replies and went on to claim: 'it cannot be said that they revealed any very definite body of opinion as to agricultural policy based on a study of what is practicable as well as desirable'.[38]

35 *Voice of Labour*, 30 Aug. 1919. **36** *Irish Independent*, 28 Aug. 1919. **37** *Voice of Labour*, 25 Mar. 1922. **38** Devine, *Organizing history*, p. 141; *Report of the twenty-sixth annual meeting of the Irish Labour Party and Trade Union Congress* (1920), p. 22.

Perhaps the labour representatives on the Commission were in fact poor judges of what was practicable as their contribution to the Commission was effectively side-lined. This contribution was concerned with, among other things, more indigenous agri-processing and less simple export of cattle on the hoof, along with compulsory tillage for holders of over 100 acres.[39] It seems strange that the appeal to what is practicable was made, when steps for the provision of land to the rural working class were already under way, and had been in the much less radical years preceding 1914.

The first labourers' cottages built under the 1883 Act providing for rural public housing had half-acre gardens attached; this was increased to one acre in 1892.[40] Tens of thousands of these houses with accompanying gardens were built in the years running up to the Great War. Additionally, in Meath a limited number of council-owned cow plots were provided, which were essentially similar to council-owned allotments, only they gave people the space to keep a cow, rather than to grow vegetables. Special circumstances prevailed in Meath as it was, almost uniquely, a county with a large proportion of agricultural workers combined with a place in the first-rank for number of cattle-drives during the ranch war, that is to say, a centre of mobilization for land re-distribution.[41]

There was a resumption of the smallholder movement for land division during the revolution. This was geographically and socially distinct from the movement discussed here, though with some overlap. Given that, and given the large scale land re-distribution enacted under the Free State, the proposal for larger cottage gardens does not seem an impracticable one. That said, it is necessary to draw a sharp analytical distinction between the demand for breaking up large farms and turning them into smallholdings. The latter was principally coming from a section of a different class and local land re-distribution was in fact often inimical to the interests of working-class people. It was large farms that provided employment. Hence the ITGWU actually intervened to prevent the letting in small portions of lands in Knockbridge and Castlebellingham in north Louth in the spring of 1922.[42] The demesne farm of Sir Edward Bellingham had sixteen men employed on it so it seems straightforward that they would not want it chopped up and let out. Perusal of the Dáil record of David Hall, Labour TD for Meath, reveals that the same issue was current after the re-distributionist 1923 Land Act. He frequently

39 Roy Johnston, *Century of endeavour*, 'Agriculture Commission 1923', http://www.rjtechne.org/century130703/1920s/agric23.htm [accessed 20 Apr. 2023].   40 John W. Boyle, 'A marginal figure: the Irish rural labourer' in Samuel Clark and James S. Donnelly Jr (eds), *Irish peasants: violence and political unrest* (Dublin, 1983), p. 332.   41 See Paul Bew, *Conflict and conciliation in Ireland, 1890–1910: Parnellites and radical agrarians*, Illus. 2: 'Cattle drives, 1907–1909'.   42 *Voice of Labour,*

raised the issue of farm workers made unemployed by land re-division – which is not to say that he was against land re-division but rather that this was not a simple issue.[43] For this reason conferences of agricultural workers that proposed land re-distribution as one of their demands always specified to whom the land was being re-distributed.[44] The demand for an extra acre, or even an extra half-acre, let alone more wholesale land disbursement, was in fact opposed from the left. Michael Donnelly of the Irish Citizen Army, and a key activist in the origins of the munitions of war dispute,[45] warned of the prospect of creating 'a lot of smallholders which will in the end be no better and some of them a lot worse capitalist tyrants than the present farmers'.[46] This may seem more than a little improbable given the small quantities of land being discussed. In 1923, Congress – the representative body of the trade unions – adopted as policy that 'the future prosperity of Irish agriculture resides in the co-operative administration and development of smallholdings and the planting of the larger farms and untenanted lands with the propertyless workers, on the basis of common ownership'.[47] There was a dissenting perspective from the secretary of the Mountcollins (west Limerick) ITGWU branch, who pointed to 'the lot of the married farm worker with a family to support':

> Golden promises that may, perhaps, take ten or twenty years to materialize will never give him the wherewithal to pay his rent or purchase the necessaries of life. We must find a present policy. What should that policy be? Why not a land campaign now at once. Give the cottier an extra acre of land and enable him to feed his family without sending them out to farmers for their feeding, as I have seen it done. Give him a chance to keep a cow.[48]

This was the same demand as was put forward by the Athy branch in November 1919, and it had, as can be seen from the survey results, a widespread popularity.

Co-operative models

The most cogent statement of agrarian policy carried in an ITGWU publication during the post-1917 expansion was written by an English guild

25 Mar. 1922. **43** 'David Hall (1891–1960)' in Charles Callan and Barry Desmond, *Irish labour lives: a biographical dictionary of Irish Labour Party deputies, senators, MPs and MEPs* (Dublin, 2010), p. 112. **44** See for example *Voice of Labour*, 3 Feb. 1923. **45** Frank Robbins, 'Introducing some friends', *Dublin Historical Record*, 25:3 (June 1972), 93–101; Bureau of Military History, Witness Statement 585, Frank Robbins. **46** *Voice of Labour*, 17 Feb. 1923. **47** *Report of the 29th ILP&TUC* (1923), p. 97. **48** *Voice of Labour*, 20 Jan. 1923.

socialist and put at its heart the centralization of capital through market competition. The author was W.N. Ewer, later a founder of the Communist Party of Great Britain and later still the writer of polemics against the Soviet Union. In the *Voice of Labour* of 3 August 1918 Ewer wrote:

> Circumstances will force the farmers through co-operation into guilds. It is the task of Trade Unionism at the same time to organize the wage-workers, and then to obtain for them, not merely better conditions, but a change of status, so that they as well as the present farmer-class shall be free and equal members of their guilds. In a word – agricultural guilds are inevitable in one or other form. It is for us to see to it that they shall be democratic in one or other form: that they shall be true guilds and not predatory trusts.[49]

The 'circumstances' were the pressure of more efficient producers in the market-place – able to produce with the benefits of economies of scale – and the squeeze created by the divergence between the prices of farm inputs and of farm outputs. The only way out for small-scale independent producers was to find forms of co-operation allowing them to scale-up, to process their own products, to buy inputs in bulk, etc. It should be noted that the perspective expressed here was contemporary with the dawn of co-operative dairy processing in Ireland and that there were experiments in co-operative farming carried out under the auspices of the Dáil government during the revolution.[50]

In any case the kind of co-operative model proposed by Ewer was the continuing thread of labour movement agrarian policy throughout these years. It was raised again, for instance, during the bacon and butter embargo of April 1920 – when the labour movement successfully forced a continuation of the food price control policies of the war period amid fears of food price inflation. This was actually as major a clash with the farmers' representative body, the Irish Farmers' Union, as any of the wage disputes. In the embargo the ILP&TUC executive issued an open letter offering a carrot to the category posited by the letter as the 'working farmer' – which it hoped to appeal to by offering a scheme of co-operative marketing – which would offer a better price for the producer by removing mercantile middlemen.[51]

---

49 *Voice of Labour*, 3 Aug. 1918.   **50** Edward N. Moran, 'The Dáil farm, Kilcumney: a social experiment, 1919–1923', *Carloviana*, 70 (2022), 161–4.   **51** *Report of the 26th ILP&TUC* (1920), pp 27–9.

Co-operative marketing: union strategy for Dublin

The co-operative marketing policy proposal was at the heart of the ITGWU's attempts to settle with Dublin farmers in 1923 and 1924 – so we have a concrete experience of how it worked in reality.

Some of the Dublin context was given by the *Irish Times* opining on 'the burdensome monopoly of rings', which is to say that fruit and vegetable marketing was conducted by monopoly practices which worked out, according to the *Irish Times*, like so:

> They buy the produce from the grower at rates which hardly repay his skill and labour: he is compelled to accept those rates because no other local market is open to him. By the time when the produce reaches the consumer its price has reached the scale with which we are painfully familiar.[52]

The ITGWU's intervention aimed at maintaining farm workers' wages, reducing the price to the consumer, and increasing farmers' profits all through the means of co-operative retail. The agenda was set forward in an Archie Heron editorial in the *Voice of Labour* of 3 March 1923:

> Labour has always expressed its willingness to co-operate with the farmers in an effort to smash the profiteers and organize direct trading between producer and consumer in the interests of the community; so far there has been no response from the farmers.
>
> The farmers of County Dublin must decide now whether they are going to line up with the capitalists who exploit them, or co-operate with the working-class, with whom they have many interests in common. There is at this moment a golden opportunity for the farmers to display broad-mindedness and social conscience in an effort in common with Labour, to establish a new social order wherein the middleman profiteer will be eliminated to the advantage of all concerned. Perhaps a postponement of reductions could be arranged while some plan on these lines is being considered. The alternative is 'immediate and terrible war', the necessary outcome of the alignment of the farmers with Big Business.[53]

---

52 Jonathan Bell and Mervyn Watson, *Rooted in the soil: a history of cottage gardens and allotments in Ireland since 1750* (Dublin, 2012), pp 82–3. **53** *Voice of Labour*, 3 Mar. 1923.

A corporate lash-up was formed called the County Dublin Agricultural Industrial Council with representation from the ITGWU, the Irish Agricultural Organisation Society (i.e., the co-operative movement), the government and the farmers (the latter now organized into the County Dublin Employers' Protection Association).

The ITGWU's own reports on the meetings of the Agricultural Industrial Council show the marked limitations of this project: 'The workers' representatives reported that progress made in regard to starting Consumer Groups or Co-operative Stores had been practically nil, the members treating the matter with indifference.'[54] Perhaps even more damning the report from another meeting throws the premise of the whole project into question and simply rejects the co-operative marketing proposal:

> It was discovered that owing to the small supplies in the markets at the present time that wholesale prices were fairly high, and that the shop-keepers prices do not show an abnormal profit. In fact, it was brought home to all present that the Shopkeepers prices very seldom fluctuate, and that profiteering exists chiefly during the period when there is a glut on the market, say, from the 1 September onwards. It was, therefore, decided that to open a store for direct trade at the present time would not form any useful purpose.[55]

It is remarkable that so much rested on what appears to be such weak foundations. It is also remarkable that this was conjoined with a rebuff of the demand that was actually popular among the rural branches – the demand for an extra acre.

Back to the land in Meath[56]

It is worth spelling out exactly what efforts at land division or re-distribution did to inequalities in the possession of land. Ultimately the process truncated the upper tier of landholders while otherwise leaving the already existing relative inequalities largely intact. Land after all had to be purchased by the new owners, whatever the rate of re-payment, and land itself is not the only means of production involved in farming – there are obviously also costs in

---

54 Irish Labour History Society, Irish Transport and General Workers' Union Papers, /T6/3/W.O'B/ Co. Dublin Councils, Farm workers 1924–1925, 'County Dublin Council. ITGWU', 3 June 1924.
55 Ibid., 'Report of committee: Co. Dublin farmers & ITGWU re co-operation', 30 Apr. 1924.

stocking and equipping a farm. Consequently, for all the talk of the landless, it was in fact often the landed who were benefiting from land re-distribution. This was exemplified by the case of the Back to the Land association in Meath, which was a more plebeian and bottom-up initiative that can be contrasted, to a degree, with the state-led re-distributions. Back to the Land was formed in the first decade of the twentieth century, and had originally been closely linked to the United Irish League and the Ancient Order of Hibernians.[57] The leading activist in Back to the Land was Father Robert Barry, the parish priest of Oldcastle, in the north-west of the county adjacent to Co. Cavan. Barry was also a frequent contributor to the local press, allowing us an insight into exactly how land division worked on a local level. In one letter to the *Drogheda Independent* in the spring of 1918, Barry actually lists all the new recipients of divided land in the parish of Oldcastle. Twenty-seven individuals can be cross-referenced from Barry's list to the 1911 census.[58] Of them the largest occupational category represented in the 1911 census (so before they received land in 1918) was 'farmer'; there was a further tier of persons with artisanal occupations, including some who were close relatives of farmers, one herdsman, one son of a gamekeeper and five or six farm labourers.[59] In other words farm labourers were a minority of land recipients in this probably unusually equalitarian land re-distribution, and their experience was in any case untypical of their cohort. Barry, perhaps unsurprisingly, recognized this, and, with rhetorical flourishes about 'the old-time custom of the "Commons"' and 'getting back to the old Gaelic State', advocated for the provision of cow plots.[60] These were lands owned by the rural district councils, the bottom tier of local government, and allotted to farm workers for them to keep cows for their own milk supply. Barry advocated for 80 acres of cow plots out of every 1,000 acres of land divided.[61] In sum land re-distribution left much of the existing rural hierarchy intact even when it was conjoined with ameliorative measures. For this reason, much of the attention of local Labour politicians, such as David Hall, was in attempting to secure the interests of working-class people within the land re-distribution programme, e.g., land allocation for former employees, or cow plots for wider use.

56 The author benefited from a discussion with local historian Úna Palcic with regard to this section. **57** Oliver Coogan, *Politics and war in Meath, 1913–23* (Navan, 2013), pp 22–5. **58** 1911 Census. **59** *Drogheda Independent*, 23 Mar. 1918. **60** *Drogheda Independent*, 15 Nov. 1913, 23 Mar. 1918. **61** Ibid., 15 Nov. 1913.

Athy lockout, 1922–3

It is fair to say that the new state was met with the expectation of reform. We can ascribe this to the influence of Irish nationalism, or British labourism, or the recent experience of unprecedented state intervention. Whichever the case, the expectation can be seen in both the resolutions of local branches, and in, for instance, the engagement of labour leaders with the Agricultural Commission. The experience of the Athy lockout of 1922–3, and other disputes of the early Free State period, shows how misplaced that expectation was.

Dan Bradley, author of the only book-length survey of farm workers' movements in modern Ireland, argued that the Athy conflict, along with its contemporaries in Waterford and Ballingarry/Kilmanagh, 'were the most prolonged and bitter farm strikes ever fought in Ireland, the outcome of which was to undermine confidence, throughout the country, in the maintenance of trade union organization amongst farm workers'.[62] In each case the Free State military was mobilized in support of employers.[63] On 2 December 1922 the conflict in the Athy district began in earnest, though it was already preceded by a smaller dispute.[64] The issue at its heart was a radical reduction in wages by 5s., from 30 to 25s. While there were reports of the decay of union organization in Kildare in the years after the 1919 triumph, this actually does not seem to have been the situation in the Athy corner of the county, where the *Voice of Labour* reported that 'non-Unionism is practically non-existent'.[65] It is likely that the proposed wage reduction related to the specific situation of barley growers. While the reduction was met with 'spontaneous hostings of agricultural workers in every branch area' in Kildare,[66] the conflict spread more westwards into some barley growing sections of Laois around Stradbally rather than into the beef-producing districts of north Kildare.[67] Barley growers had a more restricted market relative to other Irish farmers, as they were supplying a raw material to the brewing and distilling industries, as opposed to a foodstuff to the consumer's table. Moreover, it was a raw material that required an initial stage of processing before it even saw the shadow of a whiskey distillery. Consequently, the farmers involved complained of monopolistic practices by the purchasers of their outputs. Moreover, there being a well-developed Irish drinks industry, that is, a home market, barley growers, unlike

---

62 Dan Bradley, *Farm labourers: Irish struggle, 1900–1976* (Belfast, 1988), p. 65. **63** Emmet O'Connor, 'Agrarian unrest and the labour movement in County Waterford', *Saothar*, 6 (1980), 40–55; *Irish Independent*, 14 June 1923. **64** *Voice of Labour*, 9 Dec., 25 Nov. 1922; *Nationalist and Leinster Times*, 9 Dec. 1922. With regard to the strike the district encompassed farms on both sides of the Kildare–Laois border, similarly further south Ballingarry (Tipperary) was the branch but Kilmanagh (Kilkenny) was where the struck farms were. **65** Ibid., 9 Dec. 1922. **66** Ibid., 2 Dec. 1922. **67** *Leinster Express*, 16 Dec. 1922.

other farmers, were more inclined to favour protectionism over the lifting of trade barriers.[68] It is likely that reduced product prices were being passed on to the most vulnerable strata of the farming industry, the wage workers. By early January 1923, an estimated 250 workers were 'locked out', as the labour press put it, though the use of the term lockout at the time was surely meant more to stress the aggressive and extreme nature of the employer's offensive, rather than refer to what was actually not, properly speaking, a lockout. In any case events surely demonstrated what life in the Free State would be like for farm workers. Correspondence in the military archives reveal exactly how partisan parts of the government were. There was a constant lobbying by Patrick Hogan, minister for agriculture, for local labour activists to be 'arrested and interned as Irregulars', that is, imprisoned without trial as guerrillas of the Irish Republican Army. This was to be based on a list supplied by the farmers' association, despite there being, it was admitted, no evidence against these apparent suspects.[69] It was a necessary move, Hogan argued, to prevent farmers from backing down and making a negotiated settlement, or facing arbitration.[70] Ultimately branch secretary C.J. Supple was imprisoned – and while in prison farmers' representatives were allowed in to negotiate with him. All the while he could not be sent for trial, because, as the Hogan correspondence states, there was no case against him that would stand up in court.[71] Supple's imprisonment was surely a means of applying pressure in the context of negotiations. The pretext for gaoling was a number of cases of sabotage by arson in the depths of the winter of 1922–3, something which become fairly typical in winter farm strikes, along with one case where a farm steward was shot in the hand. Meanwhile Hogan counselled the military authorities to ignore any claims concerning illegal intimidation allegedly carried out by farmers.[72] The perhaps less than grievous extent of non-state violence is shown by what the military authorities claimed as a decisive victory – their supplying to the police of a list of names for prosecution of people allegedly 'unlawfully cutting timber'.[73] In the summer of 1923 the employees went back to work on their employers' harsh terms, quite some time after the military intervention so it was perhaps less than decisive. Whatever was the case the episode reveals plainly what the government of the new Free State

68 Raymond Ryan, 'Farmers, agriculture and politics in the Irish Free State area, 1919–1936' (PhD, University College Cork, 2005), pp 21, 34–5, 57, 79–80, 84, 85–7, 99, 261, 274.   69 Military Archives, P. Hogan to minister for defence, 17 Jan. 1923; Military Archives, P. Hogan to secretary of ministry of defence, A7869, P. Hogan to minister for defence, 4 Jan. 1923.   70 Military Archives, P. Hogan to minister for defence, 27 Jan. 1923; Military Archives, A1725, P. Hogan to minister for defence, 5 Jan. 1923.   71 Military Archives, P. Hogan to minister for defence, 2 Feb. 1923. 72 Military Archives, P. Hogan to minister for defence, 17 Jan. 1923.   73 Military Archives, EDC 2475, GOC Dublin Command to commander-in-chief, 25 Jan. 1923.

had in mind for the wage workers of its most important industry – a return to subordination.

Conclusion

Agriculture was the central industry in most of Ireland a hundred years ago. Even those concentrations of workers outside of agriculture tended to be connected to it, in obvious ways in agri-processing, or, in other sectors, more obliquely but also strongly, like in transport or in retail in provincial towns. Occupations that had no obvious direct link with regard to the actual processes of agricultural production were linked in terms of the social backgrounds from which those occupations recruited. Unsurprisingly then, addressing the peculiarities of the agricultural industry was a central concern of the Irish labour movement. This was a complex question for which the answers did not fall neatly along predictable lines of political partisanship. While later understandings put the focus on the national question, at the time it was the agrarian question that formed the central debate.

There are a number of striking features. First, the extent to which the leadership of the ITGWU (and of the ILP&TUC) appears detached from its rural constituency – in that little or no consideration seems to have been given to attempting to expand cottage gardens. Second, the extent to which the discussion was conducted within the premise of an imminent socialist future. Again to posterity this may seem misplaced, but to understand the period we have to understand that perspective. Third, it seems like there was a missing connection, in that nobody appears to have seen the cow plots of Meath as a possible way of marrying re-distributionist goals with opposition to economic individualism. But, while land division shaped some areas of Ireland profoundly, others were barely touched.

All that said the national question and the relationship with the new state was also an important factor. In the context of the Athy dispute the *Voice of Labour* editorialized on the limitations of Irish separatism arguing that the 'class which possesses the land and industrial machinery of a country will be politically and socially, as well as economically, dominant in that country, no matter what colour of its flag or the nature of the phrases in its constitution'.[74] But during the revolution the labour movement did its upmost to establish a state which was only going to constrain the working-class with even greater efficiency than did the British state.

74 *Voice of Labour*, 7 Apr. 1923.

'Eager to produce food': the United Irish Plotholders' Union

MARY FORREST

'At an inaugural meeting of delegates from Dublin allotment centres it was decided to form an Irish Plotholders' Union': so ran a brief front page report in the *Freeman's Journal* on 18 September 1917. Drawing on national and local newspaper reports this chapter explores how the Irish Plotholders' Union (IPU) set about achieving its aims; how it was organized at national and local level; its membership and office holders; its interaction with state and local authorities; and its involvement in local elections. Except for the text of a 1922 parliamentary question to the minister for agriculture regarding the Union and allotments, as well two originals and copies of letters from the Union, held respectively in the National Archives of Ireland and Dublin City Archives, no records of the IPU have been located.

Allotments, colloquially called 'plots', were areas of land separate to a dwelling where vegetables were grown for consumption by a plotholder and his family. With the introduction of the Labourers (Ireland) Act 1883, rural district councils, with the approval of the Local Government Board (LGB), could provide land for allotments for those living in villages and towns. For example, in the year ended 31 March 1911 the LGB received applications for 20 acres of land for allotments.[1] Philanthropic entities provided allotments in cities. In 1907, Charles Black obtained land for 'garden plots' in the Strandtown area of Belfast, which were rented by working men for vegetable cultivation.[2]

In Dublin, the Vacant Land Cultivation Society (VLCS) was founded in 1909. Land made available to the Society provided plots for casual labourers but plot numbers were low: 23 in 1910; 36 in 1911; 26 in 1912. They increased when the Society obtained Dublin Corporation land at Fairbrother's Fields.[3] In Dublin, where many working-class people were already living in poverty, wartime food shortages and price inflation led to increased privation.

---

1 *Irish Times*, 17 Aug. 1911. 2 W.H. Johns, 'Allotment gardening in Belfast', *Journal of the Department of Agriculture and Technical Instruction for Ireland* (*JDATI*), 16 (1915), 316–21. 3 Mary Forrest, 'Allotments in Dublin, 1900–1950', *Irish Geography*, 44:2–3 (2011), 265–90. See also Jonathan Bell and Mervyn Watson, *Rooted in the soil: a history of cottage gardens and allotments in*

A common foodstuff – bread – cost six pence in 1914 rising to eleven pence in 1917, a 79 per cent price increase.[4]

While from 1914 the Department of Agriculture and Technical Instruction for Ireland (DATI) had promoted increased tillage, e.g., wheat production, during 1916 the threat caused by the First World War to the supply of imported food, on which the urban population depended, became more apparent to government officials in Dublin and London. In January 1917, the DATI and the LGB introduced food production schemes, Scheme A for 'land valued over £10' and Scheme B for 'land valued less than £10, labourers' plots, town and other allotments'.[5] While the emphasis was on large-scale tillage production, provisions were made from 1917 to 1923 for small scale production of potatoes and vegetables in urban garden plots and allotments.[6] The provisions of Scheme B relating to town allotments were: 'Acquisition of land for allotments; Instruction as to management and cultivation; Measures for making available supplies of seeds, manures, spraying materials and implements; and Loans for the purchase of seed and manure.'[7]

On 3 January 1917, the LGB wrote to urban district councils stating that a council could lease land for four years in or adjacent to their town for the purpose of letting allotments to workmen resident in the district. The costs incurred by the scheme would be recouped by the rent from the allotments, with the LGB sanctioning loans to defray said costs. Each urban district council was to form a subcommittee known as a Land Cultivation Committee (LCC).[8] Following an amendment to the Defence of the Realm Act (DORA) in January 1917, the DATI could compulsorily acquire unoccupied land or rent land for cultivation.[9]

Addressing a meeting of plotholders in Waterford in July 1917, T.P. Gill, secretary of the DATI, said that the allotment movement was of greater importance than realized. In comparison to the compulsory tillage scheme (Scheme A) it looked small, however some 15,000 to 16,000 allotments cultivated produce to the value of £150,000 to £160,000. Asked about 'fixity of tenure', T.P. Gill considered that it was right to place the allotment movement in Ireland in a similar position to that in England.[10] He was referring to the Smallholdings and Allotments Act (1908), which obliged local councils in England to provide allotments for residents in their areas.

Ireland since 1750 (Dublin, 2012).   **4** Fionnuala Walsh, *Irish women and the Great War* (Cambridge, 2020), pp 70–1.   **5** Anon., 'Food production, 1917', *Journal of the Department of Agriculture and Technical Instruction for Ireland*, 17 (1916), 290–2.   **6** Mary Forrest, 'Urban food production schemes in Ireland, 1917–1923', *Studies in the History of Gardens & Designed Landscapes: an International Quarterly*, 32:4 (2012), 331–8.   **7** 'Food production, 1917', *JDATI*, 17 (1916), 302–3.   **8** *Kildare Observer*, 13 Jan. 1917.   **9** Forrest, 'Urban food production schemes'.   **10** *Cork Examiner*,

Fixity of tenure was important to plotholders. It takes time and effort to realize the potential of a plot, be it what are now termed greenfield or brownfield sites. The results of digging, manuring, sowing and planting a one eighth of an acre plot by hand are not seen in one season. One of the few women plotholders referred to her prizewinning plot as 'Cinder Hill' – an indication of the preparatory work – picking cinders or clinkers from the plot.[11] For many plotholders their plots were conveniently located near their homes.

About 75 allotment schemes with varying numbers of 'plots' were established in cities and towns in Ireland. Local associations such as the Marino Plotholders' Association and Dublin Corporation Plotholders were established. By October an umbrella organization to promote plotholding and advocate for the needs of plotholders had been founded. Fixity of tenure and legislation were to become recurring themes, which would be pursued with tenacity.

Irish Plotholders' Union: 'a young and vigorous organization'

The inaugural conference with the purpose of establishing the Irish Plotholders' Union was held on 16 September 1917. Delegates attended representing 1500 plotholders from allotment schemes in the city of Dublin, namely Kilmainham, Portmahon Lodge, Tyrconnell Road, Beach Road (Sandymount), Old Finglas, Finglas Bridge, McCaffrey Estate, Model Farm, Turvey Avenue, Whiteheather, Bull Field (Glasnevin), Pigeon House Road, Londonbridge Road, Infirmary Road, Donnelly's Orchard, Strain's Field (Inchicore), Marino, Dodder Bank and Mountain View together with Kingstown [Dún Laoghaire]. The meeting appointed a Mr Berkery secretary, and formed a committee to draft a constitution and rules. The aims of the Union were:

1. To obtain fixity of tenure, fair rent and compensation for disturbance.
2. To assist financially and otherwise plotholders who, through no fault of their own, are in distress and are in danger of being dispossessed.
3. To promote the co-operative movement generally.
4. To arrange for lectures by experts on the methods of tilling, planting, cultivation, &c.[12]

27 June 1917. **11** *Irish Times*, 9 Oct. 1916. **12** *Evening Herald*, 18 Sept. 1917.

The first provisional council and executive met on Sunday 21 October 1917 in the offices of the VLCS, at 20 Kildare Street. The council represented twenty-three groups of plotholders, in all occupying 1,847 plots.[13] The following executive committee was appointed: president, Patrick Donnelly (Old Finglas); vice president, G.H. Parnell (Marino); treasurer, John Farrelly (Marino). There were eight further committee members. Some biographical details of these office holders were located in the 1911 census returns. Patrick Donnelly, 30 Bengal Terrace (later 30 Finglas Road), Glasnevin, was a civil servant in the GPO; George Henry Parnell, 32 Xavier Avenue, North Strand, a foreman carpet layer, and John Farrelly of 86 Summerhill, Ballybough, a carpenter, who later became vice president of the Dublin Trades Council and president of the IPU.

A constitution and rules were adopted, later to be ratified by the various local associations. An annual meeting planned for January 1918 would appoint an executive which could 'claim to speak and act for the plotholders of all Ireland'.[14] A meeting of Dublin and district plotholders took place in the Mansion House on 12 November 1917 with the lord mayor presiding. He remarked that 'he looked upon the allotments scheme as the forerunner of a larger scheme for breaking up the grass of the country'. He continued, 'if the land of Ireland were tilled as it should be it would do away with low wages, which were the cause of so much disease and moral decay in our cities'. The president, Patrick Donnelly, said that the IPU was open to bona-fide plotholders, and was run by plotholders not politicians. There were twenty-four groups representing 2,000 plotholders including 120 from Kingstown, with numbers expected to rise to 4,000 by January 1918. If there were 20,000 by year's end, the IPU could demand fixity of tenure on land considered worthless before the plotholders had brought it into cultivation. He stated that 'the Union would do for plotholders what the Land League had done for farmers'.[15] It was a bold claim.

The meeting passed resolutions proposed by J.W. Murphy, Marino, and seconded by W. Martin, Kingstown, demanding an allotment act for Ireland; powers for municipalities and urban and district councils to acquire compulsorily land for purposes of allotments; fixity of tenure; an agricultural rent; compensation for disturbance; the provision of free accommodation for the holding of meetings and lectures for education purposes; and the establishment of food depots on co-operative lines for the sale of surplus produce.[16] The six resolutions passed at the first annual congress of the IPU

---

13 *Evening Herald*, 27 Oct. 1917.   14 Ibid., 13 Oct. 1917.   15 *Irish Times*, 13 Nov. 1917.
16 Ibid., 13 Nov. 1917.

held in January 1918 at Charlemont House, Marino, were more forceful and reflect the situation in which the plotholders found themselves.

1. That in view of the threatened famine the Government should enable every willing worker whole or part-time to engage in food production.
2. That as a first step towards this by controlling the rent of land, as the prices of land produce are already controlled.
3. That in Dublin and other large centres special facilities should be given to them on trams and trains to enable workers to cultivate their lots [plots].
4. That arrangements should be made at once to transfer the ranches to the unemployed who possessed the requisite agricultural knowledge and who are at present unemployed.
5. That if necessary and in the event of continued Government inactivity a national committee of representative men and women should be summoned at once to effect this transfer. Such a committee might point out to capitalists the certain profits to be derived from money invested in food production.
6. That allotments in 1918 must replace the Soup Kitchens of the awful period of '46 and '47 when our people died by the hundred thousand in this most fertile land in the world.[17]

Comments from delegates at the annual congress referred to increasing land prices, noting that while some landowners were withholding land for allotments, the Christian Brothers let land at Marino at a reasonable price.[18] Other delegates called for the takeover of land for allotments. The chairman, Patrick Donnelly, reminded those present that 'it was only by unity and extension of membership of the union that the movement could succeed'.[19] The organization of the IPU was described as follows:

> … membership is confined to bona-fide plotholders; its officers are all honorary; it recognizes neither creed nor politics, and it is run on what could be described as Trade Union lines, that is, the branch delegates for the Council, who elect from their own number the Executive. The affiliation fee is 8d per plot per year. Branches may be formed where there are at least 10 plots.[20]

---

17 *Freeman's Journal*, 19 Jan. 1918. **18** *Irish Independent*, 21 Jan. 1918. **19** *Irish Times*, 21 Jan. 1918. **20** *Freeman's Journal*, 22 May 1918.

Following the general meeting of plotholders in the Mansion House local branch meetings took place, for example at the Marino Allotment Holders' Association and Bushy Park (Rathmines UDC), which considered affiliating with the IPU.[21] In December 1917, the IPU council reported its largest meeting with representatives from Terenure, Pembroke, Booterstown and Kingstown present. Two representatives of the Union were co-opted to Dublin Corporation LCC, namely Richard Donnelly and Patrick Donnelly.[22] Requests for similar representation were being sent to other UDCs: Kingstown, Blackrock, Pembroke and Rathmines.[23] Except for Rathmines, by May 1918 these requests had been granted while in Drogheda, Co. Louth, the IPU branch had charge of the corporation plots.[24] In April 1918 the executive council passed a resolution that Dublin Corporation LCC gives the same recognition to IPU members as 'it gives to other bodies of organized workers' and second that the Corporation consider IPU members only eligible for local committees.[25] The IPU wrote to Dublin Corporation LCC, which replied, 'that as soon as the Trades Union Congress recognizes the Plotholders' Union as such the LCC will follow the example'.[26] It is noteworthy that the IPU considered itself to consist of 'workers', though plotholding was a part-time activity not a full-time occupation or trade.

Along with attending council meetings, office holders wrote to the newspapers, attended branch meetings and advocated for plotholders and plotholding. The minutes of the LCC include many letters from the IPU regarding land for allotments, seed and sprayers, fencing of plots, the reassignment of surrendered plots and rent of plots. In response to a speech made by Sir T.W. Russell, vice president of the DATI, stating that fixity of tenure of allotments should not apply in the environs of expanding towns, the president replied in a letter to the editor of the *Freeman's Journal* that the IPU 'does not aim at securing a fixity of tenure which will at any time conflict with any building scheme. It seeks to make plotholding a feature of Irish life by the enactment of an Irish Allotment Act to replace the wartime measure'.[27] A month later the IPU council urged branch delegates to hold meetings and canvas house to house to urge the LGB to use their powers to compulsorily acquire land for plots.[28]

Not all plotholders wanted to affiliate with the IPU. In January 1918, the plotholders of St Patrick's Division (a House of Commons constituency)

21 *Evening Herald*, 8 Dec. 1917; *Freeman's Journal*, 24 Nov. 1917.   22 Dublin City Council, Land Cultivation Committee LCC/R mins/01 1917, p. 334.   23 *Freeman's Journal*, 6 Dec. 1917. 24 Ibid., 22 May 1918.   25 Ibid., 18 Apr. 1918.   26 Dublin City Council, minutes of LCC, 16 Apr. 1918, p. 197 (this volume, Book 4, is not yet catalogued in the City Archives).   27 *Freeman's Journal*, 7 Dec. 1917.   28 Ibid., 15 Jan. 1918.

agreed not to affiliate with another group. They were told in a letter from the DATI that no special privileges were available to the IPU.[29] Local associations of plotholders were also established elsewhere in Ireland. In January 1918 plotholders in Fermoy, Co. Cork, formed a branch of the IPU.[30] In Sligo, where a branch was formed in February 1918, the membership fee was 1s. of which 8d. went to fund the IPU.[31] The IPU was one of thirteen bodies represented at a meeting of the Drogheda Trades and Labour Council.[32] Council members of the IPU attended local meetings to promote allotments, one example being a meeting in Blackrock, Co. Dublin, in January 1918.[33] In February 1918 the IPU president spoke at the meeting of plotholders in Ringsend, Dublin, and proposed that football grounds and areas of Ringsend Park be made available for allotments.[34]

The IPU was an advocate for local plotholders. In February 1918, VLCS plotholders decided not to sign any agreements until the terms were approved by the IPU; they also sought the transfer of lands administered by the VLCS to Dublin Corporation LCC.[35] In a letter Miss Harrison, honorary secretary of the VLCS, explained the misunderstanding – previous agreements had been legally inaccurate.[36] A month later plotholders were notified in the press of a meeting in the Mansion House to discuss a new agreement, the first notice to include the Irish title of the IPU – Cumann Luċt Ceapaċ.[37] The IPU also addressed practical matters, though in a limited way, one example being spraying potatoes for blight. Sprayers were loaned by the Dublin Corporation LCC and a sub-committee of the IPU was to arrange their use by plotholders.[38]

The IPU supported the wider plotholding movement in Dublin. Mr Donnelly wrote to the editor of the *Irish Independent* refuting the recorder of Dublin's claim that supporting plotholders from rates was a farce. In the Dublin Corporation area 3,000 plotholders from 'all walks of life' cultivated in their spare time 430 acres of land. The value of the allotment movement has been acknowledged by government, charities, clergy of various denominations, the Dublin Trades Council and the Dublin Industrial Development Council.[39] This indicates the scale and recognition of allotments in Dublin. In response to criticism of the IPU, Patrick Donnelly, then organizing secretary, referred to the annual convention held on Easter Sunday 1919 at which the following description of the IPU was given:

---

29 Ibid., 30 Jan. 1918. **30** Ibid., 15 Jan. 1918. **31** *Sligo Champion*, 16 Feb. 1918. **32** *Drogheda Independent*, 16 Feb. 1918. **33** *Irish Independent*, 25 Jan. 1918. **34** *Freeman's Journal*, 5 Feb. 1918. **35** Ibid., 25 Feb. 1918. **36** Ibid., 19 Feb. 1918. **37** *Evening Herald*, 12 Mar. 1918. **38** *Cork Examiner*, 2 May 1918. **39** *Irish Independent*, 9 July 1919.

it was a union of landless men and women run entirely by themselves, with a three-fold appeal to leaders of organized Labour, those interested in moral and physical welfare of the people, simple virtues of thrift, sobriety and industry and to the social reformer.[40]

At the adjourned convention held in the City Hall, the resolutions passed were to draw the attention of municipalities to the 'vast potentialities' of the plotholding movement, 'it being the forerunner of municipal control of land, with consequent lowering of rates, and increased prosperity.' There was a hint of the existence of a rival group, in the request that local authorities 'refuse any encouragement to the demand now being made to disrupt this Union and to so divide their forces.'[41] The concern was justifiable because in June 1919 a second plotholders' union was reported in the press. The Irish Plotholders' General Union (IPGU) had a branch at Wellpark, Whitehall, Upper Drumcondra. Having secured fixity of tenure for hundreds of plotholders, it urged people to join at the address given: 'Hon. Sec., 169 Botanic Avenue, Glasnevin'.[42]

A month later J.A. Colbert of the IPGU and S. Sloan of the IPU met with the deputy city treasurer and agreed to one plotholders' union.[43] On 8 August delegates met, and the United Irish Plotholders' Union (Cumann Luċt Ceapaċ na hÉireann, UIPU) was established. A central committee for all Ireland was elected: Thomas Shaw, chair (Old Finglas); Thomas Cahill, vice chair (Byrne's Field); Edward Kelly, treasurer (Rooney's Field) and Sean Colbert, general secretary (Croydon Park), as well as two trustees, Messrs Dillon and Parnell, and five committee members. Funds in hand were to be given to the new organization.[44]

United Irish Plotholders' Union

A meeting of the UIPU council with representatives of Dublin branches, as well as Templemore, Kildare, Waterford, Kingstown and Dungarvan, was held in September 1919. The president, Thomas Shaw, stated the one main objective to be 'the securing by every legitimate means, of the town workers, in peaceful possession and enjoyment of his plot'. The council was an all-Ireland executive committee (though in reality mainly a Dublin organization) with its decisions binding on all members. Resolutions passed included supporting co-operative buying of requisites and selling of produce, with

40 *Evening Herald*, 10 June 1919.   **41** *Irish Times*, 21 Apr. 1919.   **42** *Freeman's Journal*, 16 June 1919.   **43** *Irish Independent*, 14 July 1919.   **44** *Freeman's Journal*, 14 Aug. 1919.   **45** Ibid.,

surplus produce to be given to those unable to acquire plots, and fixity of tenure.[45]

In November 1919 it was decided to register the UIPU as a co-operative society and to work for direct representation on public bodies. It was also agreed to organize a concert in aid of the Dublin poor.[46] No details of the implementation of these resolutions were located.

Members of the UIPU executive visited, advised and advocated for local plotholding groups. In October 1919 Thomas Shaw addressed plotholders in Mitchelstown, Co. Cork, and a month later Patrick Donnelly met with plotholders in Naas who were considering joining the UIPU.[47] Speaking at the Rutland area (Dolphin's Barn) AGM, Shaw said that fixity of tenure was the strongest plank in their platform.[48] Following a meeting with the DATI, Mr Colbert, honorary secretary, advised Nenagh plotholders to bring their case to their local council.[49] Before land could be acquired compulsorily for allotments, a public inquiry had to be conducted by an LGB inspector. In December 1919 the Allotments Committee of Dublin Corporation applied for additional lands and legal representatives of a landowner and the UIPU appeared before the inspector.[50] In January 1920 the UIPU joined with the Dublin Corporation LCC and the local Sean Colbert Plotholders' Union to protest at a proposal to let land at Fairview, Dublin, to a local councillor rather than use the land for plots. The proposal was dropped.[51] Like the IPU before it, the UIPU participated in local representative groups. In Cork, for example, the UIPU branch was a member of the Cork Trade and Labour Council.[52] The movement held annual congresses at which similar resolutions, such as fixity of tenure, and an allotment bill were agreed each year. Some resolutions were agreed once, such as the registration of UIPU as a co-operative society under the Industrial and Provident Societies Acts, agreed at the first annual congress in February 1920.[53] There is no evidence that this actually occurred.

The fourth annual congress was held in the Mansion House on 25 February 1923 with 150 delegates present. The meeting accepted the following resolutions: that artisans' cottages built on land used for allotments be given to those dispossessed of their plots; that the promised allotment bill be passed; that money be provided to purchase land for permanent plots; that allotments be offered rent free to the unemployed. It was also agreed to hold an Allotment Holder's Hospital Day in September.[54] The UIPU council meeting held in October 1923 noted that the Hospital Day was a marked success in some

15 Sept. 1919. **46** *Irish Independent,* 10 Nov. 1919. **47** *Cork Examiner,* 2 Oct. 1919; *Kildare Observer,* 17 May 1919. **48** *Freeman's Journal,* 12 Dec. 1919. **49** *Nenagh News,* 22 Nov. 1919. **50** *Freeman's Journal,* 10 Dec. 1919. **51** Ibid., 20 Jan. 1920. **52** *Cork Examiner,* 22 Sept. 1919. **53** *Freeman's Journal,* 16 Feb. 1920. **54** Ibid., 26 Feb 1923.

districts, for example the Dolphin's Barn branch donated 45 cwt (2.25 tons) of potatoes, and cabbage, onions and other vegetables to six hospitals.[55] Letters of acknowledgment had been received from the Meath, Mercer's and the Royal City of Dublin hospitals.[56]

Willingness to let land or pay rents were recurring issues in the 1920s. In November 1922 the UIPU considered the eviction of plotholders from lands in Glasnevin, Dublin, where the landlords did not want to re-let land for the following year. A deputation had submitted a request to Dublin Corporation to retain plots at seven sites in Dublin, while two sites at Marino and Sloblands (Fairview) were designated for housing and for a public park, respectively.[57] There was a favourable outcome – Dublin Corporation LCC agreed to let lands under their control for plots in the following year. Regarding a meeting with the minister for agriculture, Thomas Cahill stated that they would confirm that rents had been paid by plotholders.[58]

At the January council meeting held at 27 Gardiner Place, a letter was read from the minister for agriculture stating that it was unreasonable for landowners to enter into agreements where plotholders would not manage areas or be responsible for rents. The UIPU agreed to be responsible for rents. One speaker, a Mr Lucas, said that while labourers paid their rents, the defaulters came in motors and took away the produce. In some areas the land would not be let in the coming year, an issue raised with the Department of Agriculture.[59] At its July meeting the council decided to take action and organize the Union in Limerick, Gort, Drogheda, Thurles, Templemore, Newtownbarry (Bunclody), Nenagh and Galway. All plotholders were asked to subscribe 1*d.* per week to meet the costs of the organization.[60] The previous affiliation fee of 8*d.* must have ceased.

In September the council of the UIPU was informed that the minister for agriculture intended to withdraw from renting land for plots in the Dublin metropolitan area. An estimated 600 plotholders would be affected.[61] In October 1923 the UIPU received a letter from Mr Rowe, town clerk, stating that the latest date for making application for 1924 was 1 October when a deposit of £1 should be paid. Though plotholders in Dublin numbered 668, only twenty-three had paid their deposit, arrears amounted to £70, and an extension for payment was agreed to 31 October.[62] In November the Union asked the minister to intervene with Pembroke UDC which wished to return lands at Vergemount, Clonskeagh, to the owner and remove plots from Herbert Park, Ballsbridge.[63] At the council meeting held on 16 December a

---

55 *Irish Independent*, 3 Oct. 1923.   **56** *Irish Times*, 15 Oct. 1923.   **57** *Freeman's Journal*, 13 Nov. 1922.   **58** Ibid., 27 Nov. 1922.   **59** *Irish Times*, 15 Jan. 1923.   **60** *Freeman's Journal*, 10 July 1923. **61** *Irish Times*, 13 Sept. 1923.   **62** *Freeman's Journal*, 15 Oct. 1923.   **63** Ibid., 20 Nov. 1923.

resolution was sent to President Cosgrave and the minister for agriculture requesting a suspension of notices of eviction to surrender plots on 31 December pending negotiation with landowners and the introduction of legislation.[64]

Land and legislation

With little assurance about the availability of land in the following year, fixity of tenure and the call for an allotment act in Ireland were constant demands at union congresses, council meetings and branch meetings. At the IPU inaugural meeting on 17 September 1917 a representative of the union was appointed to the forthcoming all-Ireland deputation to the chief secretary.[65] An act similar to the Allotment and Smallholders Act 1908 which applied in England was demanded. On 2 October 1917 representatives of the VLCS, including Miss S.C. Harrison, and plotholders associations, along with members of parliament, including William Field, member for the Dublin St Patrick's constituency, met with the chief secretary, Henry Duke, to discuss an Irish allotment bill to be brought before the House of Commons in London. Duke promised to 'give the matter careful consideration'.[66]

In June 1919 the IPU requested the DATI to make a definite statement for plotholders as to the Irish allotments bill and to give assurance about the extension of existing tenancies.[67] Notices to plotholders of evictions from plots had increased the call for legislation to ensure fixity of tenure.[68] A month later John Farrelly, IPU president and vice president of the Dublin Trades Council, Patrick Donnelly, IPU organizing secretary, and representatives of the Dublin Corporation Allotments Committee, met with the DATI to urge continuance of the plotholding movement and the introduction of an act to make the allotment scheme permanent in Ireland.[69] In reply, Mr T.P. Gill said that he was not yet able to give assurance of land for 1920.[70] In December 1919 Thomas Shaw told the annual meeting of Dolphin's Barn plotholders that the UIPU was drafting heads of a bill which would be passed by parliament.[71]

In June 1920, Thomas Shaw, Thomas Cahill and John Farrelly met with Mr Gill to urge allotment legislation. However, 'due to congestion in parliamentary business' it was unlikely that a bill would be passed in the current session. But land for plots would be made available for the year 1921.[72]

64 *Irish Times*, 29 Dec. 1923.   **65** *Evening Herald*, 13 Oct. 1917.   **66** *Weekly Irish Times*, 13 Oct. 1917.   **67** *Limerick Leader*, 16 June 1919.   **68** *Cork Examiner*, 28 Oct. 1919.   **69** Ibid., 3 July 1919.   **70** *Irish Independent*, 4 Aug. 1919.   **71** *Freeman's Journal*, 12 Dec. 1919.   **72** *Belfast Newsletter*, 16 June 1920.

However, the cost of renting plots would have to increase. By September 1921 the plotholders had agreed to a 25 to 50 per cent increase in rent and a deputation of the UIPU was to meet Dublin Corporation and the DATI again.[73] A month later 'an amicable settlement' was reached. The UIPU and allotment committees were informed that the DATI would continue the compulsory acquisition of land in 1922 with increased rents for plotholders. This was to be a temporary measure, 'legislation on the subject being at present impracticable'.[74]

In January 1922 a deputation of the UIPU met with Patrick Hogan, minister for agriculture, to discuss tenure of plots, the extension of plotholding in the country and legislation regarding same.[75] In November 1922 the UIPU wrote to Thomas Johnson TD, leader of the Labour Party, and to Alfred Byrne, an independent TD, both of whom undertook to assist in bringing legislation before the Dáil.[76] Byrne duly asked the minister for agriculture if he had had correspondence with the UIPU. He replied that he had advised the UIPU to rent land by negotiation with landowners and that legislation would be introduced in the coming year.[77] At the monthly meeting of the council of the UIPU held in May 1923, regret was expressed that the programme for government did not include the Irish allotments bill as promised by the minister for agriculture. This would affect 30,000 town workers throughout Ireland.[78]

In August 1923 a general meeting of the Glasnevin district branch passed resolutions seeking an allotment bill, promoting the advantages of allotments and seeking the views of candidates regarding the plotholding movement in advance of the forthcoming Dáil and municipal elections.[79] The council of the UIPU took the issue of the elections further, writing to the candidates in three Dublin constituencies seeking their support for an allotment bill, the emancipation of city workers from slums as well as recognition of the UIPU's aims.[80] A reply was received signed by seven Cumann na nGaedheal candidates stating that they would support the objectives insofar as they would be accepted by government.[81] In October 1923 it was announced that an allotment bill was listed in the current session of the Dáil.[82] A month later the UIPU wrote to the minister for agriculture urging a one clause bill to protect allotment holders until legislation was passed.[83] This did not happen.

73 *Irish Times*, 12 Sept. 1921.　74 Ibid., 7 Oct. 1921.　75 *Southern Star*, 28 Jan. 1922.　76 *Freeman's Journal*, 13 Nov. 1922.　77 *Evening Echo*, 30 Nov. 1922. A copy of the parliamentary question and a briefing note is held in the National Archives of Ireland, 2005/77/288.　78 *Irish Times*, 18 May 1923.　79 Ibid., 4 Aug. 1923.　80 *Freeman's Journal*, 22 Aug. 1923.　81 Ibid., 27 Aug. 1923.　82 *Irish Times*, 15 Oct. 1923.　83 *Freeman's Journal*, 20 Nov. 1923.

Though the First World War ended in November 1918, the DORA regulations for allotments had been continued on an annual basis, eventually ceasing on 31 August 1923. At the council meeting in March 1924 the UIPU demanded that the ministry of Saorstát Éireann provide facilities similar to those given by the British government to plotholders in Britain.[84] In January 1925 Thomas Shaw, president, and Mr McDonnell, honorary secretary, sent a circular to all members of the UIPU urging them to organize support for the allotment bill being introduced by the Labour Party. Members were asked to explain that the bill was not a party measure.[85]

In November 1925 a general meeting of the UIPU held at 6 Gardiner Row discussed the Acquisition of Land (Allotments) Act, 1925, which had recently been introduced by the government. The meeting advised all workers in urban districts to avail of the provisions of the Act and to co-operate with local authorities in carrying it to a successful outcome.[86] The bill however was defeated at the second reading. In 1926 the government introduced a bill which was enacted in July 1926 as the Acquisition of Land (Allotments) Act. In September the UIPU requested a meeting with Dublin Corporation to discuss the implementation of the Act.[87] The town clerk sent the UIPU a draft of a scheme, the headings were:

A: the land acquired be administered by the UIPU.
B: preparation of allotment areas and size of plots.
C: maximum rent to be paid to landowners or fixed by Land Commission by land taken compulsorily.
D: compensation payable on termination of letting.[88]

This draft scheme would suggest that the UIPU rather than the Corporation was to administer the scheme at local level. Once land was acquired it would have to be divided into plots, one-eighth or one-sixteenth of an acre in size, and fenced. The cost of renting land had been an issue for the plotholders' union since 1917 and it would have welcomed the provision of a maximum or fixed rent for land. Whether the compensation payable referred to the landowner's loss of earnings or the plotholder's loss of crops is unclear. In Dublin, two sites with 100 plots at Rutland Avenue, Dolphin's Barn and 60 plots in Glasnevin were acquired in 1927, and more sites followed in the succeeding years.[89] Shaw told those assembled at the annual congress in 1928 that the Acquisition of Land (Allotments) Act was not in the interests of town

84 *Irish Times*, 22 Mar. 1924.   **85** *Limerick Leader*, 19 Jan. 1925.   **86** *Irish Times*, 18 Nov. 1925.   **87** *Evening Herald*, 29 Sept. 1926.   **88** *Irish Times*, 19 Oct. 1926.   **89** Forrest, 'Allotments in Dublin', *Irish Geography*, 44:2–3 (2011), 265–90.

workers, rather it was fulfilling a promise made by an ex-governor general.[90] The provision of allotments by local councils was discretionary and the schemes had to be self-supporting. These provisions were altered in the Acquisition of Lands (Allotments) Amendment Act (1934). In that year the United Irish Plotholders' Union became the Irish Allotment Holders' Association. No reason was given for this name change but it may have reflected the name in the recently enacted bill. The word 'association' had been used by local plotholding groups, for example, Marino Allotment Holders' Association.

In this account of the plotholders' unions the name Thomas Shaw comes to the fore. Shaw (1855–1940) had a background in similar organizations having been first secretary of the Irish Gardeners' Association and an horticultural organizer for the then recently established Irish Agricultural Co-operative Society. Census returns give his occupation as journalist in 1901 and agricultural organizer in 1911. For many years he wrote gardening columns in national newspapers.[91] Shaw's addresses at annual UIPU congresses from 1920 cast light on his ideas for the plotholding movement. His 1920 speech addressed the importance to the plotholders of 'union', disposal of surplus material and the establishment of peoples' banks on Raiffeisen (co-operative) principles.[92] A year later, concerned about the future of plotholding in Ireland, he urged those in authority to continue 'this most important phase of Irish economics.' It was difficult to attend to a plot if eviction loomed, and again he stressed co-operation as the only solution.[93] At the fourth annual congress held in 1923, he told the delegates that membership had not declined in the previous year and urged loyalty to the UIPU. If plotholding ceased in Dublin, he stated, the workers would be deprived of two thousand tons of potatoes and vegetables. He continued that 'we plotholders had reason to fear that the big landed and grazing interests had lost none of their power in the new dispensation'. Why, he asked, had the Agricultural Commission not included intensive cultivation by town workers and taken evidence as to the yield from one acre producing food for eight families or for one bullock?[94] A year later Shaw described the 'social, physical, moral advantages of the plotholding system', which 'were seen in the lives and actions of those who had devoted themselves to the health-giving occupation of food-production'. He again questioned why the UIPU had not been included in the Commission of Agriculture – established to review and develop agriculture in the Free State – or in the new land Acts. He considered that the Senate and Dáil paid greater

90 *Irish Independent*, 5 Mar. 1928.   91 Mary Forrest, 'Mr Thomas Shaw – a 20th century promoter of horticulture', *Irish Garden Plant Society Newsletter*, 134 (2016), 4–6.   92 *Freeman's Journal*, 16 Feb. 1920.   93 *Irish Times*, 14 Feb. 1921.   94 *Freeman's Journal*, 26 Feb. 1923.

attention to farmers and cattle ranchers.[95] Shaw was well aware of contemporary issues in Irish agriculture. Apart from Thomas Cahill, who was a public official and vice president of the UIPU until 1931, no further biographical details of the UIPU council were located.

As well as a skilled president and a council, the UIPU had some steadfast supporters. Two committee members of the VLCS, William Field, MP until 1918, and its honorary secretary Sarah Cecilia Harrison, advocated on behalf of plotholders and attended UIPU annual congresses. In 1925 Miss Harrison's 'services in promoting the allotment bill' were acknowledged and she was elected to the council.[96] Her knowledge of allotment acts in England and Scotland and land acts in Ireland is evident in detailed notes she made in a school copy book signed S.C. Harrison and dated 1924.[97] Over many years the UIPU had a strong ally in Alfred Byrne who, as alderman, chaired the Dublin Corporation LCC; as a TD he supported the passage of the allotment bill and as lord mayor of Dublin championed the plotholding movement in the city.

The UIPU also acknowledged 'the Press for the interest they have manifested in the allotment movement'.[98] The press did obviously take an interest in the allotment movement, for this account is drawn from newspaper reports. Given that similar reports of the same meeting were published in several newspapers, it is clear that the UIPU supplied copy to newspaper editors. Shaw, with his expertise in journalism, may well have written these reports.

Was the UIP or UIPU representative of plotholders? Was it country-wide?

In 1920 there were 3,000 plotholders in thirty-seven areas in the Dublin metropolitan district. 2,270 plotholders in twenty-eight areas were affiliated to the UIPU, with fees paid in respect of 1,382 members. There were branches in Tipperary and Kilkenny with promises of others in Cork, Wexford, Westmeath, Queen's County (Laois) and Kildare.[99] Based on newspaper reports in these years it appears that there were branches also in Sligo, Kerry, Louth and Limerick. With references to only ten counties the UIPU was hardly countrywide. While the introduction of legislation would apply to all

---

95 *Irish Times*, 25 Feb. 1924.   96 *Evening Herald*, 26 Mar. 1925; *Irish Times*, 30 Mar. 1925.
97 Dublin City Archives (Dublin City Council/History Allotments Shelf), location BF R1/01/03.
98 *Evening Herald*, 26 Mar. 1925.   99 *Irish Times*, 14 Feb. 1921.

plotholders, the issues addressed by the UIP and UIPU were generally Dublin-centred. They held many of their annual congresses and council meetings in significant Dublin Corporation properties, namely, the Council Chamber, City Hall; the Mansion House; and the Lord Mayor's Court, South William Street. In 1925 and 1928 the UIPU held meetings at 6 Gardiner Row, then the headquarters of the Irish Craftworkers' Union, now those of the Connect trade union. Newspaper reports indicated that the IPU and the UIPU were primarily involved with the immediate issue of securing plots for plotholders and an allotments bill. Almost annually UIPU delegations met with Dublin Corporation officials and the secretary of the DATI to discuss, in particular, the provision of allotments for the following year. From 1922 they met with and wrote to the minister for agriculture to demand legislation.

References by the IPU or UIPU to the political situation in the country in the years from the establishment of the IPU and the enactment of legislation were few. Following the death of Tomás Mac Curtain, the North-West Ward (Cork) branch offered their condolences to his widow.[100] Speaking to plotholders in Croydon Park, Dublin, in August 1921, Thomas Shaw expressed the view that 'when a settled government was established in the country the claims of the plotholders would be recognized.'[101] In 1928 the UIPU urged support for a campaign for peace and disarmament. A letter dated 25 June 1928 from Mr McDonnell, honorary secretary, 6 Gardiner Row, urged support for a committee in Saorstát Éireann that was promoting a 'A World-wide campaign for the Renunciation of War and Disarmament'. He continued: 'as the Plotholding Movement is essentially a Movement of the people, the United Irish Plotholders' Union is convinced that it has not gone outside its province in pledging its support to a Movement which is primarily for the betterment and advancement of Democracy'.[102]

While one of the aims of the IPU was to arrange 'lectures by experts', instruction for plotholders and the supply of requisites, part of the DATI's Scheme B, mentioned earlier, was undertaken by the DATI and Land Cultivation Committees. Newspapers also published lists of prizewinners at horticultural shows where some notable members of the IPU, e.g., G.H. Parnell, were listed.[103] At a plotholder's show organized in September 1920 by the UIPU and VLCS, Wm Martin, Kingstown, and Thomas Shaw were among the prize winners.[104]

---

100 *Cork Examiner*, 26 Mar. 1920. 101 *Freeman's Journal*, 29 Aug. 1921. 102 Dublin City Archives (Dublin City Council, History allotments, BF R1/01/03). On 20 February 1929 Dáil Éireann approved of the Treaty for the Renunciation of War signed in Paris in 1928. 103 *Irish Times*, 4 Sept. 1917. 104 Ibid., 2 Oct. 1920.

Similar plotholders' unions were also established in Britain. The Scottish National Union of Allotment Holders was founded in 1917. In England the National Union of Allotment Holders was formed in October 1918. Apart from a reference by Mr Donnelly, IPU president, to the impending inaugural National Union congress in Leicester, England, in February 1918, there were no links between the unions in Ireland and Britain in the years to 1926.[105]

The United Irish Plotholders' Union was founded in a time of food shortage, exacerbated by food blockades during the First World War. The union continued to promote allotments in the years of the War of Independence and the Civil War. The union and its plotholder members are an example of how working men (few women had plots) sought and obtained better conditions for those cultivating vegetables for themselves and their families in a time of war and revolution in Ireland.

105 *Freeman's Journal*, 15 Jan. 1918.

'The only people who would take a risk': maritime workers and the Irish Revolution

BRIAN HANLEY

During October 1938 a meeting of the 'Old IRA' heard fulsome praise for Dublin Brigade's 'Q' Company during the War of Independence. Q Company was made up of ships' officers, sailors, stokers, dockers and carters, and one speaker suggested that if their 'operations were chronicled, they would put the best "thrillers" in the shade.'[1] However their story remains relatively little-known, certainly by comparison with other aspects of the IRA's war. Maritime workers played an important part in the revolutionary effort, transporting communications, finance and weapons across North America, Europe and Britain. Q Company was part of a wider network, connecting Hamburg, Antwerp, Genoa, New York, St John's and Montreal, Liverpool, Glasgow, London and Ireland itself. This chapter examines the role played by activists in Liverpool and New York, two of the key cities of the Irish diaspora. Here, as well as smuggling, republicans played an important role in strikes connected to the Irish struggle, though with differing results.[2]

Dockers, sailors and maritime networks

In June 1921 it was reported that submarines maintained a regular passenger service for officials of the Irish Republic between Ireland and the United States.[3] Though untrue, it nevertheless illustrated the importance of trans-Atlantic networks.[4] Communications, finance, arms and indeed people could only be brought to Ireland by sea. Rather than by submarine, Éamon de Valera, Harry Boland and many others crossed the Atlantic under false identities, working their way as stokers or firemen on board Cunard and White Star liners. These great passenger ships sailed from Liverpool, the 'most important' port for Irish revolutionaries. The IRA's commander there, Paddy Daly, recalled that 'scarcely a boat left (for) an Irish, Continental or American port which had not on board one or two Irishmen who were eager to do their

---

1 *Evening Herald*, 29 Oct. 1938. I am grateful to Gerard Shannon for this reference.   2 I am very indebted to Bruce Nelson who shared a copy of his unpublished article 'Clandestine maritime networks and the Irish Revolution: Neil Kerr's long journey' with me and inspired my interest in the subject.   3 *Cork Examiner*, 23 June 1921.   4 Buying a submarine in Germany was however

part.' Merseyside was the hub for transporting 'almost all the munitions in the other great cities like Manchester, Newcastle, Birmingham and Glasgow' to Ireland.[5] Liverpool was connected to Newry, Drogheda and Dundalk, but most importantly to Dublin. One of the central figures in Q Company, John 'Archie' Kennedy, recalled that during 1919 IRA General Head Quarters instructed him to form 'a special unit' for smuggling. Kennedy later claimed 41 Dublin dockers, stevedores and quaymen, and 58 seamen, as members of the company. But while Q Company was only *officially* formed in the spring of 1921, Kennedy identified the Dublin lockout of 1913–14 as when dock workers had first begun to smuggle material, initially for the Irish Citizen Army.[6]

By 1920 there were activists working on ocean liners as firemen, lamp trimmers, or stokers, as well as petty officers, ships' stewards and security men.[7] Daly explained that the 'Atlantic route was our most important both on account of the source of supply at New York and because of the fact that sailings were very regular and frequent. Our best boats on that line was the *Celtic* and the *Baltic*.'[8] A number of men working on these liners, including Barney Downes, Dick O'Neill, Billy Goggins and Billy Humphries, feature in many accounts. These men were not only instrumental in moving weapons and communications, but also in smuggling de Valera, Boland and others to America. They 'received payment for any risk they ran even though they were Irishmen. The payment was not, however, in proportion to the risks taken.'[9] There were also a group of republican sympathizers working on the boats that plied between Liverpool, London, Southampton, Dublin and smaller Irish ports, one of the most important being Ned Kavanagh of the SS *Blackrock*. There were activists based in Liverpool that travelled to Hamburg, Antwerp and Genoa. On Merseyside itself Neil Kerr, a former foreman on the Cunard Line, and Stevie Lanigan, a customs officer, were key figures; they were also long-standing members of the Irish Republican Brotherhood (IRB). They had contacts such as Peadar Reilly of the Sailors' and Firemen's Union who had

discussed during the Civil War. C/S to S. Moylan, 6 Feb. 1923, in Desmond FitzGerald Papers, University College Dublin Archives (UCDA) P80/791 (3). **5** Dr Paddy Daly, Ernie O'Malley Notebooks, UCDA P17b/136. **6** John Kennedy, IE/Military Archives (MA)/Military Service Pensions Collection (MSPC)/RO/611. Padraig Yeates has pointed out that the Citizen Army received very little weaponry until after the Lockout's conclusion and indeed Kennedy's dating of 'Q' Company's formation may be related to pension claims. **7** For a variety of examples see John Finn MSP34REF238; Harry Shorte W24B700; Brian McGilly MSP34REF9481; Patrick Gumbleton 24SP5328; Neil Kerr 24SP1206ADD; Hugh Early MSP34REF746; Owen Moore MSP34REF20971; John Murphy 24SP9570; John Joseph Byrne MSP34REF57066; Thomas Curran MSP34REF1085; Edward Mooney 24SP7571. **8** Dr Patrick Daly, Bureau of Military History Witness Statement (BMHWS) 814. The *Baltic* and the *Celtic* were White Star liners. **9** Michael O'Leary, BMHWS

'quite a stock of sailors' books belonging to former sailors (and) it was possible
for the friendly agents to forge new papers or change particulars to suit one
of our men who would need a job on a ship.'[10] An important figure on both
sides of the Atlantic was Louth native James (Jem) McGee, assistant manager
of the Marine Engineers' Association in New York. This position gave him
access to contacts travelling between 'Liverpool, London, Southampton, Cork,
Dublin and Belfast' and in his own words 'complete control' over 'ocean going
marine engineers on American ships.' McGee recounted that in January 1920
he was requested by Boland to 'form an organization of seamen, dock
labourer(s) and others who would be helpful.'[11] A number of those active in
America confirmed that McGee provided 'invaluable assistance' to IRA
operations there.[12]

    This network included publicans and café owners in dockland areas, some
of them running front operations established by republicans. Women ran safe-
houses and brought communications or small amounts of weapons to
Ireland.[13] Moira Kennedy O'Byrne was sometimes tasked with collecting
money, most of which, she recalled, 'came from America, brought in by
friendly members of ships' crews.'[14] Republicans working at sea gathered
intelligence. Sailors on liners calling at Montreal and republican custom
officers in that city identified the notorious Captain John Bowen Colthurst
when he arrived there on route to British Columbia in March 1921.[15]
Contacts in Hamburg included a veteran of Casement's Irish Brigade working
as a St Pauli police sergeant, a ship's captain married to an Irish woman, a clerk
at Lloyd's Shipping Bureau and a river pilot on the Elbe.[16]

    The make-up of the IRA's maritime network is significant. Ports were
distinctive environments, often characterized by poor living standards and
reliance on low-paid employment. The *Economic Journal* could assert in 1914
that 'dock labour all the world over has a bad name; in the popular estimation
"the scum of the earth" drifts down from trade to trade and from occupation
to occupation to form at last the dregs of our industrial system, the loaders
and unloaders of ships.'[17] But dockers also possessed a particular pride in their
relative independence and the variety of their work: 'every ship (was) a

0797; Daly, UCDA P17b/136.   10 Daly, BMHWS 814, Tom Healy MSP34REF2337.   11 James
McGee MSP34REF34671. Patrick Keegan, a ship's fireman, claimed that it was another member of
the Marine Engineers' union, Patrick Baskerville, who introduced McGee to Boland. Patrick
Baskerville MSP34REF1347.   12 Daniel Healy, BMHWS 1656, Edmond O'Brien, BMHWS 0597.
13 Richard Walsh, BMHWS 400, John Joseph Carr MSP34REF9241, Leon Speirs MSP34REF56876.
14 Moira Kennedy O'Brien, BMHWS 1029.   15 Report, 18 July 1921, Maurice Twomey Papers,
UCDA P69/217 (38–40).   16 'Hamburg', Twomey Papers, UCDA P69/217 (2).   17 L.S. Woolf,
'An experiment in decasualisation: the Liverpool docks scheme', *Economic Journal*, 24:94 (June 1914),

different factory.'[18] The decade since 1910 had seen extensive militancy among dock and maritime workers, not least in Liverpool in 1911, while dockers had been an integral and early part of the Irish Transport and General Workers' Union. The post-war period would again see dock strikes across the United Kingdom. In Liverpool at least 'the majority of (IRA) Volunteers worked at the docks'.[19] Paddy Daly explained that those who formed the core of the IRA's network on Merseyside 'were all working-class people. They were the only people who would take a risk over there.'[20] This may not be surprising given the make-up of the Irish in Britain and seems to have been the case with republican organizations there more generally.[21] But in Ireland Q Company stood out in terms of the IRA, in which so-called unskilled urban workers were generally under-represented. The port environment was also distinctive in several other ways.[22] Port cities generally had a cosmopolitan character. To a young republican from rural Galway even Dublin dockland might seem an 'awe-inspiring sight – a strange big world of noise … a place where the whole world seemed to congregate … we saw coloured men, and men from China and Japan; people crowded together like wasps in a hive.'[23] They were also rough environments. One sailor described Hamburg as 'a hungry, starving city … a city full of refugees … informers and degenerates of every kind, a cesspool of filth.'[24] Paddy Daly noted how during Prohibition many of the Liverpool sailors 'supplemented their pay by carrying whiskey to New York.'[25] One republican contact in Hamburg was described as a 'bit of a booze hound type that would do any job if paid for it.'[26] A Liverpool-born sailor was willing to 'do anything for money … a gambler, and a general all round rough character.' A seaman nicknamed 'the Arab', who played an important role in helping spirit de Valera to America, was a 'lawless type [who] cared for neither God nor man. One thing he liked, however … was to see the police get the worst of it always.'[27] Republicans found themselves working in 'very dangerous places' rubbing shoulders with 'East End crooks' and other underworld elements. Indeed one activist admitted that 'large sums of money were unaccounted for in places like Manchester and Glasgow.'[28] This again was in

---

314–19.   **18** A. O'Carroll, 'Work organization, technology, community and change: the story of the Dublin docker', *Saothar*, 31 (2006), 45–53.   **19** Col. M. O'Leary, 'The history of the Liverpool Battalion and the story of the burning in 1920, of the Liverpool docks', *An t-Óglác* (Autumn 1966). **20** Daly, BMHWS 814.   **21** Gerard Noonan, *The IRA in Britain, 1919–1923* (Liverpool, 2014), pp 72–5. Pádraig Manning, 'A mixing of social and national aspirations', *History Ireland*, 27:6 (Nov.– Dec. 2019), 40–3.   **22** For a study of Dublin port workers see A. O'Carroll & D. Bennett, *The Dublin docker: working lives of Dublin's deep-sea port* (Newbridge, 2017).   **23** Seán O'Neill, BMHWS 1219.   **24** Joseph O'Malley, BMHWS 0912.   **25** Daly, P17b/136.   **26** 'Hamburg', Twomey Papers, P69/217 (2).   **27** 'Deverant's story' (as told to Dr Moloney), Eamon de Valera Papers, UCDA P150/668.   **28** Thomas Treacy, BMHWS 1093. S. Lanigan to M. Collins, 21 June 1919 in Richard

marked contrast to the republican movement's efforts to present a respectable image in Ireland.

Liverpool

For the Irish diaspora, Liverpool was both a transit hub *and* a place of settlement. Since the 1850s that city had been a 'great commercial and human entrepot linking the old world and the new', the 'New York of Europe'.[29] By 1911, with a population of over 800,000, it was 'the premier ocean port in the British Empire' and its population reflected this: 'there is no part of the globe, however remote, whose natives may not be met on the Liverpool landing stage.'[30] In 1871, just over 15 per cent of the city's population had been born in Ireland.[31] By 1911 those of Irish Catholic descent numbered at least 200,000, of whom over 30,000 had been born in Ireland. Many of them were concentrated in north-end districts adjacent to the docks.[32] Liverpool was also unusual in that by 1900 Irish nationalists formed the opposition on its Conservative-dominated city council. The area of densest Irish settlement, Scotland Road, was represented at Westminster by a Home Rule MP, T.P. O'Connor. Reflecting the make-up of their constituency, these nationalists were often 'more concerned with problems of housing and employment than the Home Rule struggle.'[33] While a middle class was emerging among them, Liverpool's Irish were still overwhelming working class. Indeed their poverty saw them stigmatized as 'the scum left by the tide of migration between Europe and the continent of America.' Racist commentator Joseph Banister contended that Liverpool was for many years 'employed as a dumping ground for the Irish aborigines whom the United States, or our own Colonies refuse to accept ... As a result it is the most Irish, slummy, Romish, criminal and vicious city in England.'[34] Liverpool's socialists too sometimes despaired of the Irish, whose devout Catholicism seemed to inspire acceptance of poverty. One writer in the *Liverpool Forward* asserted after spending 'A day in the slums' that what most appalled him 'was the grave content amongst a people who are living their lives without knowing what life is.'[35]

Mulcahy Papers, UCDA P7/A1; Walsh, BMHWS 400.   **29** John Belchem, *Before the Windrush: race relations in 20th-century Liverpool* (Liverpool, 2018), pp 1–18.   **30** Graeme J. Milne, 'Maritime Liverpool' in John Belchem (ed.), *Liverpool 800: culture, character & history* (Liverpool, 2008), p. 258.   **31** Keith Daniel Roberts, *Liverpool sectarianism: the rise and demise* (Liverpool, 2017), p. 2.   **32** John Belchem, *Irish, Catholic and Scouse: the history of the Liverpool Irish, 1800–1939* (Liverpool, 2007), pp 8, 122.   **33** Gareth Jenkins, 'Nationalism and sectarian violence in Liverpool and Belfast, 1880s–1920s', *International Labor and Working-Class History*, 78 (Fall 2010), 164–80.   **34** Joseph Banister, *Our Judaeo-Irish Labour Party* (London, 1923), p. 21.   **35** John Belchem, 'Hub and diaspora: Liverpool and transnational labour', *Labour History Review*, 75:1 (April 2010), 20–9.

April 1920 saw an attempt by republicans to mobilize that Irish Catholic working class. In Ireland the unions had undertaken a successful two-day general stoppage in support of hunger-striking IRA prisoners. With a similar fast taking place in London's Wormwood Scrubs, Liverpool Councillor P.J. Kelly, president of the Irish Self-Determination League, argued for similar action. Tyrone-born, Kelly had been a Home Ruler before becoming immersed in labour politics during the war.[36] Asserting that there is 'no doubt Liverpool is with Ireland' Kelly demanded that the city's mayor intervene with the government on the prisoners' behalf or there would be stoppages on Liverpool docks.[37] Though union officials warned that Kelly had no right to threaten such action, on 29 April pickets, including large numbers of women, assembled at the quays.[38] Two days later Kelly would claim that 'sixteen thousand dockers, two thousand warehousemen, and two thousand coal-heavers were out.'[39] Rallies in Liverpool's 'Irish quarter' demanded 'the trial or immediate release of 174 Irishmen now on hunger strike in Wormwood Scrubs' and asserted 'that the strike declared today be continued until these men are either tried or set at liberty.' The marchers also called on 'our British fellow-workmen to uphold the true principles of liberty and democracy.'[40] At Westminster T.P. O'Connor expressed his fear of what might follow if the situation was not resolved. But the home secretary, Edward Shortt, stressed that the government 'would not yield to any sort of threat from Liverpool.' Significantly James Sexton, leader of the National Union of Dock Labourers (NUDL) and MP for St Helen's, confirmed that the strike was not recognized by his union. Indeed Sexton asserted that if 'Sinn Feiners strike they will do so without any authority from the Union, and will receive no strike pay.'[41] Of Irish Catholic ancestry, and a member of the Irish Republican Brotherhood in his youth, Sexton was now a union leader 'opposed to strikes if they can be avoided.'[42] Despite these warnings, republicans, including women, continued to picket the docks. On 3 May 1920, a mass meeting of strikers announced that because of news of the release of a number of prisoners there would be a return to work the following day. About 5,000 people took part in a subsequent parade.[43]

Coverage of the dispute varied dramatically according to the politics of the press. Liverpool newspapers refused to carry strike notices while the Unionist press described the stoppage as an 'ignominious failure' and 'a very partial

36 Sam Davies, 'A stormy political career: P.J. Kelly and Irish nationalist and labour politics in Liverpool, 1891–1936', *Transactions of the Historic Society of Lancashire and Cheshire*, 148 (1999), 147–89. 37 *Evening Herald*, 27 Apr. 1920. 38 *Belfast Newsletter*, 28 Apr. 1920. 39 *Cork Examiner*, 1 May 1920. 40 *Belfast Newsletter*, 30 Apr. 1920. 41 *Freeman's Journal* and *Belfast Newsletter*, 29 Apr. 1920. 42 Belchem, 'Hub and diaspora', p. 26. 43 Ibid., 4 May 1920.

affair' with 'little inconvenience caused.' The *Belfast Newsletter* claimed that despite pickets and speeches from the 'dinner-hour agitators' 80 per cent of the men remained in work and that 'there was no lack of substitutes for the Irishmen who struck.' But it admitted that the 'work of unloading the Irish steamers was, however, held up.'[44] The *Freeman's Journal* in contrast described how 'despite the miserable weather, throngs of Irishwomen picketed the dock gates (and) induced hundreds to strike. Carrying Sinn Fein colours along the line of docks, they brought out many more. Some success was also achieved at Birkenhead.'[45] That paper claimed that despite the 'continued assurances of newspapers that the Irish dock strike has dismally failed … on Saturday, owing to a lack of labour, the British and Irish and Tedcastle Line, the City of Cork Line, the Dundalk and Newry and Waterford services were suspended.'[46] Other reports noted that, although 'the strike is mainly confined to the men engaged on the Irish boats', some ocean sailings had been postponed, because 'a fair percentage of the strikers are coalheavers.'[47]

Strike rallies heard 'bitter attacks' on Sexton, who Harry Hart of the NUDL executive claimed, 'sat coldly in the House of Commons while his countrymen were dying in prison.'[48] Sexton by contrast explained:

> our Union is composed of a very mixed political crowd … We have English members who have no views on the Irish question, and some whose views are very pronounced on one side or the other … probably Liverpool dockers are half Sinn Feiners and half the other way of thinking, but as a union we can do nothing at all.[49]

At a Labour meeting at St Helen's, Sexton was heckled as a 'liar' and a 'traitor' but responded by asking 'why Irishmen did not call out their own trade unions … he refused to bow his knee to a lot of body snatchers, who wanted him to sacrifice his manhood and conscience to satisfy their inclination.'[50] Sexton's views were not shared by all his members. Patrick O'Farrell, an NUDL activist from Bootle, warned Sexton and 'so called Labour leaders in England, not to make scarecrows in the hope that they would justify their own inactivity.'[51] Indeed the labour press in Ireland had also seen potential in the movement, suggesting that during the April general strike,

44 *Belfast Newsletter*, 30 Apr. 1920.   **45** *Freeman's Journal*, 1 May 1920.   **46** Ibid., 3 May 1920.
47 *Cork Examiner*, 1 May 1920.   **48** *Freeman's Journal*, 3 May 1920.   **49** Ibid., 29 Apr. 1920.
50 *Derry Journal*, 3 May 1920.   **51** *Watchword of Labour*, 19 June 1920.

Liverpool dockers were becoming restless; certain branches of railwaymen were making ominous sounds. Our friends of the Irish Labour groups on the Tyne and Clyde began to move. Another day and who knows what might have happened? ... it may be that the historian will name our iron-hearted, fool-headed obstinacy as the prime factor in forcing on the British Revolution![52]

Republicans remembered the strike as a great success. Manchester activist Gilbert Lynch recounted that 'we were very successful in Liverpool and practically held up the port. For nearly a week it was at a standstill.'[53] Hugh Early noted that 'we got about 5,000 dockers out on strike and held up the Cross Channel services.'[54] Michael O'Leary recounted:

we decided to call an unofficial strike at the docks, (the) dock labourers and the crews of the cross-Channel boats – B&I, Cork, Limerick, Dundalk and Newry – came out to a man; and several of the Transatlantic ships, if not actually tied up, had their personnel very much reduced. In the case of the coal-heavers, every man came out with the exception of eight. The number employed was 5,024 and out of that number 5,016 came out on strike, completely crippling the movement of all ships in the Port of Liverpool. Our pickets (Volunteers) were at work at each dock, and the docks only looked a shadow of what they once were.[55]

But these memoirs are partial. In the strike's aftermath a number of activists were dismissed including Kit McQuale, a stevedore at B&I, and James McNance, who was sacked from his position in a warehouse.[56]

Notably absent from republican accounts was any reaction by other workers to the strike, a factor Sexton feared would produce violence. Liverpool's politics was sharply divided along religious lines, the city containing a 'strong Orange tendency ... unmatched anywhere in Britain.' This was part of the city's 'civic culture in ways that even Glasgow did not match ... Orangemen contributed much to the electoral dominance of Conservatism in Liverpool.'[57] Indeed during June 1909 the city had seen 'sectarian civil war' after a Protestant counter demonstration to a Catholic procession near Scotland Road. In the aftermath *The Times* bemoaned how,

52 Ibid., 24 Apr. 1920. 53 Gilbert Lynch, MSP34REF41334. 54 Hugh Early, MSP34REF746. 55 O'Leary, BMHWS 0797. 56 Ibid. James McNance MSP34REF49899. 57 John Belchem and Donald MacRaild, 'Cosmopolitan Liverpool' in Belchem (ed.), *Liverpool 800*, p. 328.

the Roman Catholics have driven the Protestants from the Scotland Road area; the Protestants have swept Netherfield Road clean of Roman Catholics. It is almost incredible in regard to a great English City, but these clearances are affected by actual violence.[58]

While a great transport strike of 1911 created hope that sectarian division among the Liverpool working class might be overcome, the following year 250,000 took part in a giant anti-Home Rule rally in the city.[59] Yet O'Leary could assert years later that 'our parades and meetings went ahead without any interference from the police or the Orangemen. In fact, during my three years' experience in Liverpool I never witnessed or heard of an Orange demonstration.'[60] But just prior to the 1920 strike, some 5,000 people were reported to have attended a demonstration in Sheil Park, organized by a body calling itself the 'Loyal British Patriotic Labour party'. Security sources thought the demonstration, which they described as the 'first real attempt to combat Sinn Fein-Bolshevik propaganda', was a great success. A resolution was passed attacking the Labour Party for its perceived sympathy for 'crime and disorder and the brutal murder of police and soldiers and law-abiding persons in Ireland.'[61] Such Loyalist sentiment was clearly a factor in how the strike call was received by those outside the Irish community. Indeed British Intelligence had already noted a 'growing hostility against Irishmen on the part of British Labour' and, significantly, that in Liverpool 'the feeling of Englishmen against Irishmen (is) growing: they allege that Irishmen can always get a job whereas they are dismissed.'[62]

The security services concluded that the dispute actually offered a 'severe check to the local Irish extremists.' In a detailed analysis they suggested that 'the feeling among non-Irish men in the port is raised to fever heat and there has been considerable difficulty in avoiding a clash.' Posters in support of the strike had been torn down or covered with anti-Irish slogans. Ex-servicemen painted 'Strike and lose your pay for the Irish. They won the War', and 'Another injustice to Ireland – Conscription they didn't get' on dockside walls. Intelligence sources reported that a trade union activist had stated that 'it's the Irish roughs that's the trouble here, they want the chance to make a row and pinch something'. Another dock worker was alleged to have asserted that if the authorities tried to ship arms 'by the Irish Companies' boats they will get trouble as they are manned by the Irish' but if munitions were transported

58 Roberts, *Liverpool sectarianism,* pp 27, 54.   59 Daniel Jackson, *Popular opposition to Home Rule in Edwardian Britain* (Liverpool, 2009), pp 101–31.   60 O'Leary, BMHWS 0797.   61 Report on revolutionary organizations in the United Kingdom, 20 May 1920, in CAB 24_106_29, National Archives United Kingdom (NAUK).   62 Report on revolutionary organizations in the United

'from our end of the North docks we'll ship them all that's wanted to blow hell out of the lot of them.' The Secret Service believed that P.J. Kelly had overplayed his hand by attempting to by-pass the local unions. At one stage Kelly had provocatively asked 'who was responsible for the crimes and atrocities committed in Ireland? ... the men who did these things were the sons and brothers of British trade unionists.'[63] Now, Liverpool Trades Council, which had supposedly given the Irish unions a 'half promise' that during another general strike in Ireland they would take sympathetic action, perceived the stoppage as an attack on them.[64] British Intelligence was satisfied that the prospect of solidarity action by Liverpool workers was now 'remote'. While a significant example of working-class mobilization involving republicans, such strikes also complicated the IRA's smuggling. Weapons or communications could not be moved while ships lay idle. In May 1919 Stevie Lanigan had complained of a wave of industrial action, that 'these damned strikes are going to upset all our arrangements'.[65] Yet republicans would be involved in similar action again during 1920, in a dispute that garnered international attention.

New York

New York was the centre of Irish America, the Irish making up 22 per cent of the population of the city in 1900.[66] Indeed in that period 'the Irish ruled New York ... they controlled its government and politics, dominated construction and building, moved into the professions and managerial classes, and benefitted, perhaps disproportionately, from the general prosperity of the times.'[67] Nevertheless there remained a large Irish working class, many of them poor, a significant number of whom were employed on docks in Manhattan and Brooklyn. That waterfront was 'a cauldron of competing ethnic and racial groups' and at the top were Irish longshoremen, whose 'main power base was along the west side of Manhattan where Irish-Americans controlled the docks and the representative trade union'. Irish cohesion was maintained by 'keeping other ethnic and racial groups out of their areas of operation.'[68] Indeed despite residing in one of the 'most cosmopolitan cities in the world, Irish-Americans could exhibit strikingly parochial worldviews ... Irish longshoremen seemed to cling desperately to the inward-looking slum neighbourhoods they had

Kingdom, 8 Apr. 1920 in CAB 24_103_39, NAUK. **63** Davies, 'A stormy political career', p. 169. **64** Report, 20 May 1920, CAB 24_106_29 ibid. **65** S. Lanigan to M. Collins, 22 May 1919 in Mulcahy Papers, UCDA P7/A/2. **66** Lawrence J. McCaffrey, 'Looking forward and looking back' in Ronald H. Bayor & Timothy J. Meagher (eds), *The New York Irish* (Baltimore, 1996), p. 217. **67** Chris McNickle, 'When New York was Irish, and after' in Bayor and Meagher (eds), *New York Irish*, pp 337–8. **68** Colin J. Davis, '"Shape or fight?": New York's black longshoremen, 1945–1961',

created for themselves on Manhattan's West Side' in areas such as Chelsea and Hell's Kitchen.[69]

But as the 'seat of an emergent economic empire' with 'material and capital connections around the world' New York was also 'fertile ground for international protest movement (and) for the connections forged between anti-colonialisms.' Irish republicans could not afford to be parochial. Manhattan was never 'just the stronghold of the Irish, it was also the home of socialism, communism and Zionism.'[70] Harry Boland was among the Irish sponsors of the League of Oppressed Peoples, launched in late 1919, which linked the Irish cause with those of India, Egypt, Persia, Korea, Russia and China and with Jews facing persecution in Europe.[71] Some of this interaction was also apparent in May 1920 when the Central Federated Union of New York held an event in support of Ireland. The audience was 'composed largely of laboring men and women not only of Irish descent, but of every race … Italians, Irish, Jews, Americans and a sprinkling of Hindus.' The meeting decided to appoint a group 'composed' largely of representative seamen and longshoremen' to direct Irish solidarity work. Among those involved were Joseph Ryan of the International Longshoremen's Association; Captain William A. Maher of the Association of Masters, Mates and Pilots; Thomas B. Heely of the Marine Engineers and Thomas Rock of the Pavery and Hammers Union.[72] Some of this organization would be apparent three months later.

In late August dock workers and seamen responded to pickets by female Irish activists by walking off on several piers on the west side of Manhattan. This 'Irish Patriotic Strike' had complicated origins.[73] The initial pickets were associated with the American Women Pickets for the Enforcement of America's War Aims, a group which included activists from diverse backgrounds. At various stages the IRB, the Friends of Irish Freedom (FOIF), the Irish Progressive League (IPL) and Marcus Garvey's Universal Negro Improvement Association (UNIA) would be involved. The roots of the strike lay in protests during late July. Then a crowd of up to 15,000, including Éamon de Valera, had gathered at Pier 60 in Chelsea to see off the pro-

International Journal of Labor and Working Class History, 62 (Fall 2002), 143–63.   **69** James R. Barret & David Roediger, 'The Irish and the "Americanization" of the "new immigrants" in the streets and churches of the urban United States, 1900–1930', *Journal of American Ethnic History*, 24:4 (Summer 2005), 3–33.   **70** Mathew Pratt Guterl, 'The new race consciousness: race, nation and empire in American culture, 1910–1925', *Journal of World History*, 10:2 (Fall 1999), 307–32.   **71** *Irish Press* (Philadelphia), 8 Nov. 1919.   **72** *Irish World* (New York), 29 May 1920.   **73** For various accounts see Joe Doyle, 'Striking for Ireland on the New York docks' in Bayor and Meagher (eds), *New York Irish*, pp 337–73; Bruce Nelson, *Irish nationalists and the making of the Irish race* (Princeton, 2012), pp 226–241; David Brundage, *Irish nationalists in America: the politics of exile, 1798–1998* (Oxford, 2016),

republican Archbishop Daniel Mannix of Melbourne, who was intending to travel to Ireland. There were rumours that some of the English seamen on the *Baltic* would refuse to allow Mannix sail. According to one report 'militant West street longshoremen' heard about this. They held 'an impromptu meeting and sent a delegate to the cooks and stewards of the *Baltic*' warning them that the longshoremen would 'be waiting for them outside the pier for unspecified reasons if they walked out.' The British sailors sent back a 'hasty reply' claiming that they were merely 'spoofing'. A fracas erupted when Joseph Shaw, a coal merchant from Leeds, was set upon after allegedly insulting Mannix. Shaw reportedly would 'have been torn limb from limb but for intervention of the Archbishop'.[74] But though he was allowed sail, Mannix did not reach Ireland, being taken into custody by the Royal Navy off Cornwall.

News of this reached New York along with reports of Terence MacSwiney's hunger strike. Women pickets had been protesting about MacSwiney at the British Consulate but hearing the *Baltic* was due to return transferred their protest to the docks. Leaflets were distributed calling on 'longshoremen, stokers, oilers, seamen, trimmers' and 'every Red-Blooded Workingman' to boycott British shipping.[75] In one vivid account the 'pickets then started to tie up the work of every other British ship in the port, and a scene of the wildest confusion ensued. Hundreds of excited men and women swept through the streets on to the sea front, gathering recruits as they dashed up from one pier to another, swarming up the gangways and shouting: "All off"'. When the *Baltic* docked it was 'greeted by women pickets carrying banners denouncing England's attitude towards Ireland, and taunting the British sailors with cowardice for allowing passengers to be removed from their decks.'[76] Up to 130 stokers and firemen were reported to have left the ship, stating that 'they will not return until Archbishop Mannix is allowed freedom of movement.' Altogether 2,000 longshoremen were reported to have left the Chelsea Pier.[77] A statement from the strikers pledged 'solidarity in the dock strike against British ships until Lord Mayor MacSwiney and his companions are released, and Dr Mannix free.' The men also appealed to 'our brothers in every port where British ships enter to refuse to unload them. We particularly call on Labour in Great Britain, Canada, and Australia to help in this fight for justice and civilization.'[78] Some 3,000 dock workers also took action in Brooklyn and heard speakers assert 'that Labour in ports throughout the world would soon combine to humble Great Britain, and compel her to recognize the Irish Republic'. Telegrams of support were read from 'Boston,

pp 156–61. **74** *Irish World*, 7 Aug. 1920. **75** 'Mass meeting', copies in Peter Golden Papers, National Library of Ireland (NLI) MS 13,141. **76** *Freeman's Journal*, 28 Aug. 1920. **77** *Belfast Newsletter*, 28 Aug. 1920. **78** *Irish Independent*, 4 Sept. 1920.

Philadelphia, Baltimore, New Orleans ... pledging the support of the local Waterfront Unions for the movement.'[79] The stoppage gained press coverage across the United States, one report describing it as the 'first purely political strike of workingmen' in the country's history.[80] A mass meeting in support of MacSwiney was held at Manhattan's Lexington Theatre. A delegation of strikers arrived during a speech by de Valera and were invited onto the stage where labour lawyer Frank P. Walsh lauded them as the 'people's guarantors of the Freedom of the Seas.' He also asserted that 'these men ... symbolize the resistless force of labor in the world ... the real power that comes from the stokers' holes and fires.'[81] Several other rallies in New York heard claims that dockers across America would join the strike. There were reports of a stoppage at San Francisco, which 'held up British shipping for several days.'[82] In Boston, where women pickets also called out longshoremen, 'fists flew violently during a battle in Marginal Street' though large numbers were reported not to have turned up for work. A notable feature of the strike had been the willingness of some non-Irish workers to support it. Walsh had told the Lexington rally that many of the strikers 'were not men through whose veins coursed the same blood that rushes through ours tonight.'[83] Other reports also stressed that 'Negroes went out, Italians and Slavs went out, Englishmen went out, every race was represented in the protest'.[84] Many accounts of the first day of the strike reported that 'two hundred and fifty negros unloading a Cunard liner have also struck.'[85] The participation of African American and Italian workers was notable given the long history of rivalry between these groups and the Irish. But from an early stage black workers were also being used as strike breakers. Special appeals were made to them with leaflets declaring 'Brothers if you scab Ireland, you scab the Negro Race' and 'Ireland's Fight is the Negro's Fight. Up Liberty! Down Slavery!'[86] Nevertheless at least some black workers continued to cross picket lines, despite efforts by supporters of the strike among the African American community. Newspapers reported how 'a novel feature ... was the presence of numerous negresses, who endeavoured to lure the negro longshoremen away from work. Order is being maintained on the piers, but elsewhere numerous encounters between blacks and whites over negroes replacing white longshoremen, have taken place.'[87] The strike was unofficial. One republican account noted how

79 *Evening Herald*, 4 Sept. 1920. 80 Quoted in *The Sinn Féiner* (New York), 4 Sept. 1920. 81 *Irish World*, 4 Sept. 1920. 82 *Irish Independent*, 31 Aug. 1920. 83 *Irish World*, 4 Sept. 1920. 84 *The Sinn Féiner*, 4 Sept. 1920. 85 *Irish Times*, 30 Aug. 1920. 86 'Handbill for colored Longshoremen' in Peter Golden Papers. 87 *Irish Times*, 13 Sept. 1920.

Union leaders, Ryan and Reilly, acted cautiously and held to their contracts. They did not denounce the strike but declared it without the union's authority, which made the affair all the more serious, since it proved that the cause was greater than the power of the unions.[88]

But one report suggested that a union official had initially asserted that the 'men will be back to work this morning, a good night's sleep will cause them to forget all about Ireland.' Some news reports claimed in fact that the Longshoremen's Union had 'denounced' the action early on. Despite his presence at Irish events earlier in the year, union leader Joseph Ryan seems not to have been sympathetic to the strike. Indeed one veteran suggested in later years that Ryan led second-generation Irish Americans across picket lines that Irish-born men were honouring.[89] Ryan was a product of a Chelsea upbringing who in his own words 'strayed into the labor business.' His union was notable for its lack of militancy and tolerance of the 'shape-up' system, a form of casual hiring which was often humiliating as men competed for the day's work.[90] But Ryan was not the only official charged with lack of enthusiasm. One Boston longshoreman claimed that though,

> we have all the Irish dockers of Boston on strike (and) we have also brought out Swedes, and Englishmen, and Negroes … Irish-American politicians and Irish-American Labour fakirs are fighting us. A Labour fakir of the Longshoremen's Union named Dempsey (a good German name!) is trying to secure Negroes to scab the job on the striking Irish dockers who are out in protest against England's conduct in Ireland.[91]

If the International Longshoremen's Association were not officially involved in the strike then who was? James McGee of the Ship Engineers would later claim that it was he who 'organized the strike' by taking firemen off the British ships, which 'crippled them for days'. McGee also asserted that 'the men I took off I housed in New York (and) paid for them with money (from) the public meeting held for that purpose.' But Fr Timothy Shanley, a cleric well connected to republican circles, recounted how McGee and Boland had approached the Friends of Irish Freedom and obtained $15,000 from their 'Victory Fund' to pay the New York strikers, while another $15,000 was sent to the men in Boston in order to 'cripple British shipping' there.[92] Boland was

88 *The Sinn Féiner*, 4 Sept. 1920. **89** *New York Times*, 28–9 Aug. 1920; Doyle, 'Striking for Ireland', pp 366, 665. **90** Bruce Nelson, *Divided we stand: American workers and the struggle for Black equality* (Princeton, 2001), pp 54–7. **91** *Watchword of Labour*, 9 Oct. 1920. **92** Report in de Valera Papers (N/D) UCDA P150/1309.

very pleased with the strike, writing to Cathal Brugha that 'the Mannix incident gave us an opportunity to test the spirit of the men along the New York Docks, and their response was magnificent.' Boland later told Michael Collins that 'the anti-British strike here' was 'a very augury for our work and I have ever in mind your ideas along this line.'[93] The IRB's activists on the liners certainly played a significant role. According to Fr Shanley the protest was originally planned in the case of Archbishop Mannix not being allowed board the *Baltic*. Boland instructed McGee to liaise with a group of oilers and firemen from the ship. They agreed to stop the *Baltic* sailing if Mannix was prevented from boarding it. When the archbishop was allowed travel, Boland and his allies then planned a new protest in response to news of MacSwiney's hunger-strike and the Royal Navy's interception of Mannix.[94]

But the IRB's involvement was subterranean. The public face of the strike had initially been the women pickets. They were a diverse group, the idea of which had initially been conceived to garner positive media attention for the Irish cause.[95] During the strike women such as Gertrude Corless, Kathleen O'Brennan, Dr Gertrude Kelly, Leonora O'Reilly and Helen Golden were associated with the pickets. In reality there were deep disagreements between them all on strategy, even if to outsiders they seemed to be a cohesive force.[96] Significantly the strike took place when Irish American republicanism was in the midst of a major split between supporters of de Valera and John Devoy. In this vacuum the Irish Progressive League (IPL), a small leftist group, was able to punch well above its relative weight. Its contacts meant that socialists such as Norman Thomas and Joseph Cannon were prominent speakers at events in support of the stoppage.[97] Not surprisingly, who had actually called the strike, and on whose authority, became a bone of contention among the rival Irish factions. One striker later claimed that the men had not received any money from Irish societies, while others asserted that a protest rather than a strike had been the intention of activists. There were claims that longshoremen had been told that the Friends of Irish Freedom would pay them $50 a week if they struck. Dr Gertrude Kelly was also accused of 'seeking the limelight by appointing herself treasurer of a fund which she had started without authority from anybody.'[98] Some of these allegations reflected the

---

93 Harry Boland to Cathal Brugha, 11 Aug. 1920 in de Valera Papers, UCDA P150/1128; Boland to M. Collins, 22 Sept. 1920, ibid., P150/1125. 94 Fr Timothy Shanley, BMHWS 0913. 95 Kelly Anne Reynolds, 'Irish nationalist, progressive activist or British spy? A portrait of William J.M.A. Maloney' (MA, New York University, May 2019), pp 49–51. 96 Catherine M. Burns, 'Kathleen O'Brennan and American identity in the transatlantic Irish Republican movement' in David T. Gleeson (ed.), *The Irish in the Atlantic world* (South Carolina, 2010), pp 176–94. 97 Material relating to the strike in Peter Golden Papers. 98 *Gaelic American*, 2 Oct. 1920.

bitterness of Devoy's supporters at being undercut by Boland, but they also illustrated the complex range of actors involved.

The Irish Progressive League's connections were also significant for the involvement of non-Irish workers in the strike. A leaflet in Italian asserting 'Trouble with British Ships ... Everybody keep away, Don't Be Scabs!' had been distributed early on.[99] One of the Irish pickets, Sidney Gifford, later claimed that this was 'largely the work' of the Italian anarchist Carlo Tresca, who had connections with Irish American leftists like Elizabeth Gurley-Flynn.[100] Gifford recounted how

> I had a placard which read ... 'Hear the call of the blood and refuse to work on British ships'. I realized that the call of the blood was addressed to Greeks, Italians, Lascars, etc., and when they saw a young woman with a placard they came up to enquire what the strike was about. My efforts to translate 'Hear the call of the blood' into Italian were funny, but I found one word which they all seemed to know was 'tyranny-Irlanda', and smiling and nodding, they would all walk away.[101]

Even more complicated was the role of African American workers. The left-wing black journal *The Messenger* had reported that some 250 black workers had joined the strike and, asserting 'Long love the solidarity of labor! Only labor can free Ireland!', expressed the hope that 'later on, Negroes will be having their own Irish brothers strike for Negro freedom.'[102] Here Marcus Garvey's influence was significant. Preachers allied to Garvey's movement urged black workers to strike and his *Negro World* reported positively on the action, while important discussions about the strike took place at his Harlem HQ.[103] But the use of black strike-breakers had led to violence in New York as well as Boston where on 2 September there were clashes between 1,000 white strikers and 500 recently hired black longshoremen.[104] Indeed by September Irish newspapers carried reports that 'Negroes have replaced the Irish longshoremen who deserted from the White Star piers a fortnight ago as a protest against the treatment of Cardinal Mannix and Mr MacSwiney.'[105] Some of those who crossed the picket lines explained their decision in talks facilitated by Garvey's organization. Some 400 black dockers attended a

99 Copy in Peter Golden Papers, ibid.   **100** Niall Whelehan, 'Sacco and Vanzetti, Mary Donovan and transatlantic radicalism in the 1920s', *Irish Historical Studies*, 44:165 (2020), 131–46. **101** Sidney Gifford, BMHWS WS909.   **102** Arnold Shankman, 'Black on green: Afro-American editors on Irish independence, 1840–1921', *Phylon*, 41:3 (1980), 284–99.   **103** Robert A. Hill (ed.), *The Marcus Garvey and Universal Negro Improvement Association Papers*, vol. 11, Sept. 1920–Aug. 1921 (Berkeley, 1984), pp 12–13.   **104** *New York Times*, 3, 4 Sept. 1920.   **105** *Nenagh News*,

meeting at Harlem's Liberty Hall and asserted that while willing to 'participate with the Irishmen in the strike for Liberty by virtue of it being a Common Cause akin to that of the Aethopian people', due to 'apathetical treatment extended to them in normal times on various piers on which they claim wages were highest, they desire that some proper arrangements be made to ameliorate their period of unemployment and to guarantee them a con-fraternal consideration with the Irish Workers in the Cause of Liberty which they conjointly are striving to attain.' Black longshoremen were normally effectively restricted to just one Manhattan pier. The strike had given them the opportunity to work Pier 60, formally the preserve of the Irish. Garvey told Irish activists that he 'did not take into consideration small matters arising from color predjudicism [sic], since Liberty was common to all mankind ... but allowance had to be made to meet the shortcomings of narrow-minded individuals of both parties concerned.' In contrast one of Garvey's allies Adrian Johnson told a group from the Women's Pickets that if 'the Irish Party would take into greater consideration the sentiment and the opportunities of the Colored Longshoremen', particularly with regard to their exclusion from Pier 60, 'it would automatically convert the Colored Longshoremen into the rank of the Irish Workers as a Political and Economical Ally.'[106] However the IPL's Helen Golden asserted that while Garvey's UNIA had 'inaugurated a history-making movement' towards the 'illimination [sic] of all race prejudice' if 'the Colored Longshoremen persist in breaking this Patriotic strike ... the hope of a better understanding of the so-called race question is not happy.'[107] Both Garvey and Golden, for differing reasons, underestimated the depth of resentment among the black workers and why supporting the strike was such a difficult issue for them. The legacy of the dispute was inconclusive, though co-operation between some Irish and black activists continued, with a branch of the American Association for the Recognition of the Irish Republic, including both 'Colored and white residents', established in Harlem during 1921.[108] As for the strike itself, the British press were reporting that it had effectively ended by early September, and that as the *Baltic* sailed a 'party of the Archbishop's sympathizers, mostly women', accompanied it down the harbour in a tugboat, but 'little attention was paid to them'.[109] Joseph Ryan's lukewarm attitude to the strike did not preclude from him leading an honour guard of longshoremen to welcome Muriel MacSwiney to New York in November 1920.[110]

11 Sept. 1920; *Limerick Leader*, 13 Sept. 1920.   **106** 'Decision of colored Longshoremen engaged in the breaking of the Irish patriotic strike' and notes on Adrian Johnson meeting with Irish women pickets, 13 Sept. 1920 in Peter Golden Papers.   **107** Helen Golden to Mr Welch, 19 Sept. 1920 in Peter Golden Papers.   **108** *Irish World*, 26 Mar. 1921.   **109** *Belfast Newsletter*, 6 Sept. 1920.   **110** *Irish World*, 11 Dec. 1920.

Maritime and diaspora networks were crucial to the republican revolutionary effort between 1919 and 1921. They often involved types of workers who were under-represented in the republican movement within Ireland itself. The period also saw activists engage in industrial action to further their aims. The two most important sites of these struggles, Liverpool and New York, showed the ability of the Irish revolutionary cause to mobilize support among Irish workers and others. But they also illustrated how division within the working class, whether along religious or racial lines, could disrupt these efforts. The stories of those involved in the Irish struggle cannot be separated from the wider global radicalisms of that era.

* * *

Dedicated to Bruce Nelson, 1940–2022.

'The dreaded menace of the Red Flag': the Munster soviets of 1922

DOMINIC HAUGH

The Munster soviets emerged in April 1922 during a prolonged industrial dispute between the Cleeve's group of companies and its workforce that ranged across counties Limerick and Tipperary and into parts of north Cork and west Waterford. In total more than 3,000 workers were employed by Cleeve's in creameries, flour mills and bakeries. The dispute began when the owners of Cleeve's attempted to impose wage cuts of 33⅓ per cent and reduce its workforce by a quarter.

An article in the *Voice of Labour* indicated that the Munster soviets encompassed 'a network covering more than one hundred depots, from small auxiliaries to completely equipped factories'.[1] Furthermore, in conjunction with the occupation of the Cleeve's plants, other workplace soviets took place throughout Munster, as well as land soviets, and these need to be recognized as being part of the general class conflict that encompassed the Cleeve's soviets. O'Connor suggested that the occupations took place with 'serious revolutionary intent'.[2] Many of these soviets lasted for more than three months, with some only succumbing to suppression by either the Free State army or the Anti-Treaty IRA. This chapter will review these workplace soviets, looking at their emergence and development and placing them in the wider context of working-class struggle during the Irish Revolution. The chapter will also consider the class nature and character of this 'serious revolutionary intent', as well as reviewing the response from the nationalist movement, farmers' organizations and from the trade union leadership and the Communist Party.

In Limerick the food processing industry was central to economic activity, with Cleeve's Brothers playing a dominant role in the economic life of the region. Cleeve's owned the Condensed Milk Company of Ireland, operated a processing plant in Lansdowne, on the western bank of the River Shannon, and had over 100 creamery and creamery-related premises operating in Limerick, Cork, Tipperary and Waterford. Thomas Cleeve and his four brothers also owned the J.P. Evans Engineering Company, which was engaged

---

1 *Voice of Labour*, 27 May 1922.   2 Emmet O'Connor, *A labour history of Ireland, 1824–1960* (Dublin, 1992), p. 112.

in dairy engineering and the supply of agricultural machinery, as well as several other businesses. By the end of the First World War, Cleeve's were employing more than 3,000 workers and processing the produce of 5,000 farmers.[3]

The Bottom Dog, a workers' paper produced in Limerick during 1917–18 under the editorship of Bakers' Union activist Ben Dineen, reported that munitions workers at J.P. Evans joined the Irish Transport and General Workers' Union (ITGWU) in late October 1917.[4] Women workers at the Cleeve's plant in Lansdowne joined shortly afterwards along with women workers in the Shannon Laundry.[5] A major advance was secured in July 1918 when the owners of Cleeve's agreed to a closed shop and to book its additional staff through the ITGWU.[6] The workers in the Lansdowne plant were to play a key role in the Limerick soviet less than a year later.

The Limerick soviet, April 1919

When the Limerick soviet emerged in April 1919 members of the ITGWU, and in particular ITGWU members at the Cleeve's-owned Condensed Milk Factory at Lansdowne on the northside of Limerick, played a prominent role. The 600-strong workforce, largely women workers, were the first workers in Limerick to stage strike action against the imposition of martial law by the British authorities. It was their actions that forced Limerick Trades Council to act and call a general strike in the city. The soviet committee established groups of flying pickets, 'red-badged guards', who wore a red armband and enforced the directives of the committee.[7] The Cleeve's workers at Lansdowne played a prominent role in the Red Guards and were largely responsible for the commandeering and distribution of food supplies throughout the city.[8] Conflict did arise between the ITGWU members and the leadership of Limerick Trades Council towards the end of the Limerick soviet and many ITGWU members, including a significant number of those employed by the Cleeve's group, initially rejected the decision by the Trades Council to call off the general strike.[9]

However, the Limerick soviet was to provide a template for future workplace soviets with many of the tactics adopted in Limerick being used to

3 David Lee, 'The Munster soviets and the fall of the house of Cleeve' in David Lee and Debbie Jacobs (eds), *Made in Limerick, history of industries, trade and commerce, Vol. 1* (Limerick, 2003), pp 297–8; *Irish Independent*, 15 May 1922. **4** *The Bottom Dog*, 3 Nov. 1917. Ben Dineen was a victim of the Spanish Flu pandemic and *The Bottom Dog* ceased publication after his death in November 1918. **5** *The Bottom Dog*, 3 Nov. 1917; *Limerick Leader*, 10 Dec. 1917. **6** *Voice of Labour*, 6 July 1918. **7** Ruth Russell, *What's the matter with Ireland* (New York, 1920), p. 135. **8** Dominic Haugh, *Limerick soviet 1919, the revolt of the Bottom Dog* (Shannon, 2019), p. 97. **9** Haugh,

significant effect in other occupied workplaces and the wider towns and villages where the workplaces were located. Furthermore, the failure of the leadership of the Irish Labour Party and Trade Union Congress (ILP&TUC) to act in support of the Limerick soviet by calling a nationwide general strike seems to have prompted the decision by Seán Dowling and others to launch the Revolutionary Socialist Party (RSP) in Belfast only days after the ending of the soviet.

Seán Dowling has been described as the 'philosophical begetter' of the Limerick soviet and was regarded as the main ideologue of the newly formed RSP.[10] There is evidence that a quarter of the ITGWU's industrial organizers were members of the RSP.[11] Others involved included English Marxist Jack Hedley, who originally hailed from Liverpool and deserted from the British navy in 1918. Hedley played a prominent role in workers' struggles in Belfast, being imprisoned on several occasions,[12] before becoming a key figure in the workplace soviets from 1920 onwards.[13] The RSP appears to have gained a base among workers in Belfast. A week before the Belfast pogrom in 1920 the RSP held a meeting in a labour hall in north Belfast attended by 500 workers.[14]

Munster Council of Action 1919

Within two weeks of the ending of the Limerick soviet a major strike broke out among the workers of the Cleeve's group, involving the Condensed Milk Company in Limerick as well as Cleeve's plants in Clonmel, Tipperary and Mallow. Agreement was quickly reached in Limerick on a wage of 45s. for a 48-hour week. The ITGWU demanded that the Limerick agreement be extended to all plants.[15] Clonmel emerged as the centre of the strike-wave. All

Limerick soviet 1919, p. 113.   **10** Ibid., p. 22. Seán Dowling was an industrial organizer for the ITGWU and played a significant role in the industrial battles and workplace soviets during the revolutionary period in Ireland. For more information see Dominic Haugh, 'Seán Dowling', in Emmet O'Connor and John Cunningham (eds), *Studies in Irish radical leadership: lives on the left*, (Manchester, 2016), pp 148–62.   **11** Ibid., p. 107.   **12** Jack Hedley was imprisoned in May 1919 for 'sedition' after organizing a series of socialist meetings in Belfast. See Charlie McGuire, '"They'll never understand why I'm here": British Marxism and the Irish Revolution, 1916–1923', *Contemporary British History*, 32:2 (2018), 154.   **13** Hedley began using the pseudonym Sean O'Hagan while in Belfast. He participated in the Belfast engineering strike in February 1919 and was one of the 'Red Bolsheviks' who led the Mayday protests in the city in May 1919. He was among the prisoners held in Mountjoy and released following the general strike in April 1920. Hedley was sentenced to six months hard labour in mid-1921 for making seditious speeches to sailors in Portsmouth. The sentence was handed down by a secret court under the Provision of Emergency Powers legislation. Hedley later joined the Communist Party and fought with the International Brigades during the Spanish Civil War.   **14** *Belfast Weekly Telegraph*, 5 July 1920.   **15** *Limerick*

labourers, clerks, foremen, engineers, automobile drivers and women workers in Clonmel were on strike, a total of 210 workers, as well as those in the thirty-five auxiliary creameries that operated under the management of the Clonmel plant. Workers at Kilmallock, Knocklong, Bruree, Askeaton and their auxiliary creameries joined the strike. A Workers' Council of Action was formed with representatives from the Cleeve's workplaces in the region.[16]

The company adopted a strategy of divide and rule. They began negotiations with individual workplaces and the first crack in the united front appeared when workers in Mallow accepted a reduced offer from the company.[17] Over subsequent days workers in other centres accepted a similar offer of 42*s.* for a 54-hour week and ended their strike, leaving the workforce at Knocklong Creamery and its twelve auxiliary creameries to fight alone for a further seven weeks.[18] During the course of the strike at Knocklong the dispute became increasingly more confrontational with acts of sabotage being committed by striking workers.[19] The inability to maintain a united front through the Council of Action and the isolation of the workers at Knocklong was a valuable lesson for the activists within the ITGWU and led to their determination to ensure that there was not a repeat during the Munster soviets three years later.

As the ITGWU advanced through 1919 and into 1920, membership of the union grew rapidly, rising to 120,000 by 1920. The syndicalist approach of the ITGWU led to widespread militant action and the winning of substantial gains for members of the union. As these gains were solidified a growing class consciousness among the working class was demonstrated during the two-day general strike that took place in April 1920.

The general strike of April 1920

A two-day nationwide general strike began on 13 April 1920 to secure the release of republican prisoners. The *Watchword of Labour* claimed that the prisoners were for 'the greater part our fellow workers and comrades in our trade unions'.[20] ITGWU activists were to the fore in organizing the strike. Workers' councils were established in cities, towns and villages throughout the country with red flags flying over commandeered town halls. Businesses were forced to close, food supplies were taken under the control of the workers'

Leader, 12 May 1919. **16** Ibid. **17** Ibid. **18** Ibid., 14 May 1919; D.R. O'Connor Lysaght, 'The Munster soviet creameries', *Irish History Workshop: Saotharlann Staire Eireann*, 1 (Dublin, 1981), 41. **19** Emmet O'Connor, 'Active sabotage in industrial conflict, 1917–1923', *Irish Economic and Social History*, 12 (1985), 59. **20** *Watchword of Labour*, 17 Apr. 1920.

councils, roads were blockaded, and transport only permitted with the permission of the workers. Flying pickets patrolled the streets in every location ensuring the implementation of decrees from the workers' councils.[21] An estimated 340,000 workers participated in the general strike.[22] In the face of the organizational strength exercised by the Irish labour movement, Sinn Féin and the IRA were forced to acquiesce to the control of the country by the labour movement. To cut across ongoing developments, the British authorities ordered the release of the prisoners. The threat posed by the establishment of workers' councils during the general strike was clearly expressed by the *Irish Times* which commented, 'A continuation of the fight which ended yesterday might have witnessed the establishment of Soviets of workmen in all parts of Ireland'.[23] As had been the case during the Limerick soviet in 1919, the Cleeve's workers played a prominent role in organizing the local soviets that were established during the general strike. In each area in Limerick, Tipperary and north Cork, where the Cleeve's workers were the backbone of local ITGWU branches, widespread control was exercised by the local workers' council. The *Voice of Labour* outlined that 'As in Charleville, so too in Ballyhea, Buttevant, Ballyagran, Bruree, Ballylanders, Galbally, Kilfinane, Bruff and Kilmallock, everywhere in fact where a Transport Union branch is found', workers' councils were established to organize the strike. The report described the situation in Kilmallock where 'traffic was completely suspended, the red-flaggers manned the castle entrances, tree-trunks and carts were used to compel compliance with the order to halt ... stock of all foodstuffs was taken by a special committee'. The town hall was commandeered for the issuing of permits and 'one was struck by the recognition of the Soviet system'. The article noted that a creamery clerk was 'distributing butter tickets'.[24]

O'Connor asserted that the general strike uncovered the social revolutionary dynamic bubbling at the base of the labour movement.[25] It is clear that the general strike demonstrated the power of the movement and the impotence of the British administration when labour moved into action on such a scale. The social revolutionary dynamic was demonstrated through 1920 with a major escalation in land seizures by landless labourers throughout the country.

---

21 Desmond Greaves indicates that a 'picket' of 'red guards' shut down shops in Naas, but he doesn't reference the source of this quote. See C. Desmond Greaves, *The Irish Transport and General Workers' Union: the formative years, 1909–1923* (Dublin, 1982), p. 266. A report from Tralee indicated that the workers formed a 'Citizen Guard' to ensure compliance with the general strike. See *The Liberator* (Tralee), 15 Apr. 1920. **22** *Irish Times*, 14 Apr. 1920. **23** Mike Milotte, *Communism in modern Ireland: the pursuit of the workers' republic since 1916* (Dublin, 1984), p. 31. **24** *Watchword and Voice of Labour*, 15 May 1920. **25** Emmet O'Connor, 'War and syndicalism, 1914–1923' in Donal Nevin (ed.), *Trade union century* (Dublin, 1994), p. 62.

Throughout the revolutionary period in Ireland cattle drives and land seizures were a common feature. With the mushrooming of union membership it is probable that union members were involved in these activities. From 1920 onwards there are indications that they took on a revolutionary intent. By mid-1920 the demands from many rural workers changed from the redistribution of land to the 'direct ownership and cultivation by local and national administrative bodies'.[26] At the ILP&TUC annual meeting in August 1920, Congress adopted a resolution from South King's County Trades Council, which represented 1,650 mostly agricultural workers, that called for 'public ownership of all land' and supported 'the exploitation of land by groups of land workers organized in co-operative societies.'[27]

The outbreak of agrarian militancy generated a sense of crisis among the leadership of the nationalist movement in the aftermath of the 1920 general strike. The Dáil Ministry for Home Affairs described developments as 'a grave danger threatening the foundations of the Republic'.[28] In relation to land seizures the Ministry went on to say that the 'mind of the people was being diverted from the struggle for freedom by a class war, and there was every likelihood that this class war might be carried into the ranks of the republican army'.[29] Fitzpatrick asserted that the mighty agitation of rural labourers in 1919–20 struck fear into the hearts of republicans.[30] Bradley stated that there was a growing working-class culture in 1920 that openly identified with the red flag and took inspiration from the Russian Revolution.[31]

The Knocklong soviet

The occupation in Knocklong began on 16 May 1920, and extended to include twelve auxiliary creameries at Ballinamona, Gormanstown, Kilteely, Elton, Knockcarron, Hospital, Knockaney, Ballingaddy, Kilbreedy, Bilboa, Lisnakilla and Ballylanders. In contrast to the Limerick soviet, which was to all intents and purposes a spontaneous affair, the Knocklong soviet was carefully planned.[32] While the occupation was primarily designed to secure an increase in wages and the removal of a hated creamery manager, Riordan, there was also a political dimension to this 'soviet'.[33] Jack Hedley was installed as

26 Emmet O'Connor, *Syndicalism in Ireland, 1917–1923* (Cork, 1988), p. 127.   **27** *Report of the twenty-sixth annual meeting of the Irish Labour Party and Trade Union Congress* (1920), pp 136–7.   **28** Ministry for Home Affairs, *The constructive work of Dáil Éireann, No. 1: The national police and courts of justice* (Dublin, 1921), p. 10.   **29** Ibid., p. 12.   **30** David Fitzpatrick, 'The disappearance of the Irish agricultural labourer, 1841–1912', *Irish Economic and Social History*, 7 (1980), 84.   **31** Dan Bradley, *Farm labourers: Irish struggle, 1900–1976* (Belfast, 1988), p. 55.   **32** O'Connor, *A labour history of Ireland*, p. 112; C. Desmond Greaves, *Liam Mellows and the Irish Revolution* (London, 1971), p. 189.   **33** O'Connor, 'War and syndicalism, 1914–1923', p. 59.

manager at Knocklong. In the office with Hedley was local ITGWU secretary John O'Dwyer, an employee of the creamery. Seán Dowling and Jack McGrath were present to 'watch progress on behalf of the union'. The workers immediately painted the green entrance door red, removed the name-plate and substituted a new one with the inscription, 'The Knocklong Soviet Creamery', and then unfurled a banner with the slogan, 'We Make Butter Not Profit'. The red flag and the tricolour were hoisted over the building. Work continued as normal in the creamery and the auxiliaries. Workers in nearby creameries refused to accept milk diverted by farmers from Knocklong forcing the farmers to supply the soviet. After several approaches from the owners the workers' committee agreed to hand back the property on the basis of a signed agreement guaranteeing the demanded wage increases and the permanent removal of the creamery manager.[34]

The Knocklong soviet enormously increased the prestige of the ITGWU in the region and John O'Dwyer indicated an increased membership, including of women workers, recruited as a result.[35] Seán Dowling and other Marxist industrial organizers within the ITGWU saw their influence rapidly expand. The soviet also encouraged similar occupations in other Cleeve's plants. In July women workers occupied the company's plant in Tipperary town in pursuit of a wage claim.[36] The following October discussions took place over the possible occupation of three creameries at Oola following their threatened closure by the English owners, Alpin & Barrett.[37] Cleeve's purchased these creameries in November resolving the issue.[38] The Knocklong soviet prompted a series of workplace soviets that were established over the following two years.

The Bruree soviet

O'Connor Lysaght described the period from mid-August to mid-September 1921 as 'the month of soviets'.[39] With the Arigna mines soviet, on the Leitrim–Roscommon border, organized by self-described Bolshevik, Geoffrey Coulter, lasting for two months from May 1921, three more significant soviets developed one after another within the space of weeks: the Bruree soviet, the Cork harbour soviet and the Drogheda foundry soviet.[40] Employers were

34 *Watchword of Labour*, 29 May 1920; *Freeman's Journal*, 22 May 1920. **35** Lee, 'The Munster soviets', p. 296; *Freeman's Journal*, 22 May 1920. **36** Lee, 'The Munster soviets', p. 296. **37** *Watchword of Labour*, 30 Oct. 1920. **38** Ibid., 20 Nov. 1920. **39** D.R. O'Connor Lysaght, 'August–September 1921: the month of soviets', *The Plough*, 1:1 (1972), 4–5. **40** Arthur Mitchell, *Labour in Irish politics, 1890–1930* (Dublin, 1974), p. 139; C. Desmond Greaves, *Liam Mellows*, p. 189. Ó Drisceoil suggested that the evidence is lacking to indicate whether Coulter was responsible for leading the 1921 Arigna soviet or a later workplace soviet at Arigna in 1922, or was involved in both.

becoming alarmed at the implications of the class nature of the struggle and were becoming particularly annoyed at the failure of the authorities to suppress law-breaking and violence during strikes.[41] Originally mooted in May 1920 in response to the butter and bacon embargo, the Farmers' Freedom Force (FFF) was intended to provide a 'permanent organized body in each branch … capable of meeting force by force … in the interests of the country and of the farmer'. In response to agricultural labourer strikes the 'FFF should take action as may be required'. The farmers' organizations made clear their priority in political terms, 'the FFF is required as a national bulwark against Labour, Socialism and Bolshevism, irrespective of whatever political developments may take place in the country'.[42] Regularly during 1922 the *Voice of Labour* was to raise the issue of 'White Guards' being organized by farmers to break strikes by agricultural labourers.[43]

The intensity of the war between the IRA and the British military caused a lull in class conflict in the first six months of 1921. However, once the Truce was agreed in June widespread strike action emerged. The economic recession that began in December 1920 was beginning to bite and employers were demanding a reversal of the gains made by workers over the previous four years. Workplace occupations became a regular occurrence. In August 1921, workers at the Cleeve's plant in Bruree occupied the flour mill and bakery, as well as the local creamery also owned by Cleeve's.[44] Seán Dowling and Jack McGrath were again instrumental in organizing the occupation.[45] Local ITGWU representative, Patrick Doherty, was appointed manager. The customary red flag and tricolour were hoisted over the plant and a banner

See Óisín Ó Drisceoil, 'The Arigna soviet of 1921', in John Cunningham, Francis Devine, and Sonja Tiernan (eds), *Labour history in Irish history: essays celebrating fifty years of the Irish Labour History Society* (Dublin, 2023), p. 147. **41** O'Connor, *Syndicalism in Ireland, 1917–1923*, p. 59. **42** *Watchword of Labour*, 5 June 1920. In March 1920 members of the National Union of Dock Labourers in Waterford declared their intention of preventing the export of butter and bacon through the port in response to the decision by the British government to remove price controls on these products. The ILP&TUC supported the embargo campaign. In response the Irish Farmers' Union proposed a Farmers' Freedom Force that would be used to force through the export of farm produce. See Emmet O'Connor, 'The Waterford soviet: fact or fancy?', *History Ireland*, 8:1 (2000), 10–12; and Terry Dunne, 'Notes on the defence of Irish country houses', *Peelers and Sheep Podcast*, Season 1, Episode 5, https://shows.acast.com/peelers-and-sheep/episodes/ep-5-notes-on-the-defence-of-irish-country-houses [accessed 20 Apr. 2023] See also Raymond Ryan, 'Farmers, agriculture and politics in the Irish Free State area, 1919–1936' (PhD, University College Cork, 2005), pp 30–1. **43** During a farm labourers strike in Old Parish, Co. Waterford, in March 1922 the farmers demanded that the Provisional Government provide them with shotguns. The *Voice of Labour*, 4 Mar. 1922, asserted that the purpose of this demand was to organize 'white guards to attack workers'. During another farm labourers' strike in Newport, Co. Tipperary, it was claimed that a local 'White Guard' was mobilized to protect 'the sacred rights of property'. See *Voice of Labour*, 11 Mar. 1922. **44** *Cork Examiner*, 29 Aug. 1921; *Freeman's Journal*, 30 Aug. 1921. **45** Haugh, *Limerick soviet*, p. 163.

proclaiming 'Bruree Workers Soviet Mills: We Make Bread Not Profits' was hung over the entrance. The workers awarded themselves a wage increase of 7s. 6d. and reduced prices for consumers. The media reported that the business proceeded with clockwork precision and a continuous stream of customers called to the bakery, 'all of whom seemed to appreciate the change'. Union officials claimed to have doubled the output of the bakery and that extra workers could be employed.[46] The *Voice of Labour* reported that during the course of the meeting between a Sinn Féin delegation and ITGWU representatives on 2 September in Liberty Hall, Constance Markiewicz threatened to use the IRA to remove the workers from the plant.[47] An agreement was reached granting all of the workers' demands in return for the workplace being returned to the control of Cleeve's. Demonstrating the control exercised by the workers, the *Limerick Leader* commented that when a reporter visited Bruree the previous Friday the 'soviet' was found to be in full control of the village, 'both industrially and otherwise'.[48]

The Cork harbour soviet

Within days of the ending of the Bruree soviet, dock workers in Cork harbour staged strike action.[49] A few days later, on 7 September, the striking workers gathered at the Harbour Board offices at the Customs House and proceeded to seize the premises. Pickets were dispatched to occupy the Harbour Board offices in Cobh with the support of the dock workers there. The IRA in Cork viewed the Cork harbour soviet with disdain. The petty-bourgeois elements within the IRA saw the raising of the red flag as an insult to the tricolour and wanted to suppress the soviet by force of arms. Strike leader Robert Day threatened to extend the strike action throughout the city if the IRA made any attempt to suppress the soviet.[50] However, within hours of the extension of the soviet on 7 September, the city's establishment were seeking a compromise. Realizing the prospect of the strike being extended into a city-wide action they made major concessions and proposed a conference to decide on the pay claim of the workers. On the evening of 7 September, a return to work was agreed pending a conference, which was to take place on 10 September. As soon as the agreement was announced the IRA moved into the occupied offices and removed the red flag, replacing it with the tricolour.

---

46 *Freeman's Journal*, 31 Aug. 1921; *Limerick Echo*, 3 Sept. 1921; *Limerick Leader*, 31 Aug. 1921.
47 O'Connor Lysaght, 'The Munster soviet creameries', p. 43; *Voice of Labour*, 10 Nov. 1923.
48 *Limerick Leader*, 5 Sept. 1921.   49 Luke Dineen, 'The Cork harbour soviet of 1921', *Saothar: Journal of Irish Labour History,* 42 (2017), 35.   50 Ibid., p. 39.

The Cork harbour soviet provoked subsequent hostility from Sinn Féin and the IRA in Cork. The Cork Sinn Féin executive charged both Day and the 'Chairman of the Soviet Board' William Kenneally, both of whom had previously aligned with Sinn Féin, with defying Dáil authority as a result of organizing the soviet. Both were tried at Cork courthouse and 'expelled' from the Republican movement. At the time there were rumours that elements within the Cork IRA were planning to assassinate Kenneally.[51]

The impact and legacy of the Cork harbour soviet were not lost on the British authorities either. In late September a military intelligence report stated 'that the danger from the extreme wing of the Irish Labour Party is a very real one cannot have escaped the attention of Sinn Féin leaders'.[52] Workplace soviets were becoming a key tactic of Irish workers as demonstrated a week later when the workers at the Drogheda foundry occupied the iron works in the town.[53]

IRA take an active role in suppressing strikes

At the same time strike action was intensifying among agricultural labourers, with strikes breaking out in many parts of the country. As employers moved to implement cuts to jobs, wages and working conditions, and the IRA took an increasingly active part in suppressing strikes and workplace occupations, the class conflict became increasingly violent. A two-month long strike by farm labourers in the Bulgaden area near Kilmallock in east Limerick, that began in November 1921, saw the IRA arrest strike leaders, including Seán Dowling, provoking a four-day general strike by workers in Kilmallock which secured their release.[54] In the course of the dispute, farm produce was destroyed, separators broken, fencing broken down and cattle driven; trees were felled across roads, bridges broken, fairs and markets held up; hay, straw and farm buildings were burned; walls were knocked and telegraph and electric light cables severed.[55] During January tit-for-tat kidnappings occurred, including the IRA kidnapping of local strike leader Michael Lenihan.[56] At the same time a deputation from the Irish Farmers' Union met with Arthur Griffith demanding action be taken against the strikers.[57] As a result, on 21

51 Ibid., p. 38. 52 Ibid. Writing in his diary, the Sinn Féin TD for Cork, Liam de Róiste, stated: 'Republicans and conservatives are united in their opposition to the Red Flag ... Republicans are so strenuously in opposition to the Red Flag and what it signifies'. He continued 'In fact, it is of intense interest to me to see how this struggle of what I may term Red Flag versus Irish tricolour has come about ... It is one of the things I anticipated but did not expect would come so soon in Cork'. 53 *Drogheda Independent*, 17 Sept. 1921. 54 *Freeman's Journal*, 22 Nov. 1921; *Limerick Chronicle*, 22 Nov. 1921. 55 *Limerick Leader*, 27 Jan. 1922; *Munster News*, 25 Jan. 1922; Mainchín Seoighe, *The story of Kilmallock* (Kilmallock, 1988), p. 287. 56 *Limerick Leader*, 16 Jan. 1922; *Irish Examiner*, 16 January 1922; *Munster News*, 21 Jan. 1922; *Limerick Echo*, 21 Jan. 1922. 57 Seoighe, *Kilmallock*,

January 1922 Donncha O'Hannigan, O/C of the East Limerick Brigade IRA, declared martial law around Kilmallock, with 200 IRA men being drafted into the area to suppress the strike.[58]

At the same time as the farm labourers strike at Bulgaden, workers at the Castleconnell Fisheries, on the River Shannon north of Limerick city, established a workplace soviet. Dowling and McGrath were again key figures in the episode which lasted almost three weeks, from 2 December to 22 December 1921. The fisheries were owned by prominent Sinn Féin councillor Anthony Mackey who repeatedly reneged on agreements over the previous eighteen months and demanded action by the IRA to suppress the soviet. Despite repeated threats from the local and national Sinn Féin leadership, the workers in Castleconnell stood fast until they achieved their demands. The nationalist leadership were wary about using the IRA to suppress the soviet in the crucial period after the signing of the Anglo-Irish Treaty.[59]

A workers' army

In January 1922 the leadership of the ITGWU initiated an attempt to establish a workers' army.[60] In January 1920 an Easter Rising veteran and member of the leadership of the Irish Citizen Army (ICA), Michael Donnelly, argued that the ICA had ceased to fight for a workers' republic and had become a 'tail of Sinn Féin'.[61] At the time the remnants of the ICA had an estimated 200 members. It was argued by some that the reason why the leadership of the ITGWU initiated this workers' army was to bring the ICA under its control and neuter its anti-Treaty position.[62] The initiative led to the formation of a committee comprising five members of the ICA and five trade unionists. The purpose of this committee was to begin recruiting workers to the new force. Branches of the ITGWU were contacted and the response was considered to be 'very encouraging'. Reflecting a growing mood among workers for an armed workers' force, by early April an army convention of the Workers' Army was held, and a number of units established.[63] Its aims were stated as being to defend Ireland against foreign aggression, protect strikers, secure the rights of workers as citizens and fight for the workers' republic.[64]

Given the widespread nature of strike action and workers' soviets that were facing repression from both pro- and anti-Treaty forces, along with farmers

p. 287.   **58** *Munster News*, 21 Jan. 1922; Seoighe, *Kilmallock*, p. 287.   **59** For further information on the Castleconnell soviet, see Haugh, *Limerick soviet*, pp 139–40.   **60** National Library of Ireland, MS 15,673/8/17, MS 15,676/1/72, MS 15,673/8/11.   **61** Brian Hanley, 'The Irish Citizen Army after 1916', *Saothar: Journal of Irish Labour History*, 28 (2003), 38.   **62** Mitchell, *Labour in Irish politics*, p. 164.   **63** Ibid., pp 161–3.   **64** Hanley, 'The Irish Citizen Army after 1916', p. 40.

organizations, the potential for building such a workers' army existed. As late as May 1922 Michael Donnelly and John Byrne, part of the organizing committee, were claiming that there was 'growing demand' among trade unionists for such a force. After this it looks like, in the run up to the general election in June, William O'Brien and the ITGWU leadership buried all plans for the Workers' Army.[65] It is not clear what their motivation was for this, but it was likely a number of factors played into their approach. There was a danger that the rank-and-file of a workers' army could not be controlled. It is also possible that elements involved in the workplace soviets who were already using arms were becoming too influential. It is likely that the union leadership were worried the emergence of such an armed force could have a negative impact on the fortunes of Labour candidates in the upcoming general election as a result of anti-socialist propaganda from both wings of the nationalist movement and from the Farmers' Party. Whatever the reason for the leadership abandoning the project, the end result is that the Workers' Army was effectively derailed by June 1922, and it played no role in the workplace soviets in Munster during the period.

The Munster soviets

During December 1921 the Cleeve's-owned Condensed Milk Company of Ireland sought lay-offs and wage cuts of one-third among its workforce in Limerick, Cork and Tipperary.[66] On 22 December 1921 the ITGWU held a conference in Limerick Junction comprising twenty-three delegates representing the workers in sixty-eight of the creameries owned by Cleeve's. ITGWU organizer, Jack McGrath, used the meeting to remind the delegates of the divisions that occurred amongst the workforce during the strike against Cleeves in 1919 and Seán Dowling outlined the current level of attacks by employers on dockers, railwaymen and farm workers all over the country. He called on the workers to stand solid and win the dispute. The workers unanimously rejected the proposed cuts in jobs and wages and a Workers' Committee of Action (also described as a Council of Action) was formed.[67] The new committee was effectively a revival of the Council of Action that emerged during the Cleeve's strike in 1919.

65 Ibid. 66 *Voice of Labour*, 7 Jan. 1922; *Irish Independent*, 18 May 1922; *Cork Examiner*, 18 May 1922; Lee, 'The Munster soviets', p. 300. 67 *Voice of Labour*, 7 Jan. 1922. Different names are assigned to it in the primary and secondary literature but the 'Workers' Committee of Action' comes from a report on the dispute in the *Voice of Labour*. In the remainder of the text the committee is referred to as the 'Council of Action'.

On 3 January 1922 a national conference, organized by the Ministry of Labour, was held in Dublin. The workers and employers were located in separate rooms and no progress was made during negotiations. Divisions did appear among the ranks of the workers. James Carr, president of the Limerick Trades Council, who was attending as a representative of the Irish Engineering Union, stated that they were willing to do a deal with the Limerick Federation of Employers. Other craft unions followed suit and it was left to the ITGWU, the Irish Clerical Workers' Union (ICWU)[68] and the Irish Automobile Drivers' and Mechanics' Union (IADMU) to oppose the employers.[69]

Later in January the minister for defence received a letter from Messrs Cleeve complaining of a soviet occupation of one of their factories.[70] The Ministry for Labour supported the employers' position that wage reductions were necessary and put in place two joint councils to arbitrate in the dispute. Cleeve's asserted that by the end of 1921 the company had debts of £100,000 with net losses amounting to £274,555.[71] The union organizers responded by stating that the company had made £750,000 in 1918–19 and were suspicious of the claims of the company, demanding that the company's books be opened for inspection.[72] The arbitration system came down on the side of the employers and the proposals were submitted to the unions for ballot.[73] When the Council of Action re-assembled on 31 March the result of the ballot showed a very large majority against the proposals. A temporary compromise proposal was made that included a one month's reduction in wages while a new buyer was sought for the Cleeve's company, after which the wages would revert back to previous levels. These proposals were subsequently passed by a small majority.[74]

Despite efforts to broker an agreement a strike broke out at the Cleeve's plant in Lansdowne in Limerick on 13 April.[75] After four weeks members of the Clerical Workers' Union accepted a wage cut but the ITGWU members continued to refuse.[76] In an escalation of the dispute, 200 workers in Clonmel occupied the Cleeve's plants in the town on 12 May. Workers in Carrick-on-Suir occupied the company's creamery and the following day the Condensed Milk factory. Before the weekend was out the Cleeve's premises in Kilmallock

---

68 The ICWU organized the office staff employed by Cleeve's in the Lansdowne factory and in the other main centres throughout the region. **69** *Voice of Labour*, 14 Jan. 1922. **70** Dáil Éireann Secretariat files 1919–1922, DE 1/4, Document No. 22, 16 January 1922. The workplace is not named in the telegram and no other evidence has been found that such an occupation was taking place. **71** Lee, 'The Munster soviets and the fall of the house of Cleeve', p. 300. **72** *Voice of Labour*, 5 Nov. 1921. **73** Dáil Éireann Secretariat files 1919–1922, DE 2/5 Documents No. 191–2, The Ministry for Labour, Report on activities of the Labour Department during the period 11 January 1922–18 April 1922. **74** Ibid. **75** *Munster News*, 19 Apr. 1922; *Irish Independent*, 17 Apr. 1922. **76** *Limerick Leader*, 15 May 1922.

and Knocklong were also under the workers' control.[77] Under direction and co-ordination by Seán Dowling and Jack McGrath, the Council of Action proceeded to organize widespread occupations throughout Limerick, Tipperary and Waterford.[78]

The reaction of the Dáil cabinet was swift. In order to prevent striking workers occupying the Lansdowne plant, a detachment of fully armed Free State troops was placed on guard.[79] Farmers demanded an immediate response from the leadership of the nationalist movement. At a meeting in Geary's Hotel in Limerick, Bartholomew Laffan, the Sinn Féin chairman of Limerick County Council, said that 'this struggle threatened the very lives and liberties of the farmers'. He claimed that all lawful government was being ignored and he proposed a resolution stating: 'we forbid our members to supply the red flag, which is the flag of revolution and anarchy ... we look for protection from our government to assert our right as free citizens'.[80] A meeting of the executive of the Irish Farmers' Union on 18 May took up the demands. Declaring that they did not want communism in Ireland, the delegates claimed that acts of sabotage were being carried out and that farmers were being forced to supply the creameries at gun-point. Mr M. Doran stated that 'if the government would not govern, they should be told to get out', while Father Maguire from Co. Monaghan made an appeal to those responsible for social order to expel those who had invaded private property.[81] On 9 June the Dáil cabinet made a decision to use troops to suppress any soviet still in existence by 21 June, but, as had been the case with the Cork railway workers, the decision was not implemented.[82]

Almost immediately violence became a feature of the occupations. In Carrick-on-Suir workers commandeered trucks and visited farms to confiscate milk supplies.[83] On 14 May the soviet creamery at Galteemore, on the Tipperary–Limerick border five kilometres south-west of Tipperary town, was intentionally burned to the ground by farmers.[84] These events were occurring precisely at the time that the country was sliding into civil war. In some areas, farmers continued to supply the creameries with full production continuing.[85] Sylvia Pankhurst reported in the *Daily Herald* that the soviets had forty tons of butter for sale and were donating a large quantity of sweetened condensed

77 *Freeman's Journal*, 15 May 1922. **78** Lee, 'The Munster soviets', p. 301; C. Desmond Greaves, *Irish Transport and General Workers' Union*, p. 312. **79** *Limerick Leader*, 17 May 1922. **80** *Irish Times*, 18 May 1922; *Cork Examiner*, 18 May 1922. **81** *Irish Times*, 19 May 1922; *Cork Examiner*, 19 May 1922. **82** Conor Kostick, *Revolution in Ireland: popular militancy, 1917 to 1923* (Dublin, 1996), p. 189. **83** *Irish Times*, 19 May 1922; *Northern Standard*, 26 May 1922; O'Connor, *Syndicalism in Ireland*, p. 130. **84** *Tipperary Star*, 20 May 1922. **85** *Voice of Labour*, 27 May 1922. The paper reported that at one soviet creamery 'long lines of farmers' cars – flat and covered with cans of new milk – queued up to the receiving platform'.

milk to the Russian Famine Fund.[86] Butter was sent to co-operative stores in Scotland and Wales, and it was asserted that the pro-Treaty administration requested the British authorities to send a gunboat to intercept the Wales-bound cargo.[87] It is not known if this request was acceded to. At the end of July, the police at Falmouth in Cornwall confiscated twenty-seven tons of butter from the soviet creameries valued at £5,400. Representatives from Cleeve's in Plymouth had reported the butter as stolen to the police and accompanied the authorities to Falmouth. The captain of the vessel carrying the butter initially refused to hand over the butter but relented when he was told he would be arrested by the police and the butter would be confiscated anyway.[88]

As farmers began diverting milk to farmer-owned co-operative creameries and purchased separators to process their own milk, sabotage and violence became a feature of the conflict. In the early hours of 19 May machinery worth £3,000 was destroyed at the soviet creamery in Grange, while the Oakleigh Creamery at Caherconlish was burnt down after receiving milk diverted from other plants.[89] Workers at unoccupied creameries were refusing to handle diverted milk.[90] However, farmers' sons had taken over the work in many of the farmer-owned co-operative creameries and the farmers' boycott began to bite. Diverted milk was being accepted at the Bridgetown Co-operative Creamery.[91] Pickets disrupted farmers' markets and prevented them from operating. A riot broke out in Clonmel when women workers from the Cleeve's plant attacked 'women of the farming classes' who were selling butter at a local market, scattering produce all over the road.[92] Meanwhile in Carrick-on-Suir, workers at the soviet prevented the distribution of foodstuffs to farmers outside the town.[93] At the same time the IFU was demanding that local councils sack road workers, claiming that farmers would not be able to pay their rates if they were not allowed to market their produce, and that the road workers were heavily involved in the workers' soviets while being paid from the rates paid by farmers.[94] The claims by the farmers indicate that involvement in the workers' soviets spread beyond the workforce of Cleeve's.

Socialist and anti-socialist rhetoric was commonplace. For the Farmers' Party there was a strong focus in the general election campaign of June 1922 on the defeat of the workplace soviets, the land seizures, and the Bolshevik elements within the Irish labour movement.[95] It became clear that the farmers

86 *Tipperary Star*, 20 May 1922.   **87** O'Connor Lysaght, 'The Munster soviet creameries', p. 45. **88** *Nenagh Guardian*, 29 July 1922; *Westmeath Independent*, 29 July 1922.   **89** *Freeman's Journal*, 20 May 1922.   **90** Ibid.   **91** *Limerick Leader*, 17 May 1922.   **92** *Freeman's Journal*, 29 May 1922. **93** *Munster Express*, 3 June 1922; *Workers' Republic*, 3 June 1922; *Cork Examiner*, 3 June 1922. **94** *Irish Independent*, 9 June 1922.   **95** *Tipperary Star*, 3 June 1922.

regarded the conflict over the Anglo-Irish Treaty as secondary to this. The farmers claimed that the ITGWU was a Bolshevik organization intent on taking over the country. With reference to the seizures that had been taking place, it was suggested that the property of farmers would be the next target for occupation by workers.[96] The *Tipperary Star* commented that 'Capitalism will see Cleeve's thro' against communism'.[97] Newspaper reports indicate the widespread distribution of 'red flag literature'.[98] During an election campaign meeting for the Waterford–Tipperary East constituency, Mr O'Kane of the Irish Postal Union offered an analysis of the situation in the country:

> He blamed capitalism and exploitation for the present position in which the working classes found themselves and for driving the people out of the country. They had got to make war upon capitalists and the exploiters – the capitalists and the exploiters and the Farmers and Ratepayers' Associations were the buttresses of British Militarism and landlordism in the country.[99]

Divisions did emerge within the ranks of the IFU. At a farmers' meeting in Clonmel at the beginning of June a number of farmers criticized the leadership of the IFU for representing only the interests of larger farmers and for being willing to sacrifice the financial well-being of the smaller farmers in their drive to defeat the soviets rather than attempting to negotiate with the Council of Action.[100] It was also implied that the leaders of the IFU in Tipperary had close associations with the managers of Cleeve's.[101] One of the farmers who opposed the strategy of the leadership of the IFU, John Mandeville, rejected the use of a Farmers' Freedom Force in the conflict.[102] These divisions were demonstrated when small farmers continued to supply the Ironmills creamery, ten kilometres north-east of Tipperary town, when larger farmers decided to boycott it. Similarly, the IFU branch at nearby Donohill agreed to continue supplying the soviet creamery.[103] Farmers also supplied the soviet creamery at Blackbridge, between Ironmills and Cashel, despite an organized boycott by the IFU with a similar situation also existing in Killenaule, five kilometres from Cashel.[104] Many of the smaller farmers were subject to intimidation in order to pull them into line.[105] In early August 1922 the IFU ejected the soviet from Blackbridge creamery and refused to accept milk from any farmer who

---

96 *The Nationalist*, 27 May 1922.   **97** *Tipperary Star*, 24 June 1922.   **98** Ibid., 29 July 1922.   **99** *Munster Express*, 10 June 1922.   **100** *Tipperary Star*, 3 June 1922.   **101** *The Nationalist*, 14 June 1922.   **102** Ibid., 31 May 1922.   **103** Ibid., 27 May 1922.   **104** *Tipperary Star*, 27 May 1922; *The Nationalist*, 14 June 1922.   **105** Ibid., 3 June 1922.

had supplied the soviet creamery, resulting in just three farmers supplying the new occupiers.[106] In 1923 Michael Heffernan, head of the Tipperary IFU, admitted that they succeeded in only getting half the farmers in the region to boycott the soviet-controlled creameries.[107]

At the end of May the striking workers at the Condensed Milk Factory in Limerick agreed to accept a pay cut of 10 per cent, with a further 2½ per cent reduction in subsequent months, but the company repudiated the agreement.[108] Cleeve's was in serious difficulty with repeated problems supplying markets as a result of military, political and class conflicts of the period.[109] The workers at Lansdowne in Limerick and in Bruree accepted the pay cut imposed by the company at the end of June.[110]

Within days of the attack on the Four Courts, Liam Lynch ordered Frank Ryan and the anti-Treaty IRA unit under his command, to suppress the soviet in Knocklong. Ryan stated that he himself climbed onto the roof of the building to remove the red flag while the workers were being evicted from the premises.[111] This wasn't the first occasion that Liam Lynch had ordered such action. Several months earlier he and his IRA unit ejected workers occupying the Mallow Flour Mills. In appreciation T.D. Hallinan, manager of the mill, paid the IRA £50 for helping with their 'recent labour trouble'.[112] Throughout the last two weeks of June vigilante gangs of farmers attacked several soviet creameries, damaging equipment, in an attempt to disrupt the work being carried out by the occupying workers.[113] The Council of Action responded with trained and armed pickets imposing boycotts of farmer-owned co-operative creameries. Retaliatory attacks were also carried out on these co-operative creameries, damaging equipment.[114]

Repeated attempts were made by the anti-Treaty IRA to suppress the different workplace occupations in Tipperary. In mid-May the anti-Treaty IRA succeeded in suppressing the soviet, in existence since February, at the Ballinacourty sawmills in the Glen of Aherlow, and ejected the workers at gunpoint.[115] The Munster soviets emerged in conjunction with widespread strikes by farm labourers as well as land seizures and occupations. The estate

106 *Tipperary Star,* 12 Aug. 1922.   **107** *Irish Times,* 16 Mar. 1923.   **108** *The Nationalist,* 31 May 1922; *Irish Independent,* 9 June 1922; *Nenagh Guardian,* 10 June 1922.   **109** Lee, 'The Munster soviets', p. 305.   **110** *Munster News,* 28 June 1922.   **111** Adrian Hoar, *In green and red: the lives of Frank Ryan* (Dingle, 2004), pp 18–19.   **112** Kostick, *Revolution in Ireland,* p. 164.   **113** *Tipperary Star,* 24 June 1922. Towards the end of May farmers indicated that they would establish a 'Citizen's Guard' to defend farmers' interests, see *The Nationalist,* 24 May 1922. In other areas, particularly during the farm labourers' disputes in Waterford, farmers were self-styled as 'White Guards'. See Emmet O'Connor, 'Agrarian unrest and the labour movement in County Waterford, 1917–1923', *Saothar: Journal of Irish Labour History,* 6 (1980), 53.   **114** *Tipperary Star,* 1 July 1922. Retaliatory attacks were carried out in Cappawhite, Ironmills and Ballybrack.   **115** Kostick, *Revolution in*

of Sir John Keane near Cappoquin in Co. Waterford was seized by striking farm labourers. Keane's cows were milked, and the milk, carried in a commandeered truck, was sold to the people of Cappoquin.[116] Keane had been one of the most vocal opponents of the seizure of the Cleeve's factories. In an earlier dispute, workers at the Shanbally estate, near Clogheen in south Tipperary, posted a Red Guard to prevent anyone using the woodlands on the estate.[117]

In Clonmel the workers had placed pickets on shops who refused the stock products from the soviet creamery. The anti-Treaty IRA arrived fully armed and demanded that the pickets and their supporters clear the streets. When the striking workers refused to leave the IRA fired several volleys of shots over their heads. In response, the workers linked arms and marched in formation towards the IRA unit, which was forced to retreat.[118] On another occasion, James Reidy, the former manager of the Cleeve's companies in Clonmel, was kidnapped in Mallow and locked in an office near the occupied Cleeve's plant in Tipperary. In response the anti-Treaty IRA demanded the release of the manager, which was rejected by the workers. This led to an exchange of gunfire 'between the irregulars and some of the workers' guards'. The report indicates that Reidy was released later the same evening, 'but firing continued, sometimes with terrific intensity, throughout the night'.[119] Probably in reference to the same incident, the *Leinster Reporter* stated that fighting occurred in Tipperary between 'irregulars and a "Red Guard"'.[120] It is clear that widespread support existed in local communities for the actions of workers, the strikes and occupations would not otherwise have been viable for the prolonged periods of class conflict.[121]

When the necessity arose for the workers to extend the soviets, the leadership of the ILP&TUC were seen to be washing their hands of the crisis. In an interview in the *Manchester Guardian* on 14 June 1922, Thomas Johnson declared that 'Labour had nothing to do with it and had no general policy of the kind'.[122] To support the soviets the trade union leadership would have been forced to confront not only the Provisional Government, but the anti-Treaty forces as well. In the run up to the election on 16 June, Johnson

Ireland, pp 188–9. **116** *Cork Examiner*, 13 June 1922. **117** *Voice of Labour*, 25 Mar. 1922. **118** *Northern Whig and Belfast Post*, 12 June 1922; *Workers' Republic*, 17 June 1922. **119** *Irish Independent*, 29 July 1922. **120** *Leinster Reporter*, 5 Aug. 1922. **121** Clark, *Everyday violence in the Irish Civil War*, p. 116. Clark talks about this in relation to cattle drives and land occupations, but it is clear that similar support existed for the soviet occupations. Farmers accused labourers and road workers of not alone supporting the soviets, but of participating in organizing support for them, while shop workers in many of the towns with occupied workplaces refused to serve farmers who were boycotting the soviet creameries and dumping their milk. **122** O'Connor, *Syndicalism in Ireland*, p. 127.

and his colleagues were doing everything to distance the Labour election campaign from the soviet occupations.

Not only did the trade union leadership abandon the workers, the Communist Party of Ireland (CPI) did the same. The CPI had a base of support in Tipperary and local members established a support group for the soviets in the town. But the national leadership of the CPI dismissed the soviets as reformist and spent this entire period trying to persuade the anti-Treaty IRA to start a civil war.[123] As the anti-Treaty IRA retreated from Tipperary town, they burnt the gasworks and blew up the water main so that the fire could not be put out. The occupied creamery was also burnt to the ground and while the anti-Treaty IRA were later blamed for this act of arson, trade union sources indicated that it was the workers themselves that set fire to the building as an act of defiance against the Free State.[124] When the Free State forces entered the town, they immediately suppressed the soviets and ejected the occupying workers.[125] The attitude of the Catholic hierarchy was also demonstrated at this time. Speaking following a visit to Kilmallock in mid-August, Irish-American bishop of Buffalo, Dr William Turner, stated that 'the forces of Bolshevism and Radical labour discontent will have to be reckoned with' by the Free State forces during the course of the Civil War.[126]

For a large part of 1922 illegal direct action by workers kept employers' ambitions to cut jobs and wages in check. Including the soviets in the Cleeve's companies, in excess of one hundred soviet occupations occurred during the year and with such minimal capacity for compromise given the economic conditions, the soviets arguably acquired a 'serious revolutionary intent'. The soviets and the strikes by farm labourers were the key issues for Farmers' Party candidates in the election with the farmers campaigning for the 'protection of life and property' and against nationalization of the land.[127] Workers armed themselves with the intent of defending the soviets and pickets from attacks by the IRA and 'civilian guards' organized by farmers.[128] This revolutionary intent spread far beyond the Munster soviets. Attempts to organize cattle-drives around Corofin, Co. Clare, resulted in several gun battles with the IRA.[129] The 600 workers who occupied the Greenmount Cotton Mills in

123 Milotte, *Communism in modern Ireland*, pp 57–8.   **124** Ibid., p. 93.   **125** Kostick, *Revolution in Ireland*, p. 190.   **126** *Tipperary Star*, 12 Aug. 1922.   **127** *Munster Express*, 10 June 1922.   **128** In August 1922 it was reported that fighting occurred between irregulars and 'a red guard' during 'labour troubles' in Tipperary town. See *Leinster Reporter*, 5 Aug. 1922.   **129** *Irish Independent*, 3 June 1922. Shooting between cattle drivers and the IRA also took place at Inch, near Thurles, in February. The following notice was posted on the lands of Major Lowe, just outside Tipperary town: 'Ireland for the Irish: the land for the people and not for ranches. The cattle were driven off the land last night. Anyone bringing them back or repairing walls or gates will be met with instant death.' And it was signed 'Captain Moonlight'. In many instances a red flag was hoisted on a tree, as in the case of a

Harold's Cross, Dublin, built sandbag fortifications at the entrances to the factory in the expectation that the IRA would attempt to remove them by force of arms.[130]

The leadership of the ITGWU gave nothing more than lip-service to these struggles and disputes emerged within the union as a result.[131] Not alone did the ITGWU leadership abandon the workers involved in the Munster soviets, they worked to undermine the struggle the workers were engaged in. During the period of the soviets, the creamery workers sent lorry loads of butter to Dublin for distribution to co-operative stores in Scotland and Wales. The butter was stored in the basement of the ITGWU headquarters in Dublin awaiting dispatch. When William O'Brien found out the butter was being stored in the ITGWU offices he ordered the caretaker to remove the butter from the building.[132] Indeed, O'Brien and the leadership engaged in a purge of the militant elements involved in the soviets from the union. The Marxist industrial organizers involved in the soviets were sacked and the ITGWU branch officers in Tipperary were expelled from the union.[133] During a court case in 1925, O'Brien stated that 'The Transport Workers' Union neither authorized nor agreed with the seizure of the factories, and had neither hand, act or part in it in any way'. During his testimony he openly attacked Jack Hedley, who he stated was 'not born in this country and had been imprisoned in England and Belfast in connection with other activities he had been carrying on'. According to O'Brien, Hedley 'had been carrying on propaganda for taking over the creameries, and ... was the mainspring of the whole thing'.[134]

As the Civil War progressed, and Free State troops advanced into Munster, the government was anxious not only to suppress armed resistance to the Treaty but also to deal decisively with 'bolshevik' agitation. One of the first acts of the troops when they arrived in a village or town was to suppress any soviet they found. Activists in the soviets were arrested by Free State troops during the suppression of the soviets and as late as December 1922 nearly all of the members of the Council of Action involved in the Munster soviets were

---

cattle drive from the grounds of Suir Castle, between Tipperary and Cashel. See *Nenagh News,* 11 Feb. 1922. Near Athlone in June, 100 armed men engaged in a gun battle with a detachment of IRA Volunteers guarding land. Overpowering the IRA unit and ordering them to return to barracks, the attackers burnt down the house on the land. See *Irish Independent,* 14 June 1922. **130** *Irish Independent,* 14 June 1922. **131** O'Connor, *A labour history of Ireland,* p. 112. **132** *Voice of Labour,* 21 Feb. 1925. **133** D.R. O'Connor Lysaght, 'The rake's progress of a syndicalist: the political career of William O'Brien, Irish labour leader', *Saothar: Journal of Irish Labour History,* 9 (1983), 54. **134** *Voice of Labour,* 21 Feb. 1925. O'Brien was giving evidence in a court case taken by a Tipperary farmer against the ITGWU. The farmer had supplied milk to the Tipperary creamery soviet. He had been paid during May and June but claimed he had not received payment for the

still in prison.[135] The Free State exacted further revenge, Cleeve's workers who were not re-employed after the return of the factories to company control were denied benefit payments by the Free State government.[136]

Revolutionary intent

The evidence suggests that occupation of the Cleeve's plants and the other workplace soviets that took place during 1922 demonstrated a serious revolutionary intent. The massive expansion of the trade union movement from 1917 to 1922 occurred during a period of revolutionary upheaval in Ireland. It was inevitable that among the working class the drive for political independence would dove-tail with a desire for economic and social emancipation for working class people.

Hanley has shown that 'there was a great deal of enthusiasm' among the Irish working class for both the February revolution in Russia and the later Bolshevik revolution.[137] On 4 February 1918 more than 10,000 people gathered at the Mansion House in Dublin to celebrate the Bolshevik revolution.[138] Weeks later the power of the trade union movement was demonstrated with the general strike against conscription. Throughout the revolutionary period national and local newspapers carried articles about the Russian Revolution and its aftermath, as well as articles about revolutionary upheavals in Germany, Hungary, Italy and elsewhere. The *Watchword* and the *Voice of Labour* regularly republished articles from Lenin, Trotsky and other Bolshevik leaders and openly advocated for the establishment of a workers' republic.[139]

On May Day 1918 workers marched in their thousands throughout the country behind red flags, expressing their support for the gains achieved by the Russian working class.[140] By 1919 the word 'soviet' had entered the vernacular. The Belfast engineering strike and the Limerick soviet increased class consciousness among the working class and demonstrated the ability of

milk he supplied in July 1922. He was suing the ITGWU for the cost of the milk he supplied in July.   **135** *Workers' Republic*, 9 Dec. 1922. *Voice of Labour*, 4 Nov. 1922, reported that Michael Shelley, branch secretary of the Tipperary branch of the ITGWU during the soviet, was in prison. **136** *Voice of Labour*, 10 Mar. 1923.   **137** Brian Hanley, 'Bolshevism in Ireland', *Centenary Ireland*, https://www.youtube.com/watch?v=KEVJ4GemLgc [accessed on 10 May 2022].   **138** *Irish Independent*, 5 Feb. 1918.   **139** See for example, Vladimir Onlianof (Lenin), 'The land revolution in Russia', *Watchword of Labour*, 15 Nov. 1919; Nicolai [sic] Lenin, 'Twixt capitalism and communism', *Watchword of Labour*, 25 Sept., and also 'Lenin on the new policy in Russia', *Voice of Labour*, 12 Nov. 1921.   **140** For example, 15,000 attended a May Day rally in the Market's Field in Limerick and unanimously passed a resolution paying tribute to 'our Russian comrades who have waged a magnificent struggle for their social and political emancipation'. See *Voice of Labour*, 11 May 1918.

working-class people to exercise power over their lives. The wave of strikes and land seizures demonstrated to the nationalist leadership that the national movement could be split along class lines, clearly showing the potential impact of the class struggle. By the second half of 1921 workplace soviets were becoming a common tactic in industrial disputes. During 1922 the scale and intensity of the class conflict escalated. Workers openly confronted the IRA during strikes and land seizures. In the aftermath of the Anglo-Irish Treaty and the establishment of the Free State, this conflict posed a serious threat to the continued existence of the Free State on a capitalist basis. Indeed, many of the leaders of Unionism in the North were convinced that Sinn Fein would be defeated by socialist revolution. As the soviets in Cleeve's and other factories developed, they did so outside of trade union structures and in defiance of the open hostility of the leadership of the trade union movement. Workers were armed to defend workplaces from attack by farmers' vigilante groups, to enforce the commandeering of vehicles and to enforce the confiscation of farm produce.

Socialist literature was widely distributed during the Munster soviets. Red flags were prominently displayed, and the idea of a workers' republic openly advocated throughout the period. Both the pro-Treaty and anti-Treaty wings of Sinn Féin recognized the threat posed by the workplace soviets and systematically moved to suppress them. This does raise the question of why the workplace soviets and widespread strikes in 1922 did not develop into a more encompassing socialist revolution. By 1922 the ILP&TUC had 250,000 members. The ITGWU was the vanguard of that organization with 120,000 members, and had a radical syndicalist programme and a largely independent rank-and-file, many of whom were influenced by Marxist industrial organizers. However, by 1922 a bureaucracy around William O'Brien had consolidated its control over the structures of the ITGWU.[141] Indeed, the ITGWU mirrored all the criticism posed by Lenin in relation to syndicalism – an organizational looseness, keeping workers keyed-up rather than creating a firm stronghold of class organization, petty-bourgeois-individualist features and an 'aversion to politics', and in Ireland that particularly resulted in an aversion to taking a stand on the national question.[142]

O'Connor Lysaght argued that the potential for socialist revolution in Ireland was hampered by developments happening too soon to learn the lessons of the Russian Revolution and that the smallness of Irish industrial

---

141 O'Brien had spent the previous two years removing opponents to his control from the leadership of the ITGWU, including splitting the Dublin Trades Council when the opposition won the officer positions on that body. **142** V.I. Lenin, *Collected works*, vol. 13 (Moscow, 1972), p. 168.

units (outside of Belfast where sectarian attacks had taken hold) made it impossible for Irish labour to learn these lessons on their own.[143] He does refer to the lack of a 'professional political vanguard', but fails to expand on the impact of the lack of a Bolshevik-type party in Ireland on the situation.[144] The potential of the Revolutionary Socialist Party evolving into a Bolshevik party was lost with its demise after the Belfast pogroms. The fledgling Communist Party of Ireland established in 1921 could, potentially, have grown rapidly on the back of the wave of workplace soviets and strikes in 1922. However, the CPI focused exclusively on agitating for the anti-Treaty nationalist leadership during this period, dismissing the soviets out of hand. It is impossible to predict what could have happened if the CPI had taken an active role in supporting the soviets, working to tap into the revolutionary intent of the soviets and expand the conflict to the rank-and-file of the trade union movement.

Conclusion: 'A serious threat to employers and the leadership of the trade union movement'

The Munster soviets posed a serious threat to employers and the leadership of the trade union movement alike.[145] The idea of workers' control and ownership became a key issue and was more concrete than during the earlier soviets. As the soviets were condemned by the trade union leadership, these actions not alone broke the law, they also resulted in the loss of strike pay. They were a manifestation of a militant rank-and-file moving outside the structure of the official trade union movement in order to exert their rights. The syndicalism advocated in propaganda by the trade union leadership was undermined by the use of soviets and ultimately led to a breakdown of the industrial unionism advocated by the likes of William O'Brien and Cathal O'Shannon.[146] Communist influences were more pronounced in the post-1921 soviets, with the Munster Council of Action being guided by Marxist ITGWU organizers. Importantly, the soviets signified a collapse in confidence in the national trade union leadership, an open questioning of the reliance on industrial trade unionism, and a demand for immediate revolutionary action instead. Unfortunately, the action was too fragmented to be effective.[147]

A significant measure of responsibility for this fragmentation must be laid at the feet of the fledgling Communist Party of Ireland. While the CPI

---

143 O'Connor Lysaght, 'The Munster soviet creameries', p. 38.   **144** Ibid.   **145** O'Connor, *Syndicalism in Ireland*, p. 127.   **146** Ibid., p. 128.   **147** Ibid., p. 131.

reported on the emergence of the Munster soviets, they were largely dismissed as irrelevant. They viewed these workers' struggles as reformist, rather than revolutionary in character, with Liam O'Flaherty, then a prominent member of the CPI, describing the soviets as 'merely incidental to the everyday struggle against capitalism'.[148] Not alone did the CPI fail to explain how these movements could develop a revolutionary character while it stood aloof from the struggles, the party seemed to hold the view that it had no role to play in attempting to develop a revolutionary class consciousness among the Irish working class. Seán Dowling, Jack McGrath and Jack Hedley were known to the leadership of the CPI, but the party made no attempt to contact them, or influence their actions, let alone recruit them to the CPI.[149] The incorrect perspectives of the CPI at this time can be demonstrated by the fact that they advocated for a 'Republic' rather than a 'Workers' Republic' as an alternative to the Free State,[150] and advocated a vote for anti-Treaty republicans rather than the Labour Party in the June 1922 election.[151] Throughout the Civil War the CPI repeatedly claimed that the Free State was on the verge of collapse and that a Republican victory was assured,[152] completely disorientating any workers who may have been looking in their direction for an understanding of developments at the time. By the time the Comintern had corrected the programme of the CPI at the end of 1922,[153] large sections of the Irish working class had gone down to defeat and the capitalist class had regained the upper hand, bolstered by the reactionary policies of the new Free State government. At a farmers' meeting in Ardfinnan, near Clonmel, in mid-September 1922, the head of the Tipperary IFU, Michael Heffernan, commended the 'stern fight that the united farmers had put up against the forces of Sovietism' and stated his belief that 'the dreaded menace of the Red Flag and all the evil things it stood for had been effectively beaten in Tipperary', and that 'the monster would not rear its head aloft for many a long year to come'.[154]

---

148 Milotte, *Communism in modern Ireland*, p. 57. 149 Ibid. 150 Ibid., p. 53. 151 Ibid., p. 56. 152 Ibid., p. 62. 153 Ibid., pp 63–4. The Comintern advocated a united front promoting 'a joint struggle of communists with all workers who belonged to other parties or groups, and with all non-party workers, in defence of the basic interests of the working class against the bourgeoisie'. Roddy Connolly and George Pollock, who represented the Communist Party of Ireland (CPI) at the 4th Congress of the Comintern in late 1922, faced sharp criticisms in private discussions for their failure to advocate an independent class position rather than giving de Valera uncritical support. Despite this, on his return to Ireland, Roddy Connolly argued that his support for republicans during the Civil War was correct, but accepted that the CPI had erred in failing to distinguish itself from the de Valera leadership. On 23 January 1923 Connolly's presidential address to the first congress of the CPI defended his previous position, but he faced criticism from rank-and-file members at the congress and subsequently failed to win re-election to the party's executive (Milotte, *Communism in modern Ireland*, pp 64–5). 154 *The Nationalist*, 27 Sept. 1922.

'Famous only as far as the wanders of a lame dog': the Volunteers of Moygownagh C Company

LIAM ALEX HEFFRON

By identifying Volunteers of a local IRA company, with their Cumann na mBan comrades, and interrogating newly available primary and secondary sources, this essay sheds light onto the activities and motivations of the men and women of the local Irish Revolution, as both they and others remembered it. In a micro-study of the period 1918–23, of a west of Ireland community, an understanding is conveyed of how these militant republicans fought Crown forces, established the local alternative to the state administration and confronted dissent within their own community. The relationship between the republican struggle and deep-seated agrarianism is also explored, as the war of liberation evolved into the local civil war, while state authority waned and waxed over the region.

Context

Joost Augusteijn's comparative study of 'ordinary Volunteers' involved in the War of Independence included members of two companies in west Mayo, which he understood to be at the core of their local communities and thus 'could count on solid support'.[1] Gavin Foster believed his wider findings of the pre-Truce IRA tending to be 'urban, middle class, educated, and skilled' ran counter to studies in other counties, which 'suggest a more rural, lower-class membership'.[2] However, here Augusteijn was specifically referring to the Dublin city context. For his Mayo study, he claimed poorer farmers and labourers tended not to join, except in the final period of 1920–1, 'when something real was at stake', but otherwise the movement appealed to all but 'the most well-to-do'.[3]

Fergus Campbell argued with David Fitzpatrick's 'old wine in new bottles' view of Sinn Féin members inheriting the old UIL mantle.[4] Instead, he saw

---

[1] Joost Augusteijn, *From public defiance to guerrilla warfare: the experience of ordinary volunteers in the Irish War of Independence, 1916–1921* (Dublin, 1998), pp 176, 356–7. See also Joost Augusteijn, *Mayo: the Irish Revolution, 1912–23* (Dublin, 2023). [2] Gavin Maxwell Foster, *The Irish Civil War and society: politics, class, and conflict* (London, 2015), p. 15. [3] Augusteijn, *From public defiance*, pp 360, 363. [4] David Fitzpatrick, 'The geography of Irish nationalism 1910–1921', *Past & Present*, 78

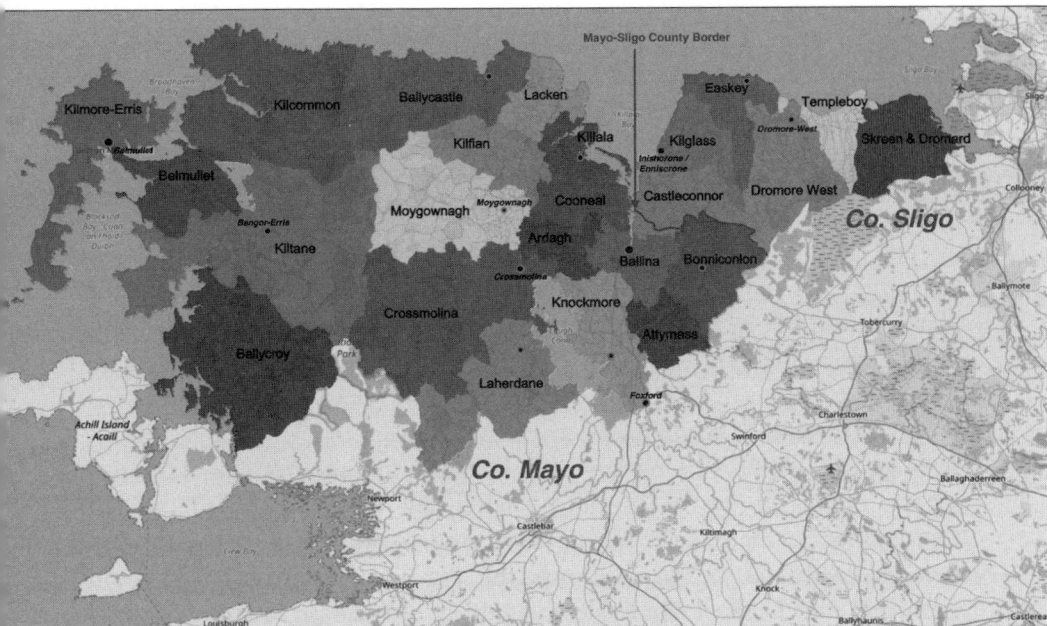

6.1 Moygownagh and neighbouring parishes in north Mayo.

change rather than continuity, with younger, poorer republicans melding with a more Fenian tradition than Fitzpatrick allowed.[5] Reflecting on his original *Land and revolution,* Campbell distilled his primary argument, in a contrary examination of the Irish Revolution in terms of 'class rather than faction or ethnicity, the ongoing importance of agrarian conflict and anti-landlord agitation, the potential for social radicalism among rank-and-file republicans and so on'.[6]

He also discounted claims for Sinn Féin's innate conservatism, with his east Galway study directly countering Fitzpatrick's findings in Co. Clare.[7] Foster refined Campbell's examination, arguing that the concept of social status rather than economic class is more flexible and historically accurate, which better explains 'deeper social identities, interests, and conflicts that divided Irish society'.[8] Yet, the IRA experience may have had significant regional variation, as suggested by Peter Hart's findings that pre-Truce IRA violence levels were not an indication of post-Treaty activity – where counties such as Mayo and Sligo were among the few 'significantly more active in 1922–3, than

(1978), 135.   **5** Fergus Campbell, 'Land and revolution revisited' in Fergus Campbell and Tony Varley (eds), *Land questions in modern Ireland* (Manchester, 2013), p. 338.   **6** Ibid., p. 346.   **7** Ibid., p. 348.   **8** Foster, *The Irish Civil War and society*, p. 18.   **9** Ibid., p. 13.

before'.[9] Within the (often conflicting) historiography, this examination of the motivations and background of the Moygownagh republicans intends to shed sharper light on the evolving, subaltern understanding of the local Irish Revolution, as found in this north Mayo rural parish.

Sources

This study uses primary sources in the vein of Augusteijn's 1998 research, but benefits from the recent releases of the Military Service Pension Collection, by the Irish Military Archives. The MSPC contains applications from seventeen members of C Company (Moygownagh) IRA, for military pensions or service medals, based on their active service during 1916–23. Extracts from their applications have been transcribed by this author in a 109-page narrative report, published by St Cormac's Society, under the Mayo Decade of Centenaries Scheme 2021, administered by Mayo County Council.[10] The National Archives of Ireland and the National Archives (UK) hold compensation claims of twenty-six individuals for financial loss, as a result of military action in the Moygownagh area, in both pre- and post-Truce periods. Within an understanding of their context and compilation, all these claims reveal details of the heretofore undocumented local Revolution experience.

Supplementary contemporary sources include Royal Irish Constabulary (RIC) Mayo county inspector reports (1917–21), Free State military and intelligence reports (1922–4), 1911 census returns for households, Valuation Office cancellation books, national schools registers and local newspapers. Moygownagh-connected individuals were interviewed for family memories of events and of the participants involved. Mayo County Library published the author's narrative of the north Mayo revolutionary period and it is referenced, where appropriate. All the above sources were used to create a dataset identifying and characterizing each Moygownagh Volunteer or Cumann na mBan member.[11] Unfortunately, the dearth of records of activities for the latter narrows this study's focus to their male comrades.

Who were the Moygownagh republicans?

A hundred years ago, Moygownagh parish had no central village settlement and without industry or services its sparse population was mainly employed

10 Liam Alex Heffron, *Transcription of Moygownagh C Company IRA claims in the Military Service Pension Collection (tenth release)* (Ballina, 2022), https://www.stcormac.ie/decade-of-centenaries.
11 Liam Alex Heffron, 'Appendix 6, Background statistics to the local Irish Revolution in north

in pastoral farming on fertile hilly lowlands stretching up into western 'broken country of vast moor and bogland'. Moygownagh comprised fifty-four townlands, situated a few miles north of Crossmolina town, in north Mayo, and contained the estates of Glenmore (Fetherstonhaugh) and Owenmore (Orme) with a Catholic church, post office and three national schools.[12] Between 1901 and 1911, its population stabilized after five decades of decline. All bar thirty-nine were Catholic and living mainly in the lowlands, with thirty-six members of the Church of Ireland and three Presbyterians. Twenty-seven Catholic families lived in the 'mountain' community, served by Crocnacally national school, only opened in 1907.[13]

The nominal rolls for C (Moygownagh) Company, IRA, reveal a membership of forty-two on 11 July 1921 and seventy-five on 1 July 1922.[14] Within north Mayo, C Company was one of the smallest during the War of Independence.[15] Notably, the large Volunteer influx during the post-Truce period fell away as the Civil War broke out, according to the company captain, Martin Gallagher.[16] The Cumann na nBan rolls for Moygownagh reveal continuity with the same fifteen members in both periods.[17] At least three pre-Truce Volunteers were not recorded on the rolls, revealing some compilation errors.[18]

The Moygownagh Sinn Féin club was formed prior to the attendance as delegates at a north Mayo executive of Volunteer James Browne and club secretary John Ruane in Crossmolina, on 19 January 1918. Ruane became a rural district councillor in the May 1920 local elections, with Sinn Féin virtually unopposed. Martin 'Darby' Gallagher of Gortnahurra, was C Company captain from its establishment in January 1918, with members initially trained by officers of other companies. The parish Cumann na nBan was formed by 1919, with Elizabeth Ruane, John's sister, as captain.[19]

Mayo', www.liamheffron.com/contested_space [accessed 25 Mar. 2022]. **12** Conor O'Brien, *Irish Tourist Association survey, Moygownagh parish, County Mayo (north)* (Dublin, 1942), https://www. mayo.ie/irish-tourist-association-survey [accessed 21 Aug. 2020]. **13** Liam Alex Heffron, 'The formation of the parishes of Killala diocese', *Cathair na Mart, Journal of the Westport Historical Society*, 37 (2020), 66–76. While technically in Doonfeeny civil parish, Inagh and Muinganierin are effectively in the Moygownagh parish mountain district. The population of the latter parish was 1,356 according to the census of 1911, slightly up from 1,350 in 1901. **14** 'IRA nominal rolls – 4th Western Division, 2nd Brigade (north Mayo) 3rd battalion (Ballycastle)', *Military Service Pension Collection (MSPC)* (16 Jan. 1936), Military Archives, MA/MSPC/RO/335. **15** 'IRA nominal rolls – 4th battalion (Crossmolina)', MA, MA-MSPC-RO-336. **16** *Transcription of Moygownagh C Company IRA claims*, p. 35. **17** 'Cumann na mBan nominal rolls – Killala/Ballycastle/Lacken District Council, North Mayo Brigade area' (14 Dec. 1937), MA, MA/MSPC/CMB/37. **18** *Transcription of Moygownagh C Company IRA claims*, pp 12–14, 47–57. The C Company nominal rolls exclude three pre-Truce Volunteers who provided evidence of their pre-Truce membership, i.e., Joseph Kelly and Patrick J Cronin, while the latter corroborated Thomas Dooher's enlistment at the same time. **19** C. na mBan Rolls – K/B/C Dist.; '1911 Census (Mayo)', Michael Ruane, Carn,

Most families of these republicans were Orme or Fetherstonhaugh estate tenants, although eleven held smallholdings purchased outright before the outbreak of the Great War. However, family farm size rather than ownership status was their most indicative characteristic.[20] Of the forty-five pre-Truce Volunteers, forty were sons of small farmers, with twenty-six from congested holdings (within parameters as defined by Fergus Campbell, based on rateable land valuations [hereinafter termed simply 'value'], with 'Congested' at less than £10, 'Small Farmer' at less than £20 and a 'Strong Farmer / Grazier' over £50).[21] Two volunteers were from middling farms, with only Capt. Michael Joseph Kelly from a prosperous farming family. He was atypical of the local Volunteer: his father Hugh, and grandfather Michael were renowned cattle dealers and district councillors, while he was the only Volunteer with a secondary school education, having attended St Muredach's College, Ballina.[22]

David Fitzpatrick highlighted the blurred definition of occupational classification as some 'small farmers' were also occasional farm workers, such as John 'Sonny' McHale's father, recorded as a farmer in the 1911 census but as a labourer in the civil registration of his son Martin's birth, three years later.[23] Many 'farmer's sons' laboured on the homestead, awaiting emigration, inheritance or a favourable marriage.[24] While seventy-four men were described in the 1911 census as (agricultural) labourers, Moygownagh lacked an ITWGU branch unlike nearby Ballycastle, Crossmolina or Killala and only two labourers, James Molloy and Michael Fleming, were pre-Truce Volunteers.[25] However, Thomas Carden, labourer on Anthony Finnerty's farm, is likely the same man who joined Capt. Michael Joseph Kelly on Carn road, on 20 July 1922 and seized William Orme Bourke's bicycle on behalf of the IRA.[26] Considering his employer's attitude to the Volunteers, Carden would have been dissuaded from public involvement.

Kilfian South DED. **20** 'Cancellation Books for rateable valuations in Ireland – County Mayo', *Books of survey revision* (Valuation Office of Ireland, 1850–2002), parish townlands within DEDs of Fortland, Crossmolina North, Deel, Kilfian South, Kilfian West, Kilfian North, Kilfian East and Beldergmore (1913–23). **21** Fergus Campbell, *Land and revolution: nationalist politics in the west of Ireland, 1891–1921* (Oxford, 2005), p. 233. **22** *Western People*, 1 Nov. 1919; *St Muredach's College, Ballina; a complete roll of past pupils (1906–1979)* (Ballina, 1979), pp 103–7. **23** 'Birth of Martin to James and Anne McHale, Rathglass', digital scan in the *Civil records of births, deaths & marriages in Ireland* (Ballina District Registry Office, 9 Feb. 1914), https://civilrecords.irishgenealogy.ie [accessed 14 Apr. 2021]. **24** David Fitzpatrick, 'Class, family and rural unrest in nineteenth-century Ireland' in P.J. Drudy (ed.), *Ireland – land, politics, and people* (Cambridge, 1982), p. 54. **25** Francis Devine, 'The Irish Transport & General Workers' Union in Mayo, 1918–1930', unpublished paper (Dublin, 2018); *Census of Ireland, 1911* (Mayo), Moygownagh townlands. **26** Post Truce compensation files (Co. Mayo), Department of Finance; Post Truce (Damage to Property (Compensation) Act, 1923) compensation files, 1922–1934, National Archives, FIN/COMP/2/16, no. 57, William O[rme] Bourke.

Membership had strong familial connections, as would be expected in a small rural parish. Forty-one families were represented in the nominal rolls with interconnected kinships, such as the three closely related republican families in Druminangle. Officer James Lynott (Snr) was also related to Capt. Gallagher, while John and Elizabeth Ruane were first cousins of officer Peter Quinn.[27]

While all were Catholic, and all but two had recorded national school attendance, the most striking feature was their youth, with an average Volunteer age in 1917–18 of 21, and 24 for their female comrades. ('Soldier Hegarty' was too old to have attended Crocnacally NS and labourer Michael Fleming is not found in the local school records but both were recorded as Catholic in the 1901 and 1911 census returns.)[28] Many would otherwise have expected to leave Ireland, but the Great War saw the emigration valve shut off.[29] The annual outflow of Mayo emigrants (most aged 20–24) plummeted from 2,436 in 1914, to twenty-two by 1917.[30] In a county with virtually no industrial development, aside from a woollen factory at Foxford and recently opened bacon factory at Castlebar,[31] they found themselves confined to their family's smallholdings, becoming radicalized by a vigorous republican movement.

Augusteijn did not explore the link between IRA recruitment and the number of young men confined to a parish such as Moygownagh by a prolonged pause in emigration.[32] His work used the official IRA nominal rolls compiled in the 1930s and largely agrees with the youthfulness of the interrelated Moygownagh Volunteers. However, where Augusteijn found a west Mayo IRA membership encompassing a high mobilization of available Catholic men, this study disagreed and observed that these Rolls – especially those members listed on the second critical date of 1 July 1922 – did not accurately represent the active company membership.[33] Augusteijn also

27 Interviews with: Hugh Jennings, Druminangle, Moygownagh, Co. Mayo (16 June 1993); Johnny Orme, Coreens, Moygownagh (3 Oct. 2018 and 27 Jan. 2018); Nellie Timlin (nee Ruane) and Kevin Timlin, Ballina, Co. Mayo (24 Aug. 2014). **28** Pupil registers of Carn NS, Glenmore NS, Crocnacally NS and Ballymachola NS, digitized page images in *ANSEO project – Saving our schools' records*, 2021, www.anseo.ie/digital-archive [accessed 24 June 2021]. **29** Fergus Campbell and Kevin O'Shiel, 'The last land war? Kevin O'Shiel's memoir of the Irish Revolution (1916–21)', *Archivium Hibernicum*, 57 (2003), 161. **30** *Emigration statistics of Ireland for the year 1920. Report and tables showing the number, ages, conjugal condition, and destinations of the emigrants from each county and province in Ireland during the year 1920; also the occupations of the emigrants, and the number of emigrants who left each port in each month of the year*, Cmd. 1414, HC (London, 1921) – for years 1909–19 see Cmd; 721, 77, 9013, 8520, 7883, 8230, 7313, 6727, 6131, 5607 and 5088 respectively. **31** 'Inspector general's and county inspectors' monthly confidential reports' (1926), *Dublin Castle Records (1795–1926)*, The National Archives (UK), CO 904/48–156b, No. 102, Apr. 1917 (Mayo). **32** Augusteijn, *From public defiance*, pp 265–6, 299–300. **33** Ibid., pp 353–7.

concluded that rural IRA membership in Mayo was composed predominantly of small farmers, rather than their sons as per this study – a non-semantic difference.[34]

What did the local IRA want?

Leading north Mayo Volunteers later attributed their republicanism to the influence of their national school teachers, but no Moygownagh republican left memories of their school days, or contemporary insight into their revolutionary aspirations or influences.[35] John 'Sonny' McHale's uncle, Martin, was briefly imprisoned with two other labourers, Michael Hanahoe and Pat Corrigan, for assault on 1 September 1880.[36] Aside from this tenuous connection to land war activism, none had explicit connections with past mobilizations and several had other than a revolutionary family background, including being on the 'establishment' side during previous struggles. James Browne's brother later recalled their family's antagonism towards local Fenians who had attacked their grandfather, Michael Browne, for land grabbing during the land war. John 'Soldier' Hegarty, and Michael Joseph Kelly, were British army veterans of the Great War.[37] John and Elizabeth Ruane's brother, Edward, joined the Scots Guards in 1904 and was killed in France in 1914, fighting with the British Expeditionary Forces. John kept his brother's war medals as heirlooms.[38]

Augusteijn may have understated how participation in cultural republicanism helped radicalize potential members of the IRA, for the RIC county inspector for Mayo, Steadman, believed that shared membership and the cultural interest of republican organizations fed into Sinn Féin party growth, as it encompassed the 'majority of the members of the GAA and Gaelic League [and] extremists generally'.[39] A Gaelic League branch was established in Moygownagh in 1903.[40] The parish had one of only ten senior GAA football teams affiliated with the Mayo County Board as early as the 1908/9 season.[41] The GAA was locally present from early in the century, with

34 Ibid., pp 356–7, 359–60.   35 Liam Alex Heffron, *No revolution: igniting war in north Mayo, 1917–1923* (Castlebar, 2017), pp 28–32.   36 Castlebar Prison Register (1878–1903), p. 70, NA, MFGS/51/3.   37 Liam Bruen, 'The Hegartys of Altderrig' (Longford, 1988), p. 8; Kelly, Michael Joseph, First World War Service Record, *War Office: Soldiers' Documents, First World War 'Burnt Documents' (microfilm copies), 1914–1920*, TNA, WO363, Service Record No. M-318861.   38 Kevin Timlin, 'Edward Rowane, 1882–1914', Family Genealogy Blog, *Rowane, World War 1*, 2014, https://rowaneww1.wordpress.com/2014/11/07/edward-rowane [accessed 2 Aug. 2016].   39 Augusteijn, *From public defiance*, pp 265–6, 299–300; Heffron, *No revolution*, p. 28.   40 *Western People*, 31 Oct. 1903.   41 *Connaught Telegraph*, 4 July 1908.

the annual Moygownagh sports, first recorded in 1895, being held under GAA rules by 1910. Quartermaster Peter Quinn, later remembered as the team's goalkeeper, beat fellow officer James Lynott in the two mile cycle, in the parish sports of October 1920.[42]

Fighting for the local republic

A civil servant pithily summarized Volunteer Joseph Kelly's Military Service Pension (MSP) service claim as consisting of 'all small things',[43] a lens through which officials also viewed his colleagues' applications. No C Company members were awarded service pensions, though in older age, being of little means, four were granted 'special allowances' for permanent health disabilities.[44] Most of the C Company Volunteers were active within Moygownagh parish, though several claimed wider service; moving arms between other areas, providing safe refuge for injured IRA on the run and rendering support to the Flying Column (ASU no. 1) based in the remote mountain district of the parish in the months leading up to the Truce.[45] Capt. Gallagher and James Lynott (snr) were recognized for having greater service than their comrades, but Gallagher's record was summed up by an MSP board official as 'a good deal of miscellaneous duty which is typical of this district'. Lynott's record revealed 'good services but would not appear to be up to Keyman standard'.[46]

The Volunteers did skirmish with Black and Tans who arrived without warning at their attempted ambush of an RIC bicycle patrol on Belville Bridge in April 1921 and during an IRA raid of Garranard post office the previous February.[47] In each case, the unexpected ferocity of enemy firepower quickly overwhelmed any desire for resistance on the part of the poorly armed Volunteers, who quickly retreated. They had more success disarming two sentries during an RIC search of the parish graveyard for arms, but aside from trenching roads against Crown patrols, that was the extent of their military operations against the state.[48]

The lack of any pre-Truce claims against the Crown forces from Moygownagh residents[49] contrasts with seventeen and thirty-three claims from

42 *Transcription of Moygownagh C Company IRA claims*, p. 102; Interview with Tony Finnerty, Carn, Moygownagh (2 Aug. 2014). **43** *Transcription of Moygownagh C Company IRA claims*, p. 53. **44** Ibid., pp 7–8, 14, 56–7, 67, 87–8. **45** Heffron, *No revolution*, pp 96–7; *Transcription of Moygownagh C Company IRA claims*, pp 32–7, 72, 75. **46** *Transcription of Moygownagh C Company IRA claims*, pp 35, 72. **47** Brigade Activity Reports – North Mayo Brigade, *MSPC 1916–23* (18 Dec. 1940), MA, MA-MSPC-A-35, pp 53–4. **48** *Transcription of Moygownagh C Company IRA claims*, pp 33–5, 53–5. **49** 'Compensation Commission, Mayo (Pre-Truce)', *Register of claimants*

Crossmolina and Ballycastle, respectively.[50] Volunteer John 'Sonny' McHale
and his father were violently interrogated in a shed at their Rathglass home
by a combined Black and Tan and RIC unit.[51] Similarly, Volunteer Patrick
Hegarty's home in nearby Treenagh was raided and he was dragged out to the
field by his house to be then subjected to a mock execution.[52] There must have
been other unrecorded 'visits' by Crown forces, seeking information on
republican sympathizers, but, in short, there was little actual military activity
in the parish related to the War of Independence.

Upholding civil law

With the closure of vulnerable constabulary barracks throughout 1920,
including Farmhill barracks, Kilfian, which had served most of Moygownagh
parish, the IRA extended its civil control relatively unhindered by the
Crown.[53] Dissatisfied locals – with little recourse except to republican
authorities – were likely aware of John Joseph Connolly's plight in nearby
Ardagh. He was severely boycotted on suspicion that he informed of a planned
IRA ambush. His house, farm and stock were damaged and in March 1922,
the roof of his house was forced in over his wife and 'due to the fright [...]
she lost the baby'. He was unable to keep his twenty-three-acre farm and
moved into a Rappa Castle outhouse, as caretaker. Bemoaning his plight, he
wrote: 'Revd Ml. McLoughlin P.P. stated to my wife that I should have minded
my own business and not mix up with the Black and Tans'. Father Peter Davis
shared the reticence of his Ardagh colleague. The parish priest had been
president of the local UIL branch, but by the late 1910s, his ill health,
alcoholism and a feud with mission priest Fr John J. Ruddy who had retired
to Moygownagh, saw him ill-placed to oppose republican excesses – even if
he had wanted to.[54]

   In 1920, the Moygownagh Sinn Féin arbitration court was established,
with local republicans acting as both police and judges, guarding courts,

(*Compensation (Ireland) Commission (Shaw and Wood-Renton Commission) and related bodies, 1922–
1930*), TNA, CO 905–8, no. 710, Mary Kelly.   **50** Ibid., no. 1281 (4 July 1921); nos 1349–50 (12
July 1921); no. 1351 (31 Apr.–1 May 1921); no. 1518 (10 Mar. 1921); no. 1577 (29 Oct. 1921).
The latter is incorrectly tagged in the catalogue as 'alleged Crown Forces' but corrected in John
McAndrew's Post Truce compensation claim and news report of same – see Post Truce Comp. Mayo,
no. 210, John McAndrew and *Western People*, 17 May 1924.   **51** *Transcription of Moygownagh IRA
claims*, pp 80–1.   **52** Interview with Peig Jennings, Druminangle, Moygownagh, Co. Mayo (17 Mar.
2012); Ruane, 'IRA Rolls–Ballycastle Batt.', Hegarty's name is glossed as 'raided' over his entry under
pre-Truce Moygownagh 'C' Company.   **53** Heffron, *No revolution*, p. 80; *Transcription of
Moygownagh C Company IRA claims*, p. 30.   **54** 'Compensation Commission – Loyalists (Post Truce)
Files of claimants' correspondence', *Irish Distress & Irish Grants Committee files and minutes,*

bringing offenders to trial, and enforcing the court decrees. They also prevented people attending 'British' courts, including by raiding the petty sessions clerk.[55] Capt. Gallagher confirmed his dual role as head of policing and as an arbitrator on the monthly court.[56] The relatively older Volunteer, Thomas Jennings, was also remembered as a 'Sinn Féin judge', while John Ruane, as the local rural district councillor, was likely the third justice as per convention elsewhere.[57]

These courts functioned as surrogate petty sessions, with C Company police 'enforcing civil law', which Peter Quinn saw as 'preventing poteen making', recording '[I] had several cases brought up before Dail court and collected fines in each case. [I] had to seize bicycles in a few cases before fines were paid'.[58] Val Irwin's father was remembered as having been fined £1, 'for a gun licence', in a court held under Belville Bridge.[59] Mrs Kearney reluctantly paid her fine for stealing cutlery from her neighbour (and sister) Mrs Cawley, after the IRA sat her in a cart outside her Killeenashask home, in preparation for 'bringing [her] up to Stonehall [jail]'.[60]

While no Moygownagh Sinn Féin court ledger survives, an Ardagh equivalent records fifteen cases over five sittings, between November 1921 and February 1922. Five were for rates arrears and five were brought by merchants, including one by Moygownagh Co-op, as debt recovery for goods sold. The remainder were brought by 'the company Police Officer' for poteen making, with one for 'assault on wife'.[61] William Jennings, a judge along with John Munnelly and Frank Birrane, was also the local county council rates collector – who would later plead guilty in court to embezzling rates he collected from July 1921 to November 1923.[62]

Resistance to the republicans

Despite having little establishment opposition, from their inception the IRA encountered resistance within their community. IRA companies were directed to get guns by any means, theft if necessary, and in Moygownagh this led to confrontations with locals reluctant to give up their shotguns. Volunteers

1922–1937, TNA, CO 762, no. 158/15, Connolly, John Joseph.   **55** *Transcription of Moygownagh C Company IRA claims*, pp 4–5, 11, 15–16, 20–2, 27–9, 30, 32–3, 41–3, 47–9, 51–5, 62–4, 68–73, 75–7, 94–7, 98–108; Interviews with Johnny Orme; Hugh Jennings; and Bobby Cafferty, Glenmore, Moygownagh, Co. Mayo (2 Dec. 1995); '1995-12-02, A history of the Moygownagh area'.   **56** Ibid., p. 30.   **57** Heffron, *No revolution*, pp 76–8; Ardagh parish Sinn Féin court ledger, Nov. 1921–Feb. 1922, copybook (Private Collection, 1922).   **58** *Transcription of Moygownagh C Company IRA claims*, pp 20, 51, 97.   **59** Interview with Johnny Orme.   **60** Interview with Hugh Jennings.   **61** Heffron, *No revolution*, pp 76, 78; Ardagh parish Sinn Féin court ledger.   **62** *Western People*, 22 Nov. 1924.

reported that from March 1920–1 they captured arms from parish residents 'under fire'.[63] Captain Gallagher confirmed: '[we took] part in about 40 raids for arms. There was shooting at 3 houses. The raiders were fired on an[d] those replied to the fire. [We] succeeded in getting the guns'.[64] He also admitted though, that 'some resisted by shooting at us through the windows'.[65] Corroborating Volunteers recalled forty to sixty raids, with shooting at the estate houses of Fetherstonhaugh, Orme and the latter's gate house, occupied by elderly Presbyterian gamekeeper, Ben Ireland and his family. While stern resistance may have been expected at gentry property, James Lynott (Snr) noted 'trouble' they had at non-gentry properties of the Dunleavys of Doobeha and the Munnellys of Ballintubber [Rooskey]. The IRA succeeded in breaking into Munnelly's but did not procure any guns there.[66] In the townland of Tawnywaddyduff, adjacent to Dunleavy's, it was recalled locally that the 'IRA went back to take gun off David Kelly's father, Pat, but weren't fit to take it as they had no guns, he was going to shoot them, they didn't bring it'.[67]

Hiding guns before the inevitable visit of the IRA was risky. Anthony Finnerty of Carn, aged 30 or so, hid his shotgun in the thatch of his home and defiantly faced off Volunteers seeking it, even though one of them may have been his neighbour and relation, Thomas Finnerty.[68] Others were not so fortunate. It was later recalled by Volunteer Martin Egan's son: '[The IRA] went around collecting shotguns and used force if needed [they] beat up Josie Cronin's old granddad in Cloonmeen [in Fairfield Lower]. He was an old man with an "auld" shotgun and when he refused to give it up they hit him.'[69] In the same townland disguised IRA men severely beat Pat Toohill in the hallway of his home when he refused to hand up his hidden gun. His wife recognized one of the assailants as her relation, the aforementioned Pat Hegarty of Treenagh.[70]

The 'parallel state' run by local republicans also had scope to antagonize elements of the community. Initially, Volunteers engaged in company recruiting, anti-conscription and anti-police activities. Volunteer Thomas Finnerty was active in dissuading young men from joining the RIC and preventing others from paying their dog licences.[71] The IRA enforced the local 'Belfast boycott' of goods from that city, while regularly drilling from the winter 1917/18 on – like other units across north Mayo.[72] Garranard post

---

63 *Transcription of Moygownagh C Company IRA claims*, pp 5, 20, 51–2, 66, 96, 98.   **64** Ibid., p. 33. **65** Ibid., p. 30.   **66** *Transcription of Moygownagh C Company IRA claims*, pp 75, 78.   **67** Interview with Johnny Orme.   **68** 1911 Census, Anthony Finnerty, Carn, Kilfian South DED; Interview with Tony Finnerty.   **69** Interview with 'Interviewee 110' (26 Dec. 2017), name redacted by request; 1911 census, Thomas Cronin, Fairfield Lower, Fortland DED, aged 70.   **70** Interview with 'Interviewee 101' (18 June 2022), name redacted by request.   **71** *Transcription of Moygownagh C Company IRA claims*, p. 20.   **72** Heffron, *No revolution*, p. 53; 'MSPC (1916–23), Browne, James';

office was raided and post-boys relieved of mail, with a view to censoring letters containing information that might be helpful to the enemy.[73] The community was effectively 'taxed' by Volunteers, through the imposition of levies for the Dáil loan, or for arms purchase.[74] C.I. Steadman reported that the 'prevalence by Sinn Féin's agents is very great' in the county, and that persuasion gave way to intimidation, with Volunteers going door to door at night, in their successful efforts to collect a considerable sum.[75] Capt. Gallagher admitted that C Company attempted to raise funds for arms, by imposing levies on dances, sports and collections 'but never could secure same'.[76] His enigmatic statement suggests considerable community resistance to 'tax' enforcement activities. The resistance may also have derived from a sense the IRA were not deemed to have earned their authority, as indicated by local memories:

> the IRA wouldn't even rob the rifles standing up [against the wall] from drunken Black and Tans who were passed out in the sun, outside Cafferty's [pub, yet] they would cut up the road and demand passwords before you could pass up near Convey's – they loved the passwords.[77]

Later memory assigned Free State support to 'fairly wealthy farmers, happy with [Michael] Collins's settlement [and who] just wanted to get on with life, with the business of farming'.[78] However, there was also significant pre-Treaty anti-republican feeling from prosperous farmers. C.I. Steadman had long warned that Catholic 'men of stake' in the community, traditional Irish Party supporters, were abandoning politics as they acquired ownership of their farms, within the farming boom during the Great War and as Home Rule awaited.[79] Sinn Féin's militant radicalism did not interest them. The prosperous, close-knit Munnelly families of the parish supplied local clergy, held local political office and claimed distinguished nationalist pedigrees (as per their obituaries), but stayed clear of republicanism, as did 'extensive farmer' Patrick Hegarty of Rooskey. He was a well-connected former Killala district councillor and justice of the peace, with a strong enmity of the anti-Treaty side.[80] Middling farmers also stayed aloof, with some openly hostile to the

'MSPC (1916–23), Lynott, James (Snr)'.   **73** *Transcription of Moygownagh C Company IRA claims*, pp 32, 52, 73, 76, 98, 104, 108.   **74** Ibid., pp 5, 16, 22, 28–9, 42–3, 63, 69, 73, 77, 106–8. **75** Heffron, *No revolution*, pp 58, 67.   **76** *Transcription of Moygownagh C Company IRA claims*, p. 28. **77** Interview with Johnny Orme; Cafferty's pub was beside Moygownagh chapel.   **78** Interview with Frank and Eddie Clarke, Rathoma, Killala, Co. Mayo (7 Apr. 2016).   **79** Heffron, *No revolution*, p. 34.   **80** For Munnelly, see *Western People*, 13 Apr. 1878, 13 Jan. 1900, 29 Apr. 1916, 25 May 1918, 19 Dec. 1925; for Hegarty: *Connaught Telegraph*, 22 Nov. 1913; *Western People*, 6 June 1914;

IRA, such as Anthony Finnerty above, who held sixty-two acres in Carn, valued at £26.[81]

Guarding property rights: the IRA and agrarianism

Solving the west of Ireland's endemic land hunger was long seen as a motivating factor in Irish politics – which a radical Sinn Féin party seized – but its military wing had to deal with a resultant 'prairie fire' of direct agrarian action sweeping the west.[82] In December 1918, on a Bangor-Erris fair day, future Sinn Féin TD, William Sears, urged the sons of small farmers to 'get the land for Ireland' and continue the work of 'Rory of the hills' in the land war of 1880–2, by shooting landlords and their agents.[83] A year earlier, John Ruane shared a platform in Ballina with Darrell Figgis, at 'the biggest fair of the whole year', and declared that 'the majority of the people of his parish were in favour of the Sinn Féin policy [of taking the land for the Irish people]'.[84] However, the Moygownagh IRA was remembered for taking the grazier's side against small farmers, only a few miles from Bangor-Erris: 'They came down on the men back the mountain who were trying to get Muinntarry [Ummerantarry] land of Anthony Kelly divided and drove off his cattle.'[85]

Anthony Kelly was a prosperous farmer of 129 acres in the lowlands at Ballaghamuck, on the border with Crossmolina.[86] He claimed his cattle were driven and damaged in June 1922, forcing him to abandon his mountain farm of eleven hundred acres, to be grazed by 'the cattle drivers' until 10 June 1923.[87] His herd Francis Lynn – a local man – also had six cattle driven and injured.[88] Capt. Gallagher confirmed his company's role was 'protecting Kelly's Lands at Muneneering [Ummerantarry] whose cattle were driven and tails cut. Was there on guard in turn for 2 weeks'.[89]

The Special Infantry Corp was set up in January 1923 by the Free State to deal with agrarian crime.[90] Four men were arrested by the SIC on 11 July 1923 and held by them in Ballina jail, for driving Kelly's cattle, as the Free State exerted its control over this remote area.[91] All four men, Peter and

'Pat Hegarty, Roosky', Department of Finance; Post Truce compensation files, 1922–1934, NA, FIN/1/2274. **81** Cancellation Books (Mayo), Carn, Kilfian South DED (1911–32); Interview with Tony Finnerty. **82** Fergus Campbell, *Land and revolution*, pp 221, 246. **83** *Connaught Telegraph*, 11 Jan. 1919. **84** *Western People*, 22 Dec. 1917. **85** Interview with Jimmy 'the Postman' Finnerty, Garranard, Moygownagh, Co. Mayo (20 July 2016). **86** Cancellation Books (Mayo), Ballaghamuck, Crossmolina North DED (1916–42). **87** Ibid., Ummerantarry, Kilfian West DED (1911–31); 'Post Truce Comp. Mayo', no. 297, Anthony Kelly. **88** 'Post Truce Comp. Mayo', no. 54, Francis Lynn. **89** *Transcription of Moygownagh C Company IRA claims*, p. 30. **90** Campbell, *Land and revolution*, p. 282. **91** 'Prisoners arrested by the Special Infantry Corp', *Civil War*

James Hegarty in Altderg, with Michael Carey and James Maughan in Muinganiarann, held farms valued under £5, adjacent to the Ummerantarry land.[92]

Nine miles west in the lowlands, the Stonehall grazing farm had been purchased by the Congested Districts Board prior to the Great War, as urged by Fr Peter Davis, to relieve the Fairfield small farmers, but it remained undivided, as the Great War disrupted the CDB's operations.[93] In May 1920, frustrated at the lack of progress, the North Mayo Farmers' Association's Moygownagh branch initiated the establishment of a special committee of Fairfield farmers to deal directly with the CDB.[94] Of the ten members, eight had farms valued at less than £10, as well as James Neary's at approximately £14 and Philip Forestal's at just over £16.[95] Their local Sinn Féin district councillor, John Lowther, advised that 'if these people wished to compel the Board to divide the land amongst them they would not let a single beast in on the land'.[96] This went against the stated policy of the CDB, which ruled that 'prevalence of intimidation of any form … will have the effect of delaying indefinitely instead of hastening proceedings for the acquisition of any lands in respect of which illegal practices prevail'.[97]

As the authority of the state ebbed, the patience of the local farmers ran out and C.I. Steadman reported that between 30 April and 1 May 1921, at Ballynacloy, where Stonehall farm was located, 'fences were knocked down and removed, with a grave dug on a CD Board farm, which was set in grazing to a herd. Local people wanted to expedite the dividing up of the farm'.[98] Two weeks earlier, on 16 and 19 April, the herd Thomas Kelly had his cattle driven by about seventeen men, after a public meeting headed by a North Mayo Farmers' Association organizer, on the crossroads by the farm. However, by July, four men, including Kelly, had purchased Stonehall farm from the CDB

Internment Collection (1923), MA, IE-MA-CW-P-02-02-01; 'Special Infantry Corp returns & reports: prisoners', *Civil War Internment Collection* (1923) MA, IE-MA-CW-P-02-02-02. The Maughan man is given the prefix P in the former record and J in the latter, but James Maughan held this holding in common with Michael Carey so likely the same man. The transcriptions in these copybooks appear rushed to create a summary index from (verbal?) reports by an official who was unfamiliar with the local geography and surnames. **92** Cancellation Books (Mayo), Muinganieran, Beldergmore DED (1910–22) and Altderg and Srahmeen, Kilfian West DED (1911–31). **93** Tony Varley, 'A region of sturdy smallholders? Western nationalists and agrarian politics during the First World War', *Journal of the Galway Archaeological and Historical Society*, 55 (2003), 132–3. **94** *Western People*, 15 May 1920. The members of the Fairfield committee were Anthony Gallagher, Anthony Martin, Philip Forrestal, James Neary, Peter Dooher, Martin Cronin, Pat Maughan, Ed Brogan, Michael Birrane and James McHale. **95** Cancellation Books (Mayo), Fairfield Lower, Fortland DED (1912–28). **96** *Western People*, 5 May 1920. **97** *Congested Districts Board for Ireland: Minutes of board meetings, January 1916 to December 1918*, vol. 3, 13 June 1917, as quoted in Varley, 'A region of sturdy smallholders?', 133. **98** IGCI, no. 121, Jan.–Nov. 1921 (Mayo).

for £1200.[99] In response, their lands were severely boycotted. Kelly was assaulted with two of his ribs broken and had his cattle driven by masked men on several occasions.[100] While admitting Stonehall was originally purchased in 1910 for 'striping it amongst the Fairfield tenants', Kelly claimed they had then fallen foul of the CDB, who sold it to the quartet and since then, 'the Fairfield people have never given the owners a minutes rest, including the boycott, driving and injury to animals and destruction of hay'.[101]

Kelly received the former 'mansion' and thirty-seven acres. The other three owners were republicans, with officer James Lynott (Snr), the most prominent beneficiary, also receiving thirty-seven acres. Volunteer Willie 'Bawn' Gallagher's brother, John, received seventeen acres and republican supporter, John Convey, received fourteen acres. The Fairfield agrarian agitators now found themselves attacking the IRA. Part of a song composed at the time is still remembered locally:

> Kelly, Lynott, Convey and Bawn.
> We'll root them out, we'll shoot them out
> For our lovely green fields of Stonehall.[102]

In response, during April to July 1921, C Company IRA, led by Capt. Gallagher, arrested 'people at Stonehall in [the] land dispute', and guarded them before their trial at a Dáil court,[103] as he later recalled:

> [I] carried out arrest of ten people at Stonehall land dispute and had narrow escape from death by being kicked by one of the prisoners in the stomach. Prisoners were defended at Farmhill by a solicitor (Mr Bourke Ballina) … Had them guarded for three days and nights before we could have them tried by Dail Court when they had to have [the] solicitor.[104]

Any court arbitration decision was bound to be seen by non-republicans as utterly biased, but while the result is not known, four smallholders in the Fairfield area did receive between five to eight acres each, including Kate Loftus, Martin Goff and two Fairfield committee members – James McHale (father of Volunteer John 'Sonny' McHale) and Philip Forrestal. The Fairfield agitators did not accept the arbitration and the four smallholders became a target of their neighbours. Stonehall farm was subjected to a 'boycott for a

---

99 *Western People*, 24 Sept. 1921; Post Truce Comp. Mayo, no. 33, Thomas Kelly. **100** *Western People*, 24 Nov. 1923. **101** Post Truce Comp. Mayo, no. 33, Thomas Kelly. **102** Interviewee 101 indicates the 'Bawn' Gallaghers of Behy. **103** *Transcription of Moygownagh C Company IRA claims*, pp 32, 20, 51–2, 97, 99. **104** Ibid., p. 30.

6.2 James Lynott, who became the vice captain of C Company, Moygownagh IRA, pictured with rabbits which he trapped and sold to Crossmolina grocers, *c.*1920. © private collection.

distance of two miles' with further driving and injury of cattle, with thefts and raiding,[105] from October 1921 and into July and October-November of the following year.[106] As the Fairfield farmers grew increasingly militant, C Company again provided protection for the new owners, while using the considerable outbuildings of Stonehall house as a base and training camp, over six weekends.[107] This situation was remembered elsewhere as 'agitation over land [one side] got the land in Stonehall – it was a big farm – and was divided – they [the IRA] took him [Nary]'.[108] Nary was James Patrick 'Sonny' Neary,

105 Post Truce Comp. Mayo, no. 32, Martin Goff; no. 438, Philip Forestal; no. 695, Mary Loftus; no. 878, Kate Loftus. **106** *Western People*, 17 May 1924; Post Truce Comp. Mayo, no. 33, Thomas Kelly. **107** Interview with Brendan Lynott, Carrowgarve, Crossmolina, Co. Mayo (8 July 2016); *Transcription of Moygownagh C Company IRA claims*, pp 22, 35, 52, 55. **108** Interview with Frank and Eddie Clarke: their mother was Annie Brogan, daughter of Edward Brogan of the Fairfield

of the Fairfield farmers' committee, who led the (ultimately futile) campaign of agrarian agitation by local smallholders, to force the new purchasers to throw up their claims.[109] He was targeted by the IRA and many attributed his death on 4 May 1924 to the trauma of being held and beaten by them. Aged 43, he left a widow with three young children.[110]

Radical land division: 'the Belfast Boycott'

In a letter to the editor of the *Western People* of 2 July 1921, former Ulster Unionist MP, Godfrey Fetherstonhaugh KC, resigned as justice of the peace, in disapproval of the partition that the 'Crown colony government' forced upon Ireland and:

> as I detest murder and outrage by whomsoever committed I cannot approve of the policy of reprisals by the forces of the Crown on presumably innocent people.[111]

However, Fetherstonhaugh later claimed compensation for post-Truce incidents on his Glenmore estate: the removal of fencing and extensive damage of his grazing lands as well as the driving of stock and the occupation of one hundred and twenty acres, by 'about 60 head of cattle, 5 donkeys and four horses' from the end of April 1922 until his estate was 'liberated' by Free State troops, at the end of August. It was a short respite and on 25 September (following the brief republican occupation of Ballina), agrarian incidents resumed until the end of October, with the lands 'invaded' again and notices posted warning anyone against interference. Three grazing tenants paying just over £40 removed their cattle after being 'noticed', which were replaced by the trespassing stock.[112] The incidents continued until 12 June 1923, when the SIC arrested two men, Michael Gallagher and Edward Flaherty, for driving 'Mr Fenstone's cattle'.[113]

The national anti-Treaty leadership sought to garner popular support by escalating radical agrarian action, by targeting Protestant graziers and landlords, officially prompted by the Belfast anti-Catholic pogroms.

farmers' committee. **109** *Western People*, 7 Feb. 1921. **110** Interview with Johnny Orme; 'Death of James P. Neary', *Western People*, 17 May 1924; Interviewee 101; Interview with Frank and Eddie Clarke, Rathoma, Killala; 1911 Census, Patrick Neary, Fairfield Lower, Fortland DED. **111** *Western People*, 2 July 1921. **112** Post Truce Comp. Mayo, no. 201, Godfrey Fetherstonhaugh. **113** 'Prisoners arrested by the Special Infantry Corp'; Special Infantry Corp returns & reports: prisoners; Interview with Johnny Orme who remembered that 'Fetherstonhaugh' was known locally as 'Fetherston'. Neither Flaherty nor Gallagher can be identified.

Considering the campaign against Fetherstonhaugh as part of this activism directed by the IRA (or with its tacit approval) is supported by the dates on which the incidents began, 1–3 May 1922. Northwards, on 29 April 1922, the anti-Treaty IRA occupied Capt. Newsham's Heathfield House and estate, inviting Ballycastle locals to send their animals to graze there.[114] On the same day, less than a mile away from Glenmore, merchants and graziers Rufus and William Carson had their Crossmolina grazing lands seized by Tim Jordan, Crossmolina IRA stock-master. Their cattle were sold by Jordan, with fences torn down and the lands let out to locals. Both seizures were carried out by authority of a letter signed by S. Kilcullen, O/C, North Mayo Brigade, 'in order to support and maintain refugees from Belfast' and as 'a reprisal for the murder of innocent men, women and children in Belfast. You, by supporting the Union between England and Ireland, are in sympathy with the Belfast murders.'[115]

This was a new, coordinated national strategy, later recalled by P.J Ruttledge – an Ardagh parish native – as the 'taking over of places for Belfast Boycott', while his colleague Conor Maguire was tasked 'to take over all the land and divide it up. They worked on this document. It was sent up to every [anti-Treaty IRA] unit to implement'.[116] William Carson had long defied calls to sell his grazing farms to the CDB, and resolutely faced down agrarian attacks as far back as 1914 with protection from the RIC.[117] Godfrey Fetherstonhaugh and his neighbour Guy Orme were publicly berated for not selling their lands, at political meetings in March 1913 and May 1914.[118] However, the large Orme Owenmore estate, adjacent to Glenmore, was not remembered locally, nor by Orme's grandson, as a land agitation target.[119] Neither did Guy Orme make any compensation claim for his Mayo properties.[120]

The new 'Belfast Boycott' strategy appears parallel to that involving former brigade adjutant, Patrick O'Connell, who was employed in early 1922 by republicans to manage Protestant businesses they intended seizing within the

114 'Captain and Mrs. Newsam [Newsham]', Department of Finance, Post Truce compensation files, 1922–1934, NA, FIN/1/1063; Tom Langan, 'Ballycastle seventy years ago', *North Mayo Historical & Archaeological Society Journal*, vol. 3, no. 1 (1992–3), pp 77–87. 115 Post Truce Comp. Mayo, no. 300, Carson (Reps of); no. 29, William H. Carson; CO 762, Post Truce Loyalist claims, no. 95/3, Carson, Rufus W.H. and no. 103/4, Carson, W.H. 116 Ernie O'Malley, *The men will talk to me: Mayo interviews*, ed. Cormac K.H. O'Malley and Vincent Keane (Cork, 2014), pp 264–8. 117 Synopsis of county inspectors' reports (1926); *Dublin Castle records*, TNA, CO 904/14–2, Mar. 1914 (Mayo). 118 *Western People*, 23 May 1914. 119 Interview with Harry Breen, Ballyglass, Moygownagh, Co. Mayo, by Pat Dowling, c.1990 (private collection); interview with Tony Orme, Camberley, Surrey, UK (23 Nov. 2016). 120 Compensation Commission, Mayo (Pre-Truce), *Register of claimants, Compensation (Ireland) Commission (Shaw and Wood-Renton Commission) and related bodies, 1922–1930*, TNA, CO 905–8.

Brigade area.[121] In their MSP claims, C Company Volunteers emphasize their diligence in carrying out orders as assigned to them by their commanding officers – including battalion command.[122] However, none mention any details regarding the well-organized Glenmore estate campaign, repeatedly occurring in the midst of their company area, near to Stonehall farm.[123] Considering Godfrey Fetherstonhaugh wrote his claim applications during December 1922 from Glenmore house itself, no doubt aware that his mail could be intercepted by the IRA, he judiciously did not identify his antagonists. Later reticence by Volunteers to admit their involvement in agrarianism, reflected the changed political and social situation where such radical actions did not merit mention. However their agrarian activism is remembered in one contemporary incident in the parish.

Patrick Munnelly, of Ballyglass, Ballycastle, claimed for damage to a dwelling house, outbuilding and fencing he was constructing at Killeenashask, during November 1922, by 'persons unknown'.[124] However IRA volunteers from adjacent Druminangle were remembered by judge Thomas Jennings's son as being responsible for destroying the buildings and 'throwing the roof into the [Owenmore] river'.[125] The apparent aim of preventing Munnelly residing on his farm (and thereby having a superior claim during CDB land division) had deep roots. Ten years previous, Moygownagh UIL promised to prevent Mrs Munnelly occupying a herd's house on her Killeenashask land, out of whom she had evicted seventy-three-year-old Mrs Anderson and her family. The UIL built a hut for them while awaiting the CDB board's division in her favour.[126] As with Stonehall farm, the Great War impacted the CDB's operations and by 1922, with the sixty-nine acres still undivided, local Volunteers attempted to thwart the ambitions of Mary Munnelly's son.[127] Though the dwelling house was never rebuilt, Volunteers did not mention the incident in their MSP claims.[128]

While Guy Orme was Church of Ireland, he married the daughter of Lord Killanin, of the Catholic Morris family of Spiddal, Co. Galway.[129] Kathleen

121 Post Truce Comp. Mayo, No. 29, 300 (in a loose sheet entitled 'notes of interview with Mr. O'Connell on 14 May 1927').   122 *Transcription of Moygownagh C Company IRA claims*; most volunteers repeatedly state this in their claims.   123 Post Truce Comp. Mayo, no. 201, Godfrey Fetherstonhaugh; 'Cassini 6 inch – Garraun, Co. Mayo in the Historic Environment Viewer', *Ordnance Survey maps, aerial and satellite images* (Archaeological Survey of Ireland, 1838–2021), https://maps.archaeology.ie/HistoricEnvironment [accessed 21 June 2022].   124 Post Truce Comp. Mayo, no. 293, Patrick Munnelly.   125 Interview with Hugh Jennings.   126 *Western People*, 13 Apr. 1912; 1911 Census, Bridget Anderson, Tonree, Kilfian South DED.   127 1911 Census, Mary Monnelly, Ballyglass, Ballycastle; Cancellation Books (Mayo), Ballyglass, Ballycastle DED (1910–28) and Killeenashask, Kilfian South DED (1911–32).   128 Cancellation Books (Mayo), Killeenashask, Kilfian South DED (1911–32); Interview with Hugh Jennings.   129 *Western People*,

and their three children were regular attendees at Moygownagh chapel, in their own box-pew by the altar.[130] Their religion may have been a defining reason Owenmore estate was not seized. So also with local Catholic grazier William Orme Bourke, who was similarly unmolested by the IRA. Like Kathleen Orme and her children, Bourke attended Mass in St Cormac's chapel, while farming 469 acres at Ballintubber, owned by the Scottish Provident Institution.[131] He was chairman of the North Mayo Farmers' Union, and a successful cattle and horse breeder, who claimed in 1927 of the Crown Commission, for damage to stock at his Abbey Farm in Crossmolina, which he ascribed to 'Irregulars'.[132] He also claimed for loss at Ballintubber, but did not blame republicans here. In contrast to Glenmore, the attention of the Ballintubber raiders was directed indiscriminately at the house and outbuildings, rather than at the extensive lands or cattle, with Bourke's claim for low level thefts, vandalism and three racehorses driven by a mob through a hedge.[133] The lack of mention of these incidents by Moygownagh Volunteers likely reflects their non-involvement, supported by a contrasting modus operandi to the Glenmore occupation. Instead, it appears part of local opportunism that, with civil war looming, became endemic.

The revolution ends

With the ratification of the Anglo-Irish Treaty by Dáil Éireann, the local republican administration came to a sudden end. In early 1922, north Mayo republicans abandoned civil law enforcement and 'took to the hills'. In February, Alex Boyd left his position as Brigade Police O/C, to join the Brigade in the Ox Mountains, while the last sitting of Ardagh Sinn Féin court was on 15 February.[134] In late July, Free State forces took Ballina and troops dispersed into its hinterland. However, the sense of control was illusory, with sniping and intermittent skirmishes culminating in Ballina falling briefly to the anti-Treaty forces on 12 September 1922. While Free State troops retook the town, they suffered serious casualties in mopping up operations, including the deaths of Brigadier Joseph Ring and Sergeant John Ingram at Lough Talt, with six soldiers killed in the Gortleatilla battle against General Kilroy's Volunteers at Glenamoy. State forces retreated to barracks in Ballina and

19 Jan. 1907. **130** Interviews with: Bobby Cafferty; Harry Breen; Johnny Orme; 1911 Census, Christopher Guy Orme, Correens, Kilfian South DED. **131** Cancellation Books (Mayo), all of Ballintubber and Cloontakillew townlands, Kilfian East DED (1912–28). **132** *Irish Independent*, 21 Jan. 1928, Bourke was the granduncle of former Irish president Mary Robinson (nee Bourke). **133** Post Truce Loyalist claims, no. 51 – William O. Bourke. **134** Heffron, *No revolution*, pp 113–14; Ardagh parish Sinn Féin court ledger.

Crossmolina, leaving the countryside at the mercy of low-level raiding by armed men, well into the spring of 1923. With the ever-present threat of 'the men of the mountains returning',[135] it was remembered in Moygownagh as 'the times with no law nor order'.[136] Capt. Gallagher ruefully admitted that they ultimately 'did not do very much during the Civil War'.[137] With a new Free State push in January 1923, republican resistance petered out in north Mayo and on 27 July the Claremorris Command reported:

> [while] in remoter districts people are more or less friendly [to the Irregulars], due mainly to their being unaffected by our propaganda and being led on to impossible expectations by the stories of the Irregulars [...] civil administration is not being interfered with in this area [north Mayo].[138]

The Free State had become a local reality. By 1936, of the 'core' group of sixty Moygownagh pre-Truce IRA and Cumann na mBan, seventeen had emigrated, eight had died and six had left the parish (including three as Gardaí).[139] For those remaining, the Sinn Féin club became the Fianna Fáil Cumann, but failure to secure a pension left many with bitter feelings towards their party, such as Capt. Gallagher, whose sense of betrayal is palpable in his final correspondences with the Department of Defence in May 1949:

> I was always a keen follower of F.F. until about 5 years ago. It was only then I realized some of their false promises, especially towards the old IRA, the way they were treated as regards the pensions ... In our Batt area less than 10 are getting pensions. Therefore they would not apply for medals. I am now organizing the battalion and we can assure the Interparty Government of our wholehearted support.[140]

His angst was shared by several former comrades in their own MSP applications.[141] Yet, as their files indicate, most Volunteers and their families continued to support their local Fianna Fáil TD and former commander, Phelim A. Calleary and his son Seán. Their war was still too recent and ran too deep for anything else.

---

135 Heffron, *No revolution*, pp 123–6.   **136** Interview with Peig Jennings, quoting her neighbour James Munnelly of Treenagh.   **137** *Transcription of Moygownagh C Company IRA claims*, p. 35. **138** Intelligence and Command reports, 1922 (Oct)–1924, MA, CW-OPS-03-06, General weekly reports from Claremorris Command.   **139** IRA Rolls – Ballycastle Batt.; Cumann na mBan Rolls – K/B/C Dist.'.   **140** *Transcription of Moygownagh C Company IRA claims*, p. 26.   **141** Ibid., pp 12, 65, 84–9.

Conclusion

In summary, the members of the Moygownagh IRA and Cumann na mBan were in their early twenties, the sons and daughters of small Catholic farmers, and they saw little military activity during the War of Independence or Civil War. Yet they provided the local backbone to the emerging Irish Republic. Unable to emigrate due to the Great War and without opportunities at home, with little discernible connection to earlier social mobilizations, they were radicalized by a well-organized Sinn Féin movement within a vigorous, Gaelic zeitgeist of nationalist cultural and sporting revival.

These militant republicans, with strong familial inter-relationships, ushered independence into rural north Mayo, by operating their republic as a rival to the British state. Their foremost activities involved the carrying out of orders as part of the national effort in hindering Crown administration. This evolved into enforcing civil law by replacing the local state apparatus – but this was not a radical revolution. The Sinn Féin courts functioned as surrogate petty sessions, without any clear division between police, judge and politician. Yet, from the outset there was strong passive resistance to republicans within the community. Stronger farmers and the 'men of stake in the country' stayed aloof to work on their farms, while the abrasive and violent methods of the IRA ran foul of others, including land-hungry small farmers and those who did not believe the Volunteers had earned their authority over them. Labourers, working on larger farms and without a local ITGWU branch organization, kept their heads down in the struggle – in public at least, being too dependent on their employers, as shown by Augusteijn.[142]

For a local republican movement forged on the basis of 'land for the people', land reform would seem a core ambition for any republican. However, beyond the rhetoric, a common theme of the members of C Company was their innate conservatism. When confronted with the opportunity to divide grazing farms, in favour of agitating small farmers, the local IRA protected the graziers' interests. It was only in late spring 1922 that republicans directed the occupation of grazing lands, under brigade orders, and then only against the estate of Protestant and ex-Unionist MP, Godfrey Fetherstonhaugh. In the case of Stonehall farm, the IRA supported the effective dispossession of neighbouring small farmers holding the CDB promise of land division in favour of their own members and supporters. The subsequent protracted and violent struggle between both factions was at odds with the contemporary pronouncements of local Sinn Féin leaders, who had encouraged radical direct

---

142 Augusteijn, *From public defiance*, p. 360.

action to relieve land congestion. For many smallholders, this republican self-interest ensured their lasting enmity.

Further examination is needed to ascertain how much Moygownagh was representative of the west of Ireland in the revolutionary period. It is clear that military operations played but one part in the local IRA experience and more attention should be paid to the effect of their activities in managing the 'parallel state' to the British administration. This study's conclusions differ markedly from Augusteijn's findings of IRA companies being set at the 'heart of the community'.[143] Instead, republicans were often struggling for legitimacy with opposing factions, along existing fissure lines that had opened during the Civil War in an absence of state authority. They also likely explain Hart's observation of increased violence in Mayo and Sligo post-War of Independence. This study also suggests that while young and relatively poor (though not of the poorest such as labourers) rural republicans were much more conservative than Campbell allows, in spite of their radical and vocal rhetoric. In Moygownagh, smallholders seeking the break-up of grazing farms for land distribution were at the root of violent protest, but the IRA found itself upholding the establishment side in these agrarian wars. This indeed was national policy, mediated through Dáil courts, as documented by Kevin O'Shiel in his account of his experience as a land arbitration judge, and it remained so until anti-Treaty command belatedly sought to harness this hunger for direct action on land reform.[144] Further work also needs to be done to understand the extent that tradition, status, emigration and generational conflict underpin Irish revolutionary behaviour, overlaying the deep-rooted status structure permeating such rural communities; Foster's characterization of a status-driven conflict thus appears a better lens to view the revolutionary period at local level.

In their later Military Service Pension claims, the lack of mention of Volunteers directing agrarian agitation is instructive of the contemporary social climate of intolerance for such direct radicalism. When the Free State came into being, it continued the 'conservative revolution', upholding property rights and the continuance of the social order. It is only through social memory that other nascent revolutionary opportunities lived on, in spirit at least.

143 Ibid., pp 176, 356–7.   **144** Campbell and O'Shiel, 'The last land war?', pp 161–7.

'They were the coming men – Ireland's hope': the mobilization of agricultural labourers in Maugherow, Co. Sligo, 1917–20

MOIRA LEYDON

This local history research looks at the mobilization of agricultural labourers in Maugherow, Co. Sligo, between 1917 and 1920, in the context of the wider mobilization of the labour movement post-1916. The aim of the research was twofold: to record this neglected dimension of the history of the area, over-shadowed as it was by that of the iconic revolutionary, Constance Markievicz; second, to highlight the role of class and labour in the wider revolutionary dynamic in a local area. Finberg, a pioneer of the study of local history, observed that the local community has every right to be considered as a distinct articulation of the national life.[1] Hence a question: was this particular mobilization a microcosm of the Irish Revolution? The concluding section will strive to answer this question by looking at what was typical of the wider national experience in Maugherow and what was atypical.

For this author, a native of Maugherow, a serving trade union official and SIPTU member, the discovery of a radical labour tradition in Maugherow was simultaneously moving and motivating; moving in the sense of gaining an insight into the lives of the poorest people in the parish and the dignity that the labour movement gave – however briefly – to those lives; motivational in the sense of engaging in ongoing research into the history of the labour movement in Co. Sligo which, with the exception of Cunningham's work, remains under-researched and, to borrow the feminist phrase, 'hidden from history'.[2]

Maugherow in 1917

Maugherow is generally defined as the land area bordering the coast between Drumcliffe and Grange in north Co. Sligo, one of five parishes in the barony of Carbury.[3] Maugherow is best described as constitutive of all of the Lissadell

---

1 H.P.R. Finberg, *The local historian and his theme* (Leicester, 1965), p. 9.　2 John Cunningham, *Labour in the west of Ireland: working life and struggle, 1890–1914* (Belfast, 1995).　3 Seán Golden, *Maugherow: a much wilder place* (Sligo, 2019), p. 56.

West Electoral Division – 14 townlands – and most of the 13 townlands in the Lissadell East Electoral Division. The area was one of the poorest in a county wholly designated as a congested district. The 1891 Base line report prepared by the Congested District Boards (CDB) recorded that out of 344 families in Lissadell West, 263 were on holdings of £4 or less in valuation. (The size of a £4 holding was typically between 4 and 6 acres.) It also noted that in the north Sligo area more generally, 'there was no constant employment in the area other than that given by landlords and the road contractors ... There was a fair share of irregular labour'.[4] Not surprisingly, there was far more business done on the credit than on the ready money system.

'Pressure on the land' was the dominant economic concern in the area, land purchase by the CDB in Sligo being well below the national level.[5] With the exception of a small number working in a local shoe factory, the vast majority of males in Maugherow were tenant farmers with smallholdings of 10 acres or less and subsistence 'farmers' with five acres or less. The next occupational grouping was that of fishermen: in reality, many farmers were also fishermen, particularly in the coastal areas of the parish. Farmers' sons in the area were primarily classified in the 1911 census as either general or agricultural labourers – and there were many of them. Notwithstanding steady emigration from the area, there was endemic under-employment. Townshend's observation, cited in Terence Dooley's landmark study on the land question, that perhaps 'the real dynamism that underlay the national movement remained the pressure of the population on the land' has a strong resonance in records of the Maugherow branch of the United Irish League (UIL).[6] In June 1915, the weekly UIL 'Branch Notes' in the *Sligo Champion* stated that its purpose was to: 'Wrest the land from the greedy and rapacious landlords and to restore it to the people for whom it was intended ... No doubt when war was over, the nation would see the dying prayers of the heroes of '98, '48, '67 realized'.[7] The pressure on the land was well illustrated by the parliamentary contribution of Thomas Scanlan, MP for Sligo North and a native of Drumcliffe, in November 1909:

> I speak for a constituency in one parish of which alone, that is Maugherow, in the Constituency of North Sligo, there are 32 landless families, and the heads of all those landless families, I know of my own

4 *Base line reports of the Congested Districts Board for Ireland, 1892–98*, 'District of Grange' (Dublin, 1898), pp 281–92 (in the library of Trinity College Dublin).   **5** Michael Wheatley, *Nationalism and the Irish Party: provincial Ireland, 1910–1916* (Oxford, 2003), p. 23.   **6** Terence Dooley, *'The land for the people': the land question in independent Ireland* (Dublin, 2004), p. 17. The Maugherow UIL branch was formed in January 1890 and remained active up to 1918.   **7** *Sligo Champion*, 15 June 1915.

knowledge and from personal experience, are people who are capable of managing economically and wisely any holdings that might be offered to them. On the other hand, I know that there are in that parish, and adjacent to the place where those people live, large tracts of land used for grazing purposes which might be advantageously split up in order to settle the question of congestion.[8]

The biggest employers of agricultural labour were the Protestant farmers, most notably the resident landlord at Lissadell, Sir Josslyn Gore-Booth, who retained a highly productive demesne of 4000 acres after the sale of 27,000 acres under the 1903 Wyndham Land Act. After Sir Josslyn, two Protestant farmers, C.J. Henry and R. Ferguson, provided seasonal tillage employment for agricultural labour. There was also a large grazing farm in the west of the parish, belonging to a Captain Gethin, which was the subject of much of the lobbying work by the UIL through the two Sligo MPs in Westminster.

Communal life in Maugherow was rich and included the UIL, the Ancient Order of Hibernians, the Gaelic League, the National – and later the Irish – Volunteers, a Temperance League and the Gaelic Athletic Association. Unusually, the Ancient Order of Hibernians had a women's league and several meetings of a local women's franchise society, established by Eva Gore-Booth, are recorded in the *Sligo Champion*. The first branch of Sinn Féin was established in January 1918. These 'social actors' were explicitly nationalist and were cross-populated by the same individuals.[9] The cessation of emigration during the war had a dramatic impact on Maugherow in that it resulted in a surplus of restive unemployed young men – and young women – who were open to political ideas far in advance of the 'constitutionalism' of their fathers in the UIL.

The mobilization of agricultural labourers

Fitzpatrick has written about the disappearance of the Irish agricultural labourer and its significance for the course of Irish politics during the last decades of the nineteenth century.[10] Between 1841 and 1911, the ratio of farm workers to farmers halved nationally and quartered in Connaught. Most farmers' sons (and other 'assisting relatives') were required to engage in

---

8 'Irish Land Bill', Hansard, vol. 13, 23 November 1909. 9 A parallel social world prevailed for the Protestant community, primarily unionist or 'loyal' in outlook. See Terence Dooley, *The decline of the Big House in Ireland: a study of Irish landed families, 1860–1960* (Dublin, 2001). 10 David Fitzpatrick, 'The disappearance of the Irish agricultural labourer, 1841–1912', *Irish Economic and Social History*, 7 (1980), 66–92.

labouring to sustain the family subsistence. Except for herdsmen and resident servants of the landed gentry, few labourers were kept throughout the year.

Bradley has underlined the variegated nature of this workforce that included the live-in servant, the married labourer living in a house on the farm, the labourer occupying a cottage provided under the Labourers' Acts, and the smallholder who worked most of the time for the bigger farmer.[11] He also provides a plausible explanation for their marginality to the nascent labour movement. Not only were they employed in isolated workplaces, their relationship with their employer was complex comprising the spectrum from exploitation to paternalism. Under-employment, compounded by the seasonal nature of agricultural work and the proliferation of 'assisting relatives', made it extremely difficult to generate a collective class consciousness. However, as discussed below, Maugherow was atypical in that unlike other areas in the county it had a labourers association, the Maugherow Labourers' Union, indicating a level of class consciousness.

Stalemate in the war in Europe impelled unprecedented government intervention in the economy, commencing with control of the railways and shipyards and the payment of war bonuses. This new industrial relations context of arbitration boards comprising employers and unions immediately mobilized workers to join unions. At national level, the union movement grew from 100,000 in 1916 to 250,000 in 1920, representing 27 per cent of the workforce. What O'Connor called disparate 'wage movements' converged into a national 'wages movement' largely driven by the Irish Transport and General Workers' Union (ITGWU).[12] A huge part of the ITGWU's attraction for workers was its syndicalist tactics and the articulation of an explicit working-class identity. Poor, marginalized and maligned, James Larkin and his radical brand of direct trade union action, premised on the great clarion call of 'an injury to one is an injury to all', gave them self-respect: a loaf on the table, a flower in the vase.[13] From 1917 to 1921, almost every industry and trade experienced strikes, stoppages and sympathetic action.[14] The RIC chief inspector's monthly report for June 1919 is indicative of the state of labour mobilization in that month alone:

ITGWU continued to spread its branches throughout the country, promoting discontent among all classes of workers, and incessant

---

11 Daniel Bradley, *Farm labourers: Irish struggle, 1900–1976* (Belfast, 1988), p. 7.   **12** Emmet O'Connor, 'War and syndicalism 1914–1923' in Donal Nevin (ed.), *Trade union century* (Dublin, 1994), pp 54–66.   **13** James Plunkett, 'Big Jim: a loaf on the table, a flower in the vase' in Donal Nevin (ed.), *James Larkin, lion of the fold* (Dublin, 1998), pp 110–15.   **14** Emmet O'Connor, 'War and syndicalism'; F. Devine, *Organizing history: a centenary of SIPTU* (Dublin, 2009), Ch. 8.

demands for increased wages. List of strikes – Belfast, Counties Antrim, Armagh, Cavan, Donegal, Down, Kerry, Carlow, Dublin, Kilkenny, King's County, Louth, Wexford, Galway, Mayo, Roscommon, Clare and Cork, nor were they confined to factory hands but farm labourers and shop assistants, County and District Council employees, artisans. In some cases, disputes settled quickly by considerable concessions on the part of employers.[15]

The turning point for agricultural labour was the introduction of compulsory tillage in January 1917 by the Corn Production Act in response to food shortages. In December 1916, the Irish Trade Union Congress convened a special conference to demand price controls and a ban on the export of food. The *Sligo Champion* editorial of 6 January 1917 underlined the need for the Act, 'if famine is to be averted'.[16] The Act required farmers of ten or more acres to put 10 per cent of the land 'under the plough' and a further 5 per cent in 1918 with guaranteed prices for wheat and oats up to 1922. (Otherwise, they had to rent or sell the equivalent to those who would.) Not only were farmers unwilling to comply with these demands, given the profitability of livestock exports, a serious rural manpower shortage had emerged. The 1915 Report of the Department of Agriculture and Technical Instruction (DATI) stated that the best labour had left the country and farmers complained of the lack of efficiency as well as the difficulty in getting labourers. The latter had multiple causes but chief among them was the subsistence wage rates. On 9 March, the Agricultural Wages Board (AWB) was established to address the labour shortage by fixing minimum rates of pay and working hours. The implication of this move was immediately evident to the leadership of the ITGWU: a fortnight later, acting general secretary, Thomas Foran, called for 'getting all of the agricultural workers of Ireland organized'.[17]

The dire state of the agricultural labourer in 1917 was well comprehended by the AWB: its final report in 1921 stated that 'the question of fixing allowances was one of extreme difficulty, and complexity, having regard to the prevalence in Ireland of the practice of paying wages partly in cash and partly in perquisites'.[18] Between November 1917 and May 1921, the Board issued six orders fixing wage rates across the District Wages Committees, which involved local Farmers' Union representatives and ITGWU representatives,

15 Irish National Archives, CO904 (The British in Ireland) MFA/54/1–136. **16** *Sligo Champion*, 6 Jan. 1917. **17** Bradley, *Farm labourers*, p. 33. **18** *Report on the operation of the Agricultural Wages Board for Ireland during the period September 1917 to September 1921* (HMSO, 1921). In its December 1917 order, the Board agreed to define perquisites – allowance or benefit additional to the main income – and fix maximum values for same.

thus consolidating the spread of trade unionism across the country.[19] In 1917, the average agricultural wage was 19s. 3d. In 1920, it was 32s. 2d.[20] The impact on agricultural labourers was dramatic; they joined the ITGWU in their thousands so that by 1920 they constituted almost 60 per cent of the membership. This remarkable mobilization was summed up by the ITGWU's acting general secretary, William O'Brien, in July 1919 when he stated that 'all over the country agricultural workers are now threatening for their demands to be made on their behalf. In some counties, Meath and Kildare, the war is already on.'[21]

Labour mobilization in Maugherow

Cunningham has documented the dramatic history of the ITGWU in the town of Sligo.[22] The fifth branch of the Union was established there on the initiative of the Sligo Trades Council on 17 September 1911, the dock labourers constituting most of the membership followed by labourers in the mills and merchants' yards. This event was attended by P.T. Daly from Liberty Hall and John Lynch was elected secretary. Lynch was elected an alderman of Sligo Urban Council in January 1913 whence commenced a consistent pattern of election of labour men to the Council for the next decade. Such was the rapid growth of the union among the town's workers that when Larkin visited the town in March 1912 Bishop Clancy denounced his socialist tendency – 'lest silence on my part in such an emergency might be interpreted … as tacit approval'.[23]

Shortly after Larkin's visit, there was a 56-day strike and lockout of dock workers and others, which presaged the violence and bitterness of the Dublin lockout later in the year. (An earlier strike in June 1912 was settled quickly to the advantage of the dockers, greatly consolidating the status of the union.) The strike resonated strongly with the mass of the townspeople who offered 'their entire support to the workers in their fight against the tyranny of the employers'.[24] It concluded with improved pay and conditions for the dockers with the RIC county inspector reporting that 'the Irish Transport Union has won a complete victory'.[25] Interestingly, in light of the later ITGWU strike on his own estate, not only did Sir Josslyn Gore-Booth provide food to the

19 C.L. Curtis, 'The agricultural labourer and the state in independent Ireland, 1922–1976' (PhD, NUI Maynooth, 2007), p. 79. 20 Ibid. 21 Ibid., p. 39. 22 John Cunningham, 'The men who wear the Transport badge: labour conflict in Sligo, 1911–1913' in Francis Devine and Fearghal Mac Bhloscaidh (eds), *Bread not profits: provincial working class politics during the Irish Revolution* (Dublin, 2022), pp 1–20. 23 Devine, *Organizing history*, p. 40. 24 Ibid., p. 41. 25 Michael Farry, *Sligo: 1914–1921: a chronicle of conflict* (Trim, 1992).

families of the striking dockers during the lockout, the 'honourable settlement' that ended the strike was facilitated by Sir Josslyn's agent, T.A. Cooper.[26] Gore-Booth's benevolence and sympathy with the downtrodden workers in the town was again evidenced in 1916 when the Sligo ITGWU branch passed a motion 'that we tender to Sir Josslyn Gore-Booth our heartfelt thanks for his generosity in sending supplies of potatoes to alleviate the distress that presently exists in the town.'[27]

Indicative of the emerging class tensions in the countryside, at its January meeting in 1917, the Maugherow UIL passed a resolution:

> … earnestly hoping that the government officials will see that the owners of the farms in this district who devoted almost all of their lands to the grazing of bullocks will be compelled to comply with the law and not be asking exemption orders or any other orders either by fear or faction or the want of labour. If they pay a fair wage, they are sure to get plenty of labour.[28]

At the same meeting a deputation was appointed to 'wait' on Sir Josslyn to seek plots as conacre for tillage for labourers in his employment who had no land. The *Champion* also reported that owing to the scarcity of labourers in the district, the Maugherow Potato Growers' Association had raised funds to purchase a picking machine.[29] The scarcity of labour is interesting given that emigration had been prohibited once the war commenced. A plausible explanation is the fact that many young men had already emigrated, as evidenced in an earlier *Sligo Independent* editorial that fear of conscription had led to a 'wild emigration rush', with hundreds of young men leaving by railway from Galway, Mayo and Sligo.[30] The UIL 'Branch Notes' in November 1915 stated that a bundle of recruiting posters had arrived in the area and that the emigration ship had 'done its share in taking the youth of our country to other lands to earn a decent living that was denied to them in Ireland'.[31]

It is interesting to note that the Maugherow Labourers' Union raised the issue of amalgamation with the ITGWU during the Sligo docks strike in April 1913.[32] Notwithstanding a letter to P.T. Daly in Liberty Hall, reference to the Union in the papers is scant until February 1917 when an indignant Ancient Order of Hibernians denied that the Maugherow labourers had authority to use its hall.[33] Shortly afterwards, the first meeting of the ITGWU took place

---

26 *Sligo Independent,* 16 May 1913. **27** *Sligo Nationalist and Leitrim Leader,* 11 Mar. 1916. **28** *Sligo Champion,* 27 Jan. 1917. **29** Ibid. **30** *Sligo Independent,* 24 Oct. 1914. **31** *Sligo Champion,* 13 Nov. 1915. **32** Ibid., 26 Apr. 1913. **33** Ibid., 24 Feb. 1917.

in Maugherow on 24 March and was attended by John Lynch and P.T. Daly, thereby constituting the fourteenth branch of the union. In his address, Lynch said that 'it was inspiring and hopeful to see such a large number of youths present at the meeting. They were the coming men – Ireland's hope'.[34] They were indeed: Maugherow labourers were among the first in rural Ireland to be absorbed into the ITGWU, a development no doubt due to the growing status of the union in the town and its success in battles with employers. It is also relevant that Bernard Meehan, who was elected branch secretary and served in that role until 1922, was in all likelihood a kinsman of Lynch, whose mother was a Meehan from the same townland.[35] Reports of meetings of the Maugherow ITGWU branch regularly appeared in the *Sligo Champion* thereafter. By June 1918, the branch had 130 members.[36]

Labour mobilization was also evidenced in the formation of a branch of the union in the neighbouring parish of Cliffoney in May 1917. The subsequent report in the *Sligo Champion* stated that it would 'tolerate no blacklegs in Cliffoney'.[37] This spirit of militancy was undoubtedly driven by the growing awareness of trade union power in a situation of acute labour shortage. It was also attributable to the increasingly explicit identification of ITGWU organizers with the emerging Sinn Féin movement and its commitment to an Irish republic. Historian Desmond Greaves observed that their simultaneous involvement in union and republican activities was in part due to the cessation of emigration, their engagement with the GAA and the Volunteers: 'those with a head for politics might belong to Sinn Féin, but for industrial purposes were in the ITGWU'.[38] The RIC, indeed, was quick to observe this alliance noting in several county and national reports that Sinn Féin and labour organizations were working 'hand-in-hand'. The union's 1918 annual report stated that 'Easter Week saved the union ... it linked up the Labour Movement with the age-long aspirations of the Irish people for emancipation from political and social thraldom'.[39]

In the same month back in Maugherow, at an animated meeting, the ITGWU committee was unanimous in protesting against the actions of C.J. Henry for his conduct towards his workmen for joining the union. It was

---

34 Ibid., 31 Mar. 1917. **35** In the ITGWU annual reports, the name Bernard is interchanged with that of Bartley. The 1911 Census records Bartley Meehan, Doonfore, as aged 30, the oldest of four children and a blacksmith by occupation – like his father. They lived in a second-class house of three rooms. As many of the Doonfore men were employees of Gore-Booth, it seems plausible that Bartley quit smithing and went to work directly for Gore-Booth. As Bernard is the name most frequently mentioned in the Maugherow ITGWU reports, it is used in preference to Bartley. **36** Farry, *Sligo, 1914–1921*, p. 148. **37** *Sligo Champion*, 19 May 1917. **38** C. Desmond Greaves, *The Irish Transport and General Workers' Union: the formative years* (Dublin, 1982), p. 217. **39** ITGWU, *Annual report for 1918* (Dublin, 1919), p. 6.

alleged that Henry stated that the UIL, the AOH, and the labourers' union 'were a rot'. He was also reported as talking to the local police sergeant and two constables with a view to terrorizing his men for 'daring to raise their voice in defence of their just demands to secure wage to enable them to ward off hunger'. More damaging was the fact that he replaced a union man with a non-union man.[40]

At a later meeting in September, the branch discussed wages and reported 'it was heartening to learn that they will be paid £1 5s. per week'.[41] In November, the branch agreed that the wages set by the AWB were satisfactory as 'this part of County Sligo is as good an agricultural district as any in Ireland' and the branch secretary was instructed to talk to local employers to secure increases for all the young men who did not come under the Act.[42] In January 1918, the ITGWU 'Branch Notes' in the *Champion* recorded that 'every man had to put his shoulder to the wheel for only by a display of an alert and intelligent interest in the Union can the members hope to make it what it should be'.[43] The militant spirit of the branch was evidenced again at the August 1918 meeting at which it was stated that 'any member more than two shillings in arrears will be fined 6d. for every meeting they do not attend. The members will not work with those men if they don't clear up their books'. A classic syndicalist tactic! At the same meeting, it was announced that an inaugural meeting of the women's branch would take place at the secretary's cottage after last Mass, with 'all expected to attend'.[44] While union reports appear with less frequency in the *Sligo Champion* thereafter, in large part eclipsed by the activities of the Sinn Féin club in the parish, of which Bernard Meehan was a leading member, the *Champion* reported on the Maugherow delegation to the demonstration in Sligo town on 23 April 1918, part of the general strike of resistance to the threat of conscription, and to the first national May Day parade in 1919. In his address to the latter, Alderman John Lynch stated that the red flag was the banner of labour and under it they hoped to march to victory.[45] An indicator of the strength of the union in Maugherow is provided by the record of remittances sent to Liberty Hall. In 1918, this figure was £60 14s. 4d. compared to £51 8s. 4d. for the Sligo town branch. In 1919, the remittance was slightly lower at £58 0s. 8d. but increased substantially in 1920 to £88 10s. 5d.[46]

---

40 *Sligo Champion*, 26 May 1917.   41 Ibid., 29 Sept. 1917.   42 Ibid., 20 Nov. 1917.   43 Ibid., 19 Jan. 1918.   44 Ibid., 31 Aug. 1918.   45 *Sligo Independent*, 3 May 1919.   46 ITGWU annual reports, 1918, 1919, 1920.

The red flag in Lissadell

Arguably, the apogee of the Maugherow branch of the ITGWU was the three-week strike in Lissadell in the summer of 1920. The cause of this strike was Sir Josslyn Gore-Booth's unwillingness to pay the AWB's minimum rates. However, it is important to provide some background to Sir Josslyn Gore-Booth in order to appreciate the sheer militancy of the union at this point in time. Maugherow was somewhat atypical in that Gore-Booth was a resident landlord who like his father was universally acknowledged as 'fair'.[47] After assuming the title of 6th Baronet on the death of his father, Sir Henry, in 1900, Sir Josslyn was among the very first landlords to offer his tenants ownership of the land under the 1903 Wyndham Land Act. In the subsequent years, over 1,000 tenants purchased 28,000 acres from Gore-Booth (mostly in the south Sligo district of Ballymote). The remaining 4,000 acres formed the 'demesne' around Lissadell house, which became one of the largest and most productive farms in the west of Ireland. He was the major employer in the area with successful horticultural, agricultural and commercial forestry enterprises, namely, a saw mill and furniture factory. He continued his father's tradition of estate improvements and was an enthusiastic supporter of Horace Plunkett's co-operative movement, establishing four co-operative creameries, including one in Maugherow, the Ballinfull Co-operative Society. He expanded his father's many entrepreneurial interests including barytes mining in Ballintrellick, oyster farming in Drumcliffe Bay and was the major shareholder in the Sligo, Leitrim and Northern Counties Railway Company. He established the Sligo Co-operative Food Store to alleviate food shortages for Sligo's poor during the war and his Sligo Manufacturing Company employed almost 100 workers, mainly women, producing 800 shirts per week for the British army. His entrepreneurial talents led him to convert his mechanical workshop at Lissadell into a munitions factory producing shells in 1915.[48] Gore-Booth demonstrated his generosity by providing a 'splendid playing pitch' to the newly formed Maugherow GAA Club in August 1917.[49] (Bernard Meehan was a member of the club committee.) He was also a

47 Gerard Moran, *Sir Robert Gore-Booth and his landed estate in County Sligo, 1814–1876* (Dublin, 2006).   48 Sir Josslyn engaged in extensive correspondence with his brother, Mordaunt, an engineer with Vickers' armaments factory in Sheffield, on the persistent tooling problems encountered. His eventual output of 30 shells per month could have been fired off by a single piece of artillery in a few days. See Dermot James, *The Gore-Booths of Lissadell* (Dublin, 2004), p. 114. The author's maternal grand-parents, James Watters and Mary Kate Feeney, met while they were working in the munitions factory. James Watters continued to work for the Gore-Booths as a mechanic until his retirement in the late 1960s.   49 *Sligo Champion*, 11 Aug. 1917.

generous patron of the Maugherow annual ploughing competition, one of the largest in the county. In June 1917, he purchased one of the first tractors in the county to assist with the harvesting, being an early convert to tillage production.[50]

Needless to say, Gore-Booth was an active recruiter for the 'war effort' and hosted several tours of the Connaught Rangers in the area. As the war dragged on, the local response became increasingly hostile as is evidenced in the May 1918 *Sligo Champion* report that, at an anti-conscription meeting after Mass, Sir Josslyn Gore-Booth was repeatedly heckled as he appealed to the young men to join the British army, arguing that 'the war was as much that of the people of Maugherow as it was of any of the allies'.[51]

However, Sir Josslyn's paternalism was increasingly rejected by his workers. In 1918, the May meeting of the Sligo Trades and Labour Council discussed a dispute involving Sir Josslyn and the transportation of potatoes to Sligo port for export, wherein four men were out on strike and 'scabs' were bringing potatoes to the railway. John Lynch stated that if the Maugherow men went on strike, it was expected that the railway men in Sligo would go on strike with them.[52] This militant spirit was evident in a letter from the ITGWU in the *Sligo Nationalist and Leitrim Leader* in January 1919 which stated that the agricultural labourers wanted a 49-hour week, a minimum wage of 30s. for men and 20s. for boys (16–18 years), overtime at time-and-a half, a harvest bonus of £4 and a rate of 6d. per hour for Sunday work, the terms to come into operation in May.[53] In Lissadell, there was slow progress in meeting this demand until things came to a head in June 1920. As noted by the *Sligo Champion*, trouble was brewing on the estate.[54] The men were paid 24s. 6d. for a 45-hour week and were determined to get the minimum wage of 30s. for the same hours.[55] Sir Josslyn pleaded inability to pay and a deadlock being reached, all entrances to the estate were picketed the following Monday and 'all work brought to a standstill' by 120 union members. The *Champion* observed that the strikers were determined to hold out for what, 'in all conscience, cannot be regarded as an exorbitant wage for a 45-hour week.'[56]

The following week the paper noted that the strike was in its tenth day and that 'the utmost vigilance has been exercised in order to ensure a complete stoppage of labour'.[57] Moreover, the situation was becoming acute as many

---

50 The shortage of horses caused by the war and compulsory tillage accelerated mechanization on Irish farms. In March 1917, there were 70 tractors in Ireland: by the end of the war the number had increased to 640. Mechanization reduced the demand for agricultural labour. See Mary Daly, 'Irish agriculture and the Great War' in *Farming and country life: history talks presented at Teagasc, Athenry* (Carlow, 2016), pp 64–5. **51** *Sligo Champion*, 4 May 1918. **52** *Sligo Nationalist and Leitrim Leader*, 18 May 1918. **53** Ibid., 22 Feb. 1919. **54** *Sligo Champion*, 11 June 1920. **55** *Sligo Nationalist and Leitrim Leader*, 11 June 1920. **56** *Sligo Champion*, 11 June 1920. **57** Ibid., 18 June 1920.

acres of meadow were ready for cutting and any delay in a settlement would lead to considerable financial losses. Under the headline, 'Exciting scenes in Lissadell', a week later the paper noted that workers paraded around the estate with a band and entered the house after an 'abortive' meeting with Sir Josslyn. The workers ordered all the house servants to leave and notices to quit were also served on non-union workers.[58] The strikers occupied some of the houses on the estate and announced their intention to take over the entire estate – 'a cut and dried scheme for the working of which under the Soviet system they had prepared'.[59] The leader of the strikers, presumably Bernard Meehan, declared that 'they would fly the Red Flag in Lissadell yet', a defiant statement demonstrating a strong class consciousness and proletarian solidarity.[60] At this stage, Sir Josslyn agreed a compromise of 30s. for a 48-hour week.

Sir Josslyn's intransigence during this three-week strike is, in many respects, puzzling. From a commercial perspective, he was one of the biggest suppliers of vegetables and potatoes to shops in Sligo town and for the duration of the war exported potatoes to 'the mainland', as well as supplying the Royal Navy ships which occasionally docked. In November, 1916 a 'heated discussion' took place at the Sligo Board of Guardians when Alderman Mc Morrow claimed that potatoes from the Lissadell estate were allowed to be exported from Sligo port while the poor farmers of Maugherow, who had to carry seaweed from the shore to manure their fields, were prevented from selling potatoes for export. At the end of a long argument, it was put forward that the Lissadell potatoes were seed potatoes and not a cash crop to which one Board member tartly replied, 'Aye, but you could ate them!'[61]

It is also of note that Josslyn's two sisters, Constance and Eva Gore-Booth, were both radicals who participated in some of the most dramatic labour mobilizations in Dublin and Manchester in this period. Constance Markievicz's support for the cause of labour and the oppressed working class was evident in her humanitarian work in feeding the locked-out workers in Dublin in 1913 and later on in the Free State period. She was also the first minister for labour from April 1919 to January 1922, a role to which she was dedicated. Her identification with the cause of labour is captured in the March 1919 issue of the ITGWU's *Voice of Labour* where she exhorted the 'Comrades' as follows:

---

58 Ibid., 2 July 1920.   **59** Farry, *Sligo, 1914–1921*, p. 284.   **60** Clive Scouler (ed.), *More of that anon: the memoirs of Aideen Gore-Booth* (Dublin, 2014). Driving into the estate after the summer holidays in their holiday home in Bundoran, Aideen Gore-Booth recalled that the three driveways were all overgrown and the grass was high because the men were on strike.   **61** *Sligo Champion*, 18 Nov. 1916.

The best and last of the long fight is before us, the watchword is 'Organize'. Every man, woman and child must be ready to take their stand for Connolly's Commonwealth. Organize politically and economically. Put your trust in God and the spirit of Republican Ireland, and full steam ahead.[62]

Eva Gore-Booth's radicalism and identification with the cause of the working class was as profound as that of her more iconic sister and equally influential. She has been described by her biographer as being at the 'cutting edge of social and political reform activities' in both Manchester and London.[63] She was a founder-member of the Salford Women's Trade Union Council in 1895. When she became its co-secretary in 1900, her role was to 'bring trade-unionism within the reach of scattered individuals working in unorganized trades, and to draft them off into their own unions once they are formed'.[64] Both sisters were also committed activists for women's suffrage and, in different ways, Irish independence. Their departure from the family home, to which they rarely returned, and their identification with radical causes most certainly distressed Sir Josslyn, who was a dedicated Unionist and supporter of the political status quo.[65]

The aftermath

This dramatic strike would appear to represent the zenith of the Maugherow ITGWU branch as there were no further reports discovered in the *Sligo Champion*. The ITGWU records for the period confirm that this was indeed the high point of the union in the area. By 1921, remittances from the branch were somewhat lower at £75 6s. 1d. In 1922 this had dropped to £22 15s. 2d. and no name was given for the branch secretary, a position occupied heretofore by Bernard Meehan. This dramatic decline in the branch membership can primarily be attributed to the 'economic slump' following the war, with food prices the first to collapse, causing a severe depression in agriculture. The decision to repeal the Corn Production Act 1917 and to abolish the AWB – in effect, abolishing the statutory minimum wage – in June 1921 empowered farmers to reduce wages, and to revert to pasturage. Without a guaranteed minimum wage, many labourers could not afford the 6d. weekly union dues. The independence struggle must also be considered as a factor: Sir Josslyn had a number of encounters with the local Volunteers, of which

62 Devine, *Organizing history*, p. 97.   **63** Sonja Tiernan, *Eva Gore-Booth: an image of such politics* (Manchester, 2015), p. 55.   **64** Ibid., p. 57.   **65** James, *The Gore-Booths*, Ch. 3.

Meehan was a member, which would have deepened his hostility to the Union. Lissadell House was raided in the same summer as the strike, shortly after which a maid was forced to leave the house, accused of being an informer. Sir Josslyn himself was kidnapped in February 1922 by the anti-Treaty IRA in response to the arrest and threatened execution of eight IRA men travelling from Monaghan to Derry. The release of the latter possibly saved Sir Josslyn's life.[66]

However, the union branch does not appear to have 'fallen away' completely, as a scathing commentary in the ITGWU's *Voice of Labour* in 1922 would indicate. In a short article, it excoriated 'Jossie the Lissadell Lollipop' for the low pay of 23*s.* per week received by his labourers who reportedly were ready to strike for an increase.[67] (The latter sum was 7*s.* less than that awarded in the summer of 1920.) The 1923 Report had no listing of a remittance from Maugherow. However, ITGWU records indicate that the Maugherow No. 14 Branch had not entirely dissolved. Extensive correspondence in 1927 is recorded between Liberty Hall, Dublin and Liberty Hall, Sligo in relation to a dispute over rights of pilotage in Sligo Bay previously retained by two pilots in Raughley townland. In March 1928, a letter from Maurice Regan, Sligo branch secretary, to the union general secretary stated that the Lissadell farm workers were again anxious to become unionized:

> Upwards of 20 men at the meeting, and promised to pay the entrance fee. I took them on at 1*s.* 9*d.* entrance fee. Upwards of 70 men employed in Lissadell but 20 is as many as are anxious to re-join union. These workers were organized on two previous occasions and 'fell away'. We should take them on as it is their own wish and we have not tried to induce them.[68]

A single line came back from Dublin: 'Regret we cannot agree to re-open this Branch at present.'[69] The next reference to the agricultural labourers in Maugherow located by the author is in the Gore-Booth archives. It is of interest that the personal or financial records of Sir Josslyn or his family, with the exception of Aideen Gore-Booth's notes for her memoir, do not contain any reference to the farm strike. This is in contrast to the detailed correspondence maintained between Gore-Booth and railway managers in relation to the 1911 British rail-workers' strike. In this instance, the company gave the staff a bonus of three days' pay for 'their attitude during the recent

---

66 Ibid., p. 115.   **67** *The Voice of Labour*, 11 Mar. 1922.   **68** Irish Labour History Society, ITGWU Archives, letter 6 Mar. 1928.   **69** Ibid., letter 7 Mar. 1928.

strike'.[70] The conclusion I draw from this lacuna is a sense of hurt on the part of Sir Josslyn who was, in many respects, a model landlord.[71] The culture of deference had been broken by the workers' assertion of the right to a minimum wage. This breach of paternalistic relationships was in all likelihood understood by Sir Josslyn as a wider threat to his economic position: he was, above all, an astute businessman and rich landowner. The records indicate that he clearly understood the nature of trade union power. In July 1930, a formal agreement was recorded with the labourers – dairy, farm and forestry – to the following effect:

> … in the event of any dispute regarding wages, hours of employment, on any other matter, there is to be no stoppage of work. Negotiations are to be carried out in a business-like manner as between employer and employees and in the event of disagreement, the Ministry of Commerce is asked to arbitrate.[72]

Was it a microcosm?

This chapter commenced with a question: was the mobilization of agricultural labour in Maugherow in Co. Sligo a microcosm of the Irish Revolution? In my opinion the answer is yes. If we understand the latter as the dynamic interplay of class, gender, ideology and nationalism in Ireland during a period of global rupture, then certainly the radicalization of the rural proletariat in Maugherow in the syndicalist, anti-imperialist and republican ITGWU was a microcosm. Kostick has documented the rise and expansion of labour militancy post-1916 and its impact on the unfolding independence struggle.[73] At national level, the organization by the Irish Trades Union Congress of a special conference in December 1916 to demand price control and a ban on the export of foodstuff was the harbinger of the lead role labour was to assume in that struggle. The coalescing of local wage struggles into the 'wages movement' spearheaded by the ITGWU constituted a unique opportunity to redress the many social and economic grievances of the people. The successful organization by the ITUC of the country's first ever general strike in support of the anti-conscription campaign on 23 April 1918 was dramatic in its impact on popular opinion and the gathering momentum of support for Sinn Féin's

70 Lissadell Papers, PRONI, D4131/E/8.   **71** In *The Gore-Booths of Lissadell* (p. 128), James records renowned Sligo historian John C. McTernan's poignant judgment of Sir Josslyn as a 'man forgotten by a country he loved … and for which he laboured so zealously'.   **72** Lissadell Papers, PRONI, 4131/A/15.   **73** Conor Kostick, *Revolution in Ireland, 1917–1923* (Cork, 2009).

version of nationalism. This was followed by the equally successful mobilization of labour the following year for a national May Day stoppage in 1919. A further mass mobilization by the ITUC in April 1920 brought the country to a halt in a two-day general strike culminating in the release of hundreds of republican prisoners, including many trade union activists. During the War of Independence, actions taken by the National Union of Railwaymen and the Automobile Drivers' and Mechanics' Union caused significant disruption to British military operations. The success of these mass mobilizations is demonstrative of widespread local labour mobilizations during the period, in particular by the agricultural workers organized in the ITGWU who, at this period, constituted almost 60 per cent of the union membership. Between 1918 to 1921, 782 industrial strikes were recorded, most of which were successful.[74] Almost 100 local 'soviets' were organized around this period, again a majority in the agricultural sector, reflecting the radicalization of union membership and a strong class consciousness.

The 'grand narrative' of a united nationalist military struggle for political independence is no longer hegemonic. Historians are increasingly identifying how local situations and conflicts impacted on the wider nationalist movement, in particular the role of class underpinning those conflicts. What motivated individuals to want to change their circumstances? What material conditions were propitious or otherwise? What collective agency was available to respond to pressing circumstances?

The account of the mobilization of agricultural labour in Maugherow from 1917 to 1920 seeks to answer these questions. Once the AWB was operationalized, the deep well of frustration and disappointment of the agricultural labourer, 'the forgotten man of Irish history', shut out of all the dispensations of the Land Acts, living in the family home with no prospect of owning their own farm, finally found an effective release.[75] The confluence of an acute labour shortage, compulsory tillage and the presence of a strong, militant ITGWU in the county constituted the auspicious environment for the Maugherow men to improve their position. The concluding observation of the last report of the AWB confirms this:

> Whatever may be said from the economic or scientific standpoint for or against the principle of fixing minimum rates of wages, it cannot be denied that when Parliament decreed that the worker in agriculture

---

74 Olivier Coquelin, 'Class struggle in the 1916–1923 Irish Revolution: a reappraisal', *Études irlandaises*, 42:2 (2017), 29.   **75** O'Connor, *Syndicalism in Ireland, 1917–1923* (Cork, 1988), p. 33.

should be given the protection of the State in this matter, the position of the Irish agricultural labourer was open to amelioration.[76]

Moreover, the agricultural labourers already had a tradition of collective agency in the Maugherow Labourers' Union. Its subsequent merging into the ITGWU and the leadership provided by Lynch and P.T. Daly from Liberty Hall greatly consolidated that collective power.[77] As noted by O'Connor, syndicalism was at its strongest among the unskilled workers in marginalized occupations.[78] Meehan and other union men were active in local organizations such as the GAA, the UIL, the Volunteers and, from January 1918, Sinn Féin and were, by any standard, politicized. Foster has documented how this cross-over of cultural and political milieus and interests formed the revolutionary generation.[79] In the context of the Maugherow union men, their membership of explicitly nationalist organizations, fused with their new found class consciousness, must have had a profoundly radicalizing impact which found a natural outlet with the establishment of a Sinn Féin branch in the parish, members of which, according to several reports in the *Sligo Champion*, had numerous boisterous 'run-ins' with the older members of the UIL.

The rapid rise and decline of the Maugherow ITGWU mirrors, in many respects, that of the other agricultural mobilizations in this period. Several factors were at play not least the organization of the farmers themselves into their own union, the Irish Farmers' Union. C.J. Henry, no friend of trade unions, was on its Co. Sligo executive and it is telling that at a meeting in 1919, he was cautioned by a John Maher that 'a poorly paid labour force was a liability to the agricultural sector'.[80] The unfolding independence struggle also impacted on conditions for trade union organization and action. Hundreds of union members were active in Sinn Féin, and were arrested and imprisoned. In September 1918, John Lynch was arrested for a seditious speech at the Arigna coal mines and spent six months in Belfast jail.

As the War of Independence unfolded, Sinn Féin leaders were increasingly aware of the need to secure the support of the farmers, large and small; not only were their sons fighting and dying for the independence cause, many of the leading activists came from such backgrounds where landownership was the very definition of what freedom from British rule meant. Sinn Féin was no fan of labour militancy on the farm that was to be the cornerstone of the new state's economic policy.

76 *Report on the operation of the Agricultural Wages Board*, op. cit.   **77** Many of the Maugherow ITGWU reports from meetings record the attendance of one or both men.   **78** O'Connor, *Syndicalism*.   **79** See Roy Foster, *Vivid faces: the revolutionary generation in Ireland, 1890–1923* (London, 2015), passim.   **80** Lissadell Papers, PRONI, 4131/A/15.

And what of Bernard Meehan? In many ways, he too was a microcosm of the radicalized generation of the period. He was active in almost all the political spaces in Maugherow – the GAA, the Irish Volunteers, and Sinn Féin. However, there is no mention of a Meehan from Maugherow in any of Farry's works on the period.[81] Neither does he appear in McGowan's account of the Civil War in the area.[82] Given his relationship with John Lynch, his disappearance from the labour and national movement is unusual. In conversation with the author, a local source stated that he was dismissed by Gore Booth and emigrated for a time to America. This is a plausible explanation, the new Free State being no country for the agricultural labourer.

81 Michael Farry, *Sligo: the Irish Revolution 1912–1923* (Dublin, 2012); *Sligo, 1914–1921;* 'Sligo 1921–1923: the aftermath of revolution' (PhD, Trinity College Dublin, 1991).   **82** Joe Mc Gowan, *Even the heather bled* (Sligo, 2021).

'No such sight has been seen in Belfast since Dissenter and Catholic united in 1791': the Workers' Union and the Belfast Labour Party

FEARGHAL MAC BHLOSCAIDH

Writing privately from his home off Belfast's Falls' Road in 1911, James Connolly asked that his famous debate with William Walker on the pages of *Forward* be published as a pamphlet 'to answer both those who declare that we are anti-national, and those who pretend that we are not international.'[1] By the year's end, Connolly told William O'Brien that the Independent Labour Party (ILP) in east Belfast, 'the largest and most active' branch, was 'strongly, in fact practically unanimously in our favour' and that his synthesis of socialism and republicanism had opened a 'new field' in 'their mental vision'. Connolly nevertheless admitted that, while his pro-Home Rule stance 'does not do me much good from the point of view of the [Irish Transport and General Workers'] Union in this Orange hole, ... at least I must take the chance'.[2]

There appeared little prospect, however, of much return on Connolly's gamble at the height of the Ulster Crisis. Yet for a fleeting moment in the twilight between the closing stages of war and the onset of slump, a wave of working-class militancy washed over Ulster, raising the temporary, tantalizing hope of an anti-sectarian, egalitarian and democratic future, before crashing on the jagged reality of loyalist counter-revolution and economic depression. Writing from the Belfast leg of her Irish sojourn in late spring 1919, the Chicago journalist, Ruth Russell, confidently and mistakenly predicted that the high cost of living had heralded the 'sickness and death of Carsonism', since it had united Protestant and Catholic workers. As evidence, she pointed to an interview with Dawson Gordon, the organizer for the Flax Roughers' and Yarn Spinners' Trade Union. From his 'dark little union headquarters', filled with 'shawled spinners and weavers', Gordon regaled Russell with colourful accounts of Ulster's ingrained sectarianism, before producing 'a much-thumbed pamphlet on the linen and jute industry' to display the

---

1 James Connolly to R.J. Hoskin, 14 June 1911, National Library of Ireland (NLI), William O'Brien Papers, MS 13,940/1/13. 2 James Connolly to William O'Brien, 7 Dec. 1911, NLI, William O'Brien Papers, MS 13,908/1/51.

material facts that explained its temporary transcendence.[3] Gordon, a Protestant Connollyite, recounted how, with 'hunger at their heels', workers,

> forgot prejudices. Catholics began to go to meetings in Orange halls. Protestants attended similar meetings in Hibernian assembly rooms; at a small town near Belfast there was a recent labour procession in which one-half of the band was Orange and the other half Hibernian, and yet there was perfect harmony.'[4]

From 400 members of textile unions in 1914, Gordon recounted how the numbers 'mounted to 40,000 in 1919', mostly based on their ability to exact higher wages.[5] That summer, the RIC inspector general inadvertently validated Gordon's analysis, reporting that 'the continued exorbitant prices of all the necessities of life is crushing the poor and persons of limited means who find it nearly impossible to make ends meet. This is no doubt a considerable factor of the discontent which is spreading in all classes of workers, and results in constant demands for increased wages.'[5a]

Gordon combined with other ILP members, most notably David Robb Campbell of the Belfast Trades Council, and Sam Kyle, James S. McKeague and Robert 'Bob' McClung, in promoting the British-based, syndicalist Workers' Union as a means of rallying Ulster's unskilled mill workers, factory hands and agricultural labourers to the socialist banner.[6] Yet despite the claims of employers and their pressmen, the demand for organization did not emerge from outside agitators or union officials but from local workers themselves. Rather, these socialists reaped a bountiful harvest as thousands of workers sensed the opportunity for genuine advancement, rupturing the thin veneer of rural and small-town class harmony.

All five men would stand (four successfully) as Belfast Labour Party (BLP) candidates in the January 1920 municipal elections. The BLP was based on 120 delegates who formed the Labour Representation Committee, including the Trades Council and two branches of the ILP.[7] Anti-partitionist and radically socialist, the BLP rejected the Irish Trades Union Congress and Labour Party (ITUC&LP) decision not to contest the 1918 general election. Having helped develop the Irish labour movement's 1916 manifesto, Campbell 'could scarcely believe that any organization of Labour in Ireland

---

3 Ruth Russell, *What's the matter with Ireland* (New York, 1920), p. 146.   **4** Ibid., pp 146–7. **5** Ibid.   **5a** RIC inspector general (IG) report, July 1919, National Archives, London (NAL), CO 904/109.   **6** I have employed the spelling McKeague throughout, although McKeag often appeared in newspaper reports; Sam Kyle would go on to be ITUC president in 1940 and 1950; D.R. Campbell was congress treasurer, 1913–18 (Donal Nevin, *Trade union century* (Cork, 1994), pp 437–41).   **7** *Irish News*, 27 Nov. 1918.

would lie down to Sinn Fein to the extent it did.'[8] Due to its record of trade union activism, its prominent role in Belfast's 44-hour general strike of 1919 and its ceaseless campaigning, the BLP carved out a significant electoral niche among the city's unskilled workers and the most progressive elements in the shipyards and foundries. As Henry Patterson has remarked: 'William Walker and his times had long been left behind'.[9] In the heat of victory, the *Watchword of Labour* may have got slightly carried away in its response to the first meeting of councillors representing the 'united working class' in City Hall, or the 'very citadel of the planters, exploiters and expropriators', but a leaven of truth buttressed the hyperbole:

> No such sight has been seen in Belfast since Dissenter and Catholic united in 1791 in the republican Belfast of the United Irishmen. Today, the man who, more than anybody else, told both of them their true history, pointed out their common exploitation and common interests, and blazed the path of Labour and that Republicanism which would lead them to freedom is no more, but the signs he saw are here, and some of them are being made by men whom he did not a little to teach and inspire… Connolly's aim and Connolly's dream are coming, and they may come fast. The ghosts of the slain are haunting Belfast, and they are taking substantial if strange shapes.[10]

In 1920, faced with a free choice, thousands of Protestant workers ignored loyalist black propaganda and BLP candidates consistently outpolled their opponents from the Ulster Unionist Labour Association (UULA), a proto-fascist group with 'its origin in the brain of the greatest patriot and one of the greatest men this country ever saw – Lord Carson.'[11] By the following summer, however, the UULA would play a decisive role in the loyalist terror that shattered this nascent movement amongst Ulster's poorest workers.

The UULA, which had a mill-owner and future Northern Ireland prime minister, J.M. Andrews, as its chair, effectively danced to the tune of the bigoted secretary of the Ulster Unionist Council, Richard Dawson Bates. The Unionist leadership and capitalist class employed this grouping and an ancillary yellow loyalist union, the Ulster Workers' Union (UWU), led by UULA committee member James Turkington, to crush socialism in Ulster.

---

8 *Irish News,* 9 Nov. 1918.　**9** In 1920, a majority of the 22 BLP candidates opposed partition, 'at least 5 of the 10 elected had a reputation as Home Rulers, while only 3 can be clearly identified as unionist'. See Henry Patterson, *Class conflict and sectarianism: the protestant working class and the Belfast labour movement, 1868–1920* (Belfast, 1980), p. 259.　**10** *Watchword of Labour,* 31 Jan. 1920. **11** *Belfast Newsletter,* 20 Jan. 1922; for the 'fascist' character of the UULA and a detailed examination

The *Watchword* claimed that, as UWU head, Turkington received £270 per annum from 'the blood money of the "profiteers of Ulster", made when the lads of the Ulster Division were shedding their blood in Flanders.'[12] An analysis of the UWU balance sheet confirmed it as a capitalist venture, which had not paid any strike, lockout or sick pay, or funeral benefits.[13] Indeed, correspondence between the Ministry of Labour and the Linen Masters' Association revealed that the employers 'would take no part' on the proposed Linen Trade Board, unless the UWU gained representation.[14]

As with the infamous example of the 1919 Caledon lockout, employers introduced UWU blacklegs, before readmitting strikers on a sectarian basis. Future BLP councillor and Irish Transport and General Workers' Union (ITGWU) organizer, Denis Houston, told the Belfast Trades Council that the UULA under Turkington had organized blacklegs, and that 'the names of men desiring employment at the mill must first be submitted to the local Orange Lodge before' they got work.[15] The UULA repudiated Houston's allegation, concluding 'that they have no connection, either direct or indirect, with any trade union or labour organization,' but the symbiotic relationship between the UWU and UULA rendered the claim unsustainable. The Caledon pattern repeated itself across Ulster, *mutatis mutandis,* at Ballymena, Banbridge, Portadown, Lurgan and Donaghmore, where a brief flowering of anti-sectarian, working-class politics lay smashed by sectarianism and reactionary violence.[16]

In the wake of the July 1920 shipyard expulsions, the *Watchword* excoriated 'the Turkington spawn', declaring: 'see vultures and you will find their bodies; see black legs or sectarian hate and you will find Turkington and his crew.'[17] Yet in January 1920, Turkington and his UULA running mate secured less than 500 votes as against Sam Kyle's poll-topping 2082 and 500 for Dawson Gordon in the overwhelmingly Protestant Shankill ward. A resilient working-class politics had demonstrated itself impervious to a year of black propaganda providing Belfast labour's 'big stride', where official Unionist candidates (including the UULA) barely registered 50 per cent of the votes in the great

---

of its role in the 1920 pogrom, see Fearghal Mac Bhloscaidh, 'The Belfast pogrom and the interminable Irish question', *Studi irlandesi*, 12 (2022), 171–93.   **12** *Voice of Labour*, 2 Aug. 1919. **13** *Watchword of Labour*, 28 Aug. 1920.   **14** Ibid., 24 Jan. 1920; *Portadown News*, 17 Jan. 1920. **15** *Irish Independent*, 9 June 1919; *Evening Telegraph*, 5 June 1919. For a detailed treatment of the Caledon lockout, see Fearghal Mac Bhloscaidh, 'The Caledon lockout: revolution and counter-revolution in rural Ulster, 1918–1922', *International Labor and Working-Class History*, 98 (2020), 193–215.   **16** UULA minutes, 21 Aug. 1919 (PRONI, D1327/11/4/1): this chapter focuses specifically on events in Belfast and its environs, yet ample evidence exists that working-class Catholics and Protestants across east Ulster's linen triangle engaged in concerted militant trade union activity, employing the Workers' Union as a vehicle, across the period.   **17** *Watchword of Labour*, 28 Aug. 1920.

Unionist citadel.[18] The spring of 1920 represented the high-water mark, as a militant wave swept across the whole island; this article will analyse the movement's activist hub amongst the narrow, red-bricked terraces and satanic mills of industrial Belfast. But to proceed it is necessary to return to Connolly and pre-war Belfast to assess this movement's origins.

Belfast beginnings

Partly as a result of joint education lectures at Danny McDevitt's shop, or the Bounders' College, on Rosemary Street in the city centre, leading Protestants in the ILP and Belfast Trades Council, chief among their number Thomas Johnson and D.R. Campbell, gravitated towards Connolly's pro-Home Rule position. Indeed, of the five Belfast ILP branches, only William Walker's in north Belfast ignored the Socialist Party of Ireland's (SPI) invitation to a unity conference in Dublin at Easter 1912.[19] Campbell and Johnson proceeded to orientate the Trades Council towards the Irish Trades Union Congress (ITUC) and then the Irish Labour Party, a bold move in the febrile atmosphere of Unionist opposition to Home Rule and the expulsion of socialist and Catholic workers from Belfast's shipyards and engineering works that summer. Nevertheless, by 1914, both had assumed prominent roles in the ITUC's campaign against partition or what Connolly famously labelled 'the carnival of reaction'.[20] Indeed, Peter Collins has argued that even the Unionist-minded delegates to the Trades Council opposed the measure in 1914.[21]

While Connolly would privately criticize both men for not backing his early, and very public, opposition to the war, the 'chance' he took in 1911 eventually bore fruit in the hothouse conditions of war.[22] Circumstance, or the Easter Rising, temporarily thrust the leadership of the ITUC&LP onto Johnson and Campbell and while the former lingered on the national stage, the latter returned to the northern metropolis intent on promoting the Irish labour movement. The outlines of this programme found expression in the ITUC&LP's October 1916 manifesto, which opposed conscription as well as partition or 'dismemberment', which 'would destroy all our hopes of achieving the unity of Ireland through the unity of the workers', before laying out a radical programme for organization and social transformation. Indeed, Dawson Gordon confided to Campbell that the sections on partition and conscription should 'have been made a little stronger'.[23] The manifesto's

---

18 *Irish Times*, 19 Jan. 1920. **19** Peter Collins, 'Belfast Trades Council, 1881–1921' (PhD, University of Ulster, 1988), pp 185–6. **20** Collins, 'Belfast Trades Council', p. 194. **21** Ibid., p. 197. **22** Connolly to O'Brien, 22 Aug. 1914, NLI, O'Brien Papers, MS 13,908/1/73. **23** Dawson Gordon

concluding paragraph encapsulates the tactics these northern socialists adopted over the following half decade: 'Let every worker become a Trade Unionist, let every branch of a Trade Union become affiliated with the local Trades Council, and every Trades Council link up with their fellows through the ITUC&LP. Thus, may the workers of Ireland become powerful for the re-building of the Irish Nation!'[24]

In essence, like worker ants, these organizers spread from their Belfast hive organizing the non-unionized across east Ulster before establishing Trade Council colonies, whose members then stood for municipal government based on their activist record. As Campbell told the 1916 ITUC Congress: 'Organization was not merely for getting a few shillings a week', but 'for the purpose of education … of educating men and groups of men to the truth … for the purpose of getting men to get rid of false doctrines,' until 'the day when the working classes would get a greater amount of control in their respective countries.'[25]

As the war progressed, these Belfast socialists organized a series of lectures, with one notable visit from Red Clydesider, Willie Gallacher, in February 1918, whose syndicalism, anti-conscription stance and 'fairly strong language' found a ready audience amongst the ILP, but received 'an unfavourable reception at the Engineers' Hall' which 'was refused to him for a second meeting'.[26] Johnson and Campbell then planned Ireland's first anti-conscription meeting on the Custom House steps on 14 April. The *Voice of Labour* heralded Belfast's 'monster protest', when around eight thousand assembled to hear the 'true voice of Ulster, the voice of the working class'. It added that Arthur Trew of the Ulster Protestant Association (UPA), who attempted to disrupt the proceedings, 'had to receive police protection'.[27] The RIC's more sombre account of the subsequent meeting at City Hall the following Saturday (17 April) noted that a 'number of men and boys from the shipyards dragged a lorry through the crowd, upset the platform and broke up the meeting', resulting in sectarian rioting on Castle Street and the expulsion of five Catholic workers from Workman & Clark's the following day.[28] Alarmed at the initial protest, the Unionist leadership and loyalist shipyard workers closed ranks, driving the socialists from the city centre, Johnson cutting a hasty retreat after being hit on the head by a 'chunk of concrete'.[29]

to D.R. Campbell, 16 Oct. 1916 (NLI, Thomas Johnson Papers, MS 17,115/3).   **24** Copy of draft manifesto by ITUC&LP opposing conscription in Ireland, Oct. 1916 (NLI, Thomas Johnson Papers, MS 17,115/5).   **25** *Workers' Republic*, 25 Mar. 1916.   **26** D.I. report, Belfast, Feb. 1918, NAL, CO 904/105.   **27** *Voice of Labour*, 20 Apr. 1918.   **28** D.I. report, Belfast, Apr. 1918, NAL, CO 904/105.   **29** Brian Feeney, *Antrim, 1912–23: the Irish Revolution* (Dublin, 2021), p. 49.

The interference by loyalists and subsequent small-scale expulsions in the 'Wee Yard' raised several important issues. First, the UPA would serve as a badge of convenience for loyalist pogromists organized by the UULA in the summer of 1920. Second, the Trades Council and BLP did not enjoy anything like majority support within the city's skilled shipbuilding and engineering aristocracy of labour. Clearly, Protestant socialists such as James Lawther and Jimmy Baird of the Carpenters' and Boilermakers' Union respectively represented prominent shipyard socialists elected as BLP councillors. Lawther was on the platform at the aforementioned anti-conscription meeting. Jimmy Baird, 'a pronounced home ruler and socialist since 1883, not in Cork, understand, but in the Queens island, Belfast', attended his first meeting of the corporation in dungarees and would subsequently lead the expelled workers in 1920 before feeling the sharp end of the southern carnival of reaction as an ITGWU organizer for the Waterford farm strike in 1923.[30]

Nevertheless, while socialism and class consciousness gained a foothold on Queen's Island and in the foundries, loyalism remained dominant. This would have crucial consequences when the economic depression, which had hit the textile industry immediately after the war, spread to other sectors in 1920, weakening the hand of labour and strengthening the fist of reaction. In general, support for the BLP's brand of socialism largely reflected the social reality for thousands of northern workers, which undermined the 'myth' of Protestant prosperity and progress that 'concealed many lags in social development: the exploited underclass of linen lasses, the marginalized Catholic workforce, or the subsistence waged labourers in agriculture, which remained the North's chief industry.'[31] This essay will focus on the activism by these Belfast socialists amongst unskilled workers – a movement built in the first instance on the unionization of the city's female mill workers – the famous Millies.

The Workers' Union and the price of living

Connolly's challenge to William Walker in 1911 found organized expression in the conflict between the ITGWU and Mary Galway's Textile Operatives' Union, which until then represented the main trade union for the city's female linen workers. Galway, however, concentrated on the skilled weavers rather than the masses of spinners and unskilled hands, who flocked to Connolly,

---

30 For self-description, see *Voice of Labour*, 19 Oct. 1918; for Corporation meeting, see *Watchword of Labour*, 31 Jan. 1920; *Belfast Newsletter*, 23 Jan. 1920; for a recent analysis of Baird as a 'rotten prod', see Conall Parr, 'Expelled from Yard and tribe: the "rotten Prods" of 1920 and their political legacies', *Studi Irlandesi: A Journal of Irish Studies*, 11 (2021), 309–11; Emmet O'Connor, *Rotten Prod: the unlikely career of Dongaree Baird* (Dublin, 2022). **31** Emmet O'Connor, *Syndicalism in*

prompting accusations of 'poaching' from Galway.[32] It was testimony to the sea-change within the ILP that by 1917, Sam Kyle, an official for Galway's textile operatives, had set his mind to organize all of Ulster's mill hands. Kyle stood in the Shankill constituency in the general election of 1918 and topped the poll in the January 1920 municipal contest just over a year later, telling voters he 'stood for the international working class and public ownership. Carson's candidates had the support of linen Lords, but real labour supported the textile workers fight for proper wages.'[33]

While Belfast's linen, shipbuilding and engineering tycoons profited handsomely from government contracts, often employing 'economic conscription' to compel men to the trenches while youths and women laboured for a pittance in their stead, the working class writhed under rampant wartime inflation. The 'Big Yard', Harland & Wolff, launched 400,000 tons of shipping during the conflict, while Workman & Clark produced 260,000. By 1919, both yards employed a combined workforce of nearly 30,000. Due to war contracts (Ulster received 160), employment in linen swelled from 76,000 in 1912 to nearly 90,000 by war's end.[34] Under these favourable conditions, trade union militancy flourished, and with it a distinctly socialist current. While strike activity and economic demands appeared general, socialism and a burgeoning class consciousness seemed strongest among the unskilled who bridled under the inflated cost of living. There is a clear correlation between an increase in unionization in the linen industry after 1916 and a relative bridging of the chasm between prices and wages. The statistics validate Dawson Gordon's anecdotal evidence to Ruth Russell.[35]

Although the Federation of Engineering and Shipbuilding Trades (FEST) largely controlled trade union politics for skilled workers in those sectors, socialists attached to the ILP made remarkable headway in the linen industry, employing strikes and the wartime arbitration process to favourable effect, winning the political loyalty of a sub-stratum of the city's working class in the process. This was largely achieved through the auspices of the Workers' Union, which had a presence amongst the swelling ranks of unskilled workers in the foundries and shipyards, but mostly served workers in the mills that dotted

Ireland (Cork, 1988), p. 173.   **32** Maria Luddy, 'Galway, Mary (1864/5–1928), trade unionist', *Oxford dictionary of national biography* [accessed 23 Sept. 2004].   **33** *Cork Examiner*, 2 Dec. 1918. **34** Between 1913 and 1920, Irish wages in most sectors more than doubled, but the increases did not significantly outpace the rising retail price of food; interestingly, nearly every ship in the German fleet sunk at Scapa Flow was equipped with 'Sirocco fans' sold by the violently partisan anti-trade unionist and sectarian bigot, Sir Samuel Davidson. Mackie's textile machinery works turned most of their production over to munition. See Collins, 'Belfast Trades Council', p. 233.   **35** W. Semple, 'Wages and prices in Belfast, 1914–23' (M.Comm.Sc. Queen's University Belfast, 1922), chapter 15, p. 1 (from Collins, 'Belfast Trades Council').

Ulster's linen triangle and rural labourers in its hinterland – a class intent on demanding its fair share of the wartime boom in agricultural prices and government contracts. Tellingly, the RIC inspector general reported in July 1918 that 'the demand for agricultural labour in some places appears to exceed the supply which is remarkable considering that emigration had practically ceased'.[36]

A 'new union' formed in 1898 by the radical socialist, Tom Mann, the Workers' Union (WU), sought to recruit casual and unskilled workers, under the pioneering ideals of a socialist society. The WU exhibited a strong left-wing ethos from the outset, but, by its zenith, also manifested the familiar tension between militant grassroots and a bureaucratic and reformist leadership. After an unspectacular first decade, the union flourished during the widespread labour militancy preceding the First World War, growing to become Britain's fifth-largest trade union by the time the lights of Europe went out. This growth relied on economic prosperity and the influence of syndicalism within British and wider European militancy.

During the war, twenty women organizers helped take female union membership from 5,000 to 80,000. Indeed, Belfast's organizers often worked in unison with their British female comrades. For instance, Gordon, Kyle and McClung shared a platform at the Dungannon May Day demonstration in 1919 with the leading British socialist and suffragette, Kate Manicom.[37] In January 1917, Gordon, by then an ITUC&LP delegate, accompanied a Miss Hanratty at an open-air meeting of mill workers on Belfast's Crumlin Road district. Hanratty emphasized 'the necessity for organization amongst the women workers in the linen industry' and the need for 'one big society, for it was only by union they would be able to get their demands conceded.' Gordon outlined how he had petitioned the Board of Trade to interfere in wage disputes as the cost of living had increased by over 80 per cent.[38] In June 1919, Gordon 'got a tremendous welcome, the audience rising and applauding for several seconds', when he introduced Ellen Wilkinson, future chair of the British Labour Party, and Margaret McCoubrey, a Belfast ILP member and suffragist, to a packed Orange Hall in Lisburn. Gordon encouraged the town's workers, whom he had already organized, to support the strike by local shop workers for recognition of their union: 'Mill workers [should] be missionaries to that cause, a holy cause, and not spend one farthing in black leg shops until the principle of the union was conceded and the dispute settled.'[39]

---

36 I.G. report, July 1918, NAL, CO 904/106. **37** *Tyrone Courier*, 15 May 1919. **38** *Freeman's Journal*, 29 Jan. 1917; for Gordon's position on the ITUC&LP, see *Evening Herald*, 29 May 1917. **39** *Lisburn Standard*, 27 June 1919.

Although the WU's bureaucracy, and its secretary the moderate Labour MP Charles Duncan in particular, may have baulked at its initial militant socialist objectives, many grassroots organizers and members clearly viewed the WU as a potential One Big Union in embryo. Indeed, in a report on a series of WU-led strikes by farm labourers in Down, Robert McClung castigated 'win the war' Duncan for the use of government scabs in a dispute at Portaferry, although Duncan did subsequently intervene in parliament on behalf of WU members in dispute with the Lurgan UDC.[40] The WU's membership exploded to almost half a million in the intoxicating atmosphere of industrial militancy in 1918, making it Britain's largest union. Indeed, fuelled by favourable economic conditions, swelled by reservoirs of non-unionized workers, galvanized by successful strike action, and operating under wartime legislation that facilitated the arbitration of disputes, thousands poured into the WU's flexible organizational structure. The post-war recession and chronic unemployment, however, corroded the membership to one hundred thousand and eventually forced the near bankrupt WU to merge with Ernest Bevin's Transport and General Workers' Union in 1929.[41]

Interestingly, most of the WU's provincial organizers in Ulster were also attached to the ITUC&LP, and Cathal O'Shannon, also a member of the SPI, provided consistent sympathetic space and coverage in the *Voice* and then *Watchword of Labour*. As Emmet O'Connor has rightly pointed out: 'By the time Dublin [the ITGWU] was ready to push northwards, British unions like the NAUL and the WU had already cornered the market'.[42] Yet the organizers for these British-based unions tended to emerge from an identifiable group shaped by 'Connolly's conversion of Belfast socialists from William Walker's pro-Union labourism to anti-partitionism'.[43]

It is possible to speculate, therefore, that the WU facilitated co-operation between Protestant and Catholic workers in a way that the ITGWU, with its overt republicanism and close relationship to Sinn Fein, could not.[44] For instance, before an audience of 200 workers at Armagh Town Hall on 23 September 1918, J.S. McKeague successfully formed a WU branch, which 'all sections of the labouring class joined'. However, the RIC described Cathal O'Shannon's 'attempt to form a branch of the ITGWU two nights later' as 'a complete failure'.[45] McKeague rightly identified himself as a 'member of a fraternity of organizers who were out to secure better conditions' for the

---

40 *Voice of Labour*, 17 Aug. 1918; for Lurgan, see *Voice of Labour*, 8 Dec. 1917; *Hansard*, HOC, 24 June 1918, vol. 107/815–16.   **41** Richard Hyman, *The Workers' Union* (London, 1971), passim. **42** O'Connor, *Syndicalism*, pp 168–9.   **43** O'Connor, *Syndicalism*, p. 179.   **44** The RIC inspector general noted the ITGWU's unpopularity in north-east Ulster, I.G. report, July 1919, NAL, CO 904/109.   **45** C.I. report, Armagh, Sept. 1918, NAL, CO 904/107.

working class.[46] The following month, the crowd had swelled to one thousand, when local Catholic mill labourer and branch president, George Carson, introduced McKeague, who urged all textile workers and general labourers to enrol.[47]

By November, the RIC noted that the 'relationship between employers and workmen is not so good', since 'strikes can be easily got up'.[48] Municipal labourers duly plunged the city into darkness, after Armagh UDC refused to hear McKeague's demand for higher wages.[49] In December, the town's carters struck for an increase, while bread servers for Inglis & Co. in Belfast merely had to threaten strike action to gain concessions.[50] In 1919, Peter McKernan, a Catholic railway clerk, chaired a meeting in the Foresters' Hall, where Dawson Gordon and D.R. Campbell gave the inaugural addresses of the Armagh Trades Council.[51] That autumn, Robert Getgood told a WU meeting that 'Labour was nearer victory than a great many people were aware of. There was going to be no peace in the industrial world until all the workers were united in one body, whereby they could control all the means by which they had to earn their living.' Felix Hughes of the Postal Clerks' Association then advocated a Co-operative Commonwealth, before Bob McClung declared that 'those who engaged in the trade union movement were going to see about sharing the wealth of the country amongst the working classes who produced it until they took all the wealth they produced.'[52] Armagh town fitted the pattern of activism outlined previously, where a symbiotic relationship between central ideological agency fused with demand on the periphery fuelled by economic necessity, resulting in a pattern of organization and subsequent politicization. This process also operated in the heart of north Armagh's linen triangle around Lurgan and Portadown and spread into east Tyrone and the industrial centres of Dungannon, Cookstown and Coalisland.

The general strike and the Belfast pogrom

The independent trade union movement in Belfast challenged Unionist hegemony among the Protestant working class. In the January 1920 municipal election in Belfast, the BLP won twelve seats, the *Newsletter* noting that 'the active supporters of the Labour candidates were jubilant after their success, and when Mr Kyle and some of his colleagues were leaving the City Hall

46 *Freeman's Journal*, 29 Sept. 1918. **47** *Belfast Newsletter*, 1 Nov. 1918; C.I. report, Armagh, Oct. 1918, NAL, CO 904/107. **48** C.I. report, Armagh, Nov. 1918, NAL, CO 904/107. **49** From an Anglican background, Getgood would lead the anti-partitionist wing of the Northern Ireland Labour Party and become chair of the ITUC in 1944. **50** C.I. report, Armagh, Dec. 1918, NAL, CO 904/107. **51** *Northern Whig*, 26 Apr. 1919. **52** *Freeman's Journal*, 25 Oct. 1919.

grounds, they were surrounded by a crowd of enthusiasts who gave vent to their feelings by singing "The Red Flag".[53] Indeed, the influential left-leaning, Protestant Sinn Féiner, William Forbes Patterson, claimed that 'so deep and wide was the rift in the Orange Lodges' during the election, 'that the Unionist leaders dared not bring out the Orange drums.'[54]

In total, explicitly anti-partitionist parties won over 30,000 votes, while official Unionist parties won fewer than 50,000. In a city where Protestants made up three-quarters of the population, this represented a hammer blow to Unionist prestige in the party's citadel. In the June rural elections, Sinn Féin won 40 per cent of the seats in Ulster's nine counties, where anti-partition groups won 55 per cent. Between the 1918 coupon election and the pogrom of July 1920, the Unionist leadership promoted violence to guarantee its provincial hegemony in anticipation of the creation of the Belfast parliament, indelibly marking the polity that emerged from the ashes.

The defeat of socialism in Belfast rested on direct masculine action by a loyalist aristocracy of labour, for 'unlike their southern colleagues, northern craftsmen had no need of an alliance with labourers to secure their bargaining power'.[55] Skilled workers in the shipyards and in engineering generally fused 'craft exclusiveness and sectarianism'; thus, two-thirds of workers were highly skilled, affiliated to British-based craft unions and enjoyed a major advantage in pay over non-skilled workers.[56] The UULA exploited the developing southern IRA guerrilla campaign as the pretext for the mass expulsion of Catholic and socialist workers from the city's main employment centres. Despite elision by many historians, political Unionism and King Carson undoubtedly inspired, directed and reaped the reactionary dividends from this pogrom.

The trajectory of the pogrom can be traced back to the 1919 Belfast general strike, which at least demonstrated 'that workers wanted a shorter working week, were not fooled by the economic and political arguments of the employers and showed massive solidarity … not threatened in any way by communal tensions'.[57] Dawson Bates, however, had little doubt that the strike 'leaders are practically all Sinn Feiners, who have taken advantage of some of the rank and file' and that 'almost a quarter of strikers were "out and out socialists".'[58] Indeed, Jimmy Baird in particular played a crucial role in

---

53 *Belfast Newsletter*, 19 Jan. 1920.   **54** *Old Ireland*, 14 Feb. 1920.   **55** O'Connor, *Syndicalism*, p. 168.   **56** Ibid., pp 168–70; O'Connor cites a ratio of 3:1; Patterson writes that in July 1914, a labourer's weekly rate of pay in shipbuilding and engineering was 51% of a plater's and 54% of a fitter's. By July 1918, the rates were 67% and 69% (Patterson, *Class conflict and sectarianism*, p. 95). **57** Austen Morgan, *Labour and partition: the Belfast working class, 1905–23* (London, 1991), p. 246. **58** Dawson Bates to James Craig, 31 Jan./1 Feb. 1919 (PRONI, D1507/A/29/7–8).

fomenting strike action the previous summer, before letting members of the Federation of Engineering and Shipbuilding Trades 'take over the business'. Baird would publicly ridicule the FEST for their political timidity and failure to confront the employers and authorities in the wake of the strike.[59] Interestingly, while the linen trade languished, shipbuilding and engineering temporarily boomed in the early peacetime market, before crashing in overproduction by the autumn of 1920. By December 1920, a quarter of Irish workers were idle.[60] Dawson Gordon informed the Belfast Trades Council that conditions meant that linen workers could not come out in sympathy with the '44-hour strikers'.[61] This downturn left militant workers in textile mills vulnerable to interventions by the UWU earlier than in other sectors of industry. It was not until the summer of 1920, that the economic conditions existed for the wholesale suppression of trade unionism, however.

Yet, in the heady days of 1919, the *Voice of Labour* hoped that, since many strikers 'are members of the Ulster Volunteer Force', in the event of a collision 'with the English forces drafted into Belfast, this body of disciplined men will be a factor of considerable importance.' The article wistfully concluded:

> much may yet be accomplished by such forces as the Ulster Volunteers, the Irish Volunteers, and the Citizens' Army. An exchange of views between these groups might show that they now have more in common than was imagined. Much has happened since the Covenant was signed.[62]

Furthermore, O'Shannon's analysis in the *Voice of Labour* editorial corresponded to that of Dawson Bates, who precluded overt Unionist party intervention against the strike to avoid a situation where workers might feel 'let down', or become 'so embittered with the Authorities that they would join hands in a universal strike for the whole of Ireland ... the consequences of which would be very far-reaching'. His proposal, an Orange manifesto, therefore, would permit 'the decent men to secede from the Sinn Fein Bolshevik element'.[63] Bates also promoted a leaflet that situated the republican movement within a global Bolshevik conspiracy, seeking to invade Ulster under a labourite cloak, echoing propaganda by the British extreme right from the Primrose League to the British Fascists. James Craig regurgitated this bile in a letter to Lloyd George, claiming that 'the rebel plans are directed towards

---

59 *Voice of Labour*, 8 Mar. 1919. **60** Emmet O'Connor, *A labour history of Ireland, 1824–2000* (Dublin, 2011), p. 119. **61** *Belfast Newsletter*, 7 Feb. 1919. **62** *Voice of Labour*, 22 Feb. 1919. **63** Bates to Craig, 31 Jan.–2 Feb. 1919 (PRONI, D1507/A/29/7–8).

the establishment of a Republic hostile to the British Empire ... working in conjunction with Bolshevik forces elsewhere towards that end'.[64] In the wake of the pogrom in August 1920, the UULA MP, Sam McGuffin, claimed that the ITGWU was a

> ... camouflaged organization for carrying out the bidding of Sinn Fein, which was linked up on the continent with the Bolshevik movement, and then India with the anarchic movement. It was all one great organization for the purpose of destroying the power of the British government.[65]

Rather than being passive observers, Unionist leaders co-ordinated a strike response based on their relative weakness vis-à-vis the popularity of the strike committee's demands during the brief post-war boom. While the victory of an independent Unionist in the subsequent East Antrim by-election hardly constituted a fatal blow to their hegemony, local Unionists blamed 'a combination between the Roman Catholics and extreme members of the Labour Party together with a considerable number of relatively moderate Protestants' for the result.[66] At the same time, Bates warned that the 'Labour question is becoming acute in Belfast and the North of Ireland ... there is a general desire to kick against all authority and all discipline all over the three kingdoms, and this found vent in the East Antrim election. We have got to face this sooner or later.'[67] Indeed, nominees of the Larne Trades Council would win five of the towns UDC seats in January 1920, the Antrim RIC county inspector bemoaning 'the return of men ... who have very little standing in the community and little experience of business' or 'intelligence'.[68]

   While the revolutionary potential of the Belfast working class should not be over-estimated, neither should we downplay Unionist disquiet at the growth of socialism. By June 1919, Bates had written to Carson, proposing to strengthen the UULA as 'many of the unions ... are controlled by officials who hold Home Rule views,' a situation that 'leads the younger members of the working class to Socialist, i.e., extreme, organizations run by the ILP [*sic*] where they are educated in views very different to those held by our body'. Interestingly, he also praised 'the vast bulk of thinking Employers, and those who have the interests of the Empire at heart,' who realized that UULA

---

64 Alan Parkinson, *Belfast's unholy war* (Dublin, 2004), p. 47.   **65** *Portadown News,* 28 Aug. 1920. **66** W. Chaine to Edward Carson, 17 June 1919, PRONI, D1507/A/30/6.   **67** 'Practically all the Roman Catholic vote was given to Hanna ... The Ulster protestant Home Ruler still exists, though in small numbers, but they can make a lot of mischief'. Bates to Captain Craig, 18 June 1919, PRONI, D1507/A/30/3.   **68** C.I. report, Antrim, Jan. 1920, NAL, CO 904/111.

10.1 Labour election leaflet for Shankill, 1920. Courtesy of Ciarán Ó Brolcháin.

advocacy had a 'most beneficial' effect.[69] In this respect, Bates merely reflected concerns from UULA members that 'some steps should be taken to enrol the younger members of the community who are liable to be influenced by opponents of the cause'.[70] Indeed, before the Belfast shipyard expulsion, William J. McDowell told a loyalist audience at Portadown that the 'socialistic or independent Labour Party had circulated the slander that the UULA was

69 Bates to Carson, 30 June 1919, PRONI, D1507/A/30/12. **70** Scott to Bates, PRONI, D1327/18/15.

out to smash the trade unions.' Rather the BLP 'posed as a true friend of labour, but they were opposed to every Unionist principle, and they tried to woo the young men in the workshops so that they might use them as tools to' discard the Union Jack 'for the flag of Sinn Fein (Never!).' In conclusion, he 'begged them not to sell their principles as Protestants and Orangemen to men who were trying to get them into a trap.'[71]

In the 1920 municipal elections, Belfast Labour secured twelve seats and matched its average share of the vote from the 1918 general election, even securing 20 per cent in the predominantly Catholic Falls ward. Apparently, a class-conscious, anti-sectarian constituency existed, whose emergence reflected the massive upsurge in trade union activism. Patterson argues that the BLP's vote merely represented 'municipal politics with a vengeance' and that 'the minority of Protestant workers who voted for the Labour candidates had not revolutionized their politics'.[72] However, this runs counter to contemporary Unionist opinion. The extremely partisan *Newsletter* lamented the 'startling' results by the BLP in 'three divisions', which were 'undoubtedly a stronghold of working-class unionism', concluding 'that there is something wrong with unionist Labour as regards municipal politics.' Indeed, while the piece identified Unionist inability to 'answer the socialist propaganda', particularly around municipal issues, which 'had been much exploited by socialist labour from an extreme class point of view', it concluded that this did 'not account for the big changes which have been made in the personnel of the City Council by this election'.[73]

Indeed, Protestant workers could hardly plead ignorance regarding the BLP's 'revolutionary' politics, since their loyalist opponents had spent a year portraying them as a republican fifth column. For instance, Turkington's speech to voters on the Shankill Road left his audience 'well-informed' about labour's intentions:

> Sinn Feiners, Socialists and Bolsheviks were going about today asking the people for their suffrages ... There was a game going on, and socialists were running candidates in all the divisions of Belfast – men ... pledged to a republic ... He wanted to draw the attention ... to the condition of the countries, which ... had republics of late, and he did not think they would be satisfied with it ... With regard to the wages question, the socialists had opposed the granting of a living wage to the police, whom they had been fighting, and slaughtering throughout the

---

71 *Portadown News*, 3 July 1920.   72 Patterson, *Class conflict and sectarianism*, pp 119–20.
73 *Belfast Newsletter*, 19 Jan. 1920.

country … to terrorize them in order that they could have a workers' republic in Ireland and rule Belfast, but that would never be. These people had also denied a living wage to the teachers, because Sinn Feiners wanted education to be in the hands of the priests. In conclusion, he said he was out against revolution, Bolshevism, and rampant Socialism.[74]

After the outbreak of violence between the IRA and a combined force of UVF and military in Derry, 'Belfast shipyard workers petitioned Carson to mobilize the UVF and take revenge'.[75] Indeed, Sam McGuffin claimed that IRA violence would 'make a Hottentot blush'.[76] Having spoken privately to the UULA, Carson then delivered an incendiary speech at the Twelfth field in Finaghy, despite his disdain for a medium that he himself described as 'the unrolling of a mummy. All old bones and rotten rags.'[77] Warning against Sinn Fein attempts to 'penetrate Ulster', by the 'insidious method' of 'tacking on' the 'Irish Republican question to the labour question', Carson claimed that 'these men who come forward posing as the friends of Labour care no more about Labour than does the man on the moon'. He continued: 'we in Ulster will tolerate no Sinn Fein … we will take matters into our own hands … And these are not mere words. I hate words without action.'[78]

In terms of this mass violence, Paul Bew reverses cause and effect (or, obscures agency) by claiming that 'shipyard workers took matters into their own hands and expelled Catholic workers and "rotten Protestants"' while James Craig merely 'sent wary signals of support to angry Protestant workers, but was fully aware of the dangers'.[79] In fact, the UULA arranged a meeting with Carson through Dawson Bates, over the Orange holiday of the Twelfth of July.[80] Carson then gave the aforementioned incendiary speech at the Orange field inciting his followers to expel Sinn Féin supporters and trade unionists. Internal minutes suggest that the UULA then organized the meeting that sparked the expulsions.[81] The police recorded how lunch-time UULA meetings, under the Ulster Protestant Association banner, resulted in younger loyalist workers engaging in a 'regular hunt' as a result 'of which Roman Catholics were badly beaten and thrown into the water. Some of these had to swim long distances in order to save their lives.' The report made it

---

74 *Belfast Newsletter*, 9 Jan. 1920.   75 Michael Farrell, *Northern Ireland: the Orange state* (London, 1976), p. 26.   76 *Portadown News*, 28 Aug. 1920.   77 Andrew Gailey, 'King Carson: an essay on the invention of leadership', *Irish Historical Studies* 30:117 (1996), 85.   78 Quoted in Jimmy McDermott, *Northern divisions: the Old IRA and the Belfast pogroms, 1920–22* (Belfast, 2001), p. 31.   79 Bew, p. 402.   80 UULA executive minutes, 1 July 1920 (PRONI, D1327/11/4/1); UULA minutes, 3 July 1920 (PRONI, D1327/11/4/1).   81 UULA executive special meeting, 15 Dec. 1920 (PRONI, D1327/11/4/1).

explicit that loyalists 'put down' Catholics 'as all Sinn Feiners'.[82] Estimates of the numbers expelled in the ensuing city-wide expulsions range from seven to ten thousand.

The UULA then broke up a meeting of Belfast Corporation called by BLP councillors for the workers' reinstatement. Dawson Bates effectively controlled the UULA, while J.M. Andrews acted as chairman. In short, the Unionist leadership left their fingerprints all over the pogrom. As the *Westminster Gazette* reported: 'It is common knowledge in Belfast, and frequently admitted by individual Unionists, that plans were matured at least two months ago to drive all Home Rule workmen in the shipyards out of their employment'.[83] In fact, the expulsions specifically targeted socialists or rotten Protestants – the 'entire cadre of working-class leaders'. One prominent trade unionist recounted how 'every man who took a part in the Trade Union movement ... had been absolutely driven from the island'.[84]

At a rally in Portadown, William Grant admitted that the UULA instigated the pogrom, which was 'bound to occur', since 'they had to take the law into their own hands'. He continued that loyalists 'had been asleep for too long. Even in the city of Belfast ... they had allowed the enemy to practically overcome them, but now he was glad to say they were aroused with a vengeance, and those who were opposed to them would have to look out (Cheers).' The leading pogromist, John Holness, erroneously claimed that when 'their fellows went to the war to defend their country, Sinn Feiners came in to fill their places.' He then stated that 'before Christmas they were boasting that it was the Protestants who would go now', before luridly recounting how loyalists 'could see the pistols sticking out of their hip pockets, and they said they were going to change the tune of the Protestant workers on the island.' Holness triumphantly concluded that 'they had bitten off more than they could chew, and they were going to get something to swallow, and they may take it from him but it would require a good drink to wash it down.'[85]

Incredibly, the British government proceeded to recruit the pogromists *en masse* into the new Ulster Special Constabulary (USC). Indeed, the city's largest shipyard, Harland and Wolff, recognized the Loyalist Vigilance Committee set up to assess the 'loyalty' of its employees.[86] The two leaders of Ulster Unionism then publicly backed the pogrom. At the unveiling of a flag in the shipyards in October, James Craig's wife wrote in her diary how he 'unfurls a big Union Jack for them and makes a splendid speech ... that he

82 D.I. report, Belfast, July 1920, NAL, CO 904/112.   **83** *Westminster Gazette*, 24 July 1920. **84** Morgan, *Labour and partition*, p. 270, estimates that 7,500 suffered expulsion; the quote is from John Hanna.   **85** *Portadown News*, 28 Aug. 1920.   **86** Geoffrey Bell, *Hesitant comrades: the Irish Revolution and the British labour movement* (London, 2016), p. 88.   **87** Diary of Lady Craigavon,

approves of their action in not allowing the disloyal element in their midst.'[87] Carson subsequently told the House of Commons that 'I am prouder of my friends in the shipyards than of any other friends I have in the whole world'.[88]

On the last day of May 1922, Lloyd George told his cabinet that Mussolini's *Fascisti* served as an 'exact analogy' for the Ulster Specials. He continued that not only had loyalists instigated the conflict, but that the brunt of subsequent violence involved the 'murder of members of the [Catholic] minority', while his government had armed 48,000 Protestants.[89] Whitehall would fully resource the USC for a subsequent two years to the tune of over £6 million, a period of little or no violence in the North.[90] Even prominent Unionists acknowledged that employment in the USC helped solidify support for partition.[91] In effect, the pogrom represented the pivotal moment in the genesis of Northern Ireland, wherein the Ulster Unionist leadership, with near-unconditional state support, effectively purged Belfast's labour market of Catholics and Protestant socialists in order to create an Orange economy that served as the material basis for a half-century of Unionist one-party rule.

Conclusion

While most Belfast and Ulster Protestants clearly continued to support the Union, thousands had demonstrated a willingness to back an anti-sectarian, socialist alternative, which clearly undermined the Unionist case for partition. The pogrom meant that Orange loyalism rapidly represented the difference between employment or poverty. After having valiantly stormed heaven, Belfast socialists were forced to eat the dust of defeat and betrayal. During 1920's winter of discontent, the *Watchword* called out J.S. McKeague for parleying with Turkington, after the UWU colonized unskilled workers across the city after the pogrom; but new political realities appeared to offer trade unionists little choice.[92] Some commentators argue that sectarian ideologies and practices in the labour movement, though predominant during the expulsions, were relatively short-lived and that progressive, secular and labourite trade union ideology quickly re-established itself on the shop floor.[93] Yet, this ignores the central point that Unionism was prepared to tolerate a brand of economistic labourism since it was not politically dangerous. For instance, in December 1920, Dawson Gordon and Sam Kyle faced the

14 Oct. 1920 (PRONI, D1415/B/39).   **88** Quoted in Morgan, *Labour and partition*, p. 277. **89** Eamon Phoenix, *Northern nationalism* (Belfast, 1994), p. 225.   **90** Michael Farrell, *Arming the Protestants: formation of the Ulster Special Constabulary and the Royal Ulster Constabulary, 1920–27* (London, 1987), pp 153; 283.   **91** Report by Ricardo, June 1922, NAL, CO 906/27. **92** *Watchword of Labour*, 6 Nov. 1920.   **93** Christopher Norton, 'Worker response to the 1920

ignominy of accompanying Sam McGuffin and the UULA to London, where Edward Carson introduced them to the Ministry of Labour to petition for the city's unemployed.[94] Faced with the reality of an Orange economy and a massive security clamp-down, these socialist organizers were reduced to what the *Watchword* sardonically labelled 'the milk and watery socialism of Sam Kyle and the Belfast ILP' – a drastic change in tone from the same organ's euphoria the previous January.[95]

No serious observer disputes the presence of a reactionary Orange ideology within sections of the Protestant working class, but this study contests the myth of the immutability of sectarian antagonism in Belfast. A brief window opened, wherein a significant minority of working-class Protestants embraced an egalitarian ideology. Orange ideology did not operate on some intangible level of the superstructure; it required material sustenance and depended on determined agency. Its reactionary triumph relied on UULA storm troopers in the first instance and its consolidation operated against the foundation of a discriminatory statelet bankrolled by imperial largesse, whose birth pangs reverberated to the pounding of the hammer of loyalist violence on the anvil of industrial slump.

Yet, for a moment, tropes about ancient hatreds rang hollow across Ulster, where thousands of working-class people demonstrated incredible solidarity under the indefatigable activism of a cohort of Belfast's Protestant socialists. After an imperialist cataclysm and amid an international atmosphere charged by hopes for a workers' millennium, the poor and marginalized seized the opportunity to make their own history, based on their own experiences, interests and understanding, not on the clarion call of ancestral voices. Sectarianism and the colonial legacy were real, but not immutable. Indeed, the examples of poor Protestants prepared to struggle with their Catholic brothers and sisters in this period have left a significant imprint on the archive, even if the enormous condescension of posterity has largely erased them from the historiography. The socialist activists of the BLP and WU did not believe that they could wish the cleavage between Planter and Gael away, they sought rather to transcend it through solidarity and struggle. At the end of his interview with Ruth Russell in the spring optimism of 1919, Dawson Gordon noted how trade unionism offered Irish people the chance to gather under Thomas Davis' motto:

> Then let the orange lily be a badge, my patriot brother,
> The orange for you, the green for me, and each for one another.[96]

Belfast shipyard expulsions: solidarity or sectarianism?', *Études irlandaises*, 21:1 (1996), 153–63. **94** *Belfast Newsletter*, 7 Dec. 1920. **95** *Watchword of Labour*, 20 Nov. 1920. **96** Russell, *What's the matter with Ireland*, p. 147.

'More militant than the men': women's activism, class and revolution in Kerry

KIERAN McNULTY

Though important research in recent decades has examined the experience of women during the Irish Revolution, much still remains to be done at national, regional and local levels.[1] This chapter aims to further this research by examining three types of female activism in Kerry during this period, showing a range of engagements and highlighting challenges faced by women who did become active.[2] Following a brief outline of circumstances in the county, the involvement of a number of individuals and groups of women will be examined in turn: female union activists; political and military women; the activism of the revolutionary, Gobnait Ní Bhruadair.

Perhaps the most remarkable example of union militancy during this period involving female workers was the dispute at the Munster Warehouse Company (MWC). The company, whose managing director was Daniel J. Murphy, was one of the few large commercial concerns in Tralee and it witnessed the most protracted industrial dispute in the town's and indeed Kerry's history, when several male and female shop assistants walked out in protest at the company's breaking of a local agreement with the Irish Drapers' Assistants' Association (IDAA) concerning the 'living-in system'.[3] This system meant that the place of work was normally also the living quarters of the firm's employees who had no choice in the arrangement. However, the roles and expectations of most women and men in the public sphere in Kerry were still subject to contemporary social norms acceptable to a society governed by an overwhelmingly male ruling class. This is clearly illustrated in the roles granted to women by both the labour movement, particularly through the policies of Tralee Workers' Council (TWC), and the republican movement in the limited activities it allowed Cumann na mBan (CnB) to undertake. This attitude is also apparent after the local elections of 1920 in the expectations Sinn Féin had of their newly elected female councillors. But, by the time of the Civil War in Kerry often the most militant and vocal section of the republican

1 See for example Margaret Ward, *Unmanageable revolutionaries, women and Irish nationalism* (London, 1983); Ann Matthews, *Renegades: Irish republican women, 1900–1922* (Cork, 2010); Linda Connolly (ed.), *Women and the Irish Revolution: feminism, activism, violence* (Dublin, 2020). 2 See Thomas Earls Fitzgerald, *Combatants and civilians in Revolutionary Ireland, 1918–1923* (London and New York, 2021). 3 *Workers' Republic*, 29 May 1915; *Kerryman*, 29 May 1915.

movement was CnB with many women defying the edicts of the Catholic hierarchy. Gobnait Ní Bhruadair (previously Albinia Brodrick), with her background in the Anglican ascendancy, was untypical of the majority of republicans. For historian Margaret Ward there was 'another dimension' to the 'struggles that were waged by women on their own behalf, both by [those] within the nationalist movement and those critical feminists who remained on the outside'.[4] This other 'dimension' also included the labour movement involving women such as Constance Markievicz, Margaret Skinnider and Helena Molony. However, Ní Bhruadair, although a nurse and thus regarded as working in an occupation traditionally reserved for women, was also committed to radical social reform but, as with James Connolly, to a large extent has been remembered only as a nationalist hero.

Kerry in the early twentieth century

At the beginning of the twentieth century, Kerry had an underdeveloped economy, based largely on agriculture. The county's population had fallen from 293,880 in 1841, to 149,171 in 1926.[5] Between 1891 and 1926 Tralee was the only town in the county to record an increase in population from 9,318 to 10,533.[6] The major factor in population decline was mass emigration with 234,716 people leaving Kerry during the years 1851–1911.[7] Between 1901 and 1926 the female population of the county dropped by 8,991 to 72,308, some 4,555 less than the male population.[8] The likely cause of this difference was a higher rate of female migration due to the relatively fewer employment opportunities for young Kerry females compared to males. Also emigration lessened the pressure on women to marry thus offering them greater career opportunities.

In 1911 the ratio of male to female workers in Kerry stood at 5:1, but by 1926 it had dropped to 3:1 with female employment increasing from 9,509 to 15,605.[9] Indoor domestic service was the sector employing by far the largest number of females engaged in work outside their homes, and was largely

---

4 Ward, *Unmanageable revolutionaries*, p. 97.   5 *Saorstát Éireann, Census of population, 1926*, vol. 1 (Dublin, 1934), p. 10. See also Kieran McNulty, '"A hard bargain": an analysis of the social and economic background to Kerry in the early twentieth century, life and work in County Kerry 100 years ago', in *The Irish story*, http://www.tara.tcd.ie/handle/2262/5520 [accessed 5 May 2023]. 6 *Census of Ireland, 1911: County Kerry* (London, 1912), p. 2; *Saorstát Éireann, Census of population, 1926*, vol. 1, p. 25.   7 T.W. Freeman, 'The changing distribution of population in Kerry and west Cork', paper read on 30 January 1942, Trinity College, Dublin, http://www.tara.tcd.ie/handle/2262/5520 [accessed 10 May 2023], p. 30; *Census of Ireland, 1911: County Kerry*, p. 1.   8 *Census of Ireland, 1911: County Kerry*, pp 1–2, *Saorstát Éireann, Census of population, 1926*, vol. 1, p. 10. 9 *Census of Ireland, 1911: County Kerry*, p. 82. *Saorstát Éireann, Census of population, 1926*,

unorganized. In 1911 there were 4,233 females employed as domestic servants in Kerry, representing 44.44 per cent of the county's female workforce.[10] One reason for such a large representation of females employed in this sector was that this type of work was seen as a natural extension of women's traditional sphere of influence in the home. Many were also young and single women who were expected to give up employment once they were married. By 1911, of the 312 people working in the drapery sector in Kerry, one third were females and in Tralee 40 out of 123 were females.[11] Females also made up over half of 'all persons engaged in professional occupations' – 971 out of 1,894. This was due mainly to the large numbers of women engaged in what was traditionally regarded as women's work, the caring professions of teaching and nursing. Significantly women's representation in the upper-middle-class professions including medicine and law was almost non-existent.[12]

However, agriculture remained by far the largest employment sector in Kerry and by 1926 accounted for 40,631 people, almost two-thirds of the workforce.[13] The only other employment opportunities in the county were in the small number of woollen mills and in firms concerned with textiles and food processing.[14] There was also the commercial activity linked to the port of Fenit. A canal connecting Tralee to the sea meant that marine traffic was able to navigate between the town and Fenit. There was also a growing tourism sector concentrated on Killarney and the fishing industry centred on Dingle.[15]

Capital versus labour: the Munster Warehouse strike

The prospects for most working-class young people in Kerry at this time were extremely limited, as Billy Mullins experienced when he started work in 1912 with Donovan's Ltd, a building suppliers in Tralee, working a twelve-hour day often six days per week.[16] Paul Dillon shows how such poor working conditions led to two strikes by Tralee labourers in the 1890s.[17] However, it was not until 1914 that Kerry's first workers' council was permanently established, Tralee Trades and Labour Council (TTLC), with a membership of 500 workers.[18] T. O'Gorman (IDAA) was elected president and Michael O'Connell (Workers' Union) elected secretary.[19] In his speech at the inaugural

Occupations, vol. 2, pp 144–5. **10** *Census of Ireland, 1911: County Kerry*, pp 82, 85. **11** Ibid., pp 88–103. **12** Ibid., p. 82. **13** *Saorstát Éireann, Census of population, 1926, Occupations*, vol. 2, pp 144–5. **14** Billy Mullins, *Memoirs of Billy Mullins: veteran of the War of Independence* (Tralee, 1983), p. 189; *Liberty* (ITGWU periodical), June 1981; *Voice of Labour*, 28 June 1919, 5 July 1919, 2 Oct. 1920. **15** *Saorstát Éireann, Census of population, 1926, Occupations*, pp 144–5. **16** Mullins, *Memoirs*, pp 189–90. **17** Paul Dillon, 'Tralee labourers' strike of 1896: an episode in Ireland's "new unionism"', *Journal of the Kerry Archaeological and Historical Society*, 2nd series, 2 (2002), 105–17. **18** Dillon, 'Tralee labourers' strike'; *Kerryman*, 29 May 1915. **19** *Liberty*, June 1981.

meeting of the Irish Transport and General Workers' Union (ITGWU) branch in Listowel on 28 March 1916, J.E. Tackaberry gave examples of workers receiving starvation wages, 'working for as little as 10/- [shillings] per week'.[20] These low wages caused considerable industrial unrest amongst small groups of workers in the county, including the strike of the Dingle railway workers, who 'gained a substantial increase in pay' in November 1915.[21]

However, it was in the retail sector – at the MWC in Tralee – that the most significant strike occurred in Kerry during these years. Women were to the forefront of this dispute as retail was one of the few occupations where a relatively large number of them were concentrated in one workplace. The workers were members of the IDAA, founded in 1901 by Michael J. O'Lehane, its general secretary and a pioneer of Irish-based trade unions.[22] Dermot Keogh states that 'O'Lehane brought a new militancy among shop assistants'[23] and was unique among most of his contemporary union officials in believing that female workers had just as much right as their male counterparts to join unions.[24] By 1913 the IDAA recorded a membership of 4,281, of which 30.6 per cent were female, and by 1915 the union had established five branches in Kerry including one in Tralee which had 129 members, 42 of whom were female.[25] Twenty-three members were on the branch committee with Thomas Howard serving as branch secretary. In 1913 four women were voted onto the committee including a Miss Fitzgerald who was employed at the MWC, of whom it was stated that she was 'a very good member of our branch, … [and] her counsel on many occasions was very beneficial.'[26]

In December 1913 an agreement was reached between the IDAA and the Tralee firms employing their members whereby, according to Elaine Sugrue, only in exceptional circumstances would the 'living-in system' be used in preference to the 'living-out system' and then only up to a maximum of 10 per cent of employees, all of whom would be females.[27] A 'living-out allowance' was also agreed in order to facilitate workers to obtain accommodation.[28] Trade unionists opposed the 'living in system' because of the adverse conditions it

---

20 *Workers' Republic*, 8 Apr. 1916.   21 Ibid., 13 Nov. 1915.   22 John Cunningham, *Labour in the west of Ireland: working life and struggle, 1890–1914* (Belfast, 1995), p. 108.   23 D.F. Keogh, 'Foundation and the early years of the Irish TUC' in Donal Nevin (ed.), *Trade union century* (Cork, 1994), p. 25.   24 Elaine Sugrue, 'Women and Irish trade unionism, a case study: the Irish Drapers' Assistants' Association, 1901–20', *Saothar: Journal of Irish Labour History*, 42 (2017), 65–74.   25 Thomas N. Crean, 'The labour movement in Kerry and Limerick', 1914–1921' (PhD, Trinity College Dublin, 1995), pp 77–81. http://www.tara.tcd.ie/handle/2262/77125 [accessed 27 Apr. 2023]; Sugrue, 'Women and Irish trade unionism', p. 71.   26 *Kerryman*, 7 Feb. 1912, 29 May 1915; quotation cited in Sugrue, 'Women and Irish trade unionism', p. 71.   27 Crean, 'The labour movement in Kerry and Limerick', p. 162.   28 Sugrue, 'Women and Irish trade unionism', p. 72.

imposed on workers. Large numbers of people from outside Tralee arrived to work in the town's drapery firms. In general these workers were forced to live in overcrowded accommodation, for example at 15 The Mall near the MWC, where three female and four male workers resided.[29] The experience of Peter Joseph Doran was not unusual for male and female employees of the company. On leaving the Saint Vincent de Paul orphanage in Dublin in 1913, Peter 'went to the Munster Warehouse ... as an indentured apprentice gent's outfitter aged 12 ... returning to Dublin in April 1918'. He had no relatives in Kerry, and little contact with his family.[30] Shop assistants at that time 'habitually worked six fourteen hour days; laboured wage free for the duration of a three year apprenticeship; enduring almost monastic restrictions'.[31] In 1910 at the conference of the Irish Trade Union Congress held in Dundalk, delegates passed a motion calling for the abolition of the 'living-in system', noting that there were no inspections, the food was often 'unfit for human consumption' and women and girls were expected to share sleeping accommodation with men and boys. There was considerable concern 'that in some cases assistants not returning before the hour of locking-up are shut out for the night, and that girls excluded are known to spend the whole night wandering about the streets'.[32] There had also been numerous fires in drapery firms around the country including in 1905 at Revington's in Tralee. These fires were used by the IDAA in its campaign against the 'living-in system'.[33] A motion at the 1914 conference declared the 'living-in system' to be 'illegal'[34] and as early as 1909, the Tralee branch declared that it 'most strongly condemns the living-in system'.[35]

In September 1914 the terms of the agreement in Tralee on the 'living-in system' were broken by Murphy when, as Sugrue reveals, 'two young male assistants in the Munster Warehouse were told that they would not be granted a living-out allowance'.[36] A strike began on 15 May 1915 when the company refused to negotiate with the IDAA.[37] In June five members of Society of Tailors employed by the MWC also joined the dispute bringing to twenty the total number of workers on strike.[38] During the dispute women demonstrated

29 *Census of Ireland, 1911*: household schedule for Donovan, The Mall, Tralee.   **30** T.P. Redmond (grandson), Duleek, Co. Meath, correspondence received by post, 14 Apr. 2016.   **31** Cunningham, *Labour in the west of Ireland*, p. 89.   **32** *Report of the Seventeenth Irish Trade Union Congress*, Town Hall, Dundalk, 16th, 17th, 18th, May 1910 (Dublin, 1910), p. 10.   **33** David Gibney, 'Michael O'Lehane: a tribute to the founder of Mandate Trade Union on the 100th anniversary of his death' (2020), https://dgibney.medium.com/michael-olehane-a-tribute-to-the-founder-of-mandate-trade-union-on-his-100-year-anniversary-d3d214668013 [accessed 31 Apr. 2023].   **34** *Report of the Twenty-First Irish Trade Union Congress (with which has been incorporated the Irish Labour Party)*, City Hall, Dublin, 1st, 2nd and 3rd June 1914 (Dublin, 1914), p. 99.   **35** *Kerry Evening Star*, 22 Feb. 1909.   **36** Sugrue, 'Women and Irish trade unionism', p. 72.   **37** *Kerryman*, 29 May 1915. **38** Crean, 'Labour movement in Kerry and Limerick', p. 163.

that they were capable of taking on leadership roles in the IDAA. Indeed
Sugrue argues that the strike 'proves that many female members of the Tralee
branch were committed to class solidarity and the objectives of the IDAA … '.
The actions of one woman in particular were singled out for praise. Nellie
Roche was described in the journal of the IDAA, the *Drapers' Assistant*, as 'one
of the most consistent members of the Tralee branch' who 'never flinched in
her duties to the organization'. Roche was employed as a buyer of millinery
and mantles and it would appear she had been active in union affairs since at
least 1911 when *The Kerryman* recorded her attending the branch AGM.[39]
When the strike began she 'not only threw her lot in with the assistants', thus
crossing sectoral boundaries but 'by wonderful spirit' of solidarity helped to
lead 'the rest of the ladies involved'.[40] However, despite this acknowledgment
of the role played by the female members, and Howard's congratulations of
the 'ladies on their gallant action on coming out on strike', Sugrue has also
revealed how the Tralee branch, in early 1916, informed the executive
committee of the IDAA that the women members were 'shirking their duties'
and 'did nothing by way of picketing'. This eventually resulted in the executive
increasing the men's strike pay to 25*s.* per week and reducing the women's
strike pay to 10*s.* per week.[41] While evidence relating to female picketing is
limited, it is quite possible that one reason they may have devoted less hours
to picket duty than their male counterparts was because they were obliged to
devote more time to domestic duties. Or perhaps it was considered 'unladylike'
by many in terms of contemporary social norms in Kerry society to be seen on
a picket. James Connolly's paper, the *Workers' Republic*, was also guilty of
displaying a negative attitude towards female union activists, referring to
workers crossing the picket line as 'blackleg ladies' despite the fact that at least
one of them was male, Bill Sullivan.[42]

Of the local newspapers, only *The Kerryman* supported the strike while the
others carried adverts for the MWC.[43] The *Workers' Republic* expressed surprise
at discovering 'that the [Tralee] Picturedome are all the time showing Munster
Warehouse advertisements'.[44] In June 1915, the *Workers' Republic* carried a
report that the Listowel branch of the IDAA 'passed a resolution in support
of the Tralee workers.[45] In October of the same year, the Tralee branch of the

39 *Drapers' Assistant*, Dec. 1917, cited by Sugrue, 'Women and Irish trade unionism', p. 72. Nellie
Roche, aged 28, of 14 The Mall, was returned as a draper's clerk in the 1911 census. In her early 30s
at the time of strike she was probably older than the other women; *Kerryman*, 18 Feb. 1911.
40 *Drapers' Assistant*, Dec. 1917 as cited by Sugrue, 'Women and Irish trade unionism', p. 72.
41 IDAA executive ordinary minutes, 20 Oct. 1915; 2 Mar. 1916; 28 June 1916, as cited by Sugrue,
'Women and Irish trade unionism', p. 72.   **42** *Workers' Republic*, 24 July 1915, as cited by Crean,
'Labour movement in Kerry and Limerick', p. 163.   **43** *Kerry News*, 31 May 1915, *Kerry Weekly
Reporter*, 21 Apr. 1917.   **44** *Workers' Republic*, 23 Oct. 1915.   **45** Ibid., 26 June 1915.

ITGWU was launched when the union's acting general secretary, James Connolly, visited the town accompanied by the IDAA's O'Lehane.[46] The Tralee Trades and Labour Council organized a rally attended by 3,000 people. It was addressed by several union officials, and finally by Connolly who encouraged all workers to join the union, and to oppose Ireland's involvement in the war in Europe.[47] Despite the success of the rally, many trade unionists were sacked from their jobs because of their involvement in it.[48] Tom Crean suggests that in the aftermath of Connolly's visit, there developed an extremely close relationship between Tralee labour and the local republican movement.[49]

The Royal Irish Constabulary (RIC) were also displaying increasing hostility to the strikers, four of whom were arrested in June 1915 for 'intimidating' employees of the WMC in their attempt to persuade them to join the strike. Those arrested included IDAA branch secretary Thomas Howard. The charges against all were eventually dismissed.[50] For its action, the RIC received support from the highest level of the government. In December 1916 in the House of Commons, the chief secretary for Ireland, Henry Duke, was asked the following question by the Irish Parliamentary Party MP for West Kerry, Thomas O'Donnell: 'Why the staff of the Munster Warehouse, Tralee, who are out on strike, were interfered with when only engaged in peaceful picketing, as they are entitled to do by law?' The chief secretary replied: 'On the occasion to which the Hon. Member refers the police considered the strikers were not acting within the law, and warned them to this effect, and I am told they desisted from the action of which complaint was made.'[51]

That such a seemingly peripheral strike was mentioned in parliament is a measure of just how much support the strikers had. Despite this hostile environment, the strikers of the Munster Warehouse continued to organize pickets and rallies to win support for a boycott of the firm's business.[52] At the Irish Trade Union Congress and Labour Party's conference in Sligo in August 1916, a resolution was passed unanimously which 'strongly condemned' the MWC for:

> ... flagrantly violating the agreement entered into with other traders in that town, as well as with the employees in connection with the 'living-in system', and it desires to place on record its appreciation of the magnificent fight which the assistants have put up during the last fifteen months.[53]

46 *Liberty*, June 1981.   **47** *Kerryman*, 23 Oct. 1915.   **48** *Workers' Republic*, 30 Oct. 1915.
49 Crean, 'Labour movement in Kerry and Limerick', pp 177–82, 361.   **50** *Kerryman*, 4 Dec. 1915.
51 *House of Commons debates* (Hansard), vol. 88, col. 1321, 19 Dec. 1916.   **52** *Workers' Republic*,
29 May 1915.   **53** Irish Trade Union Congress and Labour Party, *Report of the twenty-second annual*

Eventually both sides agreed to arbitration by the bishop of Kerry, Charles O'Sullivan, and on 25 February 1918 a settlement was negotiated resulting in significant gains for the workers. Male and female assistants, both present and future, aged over 21, were granted the option to work either under the 'living-in' or 'living-out' systems. No 'preferential' treatment would be given to those employees choosing the 'living-in system', nor would a disproportionate number of junior labourers be employed. It was also agreed that all strikers would be reinstated and that all future disputes would go before an agreed 'arbitration' panel.[54] The strike spelt the end of the 'living-in system'. It also illustrated how the IDAA 'represented', according to Sugrue, 'a radical departure from the norm in admitting women members, proving that class solidarity trumped gender antagonism for Irish drapers' assistants ... and provided female drapers' assistants ... with the opportunity to become active participants in the labour movement'.[55]

Political and military women

During the early twentieth century, women union activists such as Roche were the exception rather than the norm, with the labour movement in Kerry continuing to be characterized by paternalistic attitudes towards women workers. It is possible that this was related to the relatively low level of unionization of women in the county by comparison with the neighbouring county of Limerick, where there was even an ITGWU women's section.[56] An example of this paternalistic mentality is the attempt by the TWC (all men) to tackle the problem of female unemployment. The *Kerry People*, the only Kerry newspaper in publication at the time of the June 1922 meeting of the TWC, reported that D.D. O'Sullivan, principal of the Technical Schools, forwarded the following resolution: 'That we, the Tralee Technical Instruction Committee, request the Ministry of Labour to continue the scheme of instruction in Home Crafts for unemployed women in as much as considerable unemployment still exists in Tralee'. Likewise, J. Quinn, TWC vice president, encouraged 'unemployed women instead of getting doles at the Labour Exchange' to get instruction in 'domestic economy'. The report gives no definitions of what is meant by 'home crafts' or 'domestic economy' but the work is obviously of a type deemed suitable for women. Quinn pointed out that the scheme, which had received a grant of £500 from the Ministry

meeting, Town Hall, Sligo, August 7th, 8th, 9th, 1916 (Dublin, 1916), p. 60.   **54** *Kerryman*, 2 Mar. 1918.   **55** Sugrue, 'Women and Irish trade unionism', p. 72.   **56** Crean, 'Labour movement in Kerry and Limerick', pp 242–4, 360.

of Labour, lasted thirteen weeks and paid £1 per week with two classes of twenty women having already completed the course. The resolution was passed unanimously. The scheme relieved unemployment among Tralee's female workforce, offering a degree of financial independence and according to Quinn, 'the result of the first class was that a number of the girls got very good situations'.[57] Nevertheless, while to some extent the TWC cannot be criticized for supporting the scheme, it can be argued that the council had limited social vision in regard to women's potential to attain equal status with men in the workforce – reinforcing accepted notions of the sexual division of labour.

The membership of the republican movement in Kerry was also predominantly male, though it appeared to offer greater opportunities for expression and agency to middle-class women and women residing in rural areas. The Tralee branch of CnB was established on 26 March 1915 with a membership of 60.[58] The leadership included Cáit Breen, Liz Ann O'Brien, and Maggie Clifford.[59] Despite this apparent progress, women generally found themselves being forced to accept an inferior status to men in the republican movement in Kerry. The intention was that CnB would be a support wing to the male Volunteers, being tasked with such duties as 'ambulance work, making flags … semaphore signalling and ordinary drill'.[60] There was no suggestion that women would carry arms. For many women these restrictions were to become even more apparent after the Easter Rising, as Lisa Weihman observes: '[W]ith their best advocates within the nationalist and labour organizations dead and the Rising a military failure, women found their participation downgraded from comrade-in-arms to second-class help mates'.[61] Aideen Sheehan argues CnB essentially perceived itself 'as a body constituted to assist men in the attainment of the republic'.[62] Indeed IRA man Sean Scully from Killorglin, in his statement to the Bureau of Military History, recalled that 'Dr Joe Prendeville came and gave regular lessons in first aid' to CnB.[63]

Nevertheless from the beginning of the War of Independence through to the end of the Civil War, CnB had begun to assume a much more militant and public role within the republican movement in Kerry. In the council elections of 1920 two women, both members of CnB, won seats for Sinn Féin,

57 *Kerry People*, 8 July 1922. 58 *Kerryman*, 27 Mar. 1915; Mary McAuliffe, 'Loyalty and courage: Kerry women and Cumann na mBan' 1914–1917' in Bridget McAuliffe et al. (eds), *Kerry 1916: histories and legacies of the Easter Rising – a centenary record* (Tralee, 2016), p. 82. 59 Mullins, *Memoirs*, p. 17. 60 *Kerry's fighting story, 1916–1921: told by the men who made it* (Tralee, 1947), p. 193. 61 Lisa Weihman, 'Doing my bit for Ireland: transgressing gender in the Easter Rising', *Éire-Ireland* (Fall/Winter 2004), 228–49. 62 Aideen Sheehan, 'Cumann na mBan – policies and activities' in David Fitzpatrick (ed.), *Revolution? Ireland, 1917–1923* (Dublin, 1990), p. 97. 63 Irish Military Archives, Cathal Brugha Barracks, Dublin, Bureau of Military History, Witness Statement

Cáit Breen on Killarney Urban District Council and Gobnait Ní Bhruadair elected unopposed to Kerry County Council.[64] Ellen McGillicuddy, a 'shop keeper' in Castleisland, sheltered Volunteers during Easter Week, going on 'to procure arms and ammunition to IRA men from RIC and Free State soldiers'.[65] Margaret Pendy of Tralee, a 'telephonist', was advised by Austin Stack not to join CnB as she would be of more use to the IRA by providing intelligence from Crown forces communications and by also 'facilitating the Volunteers in their own communications'.[66] Towards the end of the Civil War in Kerry CnB members were becoming noticeably more militant. In March 1923 the National army was responsible for the massacre of twenty-five republican prisoners at Ballyseedy and elsewhere in the county.[67] When an army enquiry cleared its members of any wrongdoing CnB attempted to expose the report as a cover up. Army intelligence noted that 'hostility is displayed mostly by the female element that is in some instances more militant than the men. Tralee is a hotbed of female irregular sympathizers, who are an absolute menace to peace … They are flooding the country with vile, lying propaganda.'[68] Molly Myles, a member of CnB's Tralee Battalion who was arrested, was described as 'one of the most militant members of Cumann na mBan in Kerry.'[69]

Throughout the Civil War, the Catholic hierarchy also placed its moral force behind the Treaty. The republican press campaigned to undermine the influence of 'the pro-English clergy', whose hierarchy Peadar O'Donnell dismissed as a 'feudal remnant'.[70] In Kerry, IRA member and school teacher, Séamus O'Connor, recalled becoming so infuriated with his parish priest in Knocknagoshel that he told 'him what would happen if he would ever so preach about us again'.[71] Women were in the forefront of republican attempts to challenge the official discourse, fracturing traditional modes of deference in the process. On 27 August 1922, the congregation at Sunday Mass in Killarney Cathedral heard a letter from the bishop of Kerry accusing the IRA of 'military despotism', and 'an immoral usurpation and confiscation of the

(herafter BMHWS) 788, Sean (Bertie) Scully, NT.   **64** *Kerry's fighting story,* p. 194; *Kerryman,* 24 Jan. 1920, correctly states the Labour Party selected Michael Ashe (secretary of the Listowel ITGWU branch) as a candidate for the West Ward of Listowel UDC; it incorrectly states that Maggie Ashe not Michael was elected. See *Kerry Weekly Reporter,* 24 Jan. 1920; *Kerry News,* 2 Feb. 1920; *Kerry People,* 8 May 1920.   **65** Military Service Pensions Collection, MSP34REF58065, Ellen McGillicuddy, 30 Dec. 1938.   **66** Ibid., MSP34REF50762, Margaret Pendy, 13 Nov. 1936. **67** Michael Hopkinson, 'The guerrilla phase and the end of the Civil War' in J. Crowley et al. (eds), *Atlas of the Irish Revolution* (Cork, 2017), p. 716.   **68** BMH, Kerry Command, CW/OPS/12K, 14 Mar. 1923.   **69** BMHWS 1189, Thomas O'Conner, 15 June 1955.   **70** *Éire: the Irish nation,* 19 May 1923; Peadar O'Donnell, *The gates flew open: an Irish Civil War prison diary* (Cork, 2013), p. 4.   **71** S. O'Connor, *Tomorrow was another day* (Dublin, 1987), pp 101–13.

peoples' rights', prompting one CnB member from Kenmare to remonstrate with the bishop, promising no longer to hear Mass 'and listen to insulting remarks'.[72] Free State military intelligence reported that at Tralee, 'when the priest had left the altar at the conclusion of the night's service, members of Cumann na mBan proceeded to offer up prayers for dead Irregulars'.[73] While such acts by members of CnB were indeed defying the edicts of the clergy they were also within their traditional gender roles. However, Marie Coleman also explains the significance of CnB 'using their traditional women's role for subversive purposes', mass communal prayer 'as a form of public protest' and a way of creating 'a safe space to express messages of solidarity and defiance'.[74]

Margaret Ward has noted that until recent decades, the 'contribution' of women influencing political events in Ireland during this period 'remained hidden within historical records … [and] has at times been deliberately played down and not just simply undervalued'.[75] Indeed, in an increasingly masculine pro- and anti-Treaty political culture, female revolutionary voices became more and more marginalized from the mainstream historical narrative. For instance, Tim Horgan has revealed that when Marguerite Fleming from Kilcummin, commanding officer of CnB's Kerry No. 2 Brigade during the Civil War, died in Dublin in 1946, 'there was nothing in the proceedings to mark the fact that Marguerite Fleming had been a diehard republican'. In fact, she was interred 300 metres from the republican plot, 'forgotten, her story untold', thereby sharing 'the fate of too many heroic women of the time'.[76]

Gobnait Ní Bhruadair

Another 'heroic' revolutionary woman 'hidden within historical records' was Gobnait Ní Bhruadair (1861–1955). Her family were members of the Church of Ireland and part of the Anglo-Irish landed aristocracy. Politically they were affiliated to southern Unionism. Ní Bhruadair spent her youth on the family estate in Surrey.[77] However, as Conor J. Morrissey has noted, it was her experience during the Boer War when she was working as a secretary to her brother, the earl of Midleton, that made Ní Bhruadair an anti-imperialist.[78] Although Ní Bhruadair was untypical of the majority of republicans, historically there was a strong radical Protestant tradition throughout Ireland.

72 *Irish Times*, 30 Aug. 1922; Diarmaid Ferriter, *A nation and not a rabble: the Irish Revolution, 1913–1923* (Dublin, 2015), p. 285. **73** BMH, Kerry Command, CW/OPS/12K, 12 Mar. 1923. **74** Marie Coleman, 'Cumann na mBan and the War of Independence' in Crowley, *Atlas of the Irish Revolution*, p. 405. **75** Ward, *Unmanageable revolutionaries*, p. 142. **76** Tim Horgan, *Fighting for the cause: Kerry's republican fighters* (Cork, 2018), pp 56–7. **77** *Kerryman*, 24 Jan. 1920; Ní Bhruadair, 'Fenian graves'. **78** Conor J. Morrissey, 'Albinia Brodrick: Munster's Anglo-Irish

Morrissey argues that female Protestants like Ní Bhruadair had initially been attracted to nationalism by becoming active in the Gaelic League.[79] Protestant republican activists of the early twentieth century included Molly Childers, Dorothy Macardle, and Constance Markievicz and her sister Eva Gore-Booth. Ní Bhrudair's brother was a leader of the southern Unionists, and would later apologize for his sister's support for the Easter Rising declaring that 'she has always been very unbalanced in her views'.[80] Ní Bhruadair moved to Caherdaniel, Co. Kerry, in 1904 and after the Rising joined CnB. According to republican Bertie Scully, she 'had several of the 1916 men recuperating' there.[81] She also visited republican prisoners in Frongoch internment camp in Wales and elsewhere, and soon after joined the Irish White Cross Society, her activities resulting in her house been raided by the Black and Tans.[82] Anna Hurley-O'Mahony, a member of CnB in Co. Cork, underlines the remarkable single-minded determination of Ní Bhruadair to the republican cause even after her first cousin, 'the earl of Bandon, was captured at Castle Bernard some time before the Truce and was [held] prisoner'.[83] According to Ward, she was 'the most orthodox and unyielding of nationalists'.[84]

However, perhaps the most fascinating aspect of Ní Bhruadair's life was her activism in the area of health reform. She was appalled by the living conditions of Kerry's rural poor. In 1916, an estimated 280 people in the county died of tuberculosis, the single-biggest cause of death in Kerry.[85] In an attempt to combat rural poverty and reverse emigration, Ní Bhruadair organized classes in health and agricultural education, establishing the Kilcrohane agricultural co-operative.[86] Although 'financially independent', her efforts to raise funds to build a hospital near Caherdaniel ultimately failed due to opposition from the British government and later from the Catholic Church.[87]

After witnessing the epidemic of smallpox in 1910, Ní Bhruadair attempted to raise financial support for a hospital in Tralee. She wrote to the *British Journal of Nursing* insisting that such a hospital was necessary to care

Republican', *Journal of Cork Historical and Archaeological Society*, 116 (2011), 97.   **79** Ibid., pp 100–1.   **80** *Irish Times*, 17 Feb. 2017.   **81** Staigue Fort House http://staiguefort.com/archaeology/lady-albina-brodericks/ [accessed 15 Mar. 2020].   **82** Ní Bhruadair, 'Fenian graves'; James Wilson, 'Why did an earl's sister dedicate herself to fighting for Irish freedom?', https://www.irishcentral.com/roots/history/why-did-an-earl-s-sister-dedicate-herself-to-fighting-for-irish-freedom [accessed, 29 Apr. 2023].   **83** BMHWS 540, Anna Hurley-O'Mahony, 20 June 1951.   **84** Ward, *Unmanageable revolutionaries*, p. 142.   **85** *Census of Ireland, 1911, Kerry*, p. 160; Central Statistics Office, *Life in 1916 Ireland: stories from the statistics*, 'Table 3.7: Deaths and death rates, 1916 and 2014', https://www.cso.ie/en/releasesandpublications/ep/p-1916/1916irl/ [accessed 23 Apr. 2023].   **86** Ní Bhruadair, 'Fenian graves'.   **87** Kerry County Council, *Centenary of Irish local government, 1899–1999: local election results, 1899–1994* (Tralee, 1999), p. 36, Ward, *Unmanageable revolutionaries*,

for 'the children haunted by tuberculosis, the women tortured in childbirth, the men struck low before their time' and asked '[H]as your wife bled to death in childbirth for want of help'.[88] Eventually the Tralee Union Workhouse was converted into Saint Catherine's Hospital. Ní Bhruadair also campaigned on the need for birth control and on the dangers of sexually transmitted diseases, and their treatment. She delivered a paper entitled 'Morality in relation to public health', and chaired the National Council of Nurses Committee on the subject.[89] She also advocated for reform of Killarney Mental Hospital, opposing the use of the term 'lunatic asylum' and campaigned for training nurses in the needs of the mentally ill.[90] On all these health issues, Ní Bhruadair was considerably ahead of most contemporary health professionals. Her views also often contrasted sharply with those of the leadership of Sinn Féin in Kerry who, for example, supported the county council's campaign of opposition to the National Health Insurance Act on the grounds that it was an 'oppressive measure passed by a foreign legislature, unsuited to the needs of the people of Ireland'.[91] Later, according to Ward, Ní Bhruadair came 'into conflict with the edicts of Dáil', briefly resigning from the council in protest over the Dáil's decision to drastically reduce the number of workhouses.[92] Although Ní Bhruadair was fiercely opposed to the Treaty, as a member of the County Kerry Agricultural Committee, she was prepared to adopt a pragmatic and compassionate approach to social and economic policies. At the meeting of May 1922 she suggested that conditions of 'famine' were common in Kerry where 'the people ... were thin and hollowed-eyed and miserable, and the children had insufficient food and clothing'. Under existing conditions, she said, 'children were prey to disease', and she supported a delegation being sent to Dublin to petition the government to provide aid for the county.[93]

Ní Bhruadair also advocated for trade union representation for the nursing profession, and in 1907 joined the Society for State Registration of Trained Nurses which campaigned for parity with doctors, and demanded 'the title "nurse" be used only by certified nurses from identified training schools duly registered as such'. She declared: '[I]t is full time that we nurses should awake out of sleep and take our rightful place amongst the workers of the world in fraternal organization'.[94] Ní Bhruadair attended the International Council of Nurses Congress 1909, and later, despite fierce opposition from the Catholic

pp 141–2; Ní Bhruadair, 'Fenian graves'.   **88** O. O'Shea & G. Revington, *A century of politics in the Kingdom* (Newbridge, 2018), p. 34.   **89** Ann Wickham, 'The nursing radicalism of the Honourable Albina Brodrick, 1861–1955', *Nursing History Review*, 15 (2007), 51–64.   **90** 'Radical ruins', 8 Nov. 2017, http://aftersantacruz.blogspot.com/2017/11/feminist-and-revolutionary.html [accessed, 21 Apr. 2020].   **91** Kerry County Council minutes, 1913–1918, p. 725.   **92** Ward, *Unmanageable revolutionaries*, p. 142.   **93** *Kerry People*, 20 May 1922.   **94** Wickham, 'The nursing

and Protestant churches, in March 1919 she proposed and won recognition for 'the formation of a nurses union to be allied to the Irish Women Workers' Union'.[95] Soon after the government introduced the Nurses Registration (Ireland) Act establishing the General Nursing Council.[96] This in turn finally led to the founding of the Irish Nurses' Association with the Kerry branch of the union being launched in Tralee on 18 October 1919.[97]

Conclusion

While this period of radicalism afforded opportunities for more women to occupy public roles by winning recognition as labour activists, republican militants and politicians, it is also clear that the roles and expectation of most women and men largely conformed to the limits contemporary social norms placed on their activism. This is displayed most obviously by the attitude of local IDAA leadership to female strikers during the MWC dispute and by the TWC to unemployed female workers.

A patriarchal attitude is also shown by the republican leadership in defining the role of CnB. Unfortunately, for all their activism, by the end of the Civil War women still remained second class citizens in a Free State dominated by the writ of the Catholic Church. All the radical voices had been silenced by the victory of the counter-revolution. The words of the revolutionary Marxist James Connolly provide an apt description for the status of working-class women in early twentieth century Ireland while also providing hope for the future,

> The worker is the slave of capitalist society and the female worker is the slave of that slave ... None is so fitted to break the chains as those who wear them ... the working-class of Ireland must cheer on those efforts of those women who ... have arisen to strike them off.[98]

radicalism of the Honourable Albina Brodrick', p. 59. **95** Ibid., pp 56, 58. **96** 1919 Nurses Registration (Ireland) Act: Developments in District Nurse Training, 1890–1919, https://history. health.blog/tag/1919-nurses-registration-ireland-act/ [accessed, 16 Apr. 2023]. **97** *British Journal of Nursing*, 18 Oct. 1919. **98** James Connolly, *Collected works, volume one* (Dublin, 1987), pp 239–44.

'They felt it was their duty to stimulate that discontent': women at the Irish Trade Union Congress, 1916–23

THERESA MORIARTY

[T]he assertion of women's views on all questions of a social and public character in which women have a predominant interest such as housing, sanitation, public health, education is essential to the progress of society ...[1]

In the summer of 1916 in the assembly rooms of Sligo's town hall, the only woman trade union delegate there proposed that the phrase 'and women' should be added to a motion that described trade union members as men. This singular feminist, Marie Perolz, a member of the Irish Citizen Army (ICA), only released from prison in England weeks before, stood at the annual assembly of the Irish Trades Union Congress and Labour Party (ITUC&LP) as the acting president of the scattered ranks of the Irish Women Workers' Union (IWWU).[2] Her reminder to her listeners announced both her own and her union's presence on the floor of the hall, making visible the arrival of women within the national gatherings of Ireland's male trade unionists. The printed version of the conference proceedings mitigates the challenge of her words by recording her intervention simply as a 'suggestion'. The echo from the address to 'Irishmen and Irishwomen' in the 1916 proclamation earlier that year must have been unmistakable.[3]

Women would play an unprecedented part in making and shaping the policies of Ireland's trade unions over the next few years. But most significant was their presence. It rose – and fell – according to the prevailing political

1 Irish Trade Union Congress and Labour Party (henceforth ITUC&LP), *Official report of the proceedings of the twenty-seventh annual meeting, 1921*, Sheila Bowen, Irish Clerical Workers' Union, p. 190. Note that the ITUC&LP was renamed the ILP&TUC in 1918. 2 Marie Perolz (1874–1950) was a confidant of James Connolly as an ICA courier before the Rising. Through the 1916 conference she added 'women workers in printing and sorting trades' to a Drapers' Assistants' motion and 'by the appointment of Irishwomen' to a Belfast resolution on women factory inspectors (ITUC&LP, *Report of the twenty-second annual meeting*, 1916, p. 54–5). 3 The following year newly organized women delegates to the All-Ireland Conference proposed to Sinn Fein's executive that alongside men, 'women should be mentioned' at their autumn conference. See Margaret Ward, 'The League of Women delegates and Sinn Fein', *History Ireland*, 4:3 (1996), 37–41; and Senia Paseta,

energies at work. The all-Ireland trade unions' annual meetings, where Perolz made her stand, provide a meeting place where both the combined and cumulative impact of women in Irish public life can be seen across these tumultuous years.

Ireland's trade union movement did not offer an obviously radical venue for women. The Irish Trade Union Congress (ITUC) was formed in 1894 to advocate and examine the impact of industrial legislation and to form policies and responses through annual debate among affiliated unions. Officers and a national executive were elected from the floor. Trade union delegates assembled in a series of imposing public buildings around the country, such as Waterford's City Hall or Drogheda's Whitworth Hall. Rather grandly, they described their yearly deliberations as the 'Parliament of Labour'.

Before 1918 the central trades union leadership was still essentially voluntary, without full-time staff or permanent offices. They met with government officials in Ireland and occasionally in London as established practice. But the wartime regulation of industry had brought government authorities, employers and unions into closer contact. State arbitration and conciliation was conducted on an unprecedented scale, especially in industries where employers had previously refused any dealings with trade unions. Some trades unionists sat on a range of state boards and committees. From 1918 they looked forward to a fully-staffed head office in Dublin.

Women attended the first ITUC, when two Textile Operatives' Society of Ireland (TOSI) delegates represented Belfast's women linen workers. Two other women represented book folders from Dublin's print industry.[4] For the next eighteen years two members of the linen union were the only women in the hall. They were joined briefly in 1911 by Minnie Rodgers of the Lurgan Hemmers and Veiners. Delia Larkin, secretary of the new women's union, the Dublin based IWWU, attended in 1912. She was joined by Belfast branch delegate Ellen Gordon in 1913. Before 1918 only one woman had ever sat on the executive. The TOSI general secretary, Mary Galway, was elected each year from 1906 to 1912.[5] After 1913 no women attended from any union. In 1914, when the ITUC met as an all-male body, chairman James Larkin objected to a woman suffrage speaker because he understood she opposed trade unions, which she denied.[6]

Irish nationalist women, 1900–1918 (Cambridge, 2013), p. 227.   **4** Miss McCrory and Miss Morris were among six trades council delegates from Belfast. Miss Valentine and Miss Stanley represented book folders from the Irish National Labour Union. See Donal Nevin, *Trade union century* (Dublin, 1994), p. 357.   **5** Theresa Moriarty, 'Mary Galway' in Mary Cullen and Maria Luddy (eds), *Female activists – Irish women and change, 1900–1960* (Dublin, 2001), pp 9–36.   **6** Rosemary Cullen Owens, *Louie Bennett* (Cork, 2001), p. 65.

The world had changed drastically since then, and Ireland with it. War opened a great fissure along the fault lines of Irish life. Irish trades unionism had faltered under that pressure. Thousands of trade union members had been called up or joined up in the military. William Partridge (according to a police report quoted by David Fitzpatrick) estimated that 2,700 Irish Transport and General Workers' Union (ITGWU) members were at the front in May 1915.[7] Those remaining in Ireland were touched personally by the war. In 1916 James Flanagan, ITGWU Belfast branch delegate who had worked closely with James Connolly in the city, had three sons in the military.[8] Across the country trade union meetings were interrupted frequently to pay condolences to a war casualty's relative or in sympathy with a member killed in conflict. In 1918 the ITUC delegates remembered two colleagues from the tailors' union, Patrick Lynch and James McCarron, a founding member of the ITUC, both drowned when the *Leinster* mail boat was sunk. Dublin trade unionism, still traumatized by the violence and victimization of the 1913 lockout, was shattered by war and devastated by the deaths and executions, by military arrests, imprisonment, internment and the seizure of union records, during and since the Rising. Much of its leadership was dead or deported and the city centre workshops, stores and offices were destroyed by the fighting and fire and lay in ruins.

A British trade union journal pointed out that the 'position of women workers in particular, has not had the attention it deserves', and that 'the Irish Women Workers' Union has had to bear its share of the loss'.[9] The previous year trades unions were unable to hold the national annual conference. In 1916 the annual meeting was delayed until the high summer.

A turning point

The year 1917 marked a turning point for women across social, economic and political boundaries. The IWWU had advertised this new phase at the Sligo congress. Outside the meeting rooms and halls, a network of women stood behind Perolz, determined to save and build up the IWWU. Many were members of the Irish Citizen Army. Some were veteran members of the women's co-operative workshop on Eden Quay, where Dublin's victimized women workers found employment after the lockout, and all of them linked by their commitment to the Liberty Hall unions' members and families during the long struggle of the Dublin lockout in 1913.

---

7 David Fitzpatrick, 'Strikes in Ireland, 1914–21', *Saothar: Journal of Irish Labour History*, 6 (1980), 26–39. **8** ITUC&LP, 1916, p. 57.

Recruiting new members began before the end of 1916. Louie Bennett recalled that Liberty Hall asked her to help organize women workers in January 1917.[10] The IWWU was relaunched with a nominated committee, composed of a new president, acting president, seven vice presidents of whom Bennett was one, six executive members, two treasurers, a general secretary and clerk.[11] The postholders are familiar names in women's histories of these years. As well as Marie Perolz, Constance Markievicz, Kathleen Lynn, Annie Ginnell, Helen Chenevix, Louie Bennett, Maud Eden, Madelaine ffrench-Mullen and Sarah Harrison were all president, acting president and vice presidents. Helena Molony retained her position as the general secretary and Rosie Hackett, as union clerk. Jenny Shanahan and Mary Geraghty were the union treasurers.[12] 'Misses Bird, Caffrey, Davis, Hunt, Hackett, Murtaugh and Ryan' were the union's executive members. These nineteen women had a combined strength of years of organizing and campaigning in suffrage, nationalist and labour struggles.

Bennett targeted the print industry, 'the aristocratic one' in her phrase, where women remained outside the skilled and long-standing unions and their conditions were better than most. Women workers were still only getting between 7 and 10*s.* a week, despite the rising cost of living. Bennett recorded: 'I saw something had to be done, so I started in 1917 with a few girls of the printing trade whom I got together. And we had extraordinary success, and I got the women in the printing trade organized'.[13] Dublin women printers remained a core membership of the IWWU throughout its existence.

That summer Helena Molony, then IWWU general secretary, with Ellen Cross, later the IWWU treasurer, both attended their first Congress. Their motion, which the hall adopted, called on unions to organize the women workers in their trades or into the IWWU, and to welcome 'the co-operation of all Irish women who are prepared to accept the principles of the Irish Labour Movement and to share in the glorious task of building up an independent and self-reliant democracy in Ireland'.[14] That careful wording was designed to include those women holding office in their union, some of them unlikely trade unionists, and to deflect such criticism towards them. In the first part of their motion, they had already made it clear that this union was

9 *The Woman Worker*, Oct. 1916.   10 Louie Bennett had been asked once before to help reorganize the women's union some time after Delia Larkin, first secretary of the IWWU, left the union in the summer of 1915, but before the Easter rising.   11 William O'Brien Papers MS 13,970/1, *Saturday Post*, 3 Feb. 1917, [typed copy], quoted in full by Mary Jones, *These obstreperous lassies: a history of the Irish Women Workers' Union* (Dublin, 1988), p. 24.   12 Frank Robbins names Mary Geraghty among the Liberty Players theatre group in Liberty Hall, 1916. Bureau of Military History, Witness Statement (BMHWS) 585, p. 12.   13 Louie Bennett, *American commission on conditions in Ireland* (1921), p. 1002.   14 ITUC&LP, 1917, pp 80–1.

prepared to take in women workers of any industry. Donal Nevin pointed out that this motion was 'almost identical' to one passed at the first Congress in 1894.[15] A second matter, the need for women factory inspectors, was a regular item at earlier annual meetings. In 1917 Congress called for 'additional Female Factory Inspectors' by the appointment of an Irishwoman.

The following year IWWU delegates, once again, doubled their attendance. Four women attended, marking the union's growing membership. There were two women delegates from the 'Female Section' of the Amalgamated Society of Tailors and Tailoresses (ASTT), with Rose Timmon, of Dublin Central Teachers' Association and two INTO women delegates. All but one of the women delegates of 1918 were from Dublin.[16] These nine women were a tiny minority among 240 delegates. And they had all heard the president, William O'Brien, opening the proceedings in robust male terms, describing the 'all-Ireland organization' of 1918 as a stripling that had reached manhood. The thirty-five ITGWU delegates were all men, and no women was among that union's thirty-seven delegates at the November special congress.[17] But for the next three years Rose Timmon was elected from the floor to the national executive – the first woman to sit on the executive since 1912.[18]

At the 1918 special congress to debate the forthcoming general election, there were six IWWU delegates. Rose Timmon represented her union as well as being a national executive member. The Irish Drapers' Assistants' Association (IDAA) sent Cissie Cahalan, better remembered today as a women's suffrage campaigner with the Irish Women's Franchise League.[19] She had headed her unions 'Ladies Committee' since 1912. At her first congress she was one woman among six delegates. It was only in 1923 that a second woman, Sighle Nic Raghainn, was a delegate for the reorganized Irish Union of Distributive Workers and Clerks.[20] The change in the political climate in which Irish unions decided to switch their title around, placing Labour Party first (ITUC&LP to ILP&TUC), was the 1918 Representation of the People Act, giving parliamentary votes to all adult men, though denying women the

15 Nevin, *Trade union century*, pp 359–60.   **16** Katie Tierney, a teacher, was from Buttevant, Co. Cork.   **17** By the end of 1917 there were 17 full-time ITGWU organizers, 'of whom one was a woman'. *Fifty years of Liberty Hall* (Dublin: ITGWU, 1959), p. 73, noted in Emmet O'Connor, *Syndicalism in Ireland, 1917–23* (Cork, 1988), p. 63. Francis Devine, *Organizing history: a centenary of SIPTU* (Dublin, 2009), names two women organizers, Maire Mullen (1918–19) and Helen Hoyne (1920), pp 95, 108. IWWU minutes show Hoyne was IWWU organizer in Waterford until spring 1919, when she was followed by Kathleen McCarthy. McCarthy was an IWWU delegate at the ILP&TUC in both 1920 and 1921. Thanks to Siobhan McCarthy for information on her.   **18** Rose Timmon lived in Harold's Cross, Dublin. Few other biographical details seem to be available.   **19** Brid Smith gives the fullest account of Cissie Cahalan's biography in *Labour History News*, 8 (1992), 14–17.   **20** She may be the 'Sighle' who wrote a regular column in the union journal.

full franchise by limiting women voters to property owners over thirty years old. This promised new political possibilities and, however restricted, acknowledged women's citizenship for the first time.

New names, new faces, new organizations

This was no longer a story of the IWWU alone. Women were reshaping and reimaging Irish trade unions. The old societies and associations of skilled tradesmen had rule books restricting their membership to men only, sometimes insisting these be family members. Some unions now broadcast their willingness to admit women. The British-based Amalgamated Society of Tailors, with strong Irish branches, tagged their title with 'and Tailoresses'. In Dublin they had a women's branch. An Irish tailoring union used the same gendered words. More neutral names like the newly formed Irish Clerical Workers' Union were open to all.

Women-friendly structures were being built into those unions under pressure to admit women and provide space for them. Others, like the Association of Secondary Teachers, Ireland (ASTI) in 1920, shut down their women's branch in the name of equality. The revived IWWU had independent headquarters in Dublin, away from Liberty Hall. Other unions had longstanding women's committees, including the IDAA, and the women's branch in the Dublin tailoring trade. Among the strategies was the unique 'reserved seats' for two women on the national executive of the Irish National Teachers' Organisation (INTO) since 1907. These reserved seats were removed in 1918.

There were new names, new faces, new organizations. Women's challenge to their exclusion from public life is visible in the new groups of women workers seeking representation within the labour movement. A network of voluntary representatives within union hierarchies can be seen in the rising numbers of Congress women delegates. This attendance drew on newly released energies, evident beyond trade union meeting rooms and hallways, where women stepped out on city marches and outdoor platforms. At May Day parades women walked with their trade union banners, and their secretaries spoke from the podium at these concluding meetings – women such as Helen Hoyne in Waterford and Helena Flowers in Galway. At the 9 June 1918 *Lá na mBan* (Women's Day) nationwide protest thousands of women signed the pledge against conscription. In Dublin the largest contingent was from the IWWU, which had marched from union headquarters to City Hall to sign the pledge. Over one thousand women in tailoring unions signed too.

Teachers at both primary and secondary schools, not only white-collar workers but professionals too, had previously remained aloof from trades unionism. After the war both the INTO and the ASTI affiliated to the newly coined ILP&TUC. Wartime regulation and centralized negotiations encouraged more radical strategies, including winning a war bonus payment for women teachers that was equal to the male rate. Both unions had large numbers of women teachers. The INTO elected a woman president, Catherine Mahon, in 1912 and 1913. Women in the ASTI had held office in both regional and branch levels, with a women's branch in Dublin from 1911 to 1920. Equal pay was an urgent issue in both unions.[21]

Rose Timmon's election to the Congress' national executive from 1918 to 1922, frequently outvoting Congress veterans, demonstrated the strength of the teachers' unions at the annual gathering. Two teachers were elected to the national executive in 1919, a testimony to the support for the teachers in the hall. In 1919, although there were fewer women, more unions sent women delegates. Both Rose Timmon and Katie Tierney were there, as was Cissie Cahalan from the IDAA, the only woman on her delegation. Nora Connolly, who was working in Liberty Hall, was one among sixty-eight ITGWU delegates. Marie Mortished, secretary of the Irish Nurses' Union (INU), was there to raise the working conditions of nurses.

Public awareness of nurses had been raised during the war years. They had been twinned with soldiers as a corresponding form of gendered patriotic service. When war ended, outstanding issues of pay and the experience of their poor working conditions and long working shifts were sharpened by the state registration of nurses and midwives introduced in 1918. Nurses' training became an issue. Resources for this new union came from the IWWU, although the INU was autonomous from the start. It opened its office in South Anne Street. Today the 40,000 members of the Irish Nurses and Midwives Organisation (INMO) celebrate the origins of their union in February 1919 when twenty women agreed to form the first ever hospital nurses' trade union in any country.[22] Mark Loughrey's history of the union points to the strong trade union and socialist family background of Marie Mortished, first secretary of the INU. She was married to R.J.P. Mortished who was also well known in labour circles.[23] She shared her own outlook with her father, Adolphus Shields, a print trade unionist and journalist, and her

21 The histories of both of these teachers' unions treat women's issues and personnel within these unions; John Cunningham, *Unlikely radicals: Irish post-primary teachers and the ASTI* (Cork, 2010); Niamh Puirseil, *Kindling the flame: 150 years of the Irish National Teachers' Organisation* (Dublin, 2017). 22 Mark Loughrey, *A century of service: a history of the Irish Nurses and Midwives Organisation, 1919–2019* (Dublin, 2019). 23 In 1922 R.J.P. Mortished was appointed assistant

brother Arthur Shields, the Abbey actor, who was in the Dublin Rising and interned in Frongoch. Another brother, Will Shields, was better remembered under his stage name, Barry Fitzgerald.

On the margins

Women had always worked on the margins, sometimes barely recognized as legitimate workers, where discrimination and exploitation flourished and well beyond the reach of the trades union movement. Attempts at government regulation to fix fairer wages, reduce hours and improve conditions were viewed with suspicion by the unions as reinforcing the very grievances they were meant to tackle. Dublin's women workers were young. The capital's transport hub of port, rail stations and roads employed few women. Dublin's largest women's industrial workforce was employed in a network of clothing and food manufacturing workshops, supplying the everyday needs of Dublin's citizens. These were customarily counted in small workshops – back street businesses, tucked down lanes, operating out of side streets. Large companies like Jacob's were the exception. In 1911, just over one quarter of all industrial and manufacturing workers were women (18,596 women; 54,579 men).[24]

From 1920 competing unions in the clothing industry joined the ILP&TUC. At least four unions in the sector attended the 1921 annual conference. The new Irish Tailors and Tailoresses, with 1,500 members and a Dublin headquarters, sent two delegates, one a woman. The venerable and much reduced Amalgamated Society of Tailors, a foundation union of the ITUC, sent two delegates from the Cork branch of the renamed ASTT, one from the men's branch and one from the women's. Neither of them was a woman. After 1919 the 500 members of Walter Carpenter's Dublin union, the International Society of Tailors, Machinists and Pressers, were only allowed one delegate – himself.[25] The Amalgamated Tailors' and Garment Workers' Trade Union, with a headquarters in Manchester and 2,000 members, sent only one man from Belfast. Eighteen women are listed as delegates to the 1921 conference, including the first from a trades council.[26]

Behind the front doors of every suburban household and city residences was at least one busy domestic servant. Not all were living-in. This army of workers were always considered beyond the scope of trade union organization. A Women's Advisory Committee on the Domestic Service Problem had been

secretary to the ILP&TUC.   **24** *Census of Ireland, 1911: City of Dublin*, Table XIX, Occupations of the people (Industrial class).   **25** In 1919 Mary Clinton, a Dublin tailoress, had been a second delegate from this union.   **26** King's County [Offaly] trades council delegate is listed as Miss M.

set up by the Westminster parliament in 1918. In January 1919 newspapers reported plans to launch a domestic workers' section in the IWWU. Helena Molony, not yet a full-time official of the IWWU, had taken on the task of recruiting members in 1918, as Louie Bennett replaced her as general secretary. Molony's biographer, Nell Regan, tells how she combined regular public meetings with door-to-door house calls to talk to domestic workers. At the end of the day, she and Theresa Behan enjoyed paddling in the south Dublin beaches for their tired feet.[27]

By 1920 the Irish Domestic Workers' Union had its own premises and official, as a separate autonomous section of the IWWU. Its naming distances the union from domestic work as a service. Margaret Buckley had been president of the Irish branches of the British NFWW (National Federation of Women Workers) that had organized in the munition works in Ireland during the war. At the peace their members transferred with Buckley to the IWWU. Buckley's new office as IWWU's domestic workers section was 42 North Great George's Street.[28]

The IWWU programme for domestic workers was aimed at raising their status and eliminating their most severe grievances. Training was high on their priorities. Miss E. O'Connor, IWWU delegate, a poor law guardian and domestic worker, explained how training chimed with unemployment, and also with issues that arose from industrial unemployment. Young women were invariably told to take up domestic service if they were looking for work. 'A young woman who had been a clerk in one of the Banks, and who had been pushed out when the men came back from war, was offered domestic service.'[29] The union ran a social club and a registry office for domestic workers. Later an unemployment bureau started up. It is not clear how long this section of the IWWU survived. Mona Hearn says the Domestic Workers' Section did not long survive the citywide curfew of 1919.[30]

Revolution?

Revolution, whether in Russia or Hungary, or keenly anticipated as the outcome of the struggles outside trade union's debating chambers in Ireland's streets and countryside, framed much of the trade union rhetoric of these

Mahon, Carrig, Birr. **27** Nell Regan, *Helena Molony: a radical life, 1883–1967* (Dublin, 2017), pp 170–1. See also Jones, *These obstreperous lassies,* pp 29, 54. **28** BMHWS 821: Frank Henderson says, 'Through the co-operation of Mrs Margaret Buckley at 42 North Great George's Street', the Dublin Battalion IRA rented a room there, 'without the union's knowledge'. **29** ILP&TUC, 1923, pp 60–1. **30** Mona Hearn, *Below stairs: domestic service remembered in Dublin and beyond, 1880–1922* (Dublin, 1993), p. 87.

years. It was a time to imagine all possible futures. Election programmes were written with ambition that extended beyond the traditional working concerns of trades unions to propose a national health service or 'mother's pensions' that provided an income for women with dependants under 16 years and without male support.

The core attendance of women took the opportunities to address the specific discriminations women faced without unions, whether it was poor pay, low wages, pay cuts or discriminations directed in particular at women workers, describing how young, low paid 14-year-old school leavers were replacing older workers of 18 years who had to be paid extra.

The Flax Roughers' and Yarn Spinners' Trade Union, a small union with many women members, reported that Belfast linen was in crisis, that weavers and spinners faced short-time, and that the majority of factories had been shut since Christmas and throughout 1921. Unemployment benefits had been paid, but a special six-week extension of benefits was denied to any married women living with their husbands.[31] A young Dublin woman living with both parents whom she supported with her wages was denied any benefit because she lived with them. Resistance to wage reductions was almost impossible. As workers, women and men, were thrown out of work, trade union recruitment fell away. In 1918 the IWWU had other branches outside of the capital. Lucan, Tullamore, Edenderry, Kilkenny, Waterford, Lismore and Clonmel almost certainly transferred from the NFWW. Each year the numbers went down as the IWWU found it hard to sustain these branches.[32]

Before that pattern set in, women trade unionists, perhaps encouraged by their growing representation within the movement, took one of their boldest stands at the 1921 Congress. In a motion to the annual meeting that year two Dublin women, Sheila Bowen from the newly formed Irish Clerical Workers' Union, and Cissie Cahalan of the longer-established IDAA, announced a Women's Labour Council. Both women were seasoned activists in suffrage, labour or nationalist movements.[33] They asked, in the spirit of labour's commitment to equality, that delegates give their support, and that the executive and affiliates consult this council on all women's issues. Bowen spoke of women's discontent. 'They felt it was their duty to stimulate that discontent'. Cahalan said they were losing out on women's energy and that such a council could organize women's energy and enthusiasm. 'There was a growing spirit amongst women that had not got the proper articulation'.

---

31 ILP&TUC, 1921, p. 85.   **32** National Archives of Ireland, Registry of Friendly Societies, Irish Women Workers' Union, NAI 332T.   **33** Sheila Bowen, later Dowling (*c.*1896–1957), had been working for Michael Noyk, the republican solicitor. She was imprisoned with other anti-Treaty Cumann na mBan activists. She became an executive member of Cumann na mBan.

Helena Molony, in support of this proposal, insisted it was nothing to do with separatism. Women were not equal. She spoke of the council's educational role, and that it 'would work in perfect harmony with men's organizations', relieving them of work best done by women.[34]

The men who spoke, eight of them compared with the three women, had two responses. Some saw the council as divisive, believing equality would be best pursued in 'mixed' organizations. Others backed a proposal from Tom Johnson, to put off a decision for twelve months. Johnson was the ILP&TUC secretary but he stated he knew nothing about the proposed women's council coming before the conference delegates. Only one man approved of the idea. C. Brannigan from Dundalk spoke, he said, from 'actual experience' in the town's linen industry. Women, he said, 'found it hard to join a man's committee', whereas 'they would get them to join a women's committee'.[35]

All three women stressed that the council would have a more educational function for women than any challenge to men, anticipating the sort of opposition that P.T. Daly, secretary of Dublin's trades council, mounted 'as an advocate of women's rights'. He concluded that it would end up with 'a men's council in one room and a women's council in another room'. Sheila Bowen reassured the delegates that women's council members would have to be 'regular trades unionists'. A short procedural skirmish concluded the debate, and the council was approved by a show of hands, 118 for and 36 against. This council however did not survive long enough to have attracted much attention either at the time, or since.[36]

Much better known from the history books is the exchange between two of the leading women trade unionists that had taken place a year or so before 1921. From November 1919 to January 1920, Louie Bennett and Cissie Cahalan debated through the pages of the monthly *Irish Citizen* the merits of women's trade unionism in separate women's organizations or in 'mixed' unions of men and women members. Each took their cue from their own organizations and the industries they represented. Louie Bennett's starting point was women's unequal place at work, a point she made more than once in her opening article. She wrote of women's 'subordination' and identified 'latent antagonism' which she understood as arising from the threat to male employment from a workforce of women. Women's subordination persisted in the 'Labour world today', since any union built 'numerically and financially' on its male membership would not want to devote large scale resources to its 'weaker element', nor allow them any control over the 'business and activities' of the union. She emphasized the structural discrimination against women

34 ILP&TUC, 1921, pp 190–4. 35 Ibid. 36 Ibid.

workers, while at the same time asserting something more fundamental: that 'men have not the same aspirations for women as the women have for themselves'.[37] Cissie Cahalan based her reply on the weakness of women workers. She rejected Bennett's idea of antagonism in the workforce, citing men's fear of women lowering wages. 'It cannot be denied', she wrote, that 'this is the effect of women entering industry'. She was more concerned that union candidates were almost entirely male because of women's reluctance to stand for any position. She felt women workers were not as class conscious as men. Separate organization weakened trade unions and 'would be fatal in disputes'. She drew on her and Louie Bennett's suffrage identities and experience by pointing out that suffrage campaigners had not looked for a separate parliament for women.[38]

Their discussion, which carried over to January 1920 when Bennett replied, was based on some common assumptions, including the apathy and indifference among women workers. Neither woman addressed trade unions' meaning for women workers, overwhelmingly young and with a fragmented working life ahead of them, in which marriage, childbearing and family crisis could interrupt any long-term patterns of employment. The *Irish Citizen* debate did not take place in isolation. The difference of opinions arises from a context in which the IWWU's survival, against the relentless recruitment by the ITGWU, was at risk which combined with proposals to reorganize the Irish trade union movement as One Big Union (OBU). Such proposals had been gathering pace as trade unionism and labour politics struggled to respond to fast changing events and much larger and more unwieldy membership.

Industrial trade unionism, addressed as the OBU at the time, was the background to Louie Bennett and Cissie Cahalan's debate. There was an underlying sense that the OBU had little to offer women or would act against their interests as workers. At the IWWU executive Margaret Buckley, former organizer of the NFWW, said as much. Her opposition was echoed in Louie Bennett's published words: 'But so long as women occupy a subordinate position within the trade union movement, they will need the safeguard of an independent organization'. The debate does provide an interesting context, though, to see the form that the women's arguments took not so long afterwards, when they proposed a Labour Women's Council at the Mansion House in August 1921.

Most trade union delegations had retained their all-male composition over these years. From 1918 a woman was elected each year to the ILP&TUC executive during this period. Rose Timmon from 1919 to 1921, Helena

37 *Irish Citizen*, Nov. 1919. **38** Ibid., Dec. 1919.

Molony in 1921 and Cissie Cahalan, 1922/23. All of them were Dublin-based. The women delegates did not always act in concert. Their first duty was to their union. Nor, as is evident, did their views always coincide on industrial or legislative matters. Louie Bennett opposed trades boards, those joint committees of employers and workers' representatives. Margaret Buckley sat on one. In 1923 Bennett repeated the IWWU's opposition but backed the Congress suggestion that they be retained but reformed.

Women's attendance and participation in debates began to decline. Either they were losing interest, or unions were no longer selecting women as delegates. Eventually the IWWU would provide the only women's voices to be heard in the hall. By 1925 only one union other than the IWWU sent a woman delegate, one of the four-strong delegation from the Tailor and Garment Workers' Trade Union. The IWWU representation that year consisted of five women. During the ITUC's sixty-five years from 1894 to 1959 its only three elected women presidents all came to national prominence in the trade union movement during the tumultuous years of 1916–23. Louie Bennett was president first, in 1932 and again in 1948. Helena Molony was ITUC president in 1937 and Helen Chenevix in 1951. All three were from the IWWU.

Insisting on being equals

Almost fifty women attended the annual meetings of the ILP&TUC during the tumultuous, even hectic, years between 1916 and 1923. Fewer women found their feet to contribute to the discussions. They had reached the debating and decision-making levels of the trade unions through a variety of routes – as members of newly affiliated unions or in newly organized workforces, from women's branches or committees. They had arrived from the margins of trade unionism, where women workers were rarely or unevenly organized, to enter the framework of the trade union movement.

Irish trade unionists had opened their ranks in response to growing industrial militancy and new revolutionary energy. They aimed to build a 'labour movement' in which a labour party and the unions combined to meet the political challenges ahead. War and rebellion had stretched trade union agendas beyond the everyday issues of the workplace and combined these with radical and far-reaching programmes for change. Irish voices joined the international chorus of revolutionary challenge, in which both men and women might glimpse the possibilities of their futures.

Irish women brought formidable networks to that movement. They had established their claim to citizenship through their campaign for suffrage. They built their loyalties on their activism. Women were insisting, through both their presence and participation in the Irish trade unions, on their integration into Irish labour and society as equals.

'Welcome back Jim': the mobilization of Dublin workers on the return of James Larkin in 1923

GERRY WATTS

The 1913 lockout in Dublin augured a radical departure in Irish trade union history, and was a significant event in Europe. James Larkin, labour leader in the dispute, was essentially a trade unionist (his dabbling in politics notwithstanding), and his brand was syndicalism. When the lockout was over Larkin left Ireland for the United States and would not return until April 1923. However, Larkin's impact on Irish labour – the phenomenon of 'Larkinism' – had remained. This essay will look at how the traditions of Larkinism in Dublin and Larkin's return in 1923 combined to create a fresh resurgence in trade union and social militancy by ordinary working people. History tends, unavoidably perhaps, to focus on the *big names*. Unfortunately, a consequence of this is often to view the *big names* as being the determining agents in historical events. Thus, according to Larkin's main biographers, it was Larkin who is deemed to have caused the split within the ITGWU, which led to the formation of the Workers' Union of Ireland (WUI) in 1924. This essay will look at the other impulses that played a role in the events that split the Irish trade union movement.

The conditions prevailing in Ireland during Larkin's absence made it ripe for syndicalism.[1] The war (1914–18) had driven production, and emboldened militancy. It was followed by a post-war boom, hiking prices and wages, which was followed by a slump.[2] The Russian Revolution of 1917 had left its mark on Ireland with a series of *quasi* soviets, and the ITGWU was publishing

---

1 The word syndicalism has its origins in France (syndicalisme) in the early twentieth century, but there are antecedents for the approach that has been given that name. The notion of one big union, one of the defining developments within syndicalism, can be seen to have its origins in England with the establishment of Robert Owen's Grand National Consolidated Trades Union in 1834, and in America with the Knights of Labour in 1869. The principal offensive feature of syndicalism is the sympathetic strike. The sympathetic strike had been in existence since the early 1870s at least, and the term was first used in the South-Western Railroad strike in America (1886). Thus, the features that distinguish syndicalism were already present prior to its emergence in France. See F.S. Hall, 'Sympathetic strikes and sympathetic lockouts', *Studies in History, Economics and Public Law*, 10 (1898–9), 11–12. James Larkin and William O'Brien believed in the One Big Union, but they were poles apart politically. The terms revolutionary syndicalism and industrial unionism are also used. The Industrial Workers of the World (the Wobblies), established first in the United States in 1905, was a syndicalist union. **2** For syndicalism in Ireland, see Emmet O'Connor, *Syndicalism in Ireland:*

syndicalist tracts. On the other hand, some developments were not propitious for syndicalism. Three reasons have been identified for the demise of syndicalism. First, there was the counter-offensive to workers' demands by the employers and the state: when workers improved their conditions, the employers would find ways of recouping their losses. Second, there was the role played by the trade union bureaucracy, the reformists, in undermining syndicalism (and radical leaders like Larkin). Indeed, this was pointed out by Lloyd George in 1912, who observed: 'the best policeman for the Syndicalist is the Socialist.'[3] History has demonstrated that labour leaders tended to accommodate themselves to capitalism, and viewed reform rather than revolution as the practical path forward. Some did so reluctantly, like Thomas Foran, one of Larkin's rivals in the ITGWU; and some did so with alacrity, like Samuel Gompers, leader of the American Federation of Labor. Larkinism by definition being syndicalist, and oriented to the precepts of industrial unionism, could not accommodate itself to capitalism; if it had, it would no longer have been Larkinism. The third reason for the demise of syndicalism was the role played by the Soviet Communist International, which undermined industrial unionism (wherein workers would control society by controlling industry, with membership based on the industry rather than a particular skill) by promoting revolutionary politics as the way forward. Indeed, Sovietism attracted leading radical syndicalists like Larkin and Bill Haywood.[4]

With the War of Independence and Civil War (1919–23), the situation in Ireland was certainly volatile. But by 1923 the Irish Free State had consolidated itself somewhat. The Free State government has been described as a counter-revolutionary one; with its leading lights coming from establishment Ireland in waiting; typically, graduates of the Jesuit college, Clongowes Wood and University College Dublin.[5] The laws enacted by the new government between 1922 and 1924 were repressive. The Public Safety Act of 1923 was followed by two further Public Safety Acts in 1924: Powers of Arrest and Detention; and Punishment of Offences. Notably, this legislation was used against Larkinites at a critical juncture in their struggle with William O'Brien, ITGWU general treasurer, and *de facto* head of the union in Larkin's absence. O'Brien and Thomas Foran, ITGWU president, worked hard to facilitate the growth of the union after Larkin left in 1914, and membership would increase from 5000 to over 100,000. They also worked hard to change

1917–1923 (Cork, 1988).   **3** Cited in Ralph Darlington, *Syndicalism and the transition to Communism: an international comparative analysis* (Aldershot, 2008), p. 178.   **4** Ibid., pp 157–65; 178; 185–204 for the decline of syndicalism.   **5** John M. Regan, *The Irish counter-revolution, 1921–1936* (Dublin, 1999).

the rules and structures of the union in order to facilitate the growth of the union, and to maintain control whenever Larkin returned (Larkin and the No. 1 Branch dominated the union). But the ITGWU executive had struggled with Larkinite militancy long before Larkin returned.

Larkinite resistance to the ITGWU executive prior to Larkin's return in 1923

In 1920, Larkin's sister Delia and others formed a Larkin Release Committee (LRC) following Larkin's imprisonment in America. This stirred up trouble for the ITGWU executive. Since 1917, Delia Larkin, P.T. Daly, Barney Conway and Michel Mullen had formed the core of a Larkinite resistance to William O'Brien et al. There were many others. Indeed, when the WUI was formed, most of the Dublin workers stayed loyal to Larkin. Some of the notable Larkinites active at this time (1917–24) included John Lawlor (WUI general president in 1924), and John Kenny (general president in 1929); Michael Connolly, Richard Lynch and Patrick Brady, who brought a second action against the ITGWU executive in July 1924 (in relation to the illegality of the ITGWU's rules of 1923); Pat Murray, who was chair of the significant No. 1 Branch; John Bohan, who was secretary of No. 3 Branch (all of whose members came over to the WUI, except three officials); Seán McLoughlin (who later fell out with Larkin); Patrick Nolan, who disparaged the ITGWU in the pages of the *Irish Worker*; and Patrick Forde and Bernard Finnegan who were leaders of the gas strike committee in 1924. In Limerick, John Crotty and Jack Flood campaigned for the new union with P.T. Daly. M.P. Whittle, secretary of ITGWU in Dundalk, accompanied Peter Larkin while he campaigned in Louth for the WUI. Peter Larkin indeed was to become the WUI national organizer. Another was John Lynch, secretary of the Sligo branch, who was ousted from his position by the ITGWU executive, subsequent to which the executive was able to declare, in their 1924 annual report, that the Sligo branch was now one of the 'most loyal' branches in the land. William Gleeson was secretary of the Nenagh ITGWU branch, and when the split occurred he immediately withheld monies due to Head Office (costing him a spell in prison when he was brought to court by the ITGWU executive); he subsequently became secretary of the Nenagh WUI branch. These and many more found kindred spirits in the Larkinite milieu, and though it is difficult to trace in all its details, many would have been active in the LRC.

Barney Conway was chairman of the LRC, and Michael Connolly was secretary. The purpose of the LRC was to agitate for Larkin's release but it was, moreover, an instrument with which to beat the leadership of the ITGWU and the Irish Labour Party and Trade Union Congress. The LRC claimed the leaders of these organizations were doing nothing to get Larkin released.[6] Thus, they could propagandize on behalf of Larkin but also use the opportunity to undermine O'Brien, Thomas Johnson and others, whom they saw as self-serving careerists. Of course, O'Brien et al. could charge the Larkinites with wanting to have a 'Larkin Family Union', and there is some merit in the accusations of both sides.

During the course of its campaign, the LRC shrewdly aimed their propaganda at the Dublin working class. The strategy was to have public meetings at familiar places like Beresford Place (next to Liberty Hall), and involve as many of the Dublin workers as possible. One of their first public meetings was presided over by Richard Corish, mayor of Wexford, who, opening the meeting, said: 'Larkin was the only possible man to lead the Irish labour movement with success, and he was wanted badly [back in Ireland].' To applause, P.T. Daly declared he 'was one of Larkin's first lieutenants in the fight he waged for the working man. And as long as he lived he would continue to regard Larkin as his chief and to take his instructions from him.' The meeting approved a resolution for a cessation of work so that a petition demanding Larkin's release could be signed. Thousands signed, including notables like Countess Markievicz. Significantly, the dockers signed en masse. A series of meetings followed and it was decided to call for a national stoppage on 21 July 1920. Copies of the resolution were sent to the ITGWU and the Labour Party, neither of which responded. The day before the stoppage, the Resident Committee of the ITGWU, including O'Brien and Foran, met to discuss the matter and it was decided that they would not give any assistance to the campaign; and further, that Liberty Hall and its offices would be closed on the day of the stoppage.[7] The stoppage went ahead and the newspapers, supporting O'Brien and Foran's position, condemned it. They also sensationally reported the use of guns by Larkinites to coerce workers to down tools at the Corporation fruit and vegetable market, and Unwin's paper factory. The LRC denied that any guns had been used. The spectacle of the day took place at noon: 'a considerable procession of strikers was formed in Beresford Place, headed by pipers and a car bearing a pictorial representation of Jim Larkin in convict uniform and guarded by a United States soldier and

---

6 Thomas Johnson had written to Michael Collins on behalf of the Irish Labour Party and Trade Union Congress protesting Larkin's imprisonment. See Department of Justice, James Larkin File, JUS 8/676; National Archives, Dublin: letter dated 8 Mar. 1922. Hereafter, this file is referenced as Larkin Justice File (LJF).   **7** SIPTU archive, Liberty Hall, Dublin, ITGWU resident executive committee/executive meeting minutes 1920–23, p. 46.

warder.'[8] Although the stoppage was not widespread, the LRC achieved two things: they had put pressure on William O'Brien et al., and they had engaged the Dublin working class in an issue concerning James Larkin.

Big Jim Larkin returns to Dublin

On 26 April 1923, chief Larkinite P.T. Daly left Dublin on the mail boat from Kingstown (Dún Laoghaire) to meet Larkin in Southampton upon his arrival from America. This was no doubt to inform him first-hand of the situation with the ITGWU executive, it being widely expected that there would be a clash between Larkin and the executive members upon his return. Both Daly's and Larkin's movements were being observed by the British and Irish intelligence departments. According to Superintendent J.J. Purcell of the Irish Central Intelligence Department (CID), Daly and Larkin were expected to arrive at the North Wall in Dublin on the morning of the 29 April.[9] In fact, Larkin arrived into Kingstown early on the evening of 30 April and was met by his sister Delia, niece Esther Larkin, Michael Mullin, Patrick Lennon, Michael Lyons and Patrick Fox. They stopped off at the local Labour Hall in George's Street and then made their way to Dublin, arriving at 8.15 p.m. 'Thousands of people thronged the precincts of Westland Row station', where there were 'vociferous cheers and cries of "Welcome back Jim".'[10] According to the *Workers' Republic,* the 'so called Labour leaders [William O'Brien and Thomas Johnson] were conspicuous by their absence.'[11]

Larkin was met on the platform by other Larkinites, including John Bohan, Thomas Lawlor and John Farren. The Dublin Metropolitan Police, C and B divisions, reported on Larkin's arrival into Dublin, and the evening's activities. The reports were forwarded to Kevin O'Higgins, minister for home affairs, who was to keep a close eye on Larkin and the Larkinites in the ensuing period. Such had been the sheer number of his supporters that turned up to greet him off the train that Larkin was forced to leave Westland Row station by the back entrance in a two-horse carriage. The crowd was estimated at 5,000. At St Mark's church in Pearse Street the horses were detached and the carriage was drawn by Larkinites in a procession along Tara Street, where the fire brigade workers had hung a large banner on the fire-station tower:

---

8 For LRC activity, see *Freeman's Journal,* 5 July 1920 and 22 July 1920; *Irish Times* and *Irish Examiner,* 22 July 1920. **9** LJF: CID report, 28 Apr. 1923. **10** *Irish Times,* 1 May 1923. **11** *Workers' Republic,* 5 May 1923. (The paper founded by James Connolly in 1898 was the organ of the Communist Party of Ireland at this time.) Larkin acknowledged that Thomas Foran was present. See ITGWU, *The attempt to smash the Irish Transport and General Workers' Union* (Dublin, 1924), p.

'Welcome Home Jim'. Finally, the carriage made its way over Butte Bridge to Liberty Hall. The procession was accompanied by several bands: the two Liberty Hall bands and the O'Connell Fife and Drum band. Taking up the rear were 'two men carrying red flags'. When he got to Liberty Hall, Larkin addressed the cheering crowds of Dublin workers from the familiar upper-storey window. He pointed out that things were 'worse than ever for the working man'; that there was a lack of 'vision' (a snipe at the ITGWU officials); and he repeated the syndicalist mantra, 'Each for All and All for Each.' He finished his speech with a call for peace and a united Ireland to much applause. While the Larkinites wanted a united Ireland, they were out for more than just nationalism. They wanted a better world for all, and working-class internationalism would be central to WUI policy.

The large Dublin branches and the ITGWU executive

Perhaps the most significant issue confronting William O'Brien was the large Larkinite Dublin branches of the ITGWU, which constituted the greater part of the union. For all O'Brien's dogged manipulation, resolve to control, and sheer hard work, he could not control the Dublin branches. This, in effect, meant he could not sever the attachment of the Dublin workers to the traditions of Larkinism; and by extension, to Larkin himself.[12] The failure of the ITGWU executive to control the Dublin branches proved costly in early June 1923 when Dublin branches No. 1 and No. 3 suspended O'Brien, Foran and others from the union pending an internal investigation as to why, among other things, the Dublin membership, the overwhelming majority of the union, had not been allowed to vote on the new rules (Foran and Thomas Kennedy acknowledged that the 1923 rules had been registered illegally); and further, why the branches had not been consulted in relation to the delegate conference convened to approve the rules in April 1923.[13]

O'Brien's reaction to the suspensions was to go to the civil courts rather than appeal his suspension within the mechanisms of the union. Aware of the

151.   **12** Hence his work in the wider country; establishing loyal branches with which he would be able to outmanoeuvre the Larkinites; it was certainly good union work, but it was also presciently *realpolitik* at work. O'Brien's work in the provinces underpinned the durability of the ITGWU in its struggle with the WUI.   **13** Historians of Larkin have tended to rely on William O'Brien's account of the suspensions; for O'Brien's account, see *The attempt to smash*, passim. The indisputable fact, however, is that it was the branches that suspended the executive members. For the statistics on what votes took place, and which branches were excluded from voting, see Gerard Watts, 'James Larkin and the British, American and Irish Intelligence Services, 1914–1924' (PhD, NUI Galway 2016, aran.library.nuigalway.ie), pp 226–8; hereafter, Watts, 'Larkin intelligence'.

sensitivity of using the state courts against the union, he claimed 'there was no other course open'.[14] Arguably, it was O'Brien's recourse to the courts that began the process that would lead to the split that occurred in 1924. O'Brien secured an interim injunction that allowed the suspended members access to the union offices. The internal dispute within the union was sent forward as a consolidated action to the high court, and would be heard in February 1924. The Larkinites continued to organize. On 8 July 1923, a large procession of Larkinites took place. A 'banner was carried by members of the crowd … bearing the words "One and Only One Leader Jim Larkin".' The ITGWU fife and drum band followed, and the procession did a loop from Beresford Place through the streets of the north inner city.[15]

On 16 June 1923, after the Dublin branches had suspended the executive members (who subsequently suspended Larkin), Larkin took the opportunity to berate the labour leadership in his paper, the *Irish Worker*: 'We return to find … [a union] manipulated by cunning time-serving, ambitious charlatans.' With this statement, the war within the union was now public. Larkin began an *Irish Worker* campaign to free the IRA prisoners, who were still locked up, despite a truce being declared. The prisoners were working-class people, and some had been former members of the union. Larkin visited the camps where the prisoners were held, with each visit requiring a letter from the minister for defence to gain admittance. Throughout May, June and July 1923 thousands of Larkinites flocked to meetings at Liberty Hall where Larkin and others criticized the executive, condemned the government, and called for the IRA prisoners to be released. On 13 May 1923, a large James Connolly memorial meeting took place in O'Connell Street; in heavy rain, some 10,000 gathered. 'The Red Flag' and 'The Soldier's Song' were sung, indicating a mix of workers' militancy and IRA sympathy. Larkin spoke of the prisoners as the 'best seed in the land'. Cathal O'Shannon, ITGWU official and TD at the time, addressed the meeting but was booed off the stage. O'Brien and Farren were listed to speak, 'but made no attempt to do so, and the mention of O'Brien's name by the Chairman was received by boohs and groans.'[16] This clearly indicated Larkinite opposition to the ITGWU executive.

The Irish Free State and the 1923 dock strike

The ministries of Home Affairs and Industry and Commerce continued to be informed of Larkin's activities through the watchful eyes of the Dublin Metropolitan Police (DMP) and the CID. Of particular interest to the

14 *Irish Times*, 18 June 1923.   **15** LJF: DMP report, 9 July 1923.   **16** Ibid., July 1923.

ministries were Larkin's pronouncements on the important dock strike that was taking place. This strike was a reaction to the employers' strategy of seeking wage cuts. The employers chose their moment well, with the movement further weakened by the emerging split. It is also significant in that it reveals the working relations between the ITGWU executive, the government, and the workers in microcosm. The dispute had begun with a reduction in the seamen's wages in April. By July the employers were looking for a reduction of 2s. in the dockers' wages. On 12 July, the executive, claiming Larkin was working behind the scenes, refused to back the seamen. On Sunday 15 July, Larkin condemned the executive for not paying the seamen and firemen their strike pay; and stated that as the dockers were against the wage cut to be enforced on Monday, they should 'down tools'. Two weeks later, on 29 July, he said that he was hopeful of the imminent outcome of a recently convened conference (the Ministry of Industry and Commerce was suggesting the cuts be suspended until January). Throughout August and September he called on the men to 'stand firm and they would never be defeated.'[17]

The employers rejected any suspension of the pay cuts, and the strike spread to the coal section. Then, on 26 October, over and above the heads of the workers, the ITGWU executive declared the strike over, accepting the proposals of President Cosgrave, which included a wage cut, as a basis for cessation of the strike. The ITGWU executive refused to accept the ballot of the dockers who voted to reject Cosgrave's proposal and continue with the strike.[18] The newspapers greeted this with smug satisfaction: 'The last shred of moral excuse has been torn from … the actions of the Larkinite minority.'[19] The ITGWU executive identified 'parties working behind the scene', making impossible demands that could not be met, as being responsible for the travesty: that is, the Larkinites and Larkin himself.[20]

On 4 November, it was reported that Larkin 'advised all the members on strike to go down the Quays on Monday and present themselves for work, telling them that they were doing this as a protest, but that no fault could be found with them as they were sold out by the executive.'[21] A copy of the above report was forwarded to the Department of Industry and Commerce by Minister O'Higgins. Doubtless, it was quite clear to the government and the employers that they could work together with O'Brien. Larkin and his Larkinites, on the other hand, were incurable: they proved time and again not to be concerned with the interests of either the employers or the Government.

17 Ibid., Aug. 1923.   **18** Emmet Larkin, *James Larkin: Irish labour leader, 1876–1947* (London, 1968), pp 242–3.   **19** *Freeman's Journal*, 24 Oct. 1923.   **20** Liberty Hall Archive, Dublin, ITGWU annual report, 1923.   **21** LJF: DMP report, 5 Nov. 1923.

Larkin expelled from the ITGWU

On 12 February 1924 the legal proceedings commenced to decide the dispute that had seen the ITGWU executive members suspended in June of the previous year. It would determine whether the ITGWU would be led by either the world-renowned revolutionist James Larkin, or the reformist William O'Brien. The courts, not surprisingly, found against Larkin.[22] The ITGWU executive then expelled Larkin from the union on 18 March 1924. In a letter penned by O'Brien, Larkin was informed that he was expelled for 'conduct unbecoming a union member'. This was not an unexpected development, as Larkin had been previously suspended by the executive (technically, the executive members were themselves suspended at the time by their own branches). Larkinite meetings were organized after the expulsion. On 27 March, a 'meeting of the Larkinite section of the ITGWU was held at Beresford Place, near Liberty Hall, to protest against the expulsion of James Larkin from the Union.' P.T. Daly, James Mitchell and Bernard Conway 'called on everyone present to do all in their power to reinstate him.'[23] Larkin, however, was never reinstated, and does not seem to have made an application for same. After Larkin was expelled, O'Brien succeeded him as general secretary. However, the battle was far from over. If O'Brien was to prevail against the Larkinites in the long term, it was necessary for him to go after Larkin's Dublin base. It is probable that O'Brien had contemplated losing a very significant number of Dublin members, rather than allow them to remain a threat to him within the union. In essence, this meant going after the numerically strong No. 1 Branch which contained staunch Larkinites like Barney Conway, Pat Forde and Bernard Finnegan.

The Dublin gas strike and Liberty Hall

A very significant strike broke out in the Dublin Alliance and Consumers Gas Company in May 1924, which was to have considerable repercussions for the No. 1 Branch. The gas workers were particularly militant, and had been knocking heads with the ITGWU executive for some time. Indeed, for a number of years they had been defying the executive. On 2 October 1921, Tom Foran, ITGWU president, addressed a mass meeting of the gas workers and told them that the gas company was insisting on a significant wage cut.

---

22 For an analysis of the court proceedings, and Judge O'Connor's self-acknowledged inversion of the crucial rule 33 (on which the case hung), see Watts, 'Larkin intelligence', pp 229–30. **23** LJF: DMP report, 28 Mar. 1924.

He advised the men to reject it, unless the company modified the wage cut. When the workers rejected his advice and any modified wage cut, Foran told them they had to be realistic, particularly as their rates of pay were higher than workers in other industries. The men disagreed, and said they were not insisting their rate of pay be higher than other workers, but they were insisting on the right to resist wage cuts. Foran met with the workers again on 9 October and told them there was no new offer from the company. The men agreed to attend a conference at the gas company's offices in D'Olier Street, on 11 October. On the morning of the conference, Foran met with the workers to discuss strategy. However, much to Foran's chagrin, they still insisted they would not accept a wage cut. At that point, Foran said he was not surprised at their attitude: 'there was something very suspicious behind it all. He believed that someone was working up an agitation against him and the union.' He threatened to call off the conference, as there was no point in attending. He then charged that there was 'some sinister influence at work behind his back, because he was losing the confidence of the men ... and he would not let the gas workers or any other section dominate either himself or the union.' The next day, the Shop Stewards Committee announced that if a pay cut was enforced, they would strike immediately. This clash between the ITGWU executive and gas workers indicates significant militancy was present in Dublin long before Larkin returned.[24]

Thereafter, threats and counter-threats continued between the company and the shop committee. In March 1922, the workers who made the gas meters went on strike, and the following week the gas company decided to form a wages committee. In December 1923 the wages committee sought a wage reduction, to start in January 1924. The ITGWU informed the company by letter that the men would not accept it. Mr Grey, secretary of the Gas Board, wrote to the union: 'It is not necessary for me to point out that equivalent reductions have been accepted, after prolonged and injurious strikes, by Dockers and Chemical workers in the city ... and it is the company's intention to put [the reduction] into operation on the appointed day.'[25]

On 14 May 1924, the gas workers were called out on strike by the executive. The strike committee was headed by Larkinites Pat Forde, secretary, and Bernard Finnegan, chair, and they immediately contacted Larkin. They used the strike to attack the ITGWU executive (the executive claimed the dispute was about union rights, and not a wage cut). When the executive

24 See *Workers' Republic*, 5 Nov. 1921, for an account of the meetings with Foran. The organ was not sympathetic to Foran of course.   **25** National Archives of Ireland, Dublin Gas minute book, 1914–26, pp 438, 464–5.

learned of Larkin's involvement, it refused to issue strike pay. The objective of the gas workers was to win the strike and associate Larkin with the victory. On 20 May, Bernard Finnegan wrote to Larkin and told him that by a vote of 407 to 41 he was requested to attend the meeting of the gas workers that evening at the Mansion House. With Larkin's approval, the gas workers voted to divert their membership contributions away from the executive to the strike committee in No. 1 Branch. This afforded O'Brien the opportunity to close Liberty Hall; and in closing Liberty Hall, he was excluding the No. 1 Branch members from their offices. On Saturday 25 May, 45 Larkinite members of No. 1 entered their offices in Liberty Hall and remained there, effectively occupying it. O'Brien rang Store Street police station and asked to have them removed. Soldiers and police accompanied by an armoured car and a machine gun mounted on a lorry surrounded the hall. The Larkinites were ordered out. Barney Conway protested: 'I am Chairman of the North Wall Workers. We are all members of the union and helped to build this place. We have as much right to be in it as "Hoofey" [O'Brien] and his crowd. This is not the last of it. We will see it out with him now.' The 45 were taken from Liberty Hall to the Bridewell police station.[26]

The Larkinites were now fighting the executive, the state forces and the employers. There was a lightning strike to 'down tools' in support of the 45. On the heels of the North Wall strike, a 'party of men [Larkinites] called to the Dock Milling Co., Barrow Street, and ordered out of work six carters and four helpers ... as a protest against the arrest of some of their members and the closing of Liberty Hall.'[27] Similar reports by the DMP noted that whole firms were idle, including Brooks Thomas, Martin Murphy's Steam Packet Company, Potter's Timber Yard and a ship belonging to Guinness's, the SS *Clarecastle*. The South Wall docks were also affected, with dockers, carters, coalmen and general labourers out. On the morning of the strike, the ITGWU fife and drum band paraded the streets of the city carrying a red flag. With the Larkinites in full revolt against the ITGWU leadership, and James Larkin on the scene, police numbers were increased. Police constables followed Larkinites who were encouraging workers to down tools and warned them they would be arrested if they interfered with anybody. D Division of the DMP, which geographically encompassed the Bridewell station where the 45 had been taken, brought in sixty recruits from Kevin Street depot 'in connection with the proceedings in the Police Courts' and established night patrols. Police reports also noted that despite the rumours of workers being forced out on strike, no 'persons could be got to come forward and make a

---

26 For more details, see Watts, 'Larkin intelligence', pp 238, 244.   **27** LJF: DMP report, 26 May 1924.

charge of intimidation'; the merest 'suggestion' was enough to bring them out. Store Street station recruited fifty civic guards, and established a night patrol. B Division reported that constables were guarding Guinness's goods that were left lying on the quayside. It was also reported that all was quiet at the Dublin Gas Company offices.[28] It was in the Dublin Gas Company, now guarded by the police, where the gas strike started which led to the jailing of the 45.

On 28 May, the Larkinites were once again in possession of Liberty Hall. One of the 45 came out of the Hall and addressed a crowd from a railway pillar at Beresford Place:

> I have not much time now, as I have to be in court. I am one of the 45. But before I go I want to tell you … it is rumoured that the Executive [of the ITGWU] is coming down to take over the Hall. Let everyone of you who is a member of the Transport Union bring your card, enter the hall and remain there and make your protest. You are paying for that Hall and own it. You are now fighting a new combination: the Chamber of Commerce, the Free State Government, and the so-called [ITGWU] Executive … I must go now. Stand firm, keep quiet and I wish you luck.

Within a few minutes, the 45, accompanied by a large number of supporters and Connolly's Own Pipers Band, marched along the quays to the court at Chancery Street. Ten Larkinites remained in the Hall.[29] As it turned out, it was not the newly-formed ITGWU fighting-corps, the One Big Union Defence League (OBUDL), which reclaimed Liberty Hall for the executive. The previous day, Police Commissioner W.R.E. Murphy had told Minister O'Higgins that he objected to William O'Brien's request to clear out a second set of Larkinites from Liberty Hall: 'I do not regard it as a duty devolving on the police.' Following this exchange, on the night of the 28 May, a special auxiliary police-squad did the dirty work for O'Brien, and cleared the Larkinites out. The Hall was then 'handed over to [the OBUDL] by the alleged defenders of liberty and the Constitution.'[30]

Birth of the Port, Gas & General Workers' Committee

With the exclusion of the Larkinites from their union branch in Liberty Hall, many of whom had helped found the union, a major development took place:

28 Ibid., 26, 27 May 1924.   **29** Ibid., 29 May 1924. For an analysis of the class-based court ruling wherein the judge jailed the 45 even though they were found not guilty of anything, see Watts, 'Larkin intelligence', pp 243, 249–51. Also, see Gerry Watts, 'The battle for Liberty Hall', *Saothar: Journal of the Irish Labour History Society*, 40 (2015), 31–44.   **30** For more details, see Watts, 'Larkin

the birth of the Port, Gas & General Workers' Provisional Committee. Prior to the exclusion of the Larkinites from Liberty Hall, the gas workers chose to pay their contributions to the Gas Workers' Dispute Committee, and not to the ITGWU. It is not clear what Larkin's ultimate objective was in all this. He may have been trying to provoke a coup, with the aim of regaining control of the ITGWU through the gas workers' section. It is almost certain he did not want a new union formed. From as early as 26 June 1923 (shortly after the suspensions), Larkin had been calling for everyone to 'stick together in one large union' because a split would suit the employers.[31] However, when Larkin left for Russia on 1 June 1924, the *Freeman's Journal* reported that Larkinite Barney Conway had said at a meeting in Dún Laoghaire that a new union had been formed.[32] On 4 June, Peter Larkin announced at Beresford Place that the 'Provisional Committee ... was formed for the purposes of carrying on the union.'[33] That is, the pre-O'Brien-led ITGWU. This development was shortly followed by the formation of the Workers' Union of Ireland.

The Provisional Committee was comprised of five members: Michael Whitty, Denis Redmond, Peter Larkin, John Kenny and James Mitchell. The trustees were Barney Conway, Patrick Forde, John Ruth, John Dempsey and Henry Fitzsimon. Outside of Dublin there were Larkinite ITGWU branches strongly sympathetic to the Port and Gas Committee in Nenagh, Roscrea, Dundalk, Bray and Abbeyfeale. On 5 June at 9.30 p.m., 200 Larkinites crossed Butte Bridge and held a meeting at Beresford Place where a crowd of about 500 was waiting. Peter Larkin addressed the assembly and criticized the government, Judge Cooper (who jailed the 45), and each member of the ITGWU executive by name. He told them that his brother James,

> was gone on a mission on their behalf, that nobody knew his next move, but that he was going to win. He urged them to obey the Orders of the Provisional Committee which was formed to carry on the work of the [ITGWU] Union: Go to work tomorrow, continue at work, commit no overt act, pay your subscriptions at Luke Street, and when a list comes out to you to subscribe to the fund for the wives and the children of the 45 men who have lost their time attending court, subscribe.[34]

intelligence', pp 246–8.   **31** LJF: DMP report, 28 June 1923. Larkin later maintained that he never drew a salary as general secretary of the WUI; and in a front-page appeal for funds for the fledgling WUI (*Irish Worker*, 30 Aug. 1924) he signed off as editor of the *Irish Worker*, not general secretary of the new union. This perhaps most indicates his dissatisfaction with the new development. Larkin's chief biographer, Emmet O'Connor, maintained that Larkin 'wanted his old union back': yes, but not necessarily for the negative reasons ascribed.   **32** *Freeman's Journal*, 3 June 1924.   **33** LJF: DMP report, 5 June 1924.   **34** Ibid.

On 8 June, there was a 1000-strong 'Larkinite section' meeting at Beresford Place. Peter Larkin told the meeting that they were winning over the Dún Laoghaire and Inchicore branches; and that the builders' labourers at Marino had sent their subscriptions in. Applications for union cards had been received from Meath, Tipperary and Wexford. James Mitchell told the meeting that the Automobile Drivers' Union was coming over to the Port Committee. The next part of the campaign was to target the No. 5 Branch, the section representing timber workers, the following Wednesday, to get 'the members to pledge their allegiance to the Provisional Committee.' A series of meetings was announced at Inchicore, Beresford Place, and the Mansion House, and all were asked to attend.[35]

On the 16 June, an estimated 1000 Larkinites gathered at a meeting outside Liberty Hall. The usual suspects were denounced, and Peter Larkin condemned the 'action of the government in giving protection to the men [ITGWU loyalists] in occupation of Liberty Hall'. In fact, unknown to those present at the time, Liberty Hall would not reopen until 1927. James Mitchell, Mr Duffy and Mr Tucker addressed the meeting 'in similar terms' to Peter Larkin; and Andy Flynn from Glasgow said that they should all follow the 'great work' done by James Larkin. The meeting was told that two delegates from the newly formed union would be stationed at the quays from 8 a.m. to 5 p.m. every day to advise workers and answer questions on the new union. Peter Larkin read out a telegram from his brother James in Russia, stating that he would be home soon. A new spectacle made its presence felt: the 'Larkin Fife and Drum Band'. The new ensemble was not called the 'Provisional Committee Band'; the focus was kept very much on James Larkin by those organizing against the ITGWU executive, aware of the attraction of the Larkin name for the Dublin city workers.

At this time there was a development in the ITGWU No. 3 Branch. The No. 3 Branch was the second-biggest branch of the ITGWU, with some 7,000 members, and solidly Larkinite. The secretary was John Bohan, a staunch Larkinite at the time. Dublin Detective Branch informed Inspector Lawlor (A Division, DMP) that men entered the office of No. 3 Branch at 74 Thomas Street and one of them produced 'a revolver and assaulted John Byrne'. They remained in the hall. Inspector Lawlor went to Thomas Street and was met by Mr Gannon who said he had been sent over by Thomas Kennedy, ITGWU vice president (to possess the hall and evict Bohan). Gannon told Lawlor that the ITGWU executive had decided 'to dispense with the services of Mr John Bohan, secretary of the No. 3 Branch, as he had failed to obey the instructions

---

35 Ibid., 9 June 1924.

of the executive.' Bohan left the hall under protest when ordered out. When the executive expunged Bohan from the No. 3 Branch, they held onto their property and the branch books; however, the executive could do nothing to stop virtually all the members switching over to the Provisional Committee, which was now morphing into the WUI.

The Workers' Union of Ireland

With the WUI established, and headquartered in Unity Hall, Marlborough Street, sporadic meetings were still held at Beresford Place near Liberty Hall. On 22 June, Peter Larkin told the 1000-strong gathering that they were 'winning, and had now purchased a hall in Marlboro Street.' In line with Larkinite *international* solidarity, rather than *national* solidarity, he called for demobilized National soldiers and republicans to leave their political party affiliations and 'unite under the banner of Labour'. James Larkin's strategy of calling for the release of the political prisoners (some 13,000) was continued in his absence. On 23 June 3,500 marched to Mountjoy Prison to protest at their continued imprisonment.[36] On 20 July, Peter Larkin condemned the government for releasing only leaders of the political prisoners, and called for the 'working class' prisoners to be released as well. It was also announced that the red hand badges of the WUI were now on sale. By this time, the WUI claimed to have 21,000 members. This was a spectacular number, boosted by Dublin membership joining en masse, but somewhat exaggerated. The real figure was probably closer to 19,000. By the end of the decade, the WUI would claim to have over 2000 more members than the ITGWU. Exaggerations aside, this was quite a remarkable achievement for a union driven by radical militancy, and with an internationalist working-class outlook.

On 25 August James Larkin returned to Dublin from Russia. Again, he was met by thousands; and with red flags, banners and bands there was a procession to the Mansion House where he told the packed audience that he had been elected to be one of the twenty-five members of the Communist International to 'rule the Earth'. The highlight of the evening was the 'unfurling of the banner presented by the Moscow Transport Workers to the revolutionary Transport Workers of Dublin.' Later, and for the first time, Larkin addressed a crowd from the unfamiliar window of Unity Hall.[37] Far from being in control of events, and with two unions now at war, Larkin found himself pushed into being leader of the new union. The reformists and

36 Ibid., 5–24 June 1924.   **37** Ibid., 26 Aug. 1924.

the Irish Free State had ensured that the Larkinites did not hold onto the ITGWU, but it was the mobilization of Larkinism from below that created the opportunity to create a new union that would rival what the Larkinites perceived to be a bureaucratic officialdom that had stymied the ITGWU. With a philosophy that went beyond nationalism, the Larkinites not only wanted bread for all, they wanted roses, too.

Contributors

ANNE BORAN is professor emerita of social science, University of Chester. Editor of 'Issues in the Social Sciences' series, she has published on globalization, poverty and crime. More recently she has focused on mining and social change in Castlecomer and published a biography of her father, Nixie Boran, the revolutionary and miners' leader, entitled *Challenge to power* (2021).

JOHNNY BURKE graduated from Dublin City University with a degree in English and history (2018), and subsequently from the University of Galway with a Masters in history (2020).

JOHN CUNNINGHAM is a lecturer in history at the University of Galway, and a former editor of *Saothar: Journal of Irish Labour History*. He has published on the moral economy, Irish local history and global syndicalism, and is currently writing a biography of Tom Glynn, an Irish-born leader of the IWW in South Africa and Australia.

TERRY DUNNE was awarded a PhD by the Sociology Department, Maynooth University, in 2015. Historian-in-Residence for Co. Laois in 2021–2, he farms in east Clare, and has published widely on agrarian and rural labour movements over the long nineteenth century.

MARY FORREST was a lecturer in University College Dublin from 1986 until 2020, where she specialized in ornamental horticulture and garden history. She has written about Irish gardens and their plant collections. Research into women's horticultural colleges has led to further publications about school gardens, Arbor Day and allotments, features of rural and urban life in early to mid-twentieth-century Ireland.

BRIAN HANLEY is assistant professor of twentieth-century Irish history at Trinity College Dublin. He has written widely on Irish republicanism and radicalism and is currently researching the global impact of the Irish Revolution.

DOMINIC HAUGH teaches history in St Patrick's Comprehensive School in Shannon. He was awarded a PhD by the University of Galway in 2020 on 'The labour movement in Limerick in the nineteenth century'. Author of *Limerick soviet 1919: the revolt of the Bottom Dog* (2019), he is currently completing a book on the revolutionary period in Ireland from a working-class perspective.

LIAM ALEX HEFFRON, historian and actor, recently earned a PhD in history from the University of Galway. He provides content authenticity advice to arts and media productions. His research interests include the social causes of rebellion, folk memory, and class/status constructs. Founder of St Cormac's Heritage Charity, he received the Explore Innovation award (2019) for his digital project archiving national school records.

MOIRA LEYDON is an assistant general secretary of the Association of Secondary Teachers, Ireland, and a member of the ICTU's Global Solidarity Committee and Women's Committee. A graduate of UCD in sociology and political economy, she holds a masters' degree from UCD (equality studies) and from the University of Maynooth (applied social studies). She is currently conducting research on the labour movement in north Sligo, her home place.

Originally from East Tyrone FEARGHAL MAC BHLOSCAIDH lectures in History at St Mary's University College, Belfast. He is author of *Fenian and Ribbonmen* (2011) and *Tyrone, 1921–25* (2014), and co-editor of *For bread not profits* (2022). He has published articles on the Caledon lockout (*International Labour and Working Class History*, 2020) and the Belfast Pogrom (*Studi Irlandesi*, 2022).

KIERAN MCNULTY, originally from Birmingham, England, graduated with a BA in history from the University of Portsmouth, and with an MA in history from Maynooth University. He has published several articles on the working-class history of Kerry, 1913–23. A resident of Tralee, Kieran is active in social movements in his community.

THERESA MORIARTY is an independent researcher. Her work includes published studies of working women's lives and of women workers in trade union history. She is an honorary president of the Irish Labour History Society.

GERARD WATTS completed a PhD in digital humanities at the University of Galway on state surveillance of James Larkin. Publishing on Larkin in various periodicals and journals including *Saothar* and *Éire-Ireland*, he has been involved in digitization projects, including of ITGWU annual reports and *The Irish Worker,* 1923–5.

Index

Abbeyfeale, Co. Limerick, 257
Acquisition of Lands (Allotments) Acts, 109, 110
Addison (Housing) Act, 62
Addison, pit manager, 42
African American, 19, 124, 126, 129
agrarian movements, 10, 12–13, 15, 44–58, 79–96, 137, 156–78
Agriculture and Technical Instruction, Department of, 56, 80, 98, 102–3, 105–8, 112, 183
Agriculture, Commission on, 87–8, 94
Agricultural Wages Board, 16, 17, 183, 187, 191, 194–5
Aherlow, Glen of, Co. Tipperary, 41, 148
Alcorn, J.G., 47, 52–3
Allotment and Smallholders Act (1908), 107
allotments, 27, 67, 79, 85–8, 93, 96, 97–113, 185
Amalgamated Society of Tailors and Tailoresses, 235, 236, 238
Amalgamated Tailors and Garment Workers' Trade Union, 238
America, see United States of America
American Association for the Recognition of the Irish Republic, 130
American Women Pickets for the Enforcement of America's War Aims, 124
Ancient Order of Hibernians, 87, 93, 181, 185, 187
Andrews, J.M., 199, 214
Annaghdown, Co. Galway, 47
Antrim, Co., 210
Antwerp, 114–15

'Arab, the', 117
Ardfinnan, Co. Tipperary, 155
Arigna, Co. Leitrim, 195
Armagh, Co., 20
army, British, 9, 16, 22n, 23, 30–1, 53, 63, 64, 65, 122, 162, 188–9, 237
army, Free State, 38, 38n, 39–41, 42n, 56, 132, 226
army, workers', 42–3
Ascension Thursday, 59–60, 63, 69–71
Askeaton, Co. Limerick, 135
Association of Masters, Mates and Pilots, 124
Association of Secondary Teachers, Ireland, 236–7
Athy, Co. Kildare, 25, 85, 89, 94–6
Augusteijn, Joost, 156, 158, 161–2, 177–8

Back to the Land movement, 14
Baird, Jimmy, 203, 208, 209
Ballina, Co. Mayo, 158, 160–1, 168, 170, 172, 175
Ballinacourty, Co. Tipperary, 148
Ballinfull Co-operative Society, Co. Sligo, 188
Ballinasloe, Co. Galway, 48–9, 52, 56
Ballintrellick, Co. Sligo, 188
Ballingarry, Co. Tipperary, 94
Ballycastle, Co. Mayo 159, 160, 164, 173, 174
Ballyhea, Co. Cork, 136
Ballylanders, Co. Limerick, 136–7
Ballyragget, Co. Kilkenny, 32
Baltimore, Maryland, 126
Banbridge, Co. Down, 200
Bangor-Erris, Co. Mayo, 168

Banister, Joseph, 118
Barbersfort, Co. Galway, 51
Barry, Fr Robert, 93
Barry, Tom, 11
Belclare, Co. Galway, 51
Behan, Theresa, 239
Belfast, 20, 90, 116, 134, 134n, 151–2,
    154, 166, 172–3, 183, 195, 197,
    217, 231n, 232–3, 238, 240;
    Belfast boycott, see boycott; City
    Hall, 202; Corporation, 214;
    Crumlin Road, 205; Custom
    House, 202; Falls, 197, 212;
    Finaghy, 213; Harland & Wolff,
    204, 214; Inglis & Co, 207; Labour
    Party, 197–216; Labour
    Representation Committee, 198;
    mill-workers, 203; pogrom, 207,
    214; Queen's Island, 203; Rosemary
    Street, 201; Shankill, 200, 204;
    Trades Council, 198, 200, 201,
    203, 204, 209; Workman & Clark,
    202, 203, 204
Belfast Newsletter, 120, 207, 212
Bellingham, Edward, 88
Belville Bridge, Co. Mayo, 163, 165
Bennett, Louie, 239, 241–3
Bernard, Denis, 51
Bevin, Ernest, 206
Bew, Paul, 213
Bird, Miss, 234
Birkenhead, 120
Birmingham, 115
Birrane, Frank, 165
birth control, 229
Black and Tans, 32, 36, 38, 73, 163–4,
    167, 228
Black, Charles, 97
Blackbridge, Co. Tipperary, 147
Blackrock, Co. Dublin, 102–3
Blanchardstown, Co. Dublin, 81–2
Bohan, John, 247, 249, 258
Boland, Harry, 114–16, 124, 127–9

Bolsheviks, 7, 18, 44, 62, 70, 77–8, 122,
    138–9, 146–7, 150–2, 154,
    209–10, 212–13
Boran, Anne, 17
Boran, Nixie, 38, 38n, 41–2
Borgonovo, John, 12
Borris-in-Ossory, Co. Laois, 14
Boston, 8, 66, 125–7, 129
Bottom Dog, The, 133
Bourke, Solicitor, 170
Bowen, Sheila, 231, 241
Bowen Colthurst, John, 116
boycott, 24, 32–3, 53, 125, 146–8, 170,
    223; Belfast, 166, 172–5
Boyd, Alex, 175
Bradley, Dan, 94, 137, 182
Bradley, Sandy, 36
Brady, Patrick, 247
Brannigan, C., 241
Bray, Co. Wicklow, 257
Breen, Cáit, 225–6
Breen, Dan, 35, 41, 41n
Brehon law, 59
Brennan, Garrett, 31–2, 38
Brennan, Michael, 73
Brennan, Mike, 40
Bridgetown Co-operative Creamery, Co.
    Clare, 146
British Columbia, 116
British Expeditionary Forces, 162
British Journal of Nursing, 228
Brooks, Thomas, 255
Browne, Michael, 16
Bruff, Co. Limerick
Brugha, Cathal, 51, 128
Bruree, Co. Limerick, 135–6, 138–40,
    148
Bryan, Loftus, 19
Buckley, Margaret, 239, 243
Bulgaden, Co. Limerick, 141, 142
Bull, Philip, 45, 48
Bureau of Military History, 12–14, 225
Butterly market garden, 81

Buttevant, 136, 235n
Burke, Johnny, 13
Byrne, Alfred, 108, 111
Byrne, John, 143, 258

Caffrey, Miss, 234
Cahalan, Cissie, 235, 241, 242, 243
Caherconlish, Co. Limerick, 146
Caherdaniel, Co. Kerry, 228
Cahill, Thomas, 104, 106–7, 111
Caledon, Co. Tyrone, 200
Calleary, Phelim A., 176
Calleary, Seán, 176
Campbell, D.R., 198, 198n, 201–2, 207
Campbell, Fergus, 44–5, 48–9, 156–7,
     160, 178
Campion, James, 38
Campion, Thomas, 34, 39
Cannon, Joseph P., 128
Cappoquin, Co. Waterford, 149
Carbury, barony of, 179
Carden Thomas, 160
Carey, Michael, 169
Carn, Co. Mayo, 168
Carpenter, Walter, 238
Carrick-on-Suir, 144, 145, 146
carters, 21–6, 38–9, 114, 207, 255
Carlow, Co., 10, 25–7, 183
Carson, Edward, 199, 204, 208, 210,
     213, 215, 216
Carson, George, 207
Carson, Rufus, 173
Carson, William, 173
Casement, Roger
Cashel, Co. Tipperary, 147
Cassidy, Michael, 35
Castlebellingham, Co. Louth, 88
Castlebar, Co. Mayo, 161
Castle Bernard, Co. Cork, 228
Castleblakeney, Co. Galway, 47
Castlecomer, Co. Kilkenny, 21–43
Castleconnell, Co. Limerick, 142
Castlegar, Co. Galway, 76

Castlegrove, Co. Galway, 47
Castlelambert, Co. Galway, 53
Catholic Church, 14, 44, 47, 54, 57,
     67–8, 70–1, 75, 118, 121, 150,
     210, 218, 226, 228–30
Catholic action, 67
cattle driving, 47–8, 55, 168, 170–2
Cavan, Co., 93, 183
Cawley, Mrs, 165
Central Intelligence Department (CID),
     249, 251
Chatsworth, Co. Kilkenny, 33
China, 117, 124
Charleville, 136
Chenevix, Helen, 234, 243
Christian Brothers, 27, 101
Church of Ireland, 50, 159, 174, 227
Civic Guard, 39, 75, 256, *see also* Gárda
     Síochána, An
Civil War, 21, 38n, 39–41, 41n 42–3,
     59, 76, 113, 115n, 145, 150–1,
     155, 155n, 159, 175, 176–8, 196,
     217, 225–7, 230, 246
Clancy, Bishop, 184
Clanricarde, Lord, 60–1, 65
Clare, Co., 12, 44, 51, 80, 150, 157,
     183
Claremorris, Co. Mayo, 176
Cleeve's, *see* Condensed Milk
     Company
Clifden, Co. Galway, 17, 73
Cliffoney, Co. Sligo, 186
Clogh, Co. Kilkenny, 24, 26, 29–30, 34,
     38
Clogheen, Co. Tipperary, 149
Clondalkin, Co. Dublin, 84
Cloneen, Co. Kilkenny, 23–4, 26
Clonfert, bishop of, 44, 55
Clongowes Wood, 246
Clonmel, 41, 134–5, 144, 146–7, 149,
     155, 240
Clonsilla, Co. Dublin, 81
Clonskeagh, Co. Dublin, 106

Coal carriers Association (Castlecomer) 26

Coalisland, Co. Tyrone, 207

Coghlan Briscoe, J.M., 65

Colbert, Seán, 104–5

Collins, Michael, 19, 51, 54, 73, 128, 167, 248n

Collins, Patrick, 50, 52

Collins, Peter, 201

Colohan, Councillor, 61, 72

Communist International, 155, 246, 259

Communist Party of Great Britain, 90

Communist Party of Ireland, 43, 74–5, 132, 134n, 150, 154, 155n, 249n

Condensed Milk Company (Cleeve's), 77, 132–6, 138–40, 143–4, 146–9, 152

Congested Districts Board, 46, 169, 180

'congests' / congested famers, 8, 10, 49, 51, 160, 178, 181

Connacht Tribune, 55, 61, 78

Connaught Rangers, 189

Connemara, 17, 51–2

Connolly, James, 16–18, 25, 30, 37, 39, 42, 60, 64, 77, 191, 197–9, 201, 203, 206, 218, 222–3, 230, 233, 249n, 251

Connolly, John Joseph, 164

Connolly, Michael, 247

Connolly's Own Pipers' Band, 256

Connolly, Roddy, 155n

Connolly O'Brien, Nora, 237

Conservative Party, 117, 121

conscription, 9, 11, 14, 30–1, 66, 72, 122, 152, 166, 185, 187, 189, 193, 201–4, 236, 262

Conway, Barney, 247, 253, 255, 257

Conway, Jim, 35

Cookstown, Co. Tyrone, 207

Coolbawn, 31, 35–6

Cooper, Judge, 257

Cooper, T.A., 185

co-operatives, 22, 79, 89–92, 99–100, 104–5, 110, 130, 137, 146, 148, 151, 188, 228, 233

Corrib, Lough, 47

Corish, Richard, 248

Corn Production Act, 17, 183, 191

Corrigan, Pat, 162

Cosgrave, William T., 67, 252

Corless, Gertrude, 128

Cork, Co., 11–12, 51, 103, 105, 111–12, 116, 121, 132, 136, 138, 143, 145, 183, 203, 228, 238; Harbour Soviet, 140–1, 141n,

Corn Production Act (1917), 16, 183, 191

Corofin, Co. Clare, 150

Corrandulla, Co. Galway, 52

Coulter, Geoffrey, 138, 138n

Coventry, 74

Craig, James, 213–14

Craughwell, Co. Galway, 45, 49

Creggs, Co. Galway, 47

Cremen, Bridget, 65

Cremen, Daisy Cleaver, 74

Cremen, Stephen, 59–78

Crettyard, Co. Kilkenny, 22, 32

Crocnacally, Co. Mayo, 159, 161

Cronin, John, 68

Cronin, Josie, 166

Cronin, Maura, 48

Cross, Ellen, 234

Crossmolina, 7, 159, 160, 164, 168, 173, 175, 176

Crotty, John, 247

Crumlin, Co. Dublin, 81–2

Crutt, Co. Kilkenny, 31, 32, 40, 41n

Cullen, Louis, 16

Culleton, James (Séamus), 31, 34, 38, 40

Cumann Lucht Ceapach na hÉireann, *see* United Irish Plotholders' Union

Cumann na mBan, 29, 31, 64, 156, 158, 176–7, 217, 226–7, 240n

Cumann na nGaedheal, 108
Cunard Line, 114–15, 126
Cunningham, John, 18, 184
Cunningham, Martin, 63

Dáil courts, 13, 15, 33–4, 44, 54, 56–8, 64, 165, 170, 175, 178
Dáil Éireann, 13, 31, 38, 44, 56–7, 63–4, 88, 90, 108, 110, 137, 141, 145, 167, 229
Daly, Christy, 51
Daly, Paddy, 114–15, 115n, 117
Daly, P.T., 184–6, 195, 241, 247–9, 253
Davis, Father Peter, 164, 169
Davis, Miss, 234
Davis, Thomas, 216
Davitt, Michael, 50, 75
Dawson Bates, Richard, 199, 208, 210, 213, 214
Deerpark, Co. Kilkenny, 23, 26, 35, 38
Defence of the Realm Act, 98, 109
Delaney, Michael, 40
Delany farm, 81
Dempsey (longshoreman), 127
Dempsey, John, 257
Derry, Co., 192
de Valera, Éamon, 17, 114–15, 117, 124, 126, 128, 155n
Dillon, Mr, 104
Dillon, Paul, 219
Dock Milling Co., 255
dock workers, 9, 66, 85, 114–29, 140, 143, 184–5, 190, 248, 251–2, 254–5
Doherty, Patrick, 139
Donaghmore, Co. Tyrone, 200
Donnelly, Michael, 89, 142–3
Donnelly, Patrick, 100–3, 105, 107, 113
Donnelly, Richard, 102
Donohill, Co. Tipperary, 147
Dooley, Terence, 180
Doonane, Co. Kilkenny, 21n, 23, 26, 38
Doran, M., 145

Dowling, Seán, 134, 134n, 138–9, 141–3, 145, 155
Downes, Barney, 115
Dreaper sisters, 36
Drogheda, 19, 93, 102–3, 106, 115, 138, 141, 232
Drumcliffe, Co. Sligo, 179, 180, 188
Druminangle, Co. Mayo, 161, 164, 174
Dublin, 12, 16, 18–19, 35, 44, 54, 56, 65, 67–8, 73, 75–6, 80–6, 91–2, 97–112, 114–17, 144, 151–3, 156, 183–4, 190, 192, 201, 206, 221, 227, 229, 232–44; 1913 Lockout, 16, 18, 83, 245; Alliance and Consumers' Gas Company, 253; Beresford Place, 248, 253, 256, 258, 259; Bridewell, 255; Butte Bridge, 250; Chamber of Commerce, 256; Corporation, 65, 97, 99, 102–3, 105–9, 111–12, 248; D'Olier Street, 254; Fairbrothers' Fields, 97; Fairview, 105–6; Gas Company, 254, 256; Greenmount Cotton Mills, 150; Harold's Cross, 151; Inchicore, 258; Industrial Development Council, 103; Kevin Street, 255; Marino Plotholders' Association, 99, 258; Metropolitan Police, 249, 251, 255; Marlborough Street, 259; Nelson's Pillar, 75–6; North Wall, 255; Pearse St, 249; St Mark's Church, 249; St Patrick's Division, 102; Store Street, 255, 256; Tara St, 249; Tenants' Association, 67, 75; Trades Council, 100, 103, 107, 153n, 241n; Westland Row, 249
Dublin Castle, 19, 64
Duncan, Charles, 206
Duke, Henry, 107
Dundalk, Co. Louth, 20, 115, 120–1, 221, 241, 247, 257
Dungarvan, Co. Waterford, 104

Dungannon, Co. Tyrone, 207
Dunkellin, Lord, 60–1, 69–70, 72n,
    75–6
Dún Laoghaire (Kingstown), 99–100,
    102, 104, 112, 249, 257–8
Dunleavy family, 166
Dunmore, Co. Galway, 47
Dunne, Terry, 13, 56
Dunne, Dr, 29
Dunshaughlin, Co. Meath, 13, 81
Dysart, Co. Kilkenny, 40

Easter Rising, 1916, 18, 39, 45, 70, 228,
    231
Ebrill, solicitor, 68, 74
Economic Journal, 116
Eden, Maud, 234
Egan, Martin, 166
Egypt, 8, 124
elections, 11, 13, 29, 31, 63, 67, 74, 97,
    108, 143, 146–7, 149–50, 155,
    159, 184, 198, 204, 207–8, 210–
    12, 217, 225, 235
England, 36, 64, 67, 74, 98, 107, 111,
    113, 118–23, 151, 173, 231, 245n
Errill, Co. Laois, 14
Ewer, W.N., 90
Eyrecourt, Co. Galway, 53

Fairfield, Co. Mayo, 166, 169–72
Falmouth, Cornwall, 146
Famine, the Great, 24, 50, 54, 62, 82
Farmers' Freedom Force, 19, 139, 139n,
    147
Farmers' Party, 143, 146, 150
farm labourers, 79–96, 139n, 141–2,
    148–50, 148n, 183, 206, 262
Farrell, Dr, 29
Farrelly, John, 100, 107
Farren, John, 249, 251
Farry, Michael, 196
Federation of Engineering and
    Shipbuilding Trades, 204, 209

Female Factory Inspectors, 235
Fenians, 32, 44–5, 157, 162, *see also*
    Irish Republican Brotherhood
Ferguson, R., 181
Fermoy, Co. Cork, 103
Fetherstonhaugh estate, 159–60, 166,
    172, 173, 174, 177
Fetherstonhaugh, Godfrey, 174
ffrench-Mullen, Madelaine, 234
Fianna Fáil, 12, 54, 57, 176, 262
Field, William, 65
Figgis, Darrell, 168
Finberg, H.P.R., 179
Finnegan, Bernard, 247, 253–5
Finnerty, Anthony, 166, 168
Finnerty, Thomas, 166
Finsboro, Co. Kilkenny, 36
First World War, 7, 23, 30, 45–6, 62,
    67, 83–4, 88, 98, 109, 113, 133,
    160–2, 167–9, 174, 177, 205
Fitzpatrick, David, 12, 44, 51, 80, 137,
    156–7, 160, 181, 233
Fitzsimon, Henry, 257
Flaherty, Edward, 172
Flanagan, James, 233
Flanders, 200
Flax Roughers and Yarn Spinners' Trade
    Union, 197
Fleming, John, 34, 38
Fleming, Marguerite, 227
Fleming, Michael (Castlecomer), 31
Michael Fleming (Moygownagh), 160–1
Fleming, Patrick, 31, 40
Flood, Jack, 247
Flowers, Helena, 236
Flynn, Andy, 258
Fogarty, John, 30
Foley, John Henry, 60
Foran, Thomas, 183, 246, 250, 253, 254
Forde, Patrick, 247, 253, 257
Forestal, Philip, 169–70
Forrest, Mary, 16
Forward, 197

Freemans Journal, 63, 97, 102, 120, 257
Friends of Irish Freedom, 124, 127–8

Gaelic Athletic Association, 16, 162–3, 186, 188, 195–6
Gaelic League, 28, 29, 70, 162, 181, 228
Gaffney, Paddy, 10
Galbally, Co. Limerick, 136
Gallacher, Willie, 202
Gallagher, Martin 'Darby', 163, 166–7, 170, 176
Gallagher, Michael, 172
Galteemore, Co. Tipperary, 145
Galway, Co., 44–58, 81, 117, 157, 174, 183, 185
Galway city / town, 18, 19, 59–78, 106, 236; Claddagh, 69; Eyre Square, 59–61, 65, 69, 71; Fr Griffin Square, 69, 71, 76; Magdalen Asylum, 70; Nimmo's Pier, 69; Pro-Cathedral, 71
Galway, Mary, 203–4, 232
Galway Observer, 69
Gárda Síochána, An, 40, 42, 42n, 176
Garranard, Co. Mayo, 163, 166
Garron, Co. Laois, 14
Garvey, Marcus, 19, 124, 129–30
general strike, 8–9, 120, 123, 133–7, 141, 152, 187, 193–4, 199, 207–9, 262
Genoa, 114–15
Germany, 8, 114n, 127, 152, 205n
Getgood, Robert, 207
Gethin, Capt., 181
Gifford, Sidney, 129
Ginnell, Annie, 234
Gill, T.P., 98, 107
Glasgow, 114–15, 117, 121, 258
Gleeson, William, 247
Glenmore estate, Co. Mayo, 159, 172, 174, 175
Goggins, Billy, 115

Golden, Helen, 128, 130
Goldsmith, Oliver, 18
Gompers, Samuel, 246
Gordon, Dawson, 197, 198, 200, 201, 205, 209, 215, 216
Gordon, Ellen, 232
Gore-Booth, Aideen, 192
Gore-Booth, Constance, *see* Markievicz, Constance
Gore-Booth, Eva, 181, 190–1, 228
Gore-Booth, Henry, 188
Gore-Booth, Josslyn, 181, 184–5, 188, 190, 192, 193, 196
Gort, Co. Galway, 106
Gortleatilla, Co. Mayo 175
Grant, Revd, 29
Grant, William, 214
graziers, 45–51, 57, 160, 168, 172–3, 175, 177
Greaves, C. Desmond, 18, 84, 136n, 186
Griffith, Arthur, 51, 141
Guinness, 255, 256
Gurley Flynn, 129

Hackett, Rosie, 234
Hall, David, 13, 88, 93
Hallinan, Bishop Denis, 75
Hallinan, T.D., 148
Hamburg, 114–17
Hanahoe, Michael, 162
Hanley, Brian, 19, 152
Hanratty, Miss, 205
Harrison, Sarah, 103, 107, 111, 234
Hart, Harry, 120
Hart, Peter, 11–12, 157, 178
Haverty, James, 54, 56
Haywood, Bill, 246
Haugh, Dominic, 15, 77
Hedley, Jack, 134, 134n, 137, 151, 155
Heffernan, Michael, 148, 155
Heffron, Liam Alex, 15
Hegarty, James, 168

Hegarty, John 'Soldier', 162
Hegarty, Patrick, 164, 166–7
Hegarty, Peter, 168
Henry, C.J., 181, 186, 187, 195
Hobsbawm, Eric, 8
Hogan, Patrick, 95, 108
Holness, John, 214
Home Rule, 25, 30, 45, 118, 119, 167,
    197, 199n, 201, 203, 210, 214
Hospital Day, 1923, 105–6
House Leagues, 65
House of Commons, 31, 102, 107, 120,
    215, 223
Housing of the Working Classes Act
    (1908), 62
Houston, Denis, 200
Howard, Henry, 49, 52
Howard, James, 52
Howard, Thomas, 220, 222–3
Hoyne, Helen, 236
Hughes, Felix, 207
Humphries, Billy, 115
Hungary, 8, 152, 239
Hunt, Miss, 234
Hurley-O'Mahony, Anna, 228
Hutcheson, James, 51

I'm forever blowing bubbles, 69
Independent Labour Party, *see* Labour
    Party, Independent
India, 8, 210
Industrial and Provident Societies Act,
    105
Industrial Workers of the World, 245
inflation, 16, 17, 86–7, 90, 97, 204
Ingram, John, 175
Inistioge, Co. Kilkenny, 36
International Council of Nurses, 229
International Longshoremen's
    Association, 124, 127
International Society of Tailors,
    Machinists and Pressers, 238
Iraq, 8, 124

Ireland, Ben, 166
Irish Agricultural and General Workers'
    Union, 183
Irish Agricultural Organisation Society,
    92, 110
Irish Allotment Holders Association,
    110
Irish Automobile Drivers' and
    Mechanics' Union, 144, 194
Irish Centre for the Histories of Labour
    and Class, 20
Irish Citizen, 241–2
Irish Citizen Army, 18, 39, 89, 115,
    115n, 142, 209, 231, 233
Irish Clerical Workers Union, 144, 236
Irish Congress of Trade Unions, 20
Irish Craftworkers' Union, 112
Irish Domestic Workers' Union, 239
Irish Drapers' Assistants Association,
    217, 219–24, 230, 235–7, 240
Irish Farmers' Union, 19, 90, 133, 139n,
    141, 145, 147, 175, 183, 195
Irish Gardeners' Association, 110
Irish Independent, 9, 18, 39, 103
Irish Land and Labour Association, 83
Irish Mechanics' and General Workers'
    Union, 73–4
Irish Military Archives, 158
Irish National Teachers' Organisation,
    18, 235–7
Irish Nurses and Midwives
    Organisation, 237
Irish Nurses' Union, 230, 237
Irish Postal Union, 147
Irish Plotholders' Union, *see* United
    Irish Plotholders' Union
Irish Progressive League, 128–9
Irish Republican Army, 10–13, 15, 29,
    31–42, 44–5, 46, 50–2, 54, 58, 64,
    87, 114–19, 123, 132, 136, 139–
    42, 148–51, 153, 156–78, 192,
    208, 213, 225–6, 239, 251, *see also*
    Volunteers, Irish

Irish Republican Brotherhood, 45, 115, 119, 124, *see also* Fenians
Irish Self-Determination League, 119
Irish Tailors' and Tailoresses Union, 238
Irish Trade Union Congress, 8, 16–17, 87, 89–90, 102, 96, 134, 137, 149, 153, 183, 193–4, 198, 201–2, 205, 207, 221, 223, 231–44, 248, 248n
Irish Transport and General Workers' Union, 10, 13, 16–20, 25, 34, 36–7, 38–9, 63, 65–8, 73, 76, 79, 82, 83–5, 87–9, 91–2, 96, 117, 133–47, 151–4, 177, 182–95, 200, 203, 206, 210, 219–20, 223–4, 226–7, 233, 235, 237, 242, 245–60
Irish Times, 91, 136
Irish White Cross Society, 228
Irish Women's Franchise League, 235
Irish Women Workers' Union, 231, 233–4, 236, 239, 242–43
Irish Worker, 82, 247, 251, 257n
Irish Workers' League, 16
Ironmills, Co. Tipperary, 147
Irwin, Val, 165
Italians, 8, 126, 129, 152

Japan, 117
Jarrow, Co. Kilkenny, 23, 41
Jennings, Thomas, 165, 174
J.P Evans Engineering, 132–3
Johnson, Adrian, 130
Johnson, Tom, 108, 149, 201–2, 241, 248–9, 248n
Jones, Anny, 48, 52
Jones, David Seth, 46
Jordan, Tim, 173

Kavanagh, Ned, 115
Keane, John, 149
Kearney, Mrs, 165
Kearns, James, 49
Kelly, Anthony, 168

Kelly, David, 166
Kelly, Edward, 104
Kelly, Dr Gertrude, 128
Kelly, Joseph, 163
Kelly, Michael Joseph, 160, 162
Kelly, Paddy, 51
Kelly, P.J., 119, 123
Kelly, Thomas, 169–70
Kenneally, William, 141
Kennedy, Archie, 115
Kennedy, Thomas, 250, 258
Kennedy O'Byrne, Moira, 116
Kenny, John, 247, 257
Kenny, Tom, 45
Kernoff, Harry, 18
Kerr, Neil, 115
Kerry, Co., 17, 111, 183, 217–30
Kerryman, The, 11, 222
kidnap, 32, 37, 141, 149, 192
Kiely, Paul, 69, 71
Kilcrohane, 228
Kilcullen, S., 173
Kildare, Co., 80–1, 84–7, 94, 104, 111, 184
Kilfian, Co. Mayo, 164
Kilkenny, Co., 10, 13, 17, 21–43, 111, 183, 240
Killaclogher, Co. Galway, 51
Killala, Co. Mayo, 160
Killanin, Lord, 174
Killarney Mental Hospital, 229
Killeen, Mrs, 53
Killenaule, Co. Tipperary, 147
Killererin, Co. Galway, 51
Killeshin, Co Laois, 10
Killimor, Co. Galway, 48
Kilmallock, 135–6, 141–2, 144, 150
Kilroy, Michael, 175
Kingstown, *see* Dún Laoghaire
Kinneavey, Nell, 50
Korea, 124
Knights of Labour, 245
Knockferry, Co. Galway, 49

Knocklong, Co. Limerick, 135, 137–8, 145, 148
Kostick, Conor, 12, 183
Kulak, 29
Kyle, Sam, 198, 200, 204, 207, 215, 216

Lá na mBan, 236
Labour Party, Irish, 13, 108–9, 141, 155, 201, 226n, 235, 243, 248, 248n, *see also* Irish Trade Union Congress
Labour Party, Belfast, 197–216
Labour Party, British, 205
Labour Party, Independent, 197–8, 201–2, 204–5, 210, 216
Labour Party, 'Loyal British Patriotic', 122
Labourers' Acts, 62, 97
labourers' cottages, 61, 67, 82–3, 85, 88, 182
labourers' cow plots, 88, 93, 96
Labour Women's Council, 242
Lacey, Dinny, 41
Laffan, Bartholomew, 145
Land Acts (1903, 1909, 1923), 27, 45, 56–8, 88, 110–11, 181, 188, 194
Land Commission, 14, 22, 46, 56–8, 109
Land Cultivation Committees, 98, 102–3, 105–6, 111–12
Land courts, *see* Dáil courts
Land League, 28, 29, 45, 100
Land War, 162, 168
Lanigan, Stevie, 115, 123
Laois (Leix, Queen's), Co., 10, 13, 21n, 27, 81, 84, 94, 94n, 111
Lardner, Larry, 51
Larkin, Delia, 232, 234n, 247, 249
Larkin, Esther, 249
Larkin Fife and Drum Band, 258
Larkin, James, 16, 18–19, 25, 39, 67, 74–6, 78, 182, 184, 232, 245–60

Larkin, Peter, 247, 257, 258, 259
Larkin, William J., 59, 62, 64, 67, 74
Larkinism, 245, 247, 250
Larne, Co. Antrim, 210
Lawlor, Inspector, 258
Lawlor, John, 247
Lawlor, Thomas, 249
Lawther, James, 203
League of Oppressed Peoples, 124
Leinster Reporter, 149
Lenihan, Michael, 141
Lenin, V.I., 29, 152–3
Lennon, Patrick, 249
Leo XIII, Pope, 75
Lewin, T.F., 47
Leydon, Moira, 16
Liberty (ITGWU periodical), 10
Liberty Hall (ITGWU HQ and synonym for ITGWU), 18–20, 65, 130, 140, 184–5, 187, 192, 195, 233–4, 234n, 236–8, 248, 250–1, 253, 255–9
Limerick, 11, 63, 68–9, 74–6, 78, 89, 106, 111, 121, 132–7, 141–6, 148, 152, 224, 247; Garryowen, 68; Lansdowne, 132–3, 144–5, 144n, 148; O'Connell Street, 69; Soviet, 68, 78, 133–4, 136–7, 152; Trades Council, 68, 133, 143–4; Workers' Housing Association, 63, 68
Limerick Leader, 140
linen, 197, 200, 203–5, 207, 209, 232, 240–1
Linen Masters' Association, 200
Linen Trade Board, 200
Lissadell, 179–81, 188–90, 192, 195
Lisburn, Co. Antrim, 205
Liverpool, 66, 67, 114–31, 134; Scotland Road, 118, 121–3; Trades Council, 123
living-in system, 217, 220–1, 223–4
Local Government Board, 63, 97

Lloyd George, David, 7, 8, 16, 62, 209, 215, 246
Lloyd's, 116
lockouts, 83, 84, 94–5, 115, 184–5, 200, 233, 245
Loftus, Kate, 170
London, 9, 98, 107, 114–16, 119, 191, 216, 232
Longshoremen, *see* dock workers
Loughlin, Mrs, 31
Loughrey, Mark, 237
Lough Talt, Co. Sligo, 175
Louth, Co., 81, 86–8, 102, 111, 116, 183, 247
Lowther, John, 169
Loyalist Vigilance Committee, 214
Lucas, Mr, 106
Lurgan, Co. Armagh, 200, 206–7; Hemmers and Veiners, 232
Lynch, Gilbert, 121
Lynch, John, 184, 186–7, 189, 195–6, 247
Lynch, Liam, 148
Lynch, Patrick, 233
Lynch, Richard, 247
Lynd, Robert, 61
Lyng, Jack, 33
Lyng, Tom, 35
Lynn, Francis, 168
Lynn, Kathleen, 234
Lynott, James, 161, 163
Lynott, James (Snr), 163, 170
Lyon, Michael, 249

Macardle, Dorothy, 228
Mac Bhloscaidh, Fearghal, 20
McCarron, James, 233
McClung, Bob, 198, 205–7
McCready, Nevil, 9
Mac Curtain, Tomás, 112
McDevitt, Danny, 201
McDonnell, Mr, 109, 112
McDonogh, Thomas & Sons, 67

McDowell, William J., 211
Mac Gamhna Padraig, *see* Gaffney, Paddy
McGee, Jem, 116, 116n, 127–8
McGowan, Joe, 196
McGrath, Jack, 138–9, 142–3, 145, 155
McGuffin, Sam, 210, 213, 216
McGuire sisters, 31
McHale, James, 170
McHale, John 'Sonny', 160, 164
McHale, Martin, 162
McKeague, James S., 198, 206–7, 215
McKernan, Peter, 207
Mackey, Anthony, 142
McLoughlin, Revd Michael, 164
McLoughlin, Seán, 247
McMorrow, Alderman, 190
McNamara, Conor, 52
McNamara, J.J., 71–2
McNamara, Fr Michael, 29, 33, 34, 40
McNance, James, 121
McNulty, Kieran, 17
McQuale, Kit, 121
MacSwiney, Muriel, 130
MacSwiney, Terence, 125
Madden, P., 53
Maguire, Conor, 173
Maguire, Father, 145
Maher, John, 195
Maher, William, 124
Mahon, Catherine, 237, 239n
Mahon, Ned, 25
Mallow, 134–5, 148–9
Manchester, 115, 117, 121, 190–1
Manchester Guardian, 17, 149
Mandeville, John, 147
Manicom, Kate, 205
Manning, Michael, 49
Mannix, Bishop Daniel, 125, 128–9
Marine Engineers' Association, 116, 124, 127
Markievicz, Constance, 140, 179, 218, 228, 234, 248

Marryat, Frederick, 18
Martin, William, 100, 112
Marxist, 128, 132, 151, 153, 154, 230
Massford, Co. Kilkenny, 22
Maughan, James, 168
Maugherow, Co. Sligo, 16, 179–96
May Day, 152, 187, 194, 205, 236
Mayo, Co., 13, 15, 156–78
Meath, Co., 13, 19, 80–8, 93, 96, 184, 258; Labour Union, 13, 83
Meehan, Bernard, 16, 186–8, 191–3, 195–6
Meelick, Co. Galway, 49
Messenger, The, 129
Midleton, earl of, 227
Military Service Pension Records, 12, 158, 163, 178, 183, 185
'Million Pound Scheme', 63
miners, 21–43
Mitchell, James, 253, 257, 258
Mitchelstown, 105
Molloy, James, 160
Molony, Helena, 218, 234, 239, 243
Monaghan, Co., 145, 192
Moneenroe, Co. Kilkenny, 25, 29–31, 33–4, 40, 42
Montreal, 114, 116
Moriarty, Theresa, 17
Morris, Kathleen, 174
Mortished, Marie, 237
Mortished, R.J.P., 237
Mountbellew, Co. Galway, 54
Mountcollins, Co. Limerick, 89
Moygownagh, Co. Mayo, 15, 156–78
Mountjoy Prison, 259
Moylough, Co. Galway, 50
Mullen, Michael, 247, 249
munitions embargo, 9, 13, 15, 89
Munnelly family, 165–7, 174
Munster Warehouse, 217
Murphy, Daniel J., 217, 221
Murphy, J.W., 100
Murphy, W.R.E., 256

Murray, Pat, 247
Murtaugh, Miss, 234
Mussolini, Benito, 215

Narraghmore, Co. Kildare, 86–7
National Amalgamated Union of Labour, 206
National Federation of Women Workers, 239
National Union of Dock Labourers, 66–7, 71, 119–20, 139n
National Union of Allotment Holders, 113
National Union of Railwaymen, 194
Navan, Co. Meath, 84
Neary, James, 169, 171
Negro World, 129
Nelson, Bruce, 114n, 131
Nelson's Pillar, 76
Nestor, Canon Andrew, 71
Nenagh, Co. Tipperary, 105–6, 247, 257
Nevin, Donal, 235
Newcastle-on-Tyne, 23, 115, 121
New Orleans, 126
Newry, 115, 120–1
Newsham, Captain, 173
Newtown, Co. Kilkenny, 32
Newtownbarry, 106
New York, 19, 114–17, 123–31
Ní Bhruadair, Gobnait, 217, 228–9
Ní Raghainn, Síghle, 235
Northern Ireland, 10, 189, 215
Northumberland Hotel, 18
Nurses Registration (Ireland) Act, 230
Nurses, National Council of, 229

O'Brien, Bill (Tipperary), 10
O'Brien, Séamus, 36, 66,
O'Brien, William, 18, 25, 36–7, 73, 143, 151, 153, 155, 184, 197, 225, 235, 246–53, 255–7
O'Brennan, Kathleen, 128

Ó Conaire, Pádraic, 18, 76, 77
O'Connell Fife and Drum band, 250
O'Connor, Art, 56
O'Connor, Emmet, 12, 132, 136, 182, 195, 206, 257n
O'Connor, Miss E., 239
O'Connor, Judge, 253n
O'Connor, Séamus, 226
O'Connor, T.P., 118
O'Connor Lysaght, Rayner, 138, 153
O'Dea, Bishop Thomas, 54
O'Doherty, Bishop Thomas, 44, 55
O'Donnell, Peadar, 42, 226
O'Donnell, Ruán, 11
O'Donnell, Thomas, MP, 223
O'Dwyer, George, 31, 35–6
O'Dwyer, John, 138
O'Farrell, Patrick, 120
O'Flaherty, Liam, 155
Offaly (King's Co.), 136
O'Halloran, Fr, 24, 24n, 29
O'Hannigan, Donncha, 142
O'Higgins, Kevin, 15, 249, 252, 256
O'Kane, Mr, 147
O'Kelly, Fr T., 51–2, 54
O'Leary, Michael, 121–2
Ó Máille, Padraic, 52
O'Malley, Ernie, 11, 36
O'Neill, Dick, 115
O'Neill, Phil, 63
O'Reilly, Leonora, 128
O'Shannon, Cathal, 18, 25, 36–7, 154, 206, 209, 251
O'Shiel, Kevin, 13, 44, 53, 56
O'Sullivan, Martin, 9–10
Oldcastle, Co. Meath, 93
Oola, Co. Limerick, 132
One Big Union, 206, 242, 245, Defence League, 256
Orange Order, 121–2, 197–8, 200, 205, 208–9, 212–13, 215–16
Orme Bourke, William, 160, 175

Orme family/estate, 159–61, 165–6, 172–5
Orme, Guy, 173
Oughterard, 49
Owenmore estate, 175
Owen, Robert, 245
Ox mountains, 175

Pankhurst, Sylvia, 145
Paris Peace Conference, 7, 8
Parnell, George Henry, 100, 104, 112
Partridge, William, 233
Patterson, Henry, 199, 212
Patterson, William Forbes, 208
Pearse, Padraic, 60
Pembroke, Co. Dublin, 102, 106
Perolz, Marie, 231–2, 234
Persia, *see* Iraq
Philadelphia, 125
plots, *see* allotments
Plunkett, Horace, 188
Plymouth, 146
Port, Gas & General Workers' Committee, 256–8
Portadown, Co. Armagh, 200, 207, 211, 214
Portarlington, Co. Laois, 84
Postal Clerks' Association, 207
Power, checkweighman, 42
Power, Revd M., 29
Presbyterian, 159, 166
priests, 29–30, 33–4, 70, 71, 86, 93, 164, 213, 226–7
Primrose League, 209
Pringle, James, 71
Prior-Wandesforde, Florence, 30
Prior-Wandesforde, Henry, 22, 25–6, 27, 29–30, 35–37, 41
process-serving, 50
prohibition, 117
Protestants, 14, 27, 52, 121–2, 172–3, 177, 181, 197–203, 206–9, 212–17, 227–8, 230

Prout, John, 41
Public Safety Acts, 246

Q Company, Dublin Brigade, IRA, 114–15, 117
Quinn, Peter, 161, 163, 165

Raffeisan principles, 110
Rahoon, Co. Galway, 47
'ranch war', 15, 47, 88
Rappa Castle, Co. Mayo, 164
Ratepayers Association, 147
Rathdowney, Co. Laois, 13–14
Rathglass, Co. Mayo, 164
Rathmines, Co. Dublin, 102
Rea, Councillor, 61, 72
Red Clydeside, 202
red flag, 36, 132, 137–40, 141n, 145, 147–8, 150n, 155, 187–8, 190, 208, 251, 255
red guards, 133, 149, 150n
Redmond, Denis, 257
Redmondism, 16, 30, 65, 67, 74
Regan, Maurice, 192
Regan, Nell, 239
Reidy, James, 149
Reilly, Peadar, 115, 127
Representation of the People Act, 235
Rerum Novarum, 75
Revolutionary Socialist Party, 16, 134, 154
Ring, Joseph, 175
Riordan, creamery manager, 137
Robinson, Séamus, 41
Rodgers, Minnie, 232
Roscahill, Co. Galway, 49–50
Roscrea, Co. Tipperary, 257
'rotten Protestants', 213–14
Rowe, Mr, 106
Roxborough, Ian, 28
Royal Irish Constabulary, 14, 31–2, 32n, 35–6, 45–6, 48, 51–3, 57,83, 85, 122, 158, 162–4, 166, 173,

182, 184, 186–7, 198, 202, 205–7, 210, 212–13, 223, 226–7, 233
Royal Navy, 120, 123, 125, 190
RTÉ, 9
Ruane, Edward, 162
Ruane, Elizabeth, 159, 161
Ruane, John, 159, 161, 165, 168
Ruddy, Fr John J., 164
Rush, Co. Dublin, 81
Russell, Ruth, 197, 204, 216
Russell, T.W., 102
Ruth, John, 257
Ruttledge, P.J., 173
Russia (and USSR), 7, 9, 18, 77, 90, 124, 137, 146, 152–3, 239, 245, 257–9
Ryan, Frank, 148
Ryan, Joseph, 124, 127
Ryan, Miss, 234

Sacco and Vanzetti trial, 66
Sailors' and Firemens' Union, 115
Salford Women's Trade Union Council, 191
St Cormac's Society, 158
St John's, Newfoundland, 114
St Kieran's College, Kilkenny, 27
St Muredach's College, Ballina, 160
Saorstát Éireann, 42, 109, 112
Scanlan, Thomas, MP, 180
Scotland, 111, 146, 151
Scots Guards, 162
Scottish National Union of Allotment Holders, 113
Scottish Provident Association, 175
Scully, Bertie, 228
Sears, William, 168
Seattle, 8
Sexton, James, 119
sexually transmitted diseases, 229
Shanahan, Jenny, 234
Shanley, Fr Timothy, 127
Shaw, Joseph, 125

Shaw, Thomas, 104–5, 107, 109–12
Shawe-Taylor, Frank, 49–53
Sheil Park, Liverpool, 122
Shields, Adolphus, 121
Shields, Arthur, 238
shipbuilding, 203, 204, 208, 209
shipyard expulsions, 200, 215
shopkeepers, 29, 32, 65, 73, 92
Shortt, Edward, 119
Sinn Féin, 13
Sinn Féin courts, *see* Dáil courts
SIPTU, 179
Skehana, Co. Kilkenny, 23, 41–2
Skehana, Co. Galway, 51
Skerries, Co. Dublin, 84
Skinnider, Margaret, 218
Sligo, 5, 14, 16, 19–20, 97, 103, 106,
     111, 157, 178, 179–96, 223, 231,
     233, 247; Co–operative Food Store,
     188; Trades Council, 184, 189;
     Manufacturing Company, 188
Sligo Champion, 180, 183, 185, 187,
     189, 191
Sligo, Leitrim and Northern Counties
     Railway Company, 188
Sligo Nationalist, 189
Sloan, S., 104
Sloyan, Thomas, 74
Soldier's Song, The, 251
Socialist Party of Ireland, 24, 201, 206
Soloheadbeg, Co. Tipperary, 35
Southampton, 115–16, 249
soviets, 13–15, 61, 63, 68, 70, 72–3,
     76–8, 132–55, 190, 194, 245
Special Infantry Corp, 56, 168, 172
Springlawn, Co. Galway, 54
Stack, Austin, 56, 226
State Registration of Trained Nurses,
     Society for the, 229
Steadman, Inspector, 162, 167, 169
Steam Packet Company, 255
Stonehall farm, Co. Mayo, 165, 169–
     71, 174, 177

Stradbally, Co. Laois, 94
submarines, 114, 114n
Swords, Co. Dublin, 82, 84
syndicalism, 154, 245, 246

Tailor and Garment Workers' Trade
     Union, 243
Taylor, Mrs, 49
teachers, 29, 33, 162, 213
Temperance League, 181
Templemore, Co. Tipperary, 104, 106
Textile Operatives' Society of Ireland,
     232
Tierney, Katie, 237
Timmon, Rose, 235, 237
Tipperary, Co., 10, 19, 40–1, 51, 63,
     94n, 111, 132, 136, 138, 139n,
     143, 145, 147–51, 152n, 155,
     258
Tipperary Star, 147
Thomas, Norman, 128
Thurles, 106, 150n
Times, The, 121
tithes, 27–8, 28n
Toohill, Pat, 166
Townshend, Charles, 180
Town Tenants' League, 16, 18, 59–78
Trades Councils, 68, 72, 100, 103, 105,
     107, 123, 133, 137, 144, 153n,
     184, 198, 200–3, 207, 209–10,
     232n, 238, 238n, 241
Tralee, Co. Kerry, 129, 217–31
Transport and General Workers
     (Amalgamated), 206
Treaty, Anglo-Irish, 40, 59, 63–4, 142,
     147, 151, 153, 175, 226, 229
Treenagh, Co. Mayo, 164
Tresca, Carlo, 129
Trew, Arthur, 202
tricolour, 48, 138–40, 141n
Trotsky, Leon, 152
Truce, 39–40, 51, 68–9, 139, 228
Tuam, 47, 51, 55, 73

Tuam Herald, 70
Turkington, James, 199, 200, 212, 215
Tyrone, Co., 119, 207

Ulster Division, 200
Ulster Protestant Association, 202–3, 213
Ulster Special Constabulary, 214–15
Ulster Unionist Labour Association, 199–200, 203, 208, 210–11, 213–14, 216
Ulster Volunteer Force, 209, 215
Ulster Workers' Union, 209, 215
Ummerantarry, Co. Mayo, 168, 169
Unionism, 30, 36, 62, 70, 119, 153, 172, 177, 191, 199–202, 207–10, 208, 212, 214–15, 227
Union Jack, 212, 214
United Irish League, 17, 25, 30, 45, 49, 53, 93, 156, 164, 174, 180–1, 185, 187, 195
United Irish Plotholders' Union, 97–113
Universal Negro Improvement Association, 19, 124
United States of America, 19, 39, 66, 74, 123–31, 114–8, 123–31, 150, 196, 245–9
University College Dublin, 246
University of Galway, 20

Vacant Land Cultivation Society, 97, 100, 103, 107, 111
Voice of Labour, 73, 90–1, 94, 96, 132, 136, 139–40, 152, 190, 192, 202, 209
Volunteers, Irish, 15, 31, 51–2, 58, 64, 70, 117, 121, 156–78, 181, 186, 191, 195–6, 209, 225–6, *see also* Irish Republican Army
Volunteers, National, 181
Volunteers, Ulster, 209
Walker, William, 197, 199

Walsh, Frank P., 126
Walsh, Dr Thomas, 60, 70, 78
Wandesforde, Charles, 23–4, 27
Wandesforde estate (see also Prior-Wandesforde), 21–2
Ward, Margaret, 218, 227–9
Ward, Martin, 65
War of Independence, 33, 35, 39, 113, 114, 156, 159, 164, 177–8, 194–5, 225, 246
Watchword of Labour, 18, 135, 152, 199–200, 206, 215–16
Waterford, Co., 41, 94, 98, 104, 120, 132, 139n, 145, 147, 148n 149, 203, 232, 235n, 236, 240
Watts, Gerry, 19
Wentworth, Thomas, 21
Western People, 172
Wexford, Co., 19, 22n, 40–1, 111, 183, 248, 258
Whitaker, Mr, 26
Whitefeet, 23, 28
'white guards', 139, 139n, 148
White Star Line, 114, 129
Whittle, M.P., 247
Whitty, Michael, 257
Wilkinson, Ellen, 205
Williams, T., 53
Women's Advisory Committee on the Domestic Service Problem, 238
Workers' Republic, 18, 42, 63–4, 77, 142, 152–3, 155, 213
Workers' Republic (periodical), 222, 249
Workers' Union, 20, 197–216, 219
Workers' Union of Ireland, 245, 257, 259–60
World War One, *see* First World War
Wormwood Scrubs, 119

Yeates, Padraig, 12, 115n
Yorkshire, 21
Young, Joseph, 70